Principles of
Real Estate
Management

Professional Review
Julia A. Banks, CPM®
Laurence C. Harmon, CPM®
Richard F. Muhlebach, CPM®
Cher R. Zucker-Maltese, CPM®

Tulie O'Connor
Manager, Education Publishing

Principles of Real Estate Management

Fifteenth Edition

IREM Institute of Real Estate Management

© Dennis Harms/Images.com

Library of Congress Cataloging-in-Publication Data

Principles of real estate management.—15th ed.
    p. cm.
  Includes bibliographical references and index.
  ISBN 1-57203-113-1 (alk. paper)
    1. Real estate management.   I. Institute of Real Estate Management.
  HD1394.P74 2005
  333.33'068-dc22   2005052020

Printed in the United States of America

[Reprint schedule]

Preface

The real estate management profession is challenging, rewarding, and fulfilling. As a career, real estate management provides opportunities to manage, lease, market, and finance residential and commercial buildings, shopping centers, and many other types of properties.

Owners of residential and commercial properties entrust real estate managers with the responsibility of managing and leasing the property based on the owners' goals and objectives. These properties range in value from a few hundred thousand dollars for a small apartment building to well over a billion dollars for a major mixed-use development. Each property, regardless of its size and value, is a significant investment for its owner.

Property owners range from the sole proprietor of a small building, to developers and investment groups, to the federal government. Each type of ownership offers the professional real estate manager options for different types of employment—from employee to self-employed, from local to international.

The real estate management industry historically consisted of local real estate firms that managed properties for local ownerships. Today real estate management firms are regional, national, and international. Real estate managers can develop and grow their own real estate management companies. Some firms provide third-party management services and work as agents of the property ownership, which may be in distant parts of the country or the world. Developers, investment groups, real estate investment trusts (REITs), and major corporations hire real estate managers to manage their properties. Government agencies, municipalities, and the federal government employ real estate managers to oversee property they own.

The United States has over 34 million multifamily, mobile home, and condominium units that need professional management. Over 36 billion square feet of office, medical, retail, and industrial space also require professional management. These buildings and properties present employment opportunities for real estate managers and for real estate management companies. Each property is an investment for its ownership, and each property is the ownership's business.

Real estate is a cyclical industry, and professional real estate managers use their expertise and experiences to manage their properties through difficult markets when rents decline, vacancies climb, and values fall and through growth periods when rents increase, occupancies soar, and values rise. To accomplish the goals of ownership and to improve their professional skills, real estate managers must continually develop their management and leasing expertise.

Principles of Real Estate Management, 15th edition, is an excellent, up-to-date introduction to the real estate management profession. The first three chapters provide an overview of the real estate management industry, real estate economics, and the various forms of property ownership. The next five chapters discuss specific management responsibilities that apply to residential and commercial properties. Separate chapters present the management and leasing of residential properties, office buildings, and other commercial properties. The last chapter details the operation of a real estate management company. This new edition of *Principles of Real Estate Management* contains information regarding the specific skills and knowledge anyone interested in the field of real estate management needs to advance in this rewarding profession.

The Institute of Real Estate Management is a leader in the real estate management field. It has been a key provider of educational resources on all aspects of the management and leasing of specific residential and commercial properties. Through its educational offerings, publications, and its Web site (www.irem.org), the Institute continues to offer resources to keep real estate managers at the forefront of their profession.

ACKNOWLEDGMENTS

The Institute of Real Estate Management gratefully acknowledges the contribution of the editorial reviewers for the fifteenth edition of *Principles of Real Estate Management,* Julia A. Banks, CPM, Cher R. Zucker-Maltese, CPM, and Richard F. Muhlebach, CPM, CRE, RPA, SCSM. These seasoned professionals, who are also real estate managers, authors, and instructors, provided a peer review of the entire manuscript for accuracy of information, timeliness of content, and ease of reading. The Institute also thanks Laurence C. Harmon, CPM, for his careful review of the legal aspects of the book.

The Institute of Real Estate Management acknowledges its gratitude to James C. Downs, (1905–1980). One of the founders of the Institute of Real Estate Management in 1933, he was the first property manager to receive the CERTIFIED PROPERTY MANAGER® (CPM®) designation. Mr. Downs firmly believed that the best means of developing qualified real estate managers is to teach them specific skills. As a starting point, he wrote the first edition of *Principles of Real Estate Management,* published in 1947. He revised the book through its twelfth edition in 1980.

The Institute of Real Estate Management also gratefully acknowledges the contributions Caroline Scoulas (1941–2005), senior editor for the Institute, made to the real estate management industry for over 17 years. She provided value to the profession by combining her editing skills and her knowledge of the real estate management industry to assist in producing many of the Institute's leading real estate management publications. Caroline was an individual and editor with high moral standards and codes of ethics. Her steadfast support, personal integrity, and work ethic influenced so many of her authors. She is dearly missed by all who had the pleasure to work with her.

The Institute gratefully acknowledges the contribution of copy editor Sherry Powley, who stepped in to complete this fifteenth edition when Caroline could no longer carry on her work with the Institute. Sherry provided unfailing dedication and care throughout the process, upholding the standards set in previous editions of *Principles of Real Estate Management.*

Richard Muhlebach CPM, CRE, RPA, SCSM

Contents

Chapter 1   **An Overview of Real Estate Management** 1

Historical Perspective on Real Property   1
Evolution of Real Estate Management   3
    The 1920s to World War II   4
    Post–World War II through the 1990s   5
    The New Millenium   8
Real Estate Management and Professionalism   11
    Founding of the Institute of Real Estate
        Management   12
    Real Estate Management Skills   13
    Primary Responsibilities of the Real Estate Manager   14
Summary   19

Chapter 2   **Real Estate and Economics** 21

Basic Economics   21
    The Marketplace   22
    The Role of Government   27
    The Business Cycle   33
Real Estate Economics   39
    The Real Estate Market   40
    Government and Real Estate   43
    Real Estate Cycles   45
Summary   49

Chapter 3   **Ownership Forms and Goals**   51

Means and Reasons for Investing in Real
    Estate   51
    Means of Investing   51
    Reasons for Investment   55
Principal Forms of Income-Property Ownership   58
    Sole Proprietorship   59
    Partnerships   60
    Corporations   63
    Real Estate Investment Trusts   65
    Joint Venture   65
Summary   66

Chapter 4   **Establishing Management Direction**   67

The Management Plan   67
    Regional Analysis   69
    Neighborhood Analysis   71
    Property Analysis   73
    Market Analysis   75
    Analysis of Alternatives   85
    Cost-Benefit Analysis   89
    Conclusions and Recommendations   89
The Management Agreement   91
    Basic Components of an Agreement   92
    Responsibilities of the Manager   93
    Obligations of the Owner   97
    Compensation for Management Services   98
Summary   98

Chapter 5   **Financial Management**   99

Evaluation of Operating Funds   99
    The Cash Flow Chart   100
    Other Considerations   105
Accounting for Income and Expenses   109
    Accounting Systems   109
    Income Categories   111
    Expense Categories   111
Reporting on Income and Expenses   118
    Accounting Software   118
    Management Reports   119
Budgeting   121
    Operating Budget   122

Capital Budget   124
Long-Range Budget   125
Summary   125

Chapter 6   **Staffing**   127

Staff Requirements   128
   On-Site Staff   128
   Employees of the Management Firm   130
   Contractors   133
   Determining Adequate Staff Size   134
Hiring Qualified Personnel   135
   Recruiting Applicants   135
   Selecting Employees   138
Orientation of New Personnel   140
Retaining Valuable Employees   141
   Compensation   141
   Communications   143
   Promoting Morale   144
   Continual Training   144
   Developing Talents   145
Employee Disciplinc   145
   Employment Policies   146
   Progressive Discipline   146
Employee Termination   147
   Facing a Layoff   148
   Dismissing an Employee   150
Employer Liability   151
Summary   151

Chapter 7   **Maintenance**   153

Schedules, Inspections, and Maintenance Tasks   155
   Schedules and Inspections   155
   Custodial Maintenance   159
   Preventive Maintenance   160
Other Aspects of Maintenance   167
   Safety   167
   Protecting the Environment   168
   Controlling Energy Consumption   171
   Maintaining Property Security   172
Managing Maintenance Work   173
   Staffing Choices   174
   Record Keeping   175
Summary   178

Chapter 8   **The Cycle of Tenancy**   180

Marketing the Property   180
　Understanding the Market   181
　Developing a Marketing Program   182
　Offering Marketing Incentives   189
　Measuring Marketing Effectiveness   191
　Using Sales Techniques   194
　Approving a Prospect for Tenancy   195
The Lease Document   197
　Fundamental Elements of Leases   198
　Types of Leases   199
Collection Policies   200
　Rental Collection   200
　Security Deposits   205
Retaining Tenants   205
　Welcoming New Tenants   206
　Handling Requests   206
　Building Goodwill   207
Lease Renewal Techniques   207
Summary   208

Chapter 9   **Managing Residential Property**   210

Rental Housing   210
　Apartments   211
　Government-Assisted Housing   213
　Selecting Qualified Residents   215
　The Residential Lease   221
Common Interest Realty Associations   229
　Condominiums   229
　Cooperatives   231
　Planned Unit Developments   232
　The Role of Management   233
Other Residential Property   235
　Single-Family Homes   236
　Manufactured Housing Communities   236
　Housing for the Elderly   237
Maintenance Issues   238
　Unit Preparation   238
　Residential Amenities   241
Insurance Issues   241
　Types of Insurance   243
　Choice of Insurance Packages   244
Summary   245

Chapter 10   **Managing Office Buildings** 246

Property Analysis 246
  Class of Structure 247
  Criterion for Classification 248
Tenant Selection 254
  Business Reputation and Financial Status 254
  Space Requirements 255
  Service Requirements 256
Office Rent 257
  Measuring Rentable and Usable Space 257
  Establishing Rates 259
  Space Planning 261
  Tenant Improvements 261
Leases and Lease Negotiation 262
  Standard Clauses 263
  Concessions 265
  Tenant Options 266
  Other Lease Issues 267
Office Condominiums 268
Summary 268

Chapter 11   **Managing Shopping Centers and Other Commercial Properties** 270

Shopping Centers 270
  Property Analysis 271
  Tenant Selection 276
  Retail Rent 279
  The Retail Lease 282
  Shopping Center Management 285
Other Commercial Properties 286
  Property Types 286
  Lease Considerations 287
Marketing Commercial Space 288
  Prospecting for Tenants 288
  Marketing on Value 289
Insuring Commercial Properties 290
  Owner's Insurance 290
  Tenant's Insurance 291
Summary 292

Chapter 12   **The Business of Real Estate Management** 294

How Management Business is Acquired 294
  Identifying Prospective Clients 295

Promoting the Management Firm   298
How Management Fees are Determined   301
   Basic Fee Structures   301
   Additional Fees   302
The Real Estate Management Office   302
   Location   303
   Office Procedures and Equipment   305
Additional Client Services   310
   Appraisal   310
   Management Consultation   312
   Real Estate Investment Counseling   313
   Corporate Fiscal Service   314
   Tax Service   314
   Insurance Service   317
Summary   317

Glossary   319
Index   351

Principles of
Real Estate
Management
Fifteenth Edition

1

An Overview of Real Estate Management

Professional real estate management means conducting a property's management, operations, marketing, leasing, and financial reporting to meet the objectives of the owner. It also involves planning for the future of the property by proposing physical and fiscal strategies that will maintain and/or enhance the value of the real estate. Real estate management as a profession is the result of three major occurrences: (1) development of a legal system that granted individuals the right to own real property, (2) increased complexity and size of buildings and their components, and (3) changing economic conditions that required professional management and advice to achieve sound fiscal operation of income-producing property. The history of real estate ownership and management has a direct bearing on the role of real estate managers today.

HISTORICAL PERSPECTIVE ON REAL PROPERTY

In the United States, individual ownership of real property is a right that U.S. citizens take for granted, but the concept of holding individual title to property is a radical departure from historical precedents. Private property rights were so important to the American colonists that many of the fundamental provisions in the United States Constitution and the Bill of Rights pertain to property ownership.

The basis of American property law came to the United States with the founders of the country. European systems of government, most notably the

1

Common Law and Property Ownership

Americans are familiar with *statute law,* which is written law that a governmental body has enacted. *Common law,* on the other hand, is court interpretation when no statute applies. These interpretations are based on precedent—the inherent beliefs of the society and previous court decisions. As the common-law interpretation of property ownership evolved, feudalism was replaced by *allodialism,* a system under which an individual can own land independently without being subject to rent, service, or acknowledgment of a superior (e.g., sovereign). Although the United States uses an allodial system, elements of the feudal system persist. In many downtown commercial areas, land occasionally is leased for long terms (e.g., 99 years). A developer who builds on leased land owns the improvement (the building) but not the land itself. The owner of the improvement has only a leasehold interest in the underlying land. This is similar to the feudal privilege to use land and will it to descendants even though the king was the absolute owner of the property.

In most states, investors can purchase real property on a fee simple basis or a leasehold interest basis. When a *leasehold interest* is purchased, the improvement (the building) is all that is owned outright; the underlying land is leased from another owner. In *fee simple ownership,* the investor purchases both the underlying land and the improvement. Buyers usually prefer fee simple ownership. Assuming locations of equal appeal, fee simple properties usually have higher values than properties built on leasehold interests.

English, had a profound influence on individual ownership of real property. In the age of *feudalism*—a period that lasted from the ninth to the fifteenth centuries in Europe—the king was the principal landowner in any sovereign state. Land was the symbol of wealth in a society that initially did not have money as a medium of exchange. The land in the country was usually divided among the king's family, who were the barons and lords of the estates. (Through *primogeniture*, a rule of inheritance, the estates could be passed to their descendants.) The barons subdivided and redistributed their land to vassals (tenants) in return for expected services—usually a military obligation and often a share of the crops or livestock raised on the land.

Eventually, agricultural surpluses and manufacturing advances made feudalism impractical. Through centuries of political and economic change, the absolute power of the king gradually diminished. Money, not land, became the primary measure of wealth, and hundreds of years of change produced a powerful merchant class whose wealth eventually surpassed that of the barons. As a result, land became another commodity that could be bought, sold, or traded.

With the founding of colonies in the New World, more merchants than barons received land rights. Although the Revolutionary War broke the bonds between the British colonies and the crown and created the United

States, many rights to land today are remnants of English common law as it was applied to and evolved in the colonies. The U.S. government retained the property tax, which was common in many societies and was a means by which states and communities could raise funds for common services. The government also retained the right of *eminent domain,* which means the state can condemn private property, give fair compensation to the owner, and redevelop the property for public service—even if the property owner is unwilling to sell the property. Restrictions on the use of land for preservation of natural resources, for economic reasons, for protection of other property owners' rights, or for other specific reasons are other carryovers.

EVOLUTION OF REAL ESTATE MANAGEMENT

After the American Revolution, cities began to increase in size and number. The intensive use of land in cities created new investment opportunities. For wealthy capitalists, real estate was an alternative to the investment of surplus funds. However, such investors were not always proficient (or successful) in managing real property because that was not their primary business; they often considered such management a burden. A few people did find real estate management a profitable opportunity in this early period, but real estate brokerage was still the more lucrative activity.

Cities continued to grow in response to the Industrial Revolution, creating greater demand for residential and commercial space. Better engineering and construction techniques led to the development of larger buildings to meet that demand. However, fewer individuals could afford to own a building because larger buildings cost more to build and maintain. Ownership by groups (pooled capital) and financing by outside sources became prevalent. Because such large buildings were no longer the concern of any single person, management became very important. Greater size meant these buildings were more valuable; they were more costly to replace than smaller buildings. They required full-time attention to maintain their value, and cash flow from the property was crucial to offset the financing costs. The complexity of the ownership arrangement created an administrative role for a real estate manager.

Beginning in the 1880s and 1890s—and continuing throughout the twentieth century—several major trends affected urban land use. Land prices in cities rose because of heightened demand for space. Among other things, this prompted the construction of larger multiple-unit residences, and over time, the upgrading of residential conditions and equipment. Central heating, air conditioning, additional bathrooms, and other improvements became standard features in apartment buildings. Maintenance requirements grew with each additional feature, increasing the need for management of residential property.

Advances in structural engineering led to the development of tall steel-frame buildings known as *skyscrapers,* the earliest of which were office buildings. With every additional floor, the possible number of tenants increased. This growth required special skills in leasing as well as a full-time staff to serve the tenants.

Improvements in transportation and electrical networks made possible the development of suburban areas and, ultimately, changed the living patterns of Americans. Local stores in the suburbs carried limited stocks of merchandise, and downtown shopping districts were inconvenient for suburban residents. To meet the needs of growing markets, shopping centers developed. The evolution of these centers from strips of independent stores to large enclosed malls with unified themes led to a parallel need for management of these complex retail properties.

Over time, these trends in residential, office, and retail development sparked an increasing demand for management and ultimately led to specialization by property type. However, in the formative years of construction of large buildings, real estate management was not very complex and owner-management was common until the 1920s. In the early years, individuals who had retired from other lines of business bought most of the buildings. Such buildings were an attractive medium of investment at retirement, and many considered real estate management a post-retirement occupation.

The 1920s to World War II

Primarily because of rapid business expansion and a consequent demand for rental space, owner-management lost favor in the early 1920s. Those who had purchased property to assure themselves a modest living after retirement were suddenly quite wealthy. Dreams had become realities, and many investors chose to travel for long periods or moved to warmer climates. Being far away from their properties prompted these absentee owners to ask real estate agents to collect rents, order fuel, pay the janitor and the utilities, and forward the remainder to them. An owner's specific authorization was usually necessary for any other expenditure, and the owner usually negotiated leases personally, so the extent of real estate management during the 1920s was still limited.

Unparalleled urban prosperity characterized the 1920s. Building construction was at a high, financed primarily by private sources such as building and loan associations and insurance companies. The U.S. economy developed at an unprecedented rate. Corporate profits and personal income expanded with improvements in production. Coast-to-coast networks of chain stores emerged, and this growth in retail business held great promise for real estate managers.

The foundation of the expanding U.S. economy totally collapsed in the stock market crash of 1929. Banks were unwilling or unable to renew loans so borrowers had only one option—to default on the loans and let the banks foreclose. As a result, most of the country's income-producing real estate (especially multiple dwellings and commercial buildings built from 1920 to 1929) was in the hands of the mortgage holders. This economic devastation was the true origin of modern real estate management. For the first time, a large amount of property was gathered under one ownership, one policy, and one common perspective.

Early in the Great Depression, the lenders-turned-owners studied the existing real estate management companies and often concluded that they could best protect their interests by creating their own management departments. Not being familiar with the complexities of building management, the lenders believed that the operation of real estate was limited to collecting rents and maintaining the physical structures.

After the first years of the Depression—years of trial and error as experience in management broadened—the operators of lender-owned real estate adopted other views. The need for analysis, market research, and an organized approach to property administration was widely recognized, and many companies began to fill that need.

Property ownership, which had been concentrated among lenders because of the mass foreclosures from 1928 to 1933, was redistributed during the recovery years. Real estate promised once again to be a profitable opportunity for investors. Individuals and partnerships (sometimes called *syndicates*) purchased property from lenders who were reducing their real estate portfolios as they prepared to resume their pre-Depression activities. In many cases, the new owners retained real estate managers to ensure the highest and best use of the properties.

An upsurge in occupancy, rental rates, and property values characterized the recovery period (1934 to 1939). When the United States entered World War II at the end of 1941, the demand for rental space was so high that owners could easily rent their own properties, and the need for professional real estate management diminished.

Post–World War II through the 1990s

From the end of World War II in 1945 to the end of the twentieth century, the United States experienced many social, political, and economic changes that affected the evolution of real estate management.

The 1940s and 1950s. Phenomenal construction from 1946 until 1956 satisfied the demands for housing after World War II and after the Korean War. At the end of those decades, the number of residential units built exceeded the demand for new space. Much of this construction occurred in newly developed suburbs, which had become more numerous because of increased automobile ownership.

For many, the suburbs became the place of choice to live, but the cities grew as well. Mid- and high-rise apartment buildings became popular in metropolitan areas beginning in the late 1950s. A towering structure could house hundreds or thousands of people in the area of a city block. Such a concentration of population intensified service requirements and consequently increased the need for real estate management.

The 1960s and 1970s.   The advent of the condominium in the 1960s and 1970s offered real estate managers still more opportunities. Professional management was usually a necessity for large multiple-owner properties.

On the commercial front, an enormous demand for office space characterized the period. The government and service industries employed large numbers of people who worked in office buildings. As companies prospered, they outgrew their existing quarters. At the same time, office operations became more complex, and companies needed more space for computers and other equipment. The heightened demand for office space dramatically increased the opportunities for professional management. Rental retail space also developed during this period, and phenomenal growth occurred in the number and size of shopping centers, especially in the suburbs.

A sharp increase in the supply of mortgage money during the 1960s and 1970s affected the real estate management industry because it permitted the development of numerous large income-producing properties. Real estate investment trusts and pension funds were among the sources of mortgage money.

In the late 1960s to the early 1970s, *real estate investment trusts* (*REITs*) became a significant source of real estate investment money. A REIT is an entity that sells shares of beneficial interest to investors and uses the funds to invest in real estate or mortgages. This form of investment permits those with limited capital to participate in large real estate investments. REIT units can be traded privately, and some of the larger ones are traded on public stock exchanges, thus providing significant flexibility. However, they are inherently subject to fluctuations in the real estate market and the stock market, the integrity of the administration of the trust, and changes in governmental policy. Many REITs became suspect in the mid-1970s and early 1980s because of imprudent loans to developers and builders that placed too much debt on properties. Many investors and lenders experienced losses.

After the passage of the Employment Retirement Income Security Act (ERISA) in 1974, pension funds and insurance companies began to take an active interest in real estate as a means of diversifying their portfolios and capitalizing on the rapid appreciation of real property developments. The role of pension funds increased in the 1980s.

The 1980s. The decade started with a booming real estate industry and ended with a crash. Between 1980 and 1982, the United States suffered the worst recession since the Great Depression. During that period of double-digit inflation, investors viewed real estate as a way to preserve capital. The recession finally gave way to a period of prosperity, and construction boomed.

One reason for the nation's rebound from recession in 1983 was the availability of credit, which resulted from changes in federal regulations related to banks and savings and loan associations (S&Ls). Previously, the federal government prohibited S&Ls (also called *thrifts*) from lending money for commercial real estate development and from investing in real estate directly, but it removed those restrictions in the early 1980s.

These changes, combined with the *Tax Reform Act of 1980 (1980 Act)*, offered numerous incentives for real estate investment and fueled unprecedented development. Large syndicates and partnerships organized to take advantage of the credit and tax opportunities. Pension funds played an increasingly important role in real estate investment, and REITs rebounded from their disfavor and again became important sources of investments.

The record growth eventually faltered because of two significant and almost concurrent events:

1. The development boom began to slow in the mid-1980s. As a result of overbuilding, the market saw an overabundance of available rentable space. Many developers lost their properties because high vacancy rates reduced their cash flow and prevented them from making their loan payments. Massive foreclosures ensued.

2. The federal government enacted the *Tax Reform Act of 1986 (1986 Act)*, which repealed most of the real-estate-related income tax incentives granted through the 1980 Act. In particular, the new law defined rental income from real property as *passive activity income*—income in which the investor does not materially participate in earning the funds. Similarly, losses from such passive activities, which had been deductible from *active income* (i.e., salary) under the 1980 Act, could no longer be deducted under the 1986 Act. The changes significantly reduced the attraction of real estate for most long-term investors.

The oversupply of vacant property, coupled with hundreds of poorly conceived developments and numerous failing syndicates and partnerships, lowered even more the value of the properties the banks and S&Ls had seized. As a result, many of the financial institutions that held the properties went bankrupt, and federal regulators took them over.

By early 1989, a significant portion of the savings and loan industry had collapsed. Thrift failures were so widespread that the U.S. government dissolved the Federal Savings and Loan Insurance Corporation (FSLIC), the agency that insured deposits in participating S&Ls. The federal government needed an organization to efficiently manage and dispose of the assets from the thrifts that were in receivership, so it created several new governmental agencies. The Resolution Trust Corporation (RTC) was among them. Upon its creation, the RTC became the largest landowner in the United States. By the time of its termination at the end of 1995, the RTC had taken over 747 thrifts with total real estate assets of all types valued at nearly $402.6 billion. Among other strategies, the RTC contracted with real estate management firms to manage and market many of those assets for disposition.

The 1990s.   Real estate managers faced many challenges during the 1990s. In many markets, office vacancy rates remained high throughout most of the decade. In addition to the consequences of earlier overbuilding, numerous corporate mergers and restructurings (workforce downsizing) reduced companies' space needs. Technological advances allowed people to work at home while being linked electronically to their places of employment. (As this strategy becomes more widespread in the future, demand for office space is likely to decrease.)

Technology also had effects on retailing. Encryption software enabled credit card purchases over the Internet, and so-called e-commerce thrived as new businesses started on the Internet and established retailers rushed to use the Internet as an additional marketing and sales tool.

Initial concerns about the Internet dominating retailing did not become a reality. Owners renovated or expanded established shopping centers, and developers built new centers. *Power shopping centers*—centers dominated by large space users that sold goods at discount prices—made major inroads.

American business experienced numerous other changes. Services flourished in the 1990s while manufacturing declined. Increasingly, manufacturers produced goods outside of the United States at lower cost. That meant fewer manufacturing jobs and less space used for production. While heavy industry declined, the development of low-rise, flexible structures that could be configured as offices or used for light manufacturing grew.

Apartments built in the 1990s often included amenities more typical of single-family homes, such as *great rooms* (combined living/dining room and kitchen), larger bathrooms, and walk-in closets. Those changes added to the appeal of renting versus home ownership and helped keep average rents high.

The New Millennium

Given the increased global reliance on technology and the failure of established programming to anticipate dates overlapping with the previous

Current and Future Challenges for Real Estate Managers

- Rapid growth of urban mixed-use developments, which are more complex to manage
- Growth in the development of condominiums, increasing the need for condominium managers
- Construction of larger, more densely populated planned unit developments (PUDs) that are more tightly controlled
- Increased demand for rental apartments as baby boomers who reach retirement age choose not to maintain single-family homes
- Reorganization or change of use of major retail centers that were overbuilt in the 1990s
- Development of rural distribution centers
- Continued foreign investment in U.S. real estate and vice versa
- Increased reliance on low-cost, instantaneous global communications via cellular telephone and e-mail
- Growth of electronic business activities, increasing the need for protection from computer viruses and other problems
- Increased reliance on electronic transfer, direct deposit, and debit cards rather than cash and checks for financial transactions
- Growing need to protect personal and financial data to safeguard individuals' privacy and companies' proprietary information
- More complicated management of human resources to ensure employee retention, including flexible work schedules (part-time and shared jobs) to accommodate employees with families
- Increased immigration fueling a need to be bilingual to communicate with employees and tenants
- A growing market for real estate managers as corporations outsource real estate activities and use independent professionals to supplement (or replace) in-house personnel resources
- Environmental problems that can impact property operations as well as buy/sell transactions (e.g., mold and its remediation)
- Concerns about future acts of terrorism and being prepared to respond
- Insurance industry reacting to terrorism by reducing availability and increasing limitations on types of coverages
- Need to keep up with frequent daily technological changes

century, the world expected the crashing of computers around the world to herald the dawn of the twenty-first century. While that issue did not materialize on any scale, other problems loomed on the horizon.

The Year 2000. The economic growth of the 1990s slowed after 2000. Even though the economy slowed, productivity increased. The increase in productivity kept job growth low, and that affected the office and industrial real estate markets by keeping the demand for additional office space low. However, the discipline of lenders slowed new development and prevented the recession in real estate from being as deep as it had been in the 1990s.

The United States continued to maintain a *negative balance of trade*—importing more goods than were exported—which resulted in the loss of even more manufacturing jobs. At the same time, many corporations increasingly outsourced professional jobs, many in technology fields, to developing countries where educated populations would work for low wages. The year 2000 saw another wave of bankruptcies as Internet service providers and online retailers (dot-com companies) found they were unable to generate sufficient revenue or obtain needed capital to sustain their operations.

The Year 2001 and Beyond.   The terrorist attack on the United States, on September 11, 2001, (referred to as 9/11) was a defining moment in U.S. history. The repercussions of that event continue to resonate, and the American way of life has changed forever.

The slow growth of the economy continued in 2001 and slowed the pace of hiring—companies that are not growing do not hire new staff. In most industries, wage increases were small or nonexistent. Employees in some industries had to accept pay reductions. The travel and tourism industries were especially hard hit. Increased security checks after 9/11 made travel an aggravation, and major airlines went through bankruptcy proceedings. On the other hand, manufacturers of security devices and providers of security services experienced a business boom.

During the early 2000s, management opportunities in all types of commercial and residential properties increased—as did the challenges they offered. Developers built and renovated shopping centers, which often included multiscreen movie theaters and other entertainment venues along with the traditional mix of fashion, jewelry, and gift retailers. Developers and REITs tended to employ in-house managers, while corporations tended to outsource real estate management. This period also saw mergers and acquisitions of many real estate companies.

The array of high-tech equipment used in business demanded office buildings that could support state-of-the-art technology. Developers designed new office buildings to meet those requirements. If retrofitting older office buildings for tenants' technology needs was costly or otherwise impractical, owners and developers converted the old buildings to other uses, including hotels, condominiums, and apartments.

Trends toward urban living as well as neighborhood and downtown retailing increased. By encouraging downtown residential development—both as new construction and by conversion of commercial buildings—major cities became desirable places to live, work, and play. Suburban areas saw increasing numbers of *common interest developments (CIDs)* such as townhouse communities and low- and mid-rise condominiums. Single-family homes were increasingly built in gated (common interest) communities as well.

Inflation was low throughout the early 2000s, and interest rates were kept low. However, beginning in 2004, the Chairman of the Federal Reserve Bank began to raise the federal funds rate and the discount rate in small increments (25 basis points—one-fourth of one percent—at a time) to control inflation as the economy continued to recover. Home buyers and home owners benefited from the low interest rates as they financed and refinanced home purchases.

The Effects of 9/11 on Real Estate Management. Real estate management changed due to the *U.S.A. PATRIOT Act,* which addressed security issues that resulted from 9/11. (The acronym PATRIOT stands for "providing appropriate tools required to intercept and obstruct terrorism.") Residential properties intensified their screening of rental applicants, in particular the verification of each prospect's identity and citizenship or immigration status. Commercial properties increased security measures and paid more attention to tenants', visitors', and guests' activities. *Executive Order 13224,* issued September 23, 2001, required those leasing commercial space to check the names of officers of prospective tenant companies against the *Specially Designated Nationals and Blocked Persons list,* which identifies individuals suspected of terrorism or related activities.

The effects of 9/11 had a lingering impact on real estate management in the form of increases in management time and property operating costs. Other challenges included finding and obtaining adequate property insurance coverage that contained provisions related to terrorism, requiring more intensive screening of prospective residential and commercial tenants (security issues as well as financial concerns), and developing more comprehensive emergency procedures that emphasized preparation against acts of terrorism.

Many of the same issues discussed here will undoubtedly affect the management of investment real estate in the future. Regulation by all levels of government will continue to grow, and new technologies will affect the way buildings are built and used. Changes will continue to challenge managers of all types of properties as they strive to keep vacancies to a minimum, operate efficiently and cost-effectively, and achieve the owner's objectives for the property.

REAL ESTATE MANAGEMENT AND PROFESSIONALISM

Compared to other professions that have existed for centuries (e.g., accounting, law, medicine), real estate management is a relative newcomer.

An early organizational step was the 1907 founding of the National Association of Building Owners and Managers, which focused on office buildings. No organization existed for those who specialized in managing rental apartments or other types of commercial properties until 1923, when the National Association of Real Estate Boards (also founded in 1907) organized its Property Management Division. Members of the Division were local real estate boards.

The professional aspects of real estate management developed virtually overnight as a result of dire circumstances. Businesses that survived the stock market crash in 1929 were in a precarious position. They had already suffered substantial losses, and poor management of their real estate holdings would have perpetuated their losses. Pioneers in the profession recognized the need to establish standard management practices and a method of accrediting real estate managers. They subsequently reorganized the Property Management Division into a different type of body.

Founding of the Institute of Real Estate Management

In 1933, one hundred real estate management firms joined together to form the *Institute of Real Estate Management (IREM®)* as an affiliate of the National Association of Real Estate Boards (today the NATIONAL ASSOCIATION OF REALTORS®). Each firm was required to pledge itself to certain practices: (1) The firm would set up separate accounts for its funds and those of its clients; under no circumstances were the funds to be commingled. (2) The firm would carry a fidelity bond on all applicable employees. (3) The firm would in no way benefit financially from a client's funds without full disclosure to and permission from the property owner.

Although the initial reason for organizing the Institute of Real Estate Management was to adopt specific ethical standards of practice, the association and the scope of its standards continue to grow. In 1938, the founders of IREM agreed that accrediting individual real estate managers was more fundamental and beneficial than recognizing the integrity of management firms—which had been the previous practice. The standards of a management firm can change with staff changes, the founders reasoned, but individuals' standards generally apply throughout their lives. Therefore, the Institute of Real Estate Management reorganized as an association of individuals and inaugurated the CERTIFIED PROPERTY MANAGER® (CPM®) designation to acknowledge individual professional achievement. A CPM member of IREM subscribes to a Code of Professional Ethics, has proven his or her ability by successfully completing a series of real estate management courses, and has worked a prescribed number of years in the profession and managed a portfolio of a required size. Other factors involving the individual's professional experience are also considered.

Nearly 19,000 individuals have achieved the CPM designation, and more than 8,600 CPM members of IREM are actively engaged in real estate property and asset management. These professionals manage more than $848 billion of real estate assets. Although the careers of many CPM members of IREM exclusively involve real estate management, some are also active in brokerage, syndication, consultation, development, and appraisal.

As the Institute has grown, it has also responded to and accommodated changes in the real estate management profession by developing two additional credentials. The ACCREDITED MANAGEMENT ORGANIZATION® (AMO®) accreditation was created in 1945 and is related to the original Institute program, which accredited real estate management companies. In addition to the original practices that were required for a firm's membership in IREM, the AMO accreditation stipulates that at least one executive of the firm must be a CPM member of IREM. It also includes insurance and financial requirements specific to the firm's operations.

A major aspect of real estate management is site management of residential properties. To recognize this specialization, the Institute established the ACCREDITED RESIDENTIAL MANAGER® (ARM®) certification in 1974. The prerequisites of successful course work, professional experience, and agreement to uphold the ARM Code of Ethics are similar to the qualifying steps for the CPM designation, except that the focus of the ARM certification centers on residential property and specific site-management responsibilities.

Real Estate Management Skills

Real estate managers work closely with tenants and property owners, and many skills are necessary to successfully serve these two groups. Diplomacy is essential to effectively negotiate delicate matters that may arise between the two parties. Knowledge of advertising and business promotion are valuable skills if the rental property is not large enough to warrant the services of an advertising agency. Familiarity with the market of the property managed—and its competition—is critical for maximizing the financial return from the property as well as its occupancy. An understanding of economics, accounting, statistics, and valuation calculations is essential to set realistic rents for the present and future and to ensure a healthy economic life for the property.

Education is a vital qualification for the professional real estate manager. Every real property is unique. Economic, social, and political changes affect each property differently. A manager trained in these areas is generally able to isolate these factors, determine how they affect the property, and create a program to respond appropriately to them. The foundation of this flexibility and foresight is education.

Even though the real estate management profession has grown exponentially since the early 1930s, it is still essentially a personal service

---

Primary Responsibilities of Real Estate Management

- Meet owner's goals
- Develop a management plan to operate the properties
- Develop and implement marketing plans
- Conduct market surveys and determine rental rates
- Develop and administer a maintenance program
- Anticipate and respond to residents' and commercial tenants' needs
- Administer the collection and deposit of rents
- Monitor and pay expenses
- Prepare comprehensive budgets and cash flow projections
- Develop and implement marketing plans
- Negotiate leases
- Communicate with property owners
- Administer the Human Resources activities of the property and the professional management company
- Assess, minimize, and mitigate risk
- Develop an emergency procedures plan

The objective of these responsibilities is to achieve the owner's goals for the property (see chapter 3).

---

profession. Because of the individual relationships they have with building owners and tenants, conscientious real estate managers are aware of the ongoing need for self-improvement and adherence to a strict code of ethics.

Primary Responsibilities of the Real Estate Manager

By definition, *real estate* refers to land and any improvements on it. While farms, mines (both underground and at the surface level), golf courses, forests, and even deserts are real estate, the definition is often limited to non-agricultural property that houses individuals or families or accommodates commerce, industry, professions, or other activities. Any changes or new trends among these property users directly affect real estate and its management. As society expands and changes, real estate managers respond to a diversity of problems—either to capitalize on or to minimize the effects of changes on the real estate in their care (depending on the projected outcome).

Real estate management is growing steadily as a profession because of three significant trends. First, simultaneous growth of the population and its requirements for space has increased the total number of all types of buildings. Second, a larger percentage of real estate is investment property. Third, the fact is widely accepted that real estate management requires special training and education.

The training, education, and duties of the real estate manager can be categorized under four different responsibilities—management of the physical site, management of on-site and off-site personnel, management of funds and accounts, and management of leasing activities and tenant services. These responsibilities are all components of the manager's overall responsibility as the agent of the owner. An *agent* is a person who enters a legal and confidential arrangement with an owner and who is authorized to act on behalf of the owner. In the role of agent, the manager is the owner's *fiduciary* and is entrusted to act in the owner's best interests. Real estate management often involves fiduciary responsibility for millions of dollars in assets and cash flow. For this reason, property owners should choose as their agents real estate managers who have strong ethical backgrounds.

Site Management.   Real estate managers regularly inspect the properties they manage using appropriate inspection checklists. Although maintenance staff members may regularly examine particular sections or components of the property, the manager should be available to consult with the staff and the owner on any problems that are noted. The manager is the one who identifies, analyzes, recommends, and implements any major maintenance or remodeling projects. Because the manager is ultimately responsible for such activity and is not necessarily an expert on every aspect that warrants attention, he or she should rely on the advice of knowledgeable staff, skilled professionals, or trustworthy contractors.

The term *site management* often implies maintaining the physical structure, but updating documents and records is also a principal aspect of this role. Aside from accounting records, real estate managers must maintain numerous other forms and documents (insurance policies, tenant files, the management agreement, and other property-related documents and information) in a logical and chronological order. All insurance records should be kept where they can be referred to immediately when the need arises, and a manager should quickly be able to retrieve the files of tenants who enter the management office. In addition, a cross-referencing system is necessary so the manager can refer to specific time-sensitive documents well in advance of their expiration. Insurance policies generally renew annually, and many residential leases follow this pattern. The effort to keep records up-to-date ensures continuity in the operation of a property and gives the manager more time to invest in other management responsibilities.

The owner has primary responsibility for compliance with governmental regulations with respect to the property, but the real estate manager must be knowledgeable in this area in order to avoid (or at least minimize) any liability for noncompliance and to advise the owner regarding applicable regulations. Changes in income tax laws, fair housing and other antidiscrimination laws, environmental regulations, zoning ordinances, or property taxation rules are just some of the ways in which government at

---

Real Estate Management Positions

Site Manager This individual is responsible for day-to-day dealings with residents, leasing, collecting rents, and overall supervision of property maintenance. The title typically applies to managers of apartment buildings or other residential properties; they are also commonly called *residential managers.* On-site residential managers often maintain basic accounting records related to rent collections and unit occupancy (tenant files), while the property manager retains control of the management agreement, insurance policies, and complete accounting records. The site manager of an office building may have the title of *building manager,* and the site manager for a shopping center may have the title of *mall manager.*

Property Manager A property manager may be responsible for operating a single large property or a portfolio of several properties. In the latter situation, if the individual properties have on-site managers, the property manager may supervise the on-site managers. The position may also be known as the *property supervisor.*

Regional Manager This individual supervises on-site residential or commercial property managers. The position may also be called *regional property manager, portfolio supervisor,* or sometimes *senior property manager.* (The title *executive property manager* is usually reserved for one or more of the officers of a management firm or its owner. The executive property manager is responsible for overseeing management, ensuring profitability, and acquiring new business.)

Asset Manager Individuals in this position are typically responsible for long-range planning for and evaluation of investment properties. Their role is more advisory than hands-on management: They often analyze a property's physical and financial condition and recommend ways to maximize the owner's return on investment (ROI). Asset managers often work for corporate and institutional owners.

Portfolio Manager This individual is responsible for assembling real estate assets to achieve specific investment plans and goals—similar to the management of a mutual fund or other pooled investment.

These are some of the more common real estate management positions. However, each employer determines the job titles and responsibilities of individual managers the firm employs. Whatever their positions, professional real estate managers must keep in mind that managing a property is managing a business. Managing a 20-unit apartment building is the same as managing a million dollar business; managing a regional mall is managing a $100 to $400 million business. For more on real estate management positions, refer to IREM's book on job descriptions.

---

all levels can affect the operation of income-producing property. The real estate manager's role includes advising the owner as to when to seek legal counsel. Such advice requires the manager to be knowledgeable about the legal and tax ramifications of certain actions.

Although the responsibilities of real estate management are broadly applicable, the skills required to carry out these responsibilities may be refined or tailored to a specific type of property. The duties and requisite skills for operating a skyscraper office building can differ substantially from the requisites for managing a 20-unit multiple dwelling in the suburbs. Perhaps the most challenging property to manage is the *mixed-use development,* which may combine office, retail, entertainment, and residential uses in a single property.

Asset Management.   An *asset manager* views a property from the perspective of its present and potential value to the owner—its ability to meet the owner's goals, whether for income-producing or for owner-occupied property. Even though an owner may consider the property solely from an investment standpoint, effective asset management requires a working knowledge of property management duties and valuation procedures. A thorough evaluation to determine highest and best use can lead an asset manager to identify and analyze alternate uses of a property. If an alternate use (e.g., conversion of an aging office building into residential units) seems feasible, the manager must be able to implement a plan to change the property's use. Yet another aspect of asset management is analysis of properties to identify and recommend what to buy, sell, refinance, or reposition in the market—possibly through a change of use. This requires knowledge of capital markets as well as local conditions.

Facility Management.   Properties owned by public (the government and the military), nonprofit (colleges and universities), and private entities (for-profit corporations) are often managed by *facility managers.* In general, facility managers coordinate the needs of people, equipment, and operational activities within the physical workplace, a role that is slightly different from that of a real estate manager. Facility managers who work for corporations have responsibilities similar to those of on-site or property managers.

Personnel Management.   Staff members in fact perform many of the duties of a real estate manager. Unless a manager's portfolio is small, one individual would have difficulty performing all of the accounting, maintenance, leasing, and administrative functions required. A support staff is usually necessary to give clients effective service. Some staff may work at a particular site; others may work at various sites; still others may not work on-site at all. Real estate managers often hire contractors to perform specific functions that are not regularly encountered or otherwise do not warrant a staff assignment.

Whether contracted or employed, staff must be managed on a daily basis. Similarly, supervision is necessary to ensure that subordinates who have staff members reporting to them comply with management standards. A manager must monitor the chain of command to verify its efficiency and maintain its flexibility to effectively serve new needs as they arise. Clear communication is crucial to the assessment of work performance and verification of adherence to specifications and safety regulations.

Staff members and contractors require operating policies and procedures to guide them in the performance of their jobs. Such policies and procedures should neither be so rigid that they stifle innovation nor so elastic that they provide no guidance at all. Management must establish, monitor, and enforce operating policies and procedures for every operating department of a property and for each job title. Policies and procedures include working hours, training procedures, productivity expectations, and accountability for tools and equipment. The property manager is responsible for the supervision of on-site and off-site personnel (including contractors) and the development of policies and procedures.

Financial Management.   Investors usually own managed property for the purpose of producing income. A large part of a real estate manager's job is to maximize that income. This mandates that a manager be capable of administering property funds and accounts. The manager should have the authority to incur expenses, up to a prescribed dollar limit for any single expense. He or she decides which items or services to purchase, determines the quality and quantity of purchases, approves invoices, and negotiates or approves contracts for services within an agreed budget.

The manager reviews all journal entries, records of accounts, bank deposits, progress reports on the collection of delinquent and slow-paying accounts, and filing of receipts to ensure consistency, accuracy, and honesty. Management information systems should include controls to safeguard receipts and disbursements. The manager prepares, reviews, or verifies the monthly operating statement and submits it to the owner. He or she meets with the owner to review financial requirements and, when appropriate, recommends sources of additional funds. The manager advises the owner of estimates of the value of the property and the implications those estimates have in comparison to similar properties.

As part of the responsibility for funds and accounts, a real estate manager determines the validity of the assessed valuation of the property (real estate taxes). The manager should also recommend that the owner consult with a qualified insurance broker regarding an appropriate insurance program for the property. (The owner, in consultation with an expert in the field of casualty insurance, determines the insurable value and related risks.)

While daily and monthly maintenance of funds is a continual process, projection of future income and expenses is also a recurring responsibility. A real estate manager must be able to develop seasonal, annual, and long-range operating and capital expenditure budgets. Even though a budget is merely an estimate, such estimates must be as accurate as possible to ensure fiscal strength and predictable cash flow. Variances will inevitably occur, however, and the manager of the property is responsible for controlling variances from the budget as much as possible.

Leasing and Tenant Management. Real estate managers do most of their work with the property owner in mind, but they must also provide their residents or commercial tenants with effective service. They must be genuinely dedicated to responding to tenants' needs because the space tenants lease is the space in which they live, work, or exchange goods. Direct attention to tenants is an indirect service to the property owner—good service fosters renewals and minimizes turnover.

Foremost among the manager's responsibilities is supervision of renting and lease renewal. In commercial properties, a separate department of the management firm or an individual leasing agent may be in charge of leasing. To maximize income from the property, the manager must determine the amount of rent to charge and authorize any deviations. If special improvements or additional resident or commercial tenant services are necessary, the manager should determine the appropriate amount of additional rent.

The real estate manager should meet routinely and personally with building occupants to discuss management matters. While this may be on an individual basis for items such as maintenance or lease renewals, the manager may also need to meet with all occupants at once (e.g., the home owner members of a condominium association). In the effort to lease available space, the manager often prepares marketing plans and selects the media, format, and volume of advertising to carry out those plans.

SUMMARY

The professional real estate manager's role is to oversee the operation and maintenance of real property according to the objectives of the owner. The development of real estate management as a function within the real estate industry resulted from a number of factors. The major demand for management expertise arose in the 1930s after lenders foreclosed on thousands of mortgages and discovered that the management of those properties required specialized skills. Since that time, the need for professional management has intensified because of absentee ownership of real estate, ownership by groups of investors through syndicates and partnerships, increased urbanization, and recognition that professional management is often necessary to maximize income and value.

Recognizing the need to establish professional standards of management, a group of real estate managers gathered during the Great Depression and founded the Institute of Real Estate Management. The Institute grants three credentials—the CERTIFIED PROPERTY MANAGER® (CPM®) designation for individuals, the ACCREDITED MANAGEMENT ORGANIZATION® (AMO®) accreditation for management firms, and the Accredited Residential Manager® (ARM®) certification for apartment managers. Recipients must meet personal education and experience requirements, and all must pledge to adhere to ethical business practices.

The primary functions of a real estate manager are management of the site, management of on-site and off-site personnel, management of funds and accounts, and management of leasing activities and tenant services. Through the educational programs offered by the Institute of Real Estate Management and from their professional experience, CPM members of IREM continually seek to improve their abilities to expand and refine the services they offer to their clients.

2

Real Estate and Economics

The goal of the manager of real property is to preserve and increase the value of the property. The manager can best accomplish this by putting the property to its *highest and best use*. In economic terms, that means the use that produces the highest yield in terms of income or value or both. To determine the highest and best use for a particular property, the manager analyzes the range of possible alternative uses. This analysis includes a study of the impact of social, political, and economic trends on each proposed use over its economic or productive life. Economic trends, in particular, have a significant impact. In order to understand the impact of economic trends on real estate, one must first understand the fundamental principles of economics.

BASIC ECONOMICS

Economics is the study of the range of activities necessary for the satisfaction of human needs. These activities include the production, distribution, and consumption of manufactured goods and agricultural products as well as the various services provided to individuals and businesses. Fundamental to all of these activities is the use of land and the construction of buildings to house these activities—real estate is an important component of economics in general. In fact, ownership of land was once the principal measure of wealth.

Today money is the measure of wealth. The material substance of wealth—an automobile, a home, furnishings, stocks, bonds, and other investments—is expressed as the money value of those items. The interrelationship between money and the goods and services it can purchase goes beyond money's role as a *medium of exchange*. Money allows comparison and measurement of the values of goods and services that are otherwise not readily comparable or measurable; it serves as a *standard of value*. Money itself has value based on its purchasing power; it serves as a *store of value* during the time between specific transactions. The value of money fluctuates over time because of changing factors in the marketplace (e.g., interest rates, inflation, money supply).

The Marketplace

In any study of economics, an important element is the *market*—the place in which the exchange of goods and services between willing sellers and buyers actually takes place. The town square market, a retail store, and a real estate office are all markets. In these markets, purchases and sales take place between people who are face to face. In other markets—e.g., the New York Stock Exchange, Chicago commodity markets, the Internet—the seller never sees the buyer. The marketplace has become complex and multifaceted. Many elements are part of or have an effect on the market for a particular item. Price, supply, and demand have direct effects on rental space and employment levels. These phenomena are themselves affected by changes in technology and in the value of money. These elements of the market are of particular interest to real estate managers.

Price.   In a complex economy where money is the medium of exchange used to measure the value of goods and services, the *price* of an item is the amount of money required in exchange for a unit of the item. Market factors determine the price of any item, and the price must be acceptable to both the buyer and the seller. If the price the seller wants is higher than the amount a buyer is willing to pay, no transaction will take place.

Supply and Demand.   Prices in the marketplace are subject to the quantity of available goods and services and the relative value of money. The availability of goods and services is called *supply*. Availability of goods and services for sale is related to price, and more goods or services are offered as prices rise. When the amount of merchandise available for sale exceeds the amount that people are willing to buy, the excess volume reduces the value of the individual units and therefore lowers the price.

Price is not the only factor that limits supply. The price of one item can affect the supply of another related item. The supply of corn drops if the price of soybeans rises because farmers choose to grow the more profitable crop. Supply of a finished product depends on the price and availability of

The Laws of Supply and Demand Relative to Price

- When demand exceeds supply, prices rise.
- If supply exceeds demand, prices drop.
- When supply equals demand, prices are stable.

its components. An increase in the number of sellers of a specific product increases the supply of that product. Reduction of import restrictions permits foreign-made goods to compete with comparable domestic products and increases the overall supply. Sellers' expectations are another consideration. For example, oil production may temporarily fall (i.e., be delayed) if prices are expected to rise in the future.

Another market factor that affects price is *demand*—the amount of goods or services for which purchasers are available. Conversely, price affects demand. Generally the amount purchased increases as prices drop. Factors other than the price of an item also affect demand. The price of related goods is one example. Demand for tea increases when the price of its substitute, coffee, rises. On the other hand, demand for sugar, a complement to coffee, drops when coffee prices rise. Because the price of coffee with sugar rises as the price of coffee rises, reduced coffee consumption will lower the demand for sugar. Another example is income. People spend more as their income rises, increasing demand. People's preferences are also a factor in demand, and advertising may alter preferences. High-fiber cereals owe their popularity to the advertisement of their health benefits. An increase in the number of buyers will increase the demand for goods or services. The baby-boomer segment of the U.S. population continues to have a high impact on product markets as it ages. Buyers' expectations are also a consideration. People tend to stock up on consumable items such as coffee when they expect prices to rise; conversely, they delay buying a car if they expect automobile prices to be lower in the future.

Over time, prices tend to be stable when supply meets or is equal to demand. When supply is less than demand, prices tend to rise; when supply exceeds demand, prices tend to fall. Taken together, these statements are the *laws of supply and demand.*

Rental Space.   These same phenomena occur in the real estate market. When demand for rental space is strong, rents go up. Growth in the number of new households increases the demand for apartments. A growing work force signals a need for more office space. Rising income encourages consumer spending, and that creates a demand for retail businesses and store space.

Rising rents stimulate investment in existing income-producing proper-

---

Employment, Unemployment, and Rent

The Bureau of the Census measures employment by surveying 58,000 households every month to gather information on their labor-market activities during the preceding week. From these data, the Bureau of Labor Statistics estimates the number of people employed and unemployed during that month. It classifies everyone over age 16 as employed, unemployed, or not in the labor force based on a specific definition of employment. The *unemployment rate* is the number of unemployed divided by the number in the labor force (the number of employed plus the number of unemployed).

For real estate managers, levels of employment and unemployment, particularly as they change within a localized area, reflect people's—and businesses'—ability to pay rent. The employment levels also indicate whether the need for housing or commercial space will increase or decrease.

---

ties (apartments, office buildings, shopping centers, industrial parks) as well as construction of new ones. New development eventually increases the supply of apartments, offices, industrial, and store spaces beyond the demand for them, and rents stabilize or decrease. The value of the real estate holding also decreases as its rental income diminishes.

Employment Levels.   The labor market, too, is subject to the laws of supply and demand. The workforce consists of all employed plus all unemployed individuals. Full employment is an unachievable ideal. As new jobs are created, other jobs are removed from the market. Unemployment can result from corporate downsizing and outsourcing of jobs, long-term decline of a specific industry, or a general downturn of the economy. Full employment (in economic terms) can only result when everyone who wants to work can find a job.

Unemployment has many negative connotations, but some types of unemployment are not negative. The voluntary changing of jobs is an active part of a dynamic economy.

Significant unemployment affects the real estate industry in several ways, most notably as a reduction of the income stream of a property. People who are not working do not have income from which to pay rent for housing. Rather than struggle to meet expenses on their own, renters may double up to share expenses, or young adults may return to their parents' homes. Inability to pay rent may force residents to vacate apartments or face eviction.

Reduction of the work force means businesses have fewer employees. For most businesses, fewer employees mean reduced work space requirements. Unemployed people are generally not consumers, so retail businesses may have to cut back on inventory and the amount of space used to display merchandise. They may opt to relocate to smaller stores. In factories, the initial reaction may be the reduction of the length or number of work shifts, but eventually manufacturers may eliminate redundant equipment and then seek smaller sites. As the slowdown of business reduces the demand for space, it also reduces the demand for new construction. The market cannot absorb additional rental space, and the market for a type of space becomes overbuilt.

The office building market is particularly affected by changes in the level of employment. High employment means that companies need more space to house their operations and personnel. The market for office space is usually healthy. However, high unemployment means companies need less space; they will also be less inclined to move because of the expense involved. If they stay and renew a lease, they may seek to reduce the amount of space rented. If they do move, it will be because they have found a smaller space that meets their needs. The ultimate effect of major unemployment on office space is higher vacancy levels and slow absorption of new space.

Technological Change   One of the most far-reaching causes of change in the marketplace is new technology. The twentieth century witnessed greater efficiency in production, improved modes of transportation, innovations in communication, and development of totally new products. New technology can affect production, distribution, supply, and demand. The jobs created by technological change have a direct impact on the labor market.

Technology also has an impact on rental space. For example, development and widespread use of computers contributed to a growing demand for new office buildings because retrofitting of older buildings for the high-tech equipment used in many businesses can be very costly. On the other hand, the use of computers and their adjuncts may increase productivity in the workplace and have a negative impact on demand. More specifically, the advent of home computing in the 1990s affected both the demand for office space and the way it is used. Computers, cellular telephones, personal digital assistants (PDAs), broadband wireless Internet access, and other new technologies made it possible for workers to perform job tasks at home or at locations other than their employers' offices. These workers could *telecommute*—connect to their office directly via telephone lines—or they could establish a *home office*, where they could use computers, facsimile (fax) machines, telephones, and the Internet (e-mail) to connect with the central office. In such situations, the employer might need less space overall. A company might not maintain office space for a particular employee but instead set aside a cluster of spaces for those staff members who only needed to work in the office periodically—a practice called *hoteling*.

Computers also altered inventories. Increased supplies of crops and manufactured goods generally increase demand for warehouse space.

However, the ability to maintain accurate counts of items in stock, coupled with manufacturers' desire not to invest large amounts of capital in inventory and their ability and willingness to ship small quantities on short notice (just-in-time delivery), reduced the need for storage space among distributors and retailers. The direct effect of this phenomenon was increased demand for *smaller* store spaces.

By-products of technology provide other examples of technology's impact on rental space. Prior to the 1980s, video stores did not exist. However, video rentals could be profitable in just about any size store, and those operations leased space in every type and size of shopping center and provided additional profits to supermarkets, drug stores, bookstores, and other businesses. On the other hand, video stores are likely to become extinct as the Internet and new technological devices make films directly available (pay-per-view). The 1990s brought the ability to transact sales securely via the Internet without specific need for a brick-and-mortar site (i.e., virtual businesses). The full impact of this change on the demand for rental retail space has yet to be determined; however, warehouse and distribution facilities have already experienced a noticeable impact. In the twenty-first century, portable devices for downloading and storing individual songs from the Internet are likely to impact the retailers who sell music on compact disks (CDs) and audiotapes.

Money.   The U.S. *money supply* comprises all of the printed currency and coinage in circulation outside of banks, plus those bank deposits that are immediately convertible to cash (savings and checking deposits owned by individuals but held in banks), plus other negotiable instruments such as traveler's checks, credit union share-draft balances, and negotiable order of withdrawal (NOW) accounts. This amount of money, referred to as *M1,* is the most frequently cited measure of the U.S. money supply. More broadly, the money supply includes less liquid funds such as money market mutual fund shares and small time deposits (e.g., certificates of deposit) on which penalties are imposed for withdrawal before a specified maturity date. Those less liquid funds are added to M1, and the result is called *M2.*

The laws of supply and demand at work in the marketplace also affect the value of money, which is a reflection of the general price level. Fluctuations in prices and in the value of money relate to the amount of currency available, the number of times money changes hands, and the amount of goods exchanged in sales and purchases. The amount of currency available includes both cash and demand deposits in banks (savings and checking accounts). The greater the volume of currency, the lower the value of the individual unit of currency—e.g., the U.S. dollar. Because money is not consumed in transactions, the number of transactions or exchanges that involve the individual unit further define the value of that unit of money. One dollar used ten times in a year has as much value in the marketplace as ten dollars exchanged only once. The need for currency is based on the *volume of trade*—the amount of goods exchanged. The greater the volume of trade, the greater the need for money and therefore the greater the value of a unit of money. A disproportionate increase in the currency in relation to the volume of goods available for purchase is *inflation*; the value of the currency decreases and prices rise. An individual needs more of the less-valuable money to make a specific purchase. On the other hand, a decrease in the currency in relation to the volume of goods is *deflation*; the value of the currency increases and prices drop. Periods of inflation and deflation result. Historically, prices were as likely to fall as to rise. Since World War II, however, deflation has been significantly absent from the U.S. economic scene. Specific changes frequently trigger inflation (or deflation) in the money supply, and governments have a key role in managing the supply of money.

The Role of Government

The U.S. government has an impact on the economy in numerous ways. Sometimes the government competes directly with private businesses, as when the Tennessee Valley Authority became a local provider of electricity. The government is also a purchaser of goods and services from private industry, and that stimulates production and fosters competition. On the other hand, specific legislation and regulatory programs add to consumer prices and skew the costs of doing business (e.g., requiring governmental agency approval of drugs, pesticides, and other products before marketing; setting minimum wage rates; taxing specific products such as tobacco, alcoholic beverages, and gasoline). *Price controls* (supported prices for agricultural products) and regulation of competition in U.S. markets (limitations on imports, subsidies for domestic products) are other examples.

In addition to its participation in the economy, the federal government also measures economic activity. It collects information on wholesale and consumer prices, interest rates, the money supply, levels of production and consumption of goods, construction starts and permits issued, sales of new and existing homes, and more. Trends and changes in these *indicators* are used to chart economic growth, inflation, and the place of the U.S. economy in the world at large.

Changes in the levels of employment and unemployment, especially in those sectors represented among residential and commercial tenants in a particular locale, signal possible changes in tenants' ability to pay rent. Growth in nonagricultural employment relates to new jobs, new businesses, and increasing demand for rentable commercial (office, retail, industrial) space. Declining employment may be the harbinger of increasing numbers of late rent payments and may lead to rental vacancies as tenants seek less-expensive space (smaller size, lower rent). It may also be a reason for tenants' unwillingness to accept rent increases at lease renewal.

Measures of Productivity

For decades, the productivity of the U.S. economy was measured as *gross national product (GNP)*. The GNP is the market value of all final goods (tangible objects such as canned food and automobiles) and services (intangible objects such as entertainment activities and transportation) produced by an economy in one year's time. It measures output attributable to U.S. residents *regardless of their geographic location.* Because foreign trade provides some of the goods and services Americans purchase, its effects are also included in the measurement of GNP. It accounts for the volume of goods and services exported to and imported from other countries. When imports exceed exports, the net value of the GNP is negative (as it was during the late 1980s in particular).

Beginning in 1991, however, U.S. productivity has been reported as *gross domestic product (GDP),* which measures the same factors for economic activity located *only within the United States.* (Nearly all other countries measure productivity as GDP, so use of GDP facilitates comparisons of U.S. economic activity with that of other countries.)

The U.S. GDP is currently measured in billions of dollars. The amount is calculated by adding together the value of personal consumer purchases (durable and nondurable goods and services) and government purchases of goods and services at the federal, state, and local levels, plus the investment of private capital in new plants and equipment, commercial buildings and residential structures (fixed investment), and new stocks of business inventory. The investment amount is adjusted for depreciation (using up) of the existing capital stock during the process of production. A rapidly rising GDP may signal rising interest rates or the beginning of a period of increasing inflation. A declining GDP may forecast falling interest rates or impending recession. (Some economists consider two consecutive quarters of declining GDP as an indicator of recession.)

Real estate is a significant portion of GDP (more than 12 percent in 2003). It comprises construction, professional services, and real estate finance and accounts for designing, building, brokering, financing, and managing real properties (residential, office, retail, industrial) built or traded for investment. It excludes building materials and construction of public facilities. Real estate's contribution to the GDP exceeds those of durable and nondurable goods manufacturing, wholesale and retail trade, and the cost of government as individual sectors.

Other indicators are also relevant to real estate and its management. Fluctuations in interest rates are a measure of the availability of funds for borrowing—for investment, construction, and operating capital. The U.S. Federal Reserve System may lower the discount rate at which it lends money to its member banks as a way to stimulate economic growth. The *Producer Price Index (PPI)* and the *Consumer Price Index (CPI)* are measures of inflation at the wholesale and retail levels, respectively. (In leases written before the 1990s, real estate managers often used the CPI for rent increases based on increased operating costs. The CPI is discussed in detail later in this chapter.) The number of building permits issued, the number and value of construction starts, and the absorption rates for newly constructed space chart the health of the U.S. real estate market. Real estate professionals in general and real estate managers in particular follow many of these economic indicators as a matter of course.

Of all the functions of government, however, taxation on income, regulation of banking, and control of interest rates are among those of greatest interest to the real estate manager. (The specific role of the various levels of government in the real estate market is discussed later in this chapter.)

Taxation.   The functions of government, including the services it provides, have inherent costs. In order to pay those costs, the government must have income. Government derives its income from various sources, the most significant of which is taxes. In the United States, the federal government taxes the income of individuals and businesses. State and local governments impose taxes primarily on property although some tax income as well.

The federal income tax, as its name implies, is a tax on personal and business income. Changes in the law have from time to time specifically encouraged or discouraged investment in income-producing property In the early 1980s, the law provided for higher tax rates on higher incomes, but it also created a variety of tax shelters. An individual or entity could invest in property that generated little or no income and still make a profit. The level of continuing inflation essentially guaranteed a selling price higher than the property's purchase price. In addition, investors could use losses from real estate investments to offset income from wages and other sources. That reduced the property owner's taxable income and in some cases lowered the tax bracket. However, the *Tax Reform Act of 1986* changed all that. Investment in real estate became less attractive because the act greatly reduced tax incentives. Property owners could no longer use losses that resulted from real estate operation to offset other income. The tax reform blocked them from sheltering that income from taxation. Owners who previously bought property for tax breaks found themselves in the position of having to use income from other sources to support their real estate investments that were operating in the red. Those who did not have extensive resources had few options, and they elected sale, foreclosure (default), and sometimes bankruptcy. Inflation slowed and property values no longer appreciated quickly, especially in overbuilt markets. As a result, the number of distressed properties on the market increased.

Changes in the federal income tax laws affect the amount of capital people are willing to invest in real estate and other assets. The *Economic Growth and Tax Relief Act of 2001* lowered individual tax rates, and the *Jobs and Growth Tax Relief Act of 2003* made further adjustments, including the reduction of the long-term capital gains tax rate from 20 percent to 15 percent. (Those capital gains rate cuts were to be effective for the tax years ending on or after May 6, 2003, through December 31, 2008.) Favorable capital gains tax rates encourage the sale of appreciated property. On the other hand, changes in the rules regarding depreciation—the method by which taxpayers are allowed to recover the cost of their investment—can encourage or discourage investment. The current long cost recovery periods for real estate investment (27.5 years for residential property; 39 years for commercial property) diminish the rate of return on the owner's investment.

Financial Regulation.   A significant role of government relates to money. Government establishes the form of money and fixes its value. It also produces the nation's money and regulates the amount in circulation. When governments mint and print additional currency, they create inflation. When they reduce the amount of currency in circulation, they cause deflation. Printed money and coinage were traditionally backed by some type of convertible commodity. Each country fixed a value of the commodity for its particular currency so that international exchange could take place. Previously, gold was the accepted standard. However, the present standard involves a mixture of floating and fixed exchange rates. The value of the U.S. dollar floats with respect to the major currencies of the world.

The U.S. government also regulates banking. Deregulation of the thrifts in the 1980s gave rise to several phenomena. Branch banking (and branch S&Ls) became widespread, and the government allowed S&Ls to offer negotiable order of withdrawal (NOW) checking accounts and to lend money for commercial investment. A large number of banks and S&Ls entered the real estate market directly, often lending money in a manner that allowed them to participate in the property ownership. Many of those institutions had no prior experience in real estate investment, and they frequently made loans for the development of marginal properties. In addition, they allowed assets held in reserve to reimburse depositors to fall below required levels (sometimes as a result of real estate assets having lost value). When the borrowers defaulted on the loans, the financial institutions foreclosed on the properties. By the end of the 1980s, the market was glutted with troubled properties. Failures of S&Ls became widespread, and the *Federal Savings and Loan Insurance Corporation (FSLIC),* which guaranteed the deposits in the institutions, was required to pay back the insured deposits. The *Financial Institutions Reform, Recovery, and Enforcement Act (FIRREA),* which the U.S. Congress enacted in 1989, transferred the responsibilities of the FSLIC to the *Federal Deposit Insurance Corporation (FDIC),* which is the insuring body for deposits in banks and in the few remaining S&Ls.

Beginning in the late 1990s, the government began allowing banks to acquire or merge with banks in other states. It modified the Bank Holding Company Act to authorize banks to underwrite and sell insurance and securities, conduct both commercial and merchant banking, and invest in and

Money and the International Arena

International trade requires the exchange of the U.S. dollar for other nations' currencies. In free markets, currency values generally *appreciate* in countries where inflation rates are lower than those in the rest of the world. Foreign demand for those countries' goods drives up the value of the currency. Likewise, in countries with lower-than-average economic activity (specifically, low imports), exchange rates (currency values) rise. Countries where interest rates are high attract investment capital from all over the world. The reverse is also true: Currencies *depreciate* in value in countries with high inflation rates, high levels of economic activity, or low interest rates. The U.S. dollar has a floating exchange rate against foreign currencies, most notably the British pound, the euro, and the Japanese yen.

In the United States, the Federal Reserve System regulates the money supply by changing the required *reserve ratio* (the amount of reserves a bank must have on hand in relation to the deposits on its books), by changing its policy on lending to banks (raising or lowering the *discount rate*), or through open market purchase and sale of government securities. To increase the money supply, the Federal Reserve purchases U.S. government bonds (treasury bills or T-bills) that pay a fixed number of dollars of interest annually for various terms (one-year T-bills, 10-year notes, 20-year bonds). Increasing the money supply results in higher bond prices and lower interest rates. Conversely, when the Federal Reserve sells bonds, the money supply decreases, and lower bond prices and higher interest rates result. As an example consider a bond that pays $90 a year. It will yield a return of 9 percent when the bond price is $1,000. However, if the bond price falls to $900, the bondholders will receive a 10-percent return.

Real estate investors and managers use the interest rate on treasury bonds as a benchmark—a *risk-free rate of return.* They use it to determine how much additional interest a real estate investment must return to compensate for its illiquidity and other risk factors. For example, if the risk-free rate of return on treasury bonds is 6 percent, a real estate investor may require an 8-percent or larger return. Internationally, the London Inter-Bank Offering Rate (LIBOR) provides a similar benchmark. The LIBOR rate quoted in *The Wall Street Journal* is an average of the rates at which five major banks would be willing to deposit U.S. currency for a set period. It compares most closely with the U.S. rate on one-year T-bills.

develop real estate, among other activities. However, the act limits the kinds of nonfinancial activities in which those new entities can engage. (Banks are not allowed to act as agents in real estate transactions.) National banks are allowed to underwrite municipal bonds.

Toward the end of the twentieth century and the beginning of the twenty-first century, consumers increasingly used electronic payments for all manner of transactions. In addition to credit and debit cards, consumers used checks as a means of electronically withdrawing money from their checking accounts. The recipients of the checks used them in the same way. *Check 21,* a law that became effective in October 2004, allowed banks, retailers, and others with whom consumers do business to speed the transfer of funds through a process called *electronic check conversion*. In other words, the paper check became a vehicle for electronic funds transfer. The information on a check—check number, account number, and financial institution identification—could be used when a check was mailed to pay a bill or when a purchase was made at a retail store. Most banks had for years provided images of canceled checks with customers' monthly statements (the originals were destroyed), and they issued a substitute check if the customer required a copy as proof of payment. Banks listed electronic transactions separately from check payments,

Interest Rates.   As part of its regulation of banking, the U.S. government controls the money supply by adjusting interest rates, and that has widespread effects. When the Federal Reserve System lowers the discount rate charged to its member banks (to stimulate economic growth), the banks, in turn, may lower the commercial *prime interest rate* they charge their most creditworthy customers for short-term loans. This can lead to a reduction in the interest rate paid on deposits as well. Conversely, the Federal Reserve System may raise the discount rate to reduce the money supply or to discourage banks from excessive leniency in their lending and investment policies.

Interest is a major inducement for people to save. When an individual's income exceeds the amount required to take care of basic needs, the surplus income can be spent immediately for personal enjoyment (to acquire possessions, for recreation, etc.) or set aside for future use. When interest rates are high, individuals are willing to save more.

Savings deposited in banks and related financial institutions do more than earn interest for the saver. That money works to produce more money. Banks use savings deposits to finance various types of lending. Consumers borrow money to purchase homes, automobiles, major appliances, recreational equipment, vehicles, etc. Businesses borrow money for operating capital, which they use to purchase raw materials for processing into finished products or to provide inventory of products for sale. Both individuals and businesses borrow money to invest in income-producing real estate. They pay the borrowed money back to the lenders with added interest. In fact, the amount borrowed often depends on the rate of interest charged.

When money is plentiful, interest rates tend to be low, and banks readily lend money to willing borrowers. Throughout the 1990s and into the 2000s, interest rates were kept low to fight inflation, despite a recovering economy. The low interest rates encouraged a boom in single-family home purchases and in refinancing, and the country enjoyed a strong economy in the latter part of the 1990s.

The exuberant purchasing and refinancing began to wane in 2004 when the Federal Reserve Bank began to raise the federal funds rate and

---

Economic Indicators

A number of economic factors measured by the U.S. government on a regular basis move upward and downward in the same pattern as the business cycle. Some of these indicators lead the cycle, some run concurrent with it, and others follow it. Of particular interest are the indexes of business activity—building permits, total output, employment, business formation, and new orders. A period of recession often follows sustained downturns in one or more of these indicators.

Indicators that relate directly to real estate include the total value of new construction put in place (all property types), nonresidential investment as a percentage of gross domestic product (GDP), total manufacturing and wholesale trade inventories, and retail sales. Other indicators of interest to real estate professionals reflect the general economy. These include consumer and producer prices, net exports, employment, and interest rates (especially the prime rate).

Indicators that tend to rise or fall in advance of a general rise or fall in business activity are called *leading indicators.* They are the most important because they give advance warning of future economic events. Normally they turn down before a recession and up before an expansion of the economy. The U.S. Department of Commerce publishes a composite *index of leading indicators* that is a weighted average of twelve of their leading indicators. Four components of this index are new building permits, net change in inventories, stock prices, and the money supply. The index of leading indicators is one of the most widely used indicators in the U.S. economy; however, its accuracy in forecasting recessions is not absolute because components of this composite index do not move together in exactly the same rhythm.

---

the federal discount rate, which in turn influenced the prime rate quoted by financial institutions. When money is tight, however, interest rates tend to rise, and individuals and businesses tend to borrow less. High interest rates encourage saving and discourage borrowing. Changes in interest rates are among the factors that contribute to inflation and deflation, and periods of inflation and deflation affect the sale and purchase of goods and services, usually in a cyclic manner. Controlling interest rates is one way the government attempts to control inflation and the amount of money available for borrowing.

The Business Cycle

Periods of economic expansion or contraction may be short-lived (a few months), or they may go on for many years. Sometimes one region of the United States or the world is affected more than another region. Occasionally a single industry or a single market is the focus of economic change, but that is rare. Businesses and industries today are interrelated in such complex ways that whatever affects one significantly eventually affects most if not all of them. Poor sales of consumer merchandise slow a retailer's business, the retailer orders less from wholesalers and distributors, and they in turn take less of a manufacturer's production. A raw material shortage curtails a manufacturer's production, less merchandise is available for wholesalers and distributors to move to retailers, and consumers cannot purchase products they desire. Changes in technology, development of new materials, and discovery of new uses for existing materials are some factors that contribute to massive economic changes. They may make current materials and technologies obsolete, or they may create entire new industries. Downsizing of computers, development of fiber-optic cables, and creation of the Internet are just a few examples.

When business is good, selling goods or services is simple. Demand exceeds supply, prices are high, and making a profit is easy. When business is poor, supply exceeds demand, prices are low, and losses often replace profits. These various periods of inflation and deflation of an economy are known as the *business cycle*. The business cycle generally has four successive stages: recession, depression, recovery, and prosperity (exhibit 2.1). By convention, professional economists look at the downside first, perhaps because its causes and effects are more readily apparent.

Recession.   During periods of prosperity, all sectors of the economy expand. The increased demand for goods and services tends to raise prices. Prosperity also results in higher wages. When personal income increases, people have a tendency to spend that income—buying a more luxurious car, paying more in rent for a larger apartment, etc.—but only up to a point. Once their needs and wants are satisfied, many people will store their surplus income in the form of savings or investments. Money held in savings is not available for spending.

When individuals actively save money, a corresponding reduction in consumer spending generally occurs. However, savings invested in banks or in stocks and bonds provide the capital for commercial investment. Spending by business firms temporarily offsets the absence of spending by consumers. The lessening of consumer spending affects businesses in two ways. Because merchants can no longer rely on the same level of sales, their income decreases, and they cannot afford to maintain the same inventory levels. Manufacturers still have to pay for raw materials, wages, and other costs of production.

Providers of services are also affected. Businesses may postpone or defer equipment maintenance and repairs. To control costs, they may have in-house staff provide services that they previously outsourced. Conversely, they may opt to reduce staff and outsource services that they can contract for less. To increase profit margins, manufacturers of consumer goods may deal directly with retailers, eliminating the wholesale distributor. Some may

Exhibit 2.1
The Business Cycle

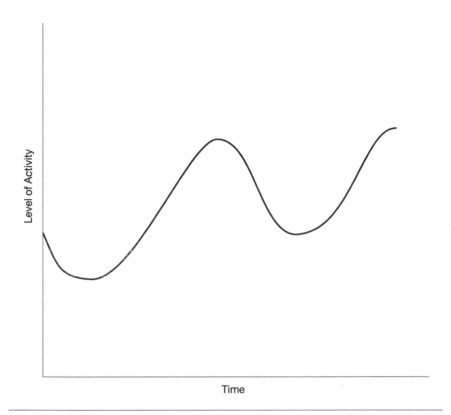

Time

The business cycle is represented by a series of troughs and peaks over time. Slowing business activity (a downward slope) is a period of *recession;* a deep trough indicates *depression.* Beginning growth or *recovery* (an upward slope) culminates in *prosperity* (the peak).

even choose to deal directly with consumers via factory outlet stores, direct mail (catalogs), and the Internet. Competition increases as businesses try to maintain or increase their share of a dwindling consumer or industrial market. In order to maintain inventories and meet payroll expenses, businesses turn to bankers. Meanwhile, the bankers become cautious; their willingness to lend money to business for expansion may not extend to providing operating capital. Tightening credit also reduces the funds available for new construction. Prices cannot continue to rise in this environment. Not enough buyers are available—demand has reduced. This slowdown in business activity signals the beginning of a period of economic *recession.*

Soon manufacturing costs catch up with selling prices. Banks raise their

---

The Business Cycle

- Recession
- Depression
- Recovery
- Prosperity

---

interest rates and may even refuse to make loans; businesses cannot borrow additional capital. The inability to obtain funds from banks leads to the failure of some businesses, and that can have a domino effect. One business may depend on payment from a second business to meet its obligations on a loan. When that payment does not come, the first business fails. Business failures mean banks and other lenders cannot collect their outstanding loans, and eventually the financial institutions themselves fail.

Depression.   A widespread reduction in business activity ultimately results. Employment drops, wages fall, and consumer demand declines. Surviving businesses try to sell all they can and buy as little as possible so they can meet contractual obligations, pay their debts, and avoid failure. As demand continues to decline, so do prices. The most serious outcome of all of these negative factors is a period of *depression*. Stocks of goods diminish as businesses sell and do not replenish their inventories. The rate of production is slow and prices are low. Interest is down and so are wages. Unemployment is widespread. Depression eliminates the weakest businesses and banks, and less competition exists in the marketplace.

Recovery.   During a depression, however, business costs also decline because rents, wages, and prices for raw materials decline. Businesses will eventually have to replace machinery and equipment they did not maintain or replace during the depression. The need for new machinery creates a demand for capital equipment, and increased demand stimulates other businesses and leads to higher prices. These are early signs of *recovery*. Once recovery gets started, employment and wages increase. Additional income increases the demand for consumer goods and services and tends to raise prices. Production costs will not rise as quickly as prices because rents, interest rates, and wages—which react more slowly to change—will remain low for some time.

Prosperity.   When prices rise faster than the costs of production, business income increases in the form of higher profits. The reviving economy heads for prosperity once again. *Prosperity* is a period of good business. Businesses foresee opportunities for profits, so they borrow capital, increase their production, and try to enlarge their share of the market. Banks are

Generational Groups

Born	Generation Names	Values
1920 to 1945	Mature Generation Matures	Duty, honor, doing a good job
1946 to 1964	Baby Boomers Boomers	Strong work ethic, personal development
1965 to 1980	Generation X Gen Xers Xers	Self-reliance, balance between rewards and costs
1980 to 2000	New Millennials Millennials Boomlets Echo Boomers	Individualism, optimism, ability to adapt to change

willing to lend money for business expansion because such loans are easy to repay. Lending expands the banks' business. The expansion of one business creates a demand for the products and services of other businesses, and that tends to raise prices. High prices in the marketplace attract other businesses to it, resulting in competition.

Population growth also fuels economic growth. In the United States, immigration has significantly affected the population. Foreign-born individuals represented 6.2 percent of the total U.S. population in 1980, 7.9 percent in 1990, and 11.1 percent in 2000. The decade from 1991 to 2000 saw a total influx of more than nine million immigrants, and another two million plus came in 2001 and 2002. More specifically, changes in the size of the population affect the size of the work force. A growing work force means larger numbers of consumers as well. The increase in immigration brings with it opportunities for specialty retailers who understand and cater to other cultures. The baby boom generation dramatically increased the size of the work force beginning in the 1970s (exhibit 2.2). However, they produced fewer offspring than their parents. As the Baby Boomers passed into middle age (in the 1990s and beyond), their children entered the work force—but in much smaller numbers. Generation X and the Millennials are expected to comprise half of the U.S. work force by 2010. Immigrants will make up the remainder. Unfortunately, this reduction in the labor pool will reduce the overall demand for consumer goods.

Prosperity tends to feed on its own momentum. Employment levels rise as businesses expand. Business expansion leads to new construction of office, industrial, and retail properties. High wages permit workers to purchase luxury items and invest in home ownership. During these times, housing starts increase, especially single-family homes. Investment, savings, and purchases on credit are on the rise. Meanwhile, rents and interest

Exhibit 2.2
Projected Population of the United States (percentage)

Age Group(s)	1970	1980	1990	2000	2010	2020	2030
Total Population (thousands)	203,235	226,546	248,791	281,422	308,936	335,805	363,584
Percent Increase	—	11.5	9.8	13.1	9.8	8.7	8.3
Under 20 years	**34.3**	*32.0*	*28.8*	28.6	26.9	26.5	26.2
20–24 years	**11.7**	**9.4**	*7.7*	*6.7*	7.0	6.2	6.4
25–34 years	12.3	**16.4**	**17.4**	*14.2*	*13.5*	13.4	12.4
35–44 years	11.4	11.3	**15.1**	**16.0**	*13.3*	*12.8*	12.8
45–54 years	11.4	10.1	10.1	**13.4**	**14.5**	*12.2*	*11.8*
55–64 years	9.2	9.6	8.5	8.6	**11.7**	**12.7**	*10.8*
65 and older	9.8	11.3	12.5	12.4	13.0	**16.3**	**19.6**

Data compiled from *Statistical Abstract of the United States*: 1999 and 2004–2005. Figures for 1970, 1980, 1990, and 2000 are actual. Aging of the baby-boom generation (those born between 1946 and 1964) is indicated in boldface.

Generation X (those born between 1965 and 1980) is indicated in italics. The population percentages for New Millennials (those born between 1980 and 2000) immediately precede the Generation X figures and overlap them by half a decade (e.g., in 2010, this group will still largely be 10–30 years old). These two generations represent the work force of the future.

rates begin to escalate as leases and contracts expire. The economy starts to slow down, checked by rising prices, wages, rents, and interest rates—all of which make money tighter—and the cycle repeats itself.

Throughout the business cycle, rents, interest, and wages do not change as quickly as other prices. Rents and interest rates usually remain fixed for a time; leases and other contracts run for months or years. Wages and salaries also remain fixed for extended periods, sometimes by contract. As general prices rise, rents, interest, and wages are slow to catch up. The disparity in these costs of production in relation to the prices commanded for goods is part of the fuel behind prosperity. Rents, interest, and wages eventually catch up with prices, however, and that has the effect of reducing profits and creating losses—ultimately fueling a recession. The numbers of potential buyers diminishes, depressing real estate prices. Unavailability of capital precludes investment in improvements, and the real estate market becomes glutted with distressed properties. In the end, the credit crunch that results promotes recovery by limiting new building.

A period of depression does not always follow a recession, and recovery is not always a separate stage in the business cycle. Sometimes periods of prosperity follow periods of mild recession; economic expansion and contraction are apparent but not pronounced. Often a scientific breakthrough or development of a promising new technology can be a

Credit Card Debt

Yet another contributor to the down side of an economy is credit card debt. With easy availability of credit, consumers are as likely—or more likely—to make purchases with credit cards than with cash. When the credit card bills come in, they have a tendency to pay only the minimum amount due, carrying forward a growing balance at a high rate of interest. Competition among credit card issuers encourages consumers to pay off an existing credit card balance using a new card at a lower interest rate. Those who continue to use credit cards without paying down the balance often end up declaring bankruptcy. Their creditors—merchants, property owners, and others—may be able to collect only a small portion of the debt owed—or nothing at all. As this book went to print, the federal government was working on legislation to change the bankruptcy laws to include provisions that would require greater repayment of debts.

Large numbers of personal bankruptcies may have little perceived impact on the U.S. economy during boom times, but in a slow economy, they mean fewer purchasers who have money to spend on consumer goods and more individuals who are unable to pay rent and other financial obligations.

significant contributor to economic recovery. The real estate industry is part of the general economy, and it reacts to the same economic pressures, but its reactions are slower and stronger. (The nature of the real estate cycle is discussed later in this chapter.)

REAL ESTATE ECONOMICS

The amount of land available for use—the earth's surface—is strictly limited. Land also has unique characteristics based on its location and its inherent qualities. These factors give value to land and affect its desirability. Value is also created when land is made *usable*—i.e., prepared for development by grading, draining, and installation of curbs, sidewalks, sewers, and streetlights.

Ultimately, the use or potential use of land determines its market value. Fertile farmland that yields more grain per acre is more valuable than less-productive acreage. However, neither will be as valuable if the grain cannot be transported to the marketplace. A location that includes ready access to transportation is a key factor in the value of farmland. Land in urban areas (city centers) is often considered more valuable than suburban land because of its intensive use. Population density is very high for residential uses—a 100-unit apartment building may occupy the same amount of land as two or three single-family homes.

In urban areas, residents accept high rents as a tradeoff against long, expensive commutes to work. They expect ready access to public transportation and the cultural and entertainment features of the city as well as the amenities of the building to compensate them for that rent. Businesses willingly pay high rents for office space in urban areas because they have access to a large labor pool and to all the services available in a city. (Exceptions do exist. Some cities have lower rents per square foot than their surrounding suburbs.) Retailers will pay high rents to have store space in an area where wealthy people shop or to have access to large numbers of potential customers. High rents mean higher property values because property returns greater profits to investors in city land.

The Real Estate Market

Markets for specific products and services exist wherever willing buyers and sellers of those products and services are. The products themselves and the people who provide the services can move from one location to another. While land is fixed in location, owners of real estate may not be local. Large commercial properties, in particular, are traded at the national level and in international markets. However, the ultimate users are local.

The value of land in the local market depends on its use and any improvements to it. Because buildings and other improvements on land have a long physical life, the commitment to a specific use is not readily subject to change. Land use is affected by many factors, among them industry, population, highways—and supply and demand.

Industry.   Changes in industry and the economy also affect land value. Inflation, wide fluctuations in the availability and cost of mortgage money, and the cost and availability of foreign crude oil are factors that affect the real estate market at the regional, national, and international levels. At the local level, empty factories and warehouses on the edge of a city may no longer be useful as industrial property. Creative developers and architects can usually find a way to convert them to other uses. Vacant warehouses that could not be sold or were no longer usable for their original purpose have been renovated and converted to housing. Factories, post offices, railroad stations, and historic buildings have been made over as shopping centers. Such changes, intended to increase the income from the property and therefore increase its value, also preserve landmarks and conserve raw materials.

Changes in a region affect land use. The growth that occurred in the *Sunbelt* (the Southwest) in the 1980s had nationwide impact. Many industries relocated there from the northeastern United States. The areas they left behind became known as the *Rust Belt*. High technology and petroleum were the booming Sunbelt businesses. They brought jobs that created demand for new office space. However, dependence on them to the exclusion of other types of industries eventually had severe effects locally. Increased importation of petroleum reduced domestic exploration and production. Higher prices for domestic oil increased the production costs of products derived from it. When the oil and high-technology industries faltered, many cities—especially Dallas and Houston in Texas—suddenly had phenomenal amounts of vacant new office space and interrupted construction. Property values declined drastically.

The 1990s brought other changes that carried over into the 2000s. Service industries flourished while manufacturing declined in the United States, and reliance on goods produced elsewhere increased. The way business is conducted continues to change as the Internet offers opportunities to buy and sell products, market and lease real estate, trade stocks and bonds, and perform similar transactions. So-called virtual businesses may need less space or use space differently than traditional businesses. On the other hand, established firms—retailers, stock brokers, and others—use the Internet as an adjunct to their traditional marketing and selling methods so they can compete effectively with their nontraditional counterparts.

Population. Changes in population size have a direct impact on land values. When the population in an area grows, land value increases. The increase in demand for the fixed amount of land leads to higher prices. Population growth is a direct result of the formation of new industries that provide jobs. New manufacturing industries attract support businesses (suppliers of raw materials or parts and distributors of finished goods), which also increase the number of available jobs. When the local population declines—particularly if significant numbers of people move away and others do not move in to replace them—demand for land decreases, land values decline, and prices fall. Population decline results when industries close down because they have become obsolete or lost their share of the market. Those satellite businesses that depended on the major industry may close down earlier because the components they supply are no longer needed or later because there are no finished products for them to distribute. These shifts in industrial activity that affect population size also affect the local economy by increasing and decreasing the amount of income available for discretionary spending.

Changes in the characteristics of a population can affect land use, and that has an impact on land value. As wages increase, individuals have more discretionary income. Home ownership, once a dream, can now become reality. The demand for housing soon becomes a demand for better quality housing as renters opt to buy or choose to pay higher rent, but only in exchange for certain amenities. Shorter workweeks (elected by employees) increase leisure time and generate a demand for recreational and entertainment facilities (e.g., golf courses, sports arenas) where the discretionary income can be spent.

Ample discretionary income and ready availability of credit encourage shopping, and that creates a demand for shopping centers. In order to meet the demand and create unique shopping environments, major malls include food courts, movie theaters, and other forms of entertainment.

The U.S. population is aging rapidly, and more people are living longer than ever before. For many, careful retirement planning provides high income after retirement. An aging population increases the demand for senior communities and retirement housing (which may be comparatively smaller and are likely to be more expensive and include recreational amenities). Such housing provides opportunities for specialty management, such as home-owner's associations. The aging population also increases the need for extended care facilities—nursing homes and health care facilities.

Highways.   New highways provide access to distant land and open new areas to development. Initial development may be housing that will draw residents away from urban areas because they can live in a less-congested environment while continuing to work and shop in the city.

Eventually commercial development will follow. Businesses will move offices and manufacturing from the city to the suburbs and even to areas once considered rural. While the areas surrounding major cities once had less congestion and a pool of labor that might not demand the same wage scale as in the city, other factors are driving this change. Computers and telecommunications have reduced the need to have all of a business's operations under one roof. While an organization may need a headquarters office in the central business district (CBD), support functions (customer service, inventory controls, storage) can be located anywhere.

Enclosed shopping malls that offer a wide range of merchandise beyond clothing not only meet the needs of suburban residents but also attract shoppers from nearby communities and cities. While highways provide suburban residents access to cities, they also create reverse commutes. Some people who live in the city cannot find jobs there, and suburban commercial areas cannot always fill their labor needs from the nearby communities. So people may travel from the city to the suburbs to work—instead of the reverse.

Highways not only open land to development, they also lead to specific land uses. Travelers between cities create demand for roadside facilities such as service stations, restaurants, and various qualities of temporary lodging (hotels, motels). Highway intersections that attract operators of roadside facilities eventually attract other businesses, and those businesses attract employees who become residents in the area. All of these factors that lead to land development also add to its value.

Supply and Demand.   In the real estate market, the laws of supply and demand are also at work. Usually the value of real estate in a given market is based on the present worth of projected future benefits to be derived from the investment. Stable values result when a balance exists between the supply of a given land use and the economic demand for that use. Supply may be limited and is not quickly increased. Supply declines because of deterioration, demolition, and destruction by hazards (e.g., fire). Change of use reduces the supply of one use while adding to the supply of another. Existing properties are part of the total supply even if they are not used. Demand changes, however, and many factors influence it. Population, income, credit, personal tastes and preferences as well as governmental actions, taxes, and cost savings all have an impact on demand. The imbalance between supply and demand means real estate investment can be riskier than other types of investments whose markets are more predictable.

When a particular use (e.g., office space, shopping centers) is in oversupply, the value of that type of property declines. An overbuilt market is a renter's market. More space is available than renters who desire such space, so prospective tenants can negotiate lower rents and other favorable terms—some or all of which can have negative long-term effects on property value. An underbuilt market is more appealing to investors because it favors the property owner. When demand exceeds supply, the available space commands high rents because less competing space exists.

Government and Real Estate

Governments at all levels affect real estate transactions in numerous ways. Local governments tax real property based on its value *(ad valorem tax)*. The tax burden affects the value of a particular parcel of land and is therefore an important consideration in the investment in real estate. Local *zoning* ordinances impose limits on land uses, and compliance with them—or efforts to change zoning—can be costly. Appropriate zoning is particularly important in real estate development.

Federal regulations that affect financial transactions have an impact on the real estate market. Acceptable interest rates and the availability of funds for mortgage loans determine how much buyers can borrow. As stated, high interest rates discourage borrowing. The amount of *debt service* (mortgage principal and interest payments) affects the return that an investor can derive from the purchase of a rental property. To meet debt service requirements, the property must generally produce more income. The amount of income needed to pay debt service reduces the amount of income the owner can keep. Note, however, that a mortgage reduces the amount of money the owner has to invest initially, and leveraging (financing) can yield a higher return on the amount actually invested.

Government ownership of land in national and state parks, highways and rights of way, public buildings, and military bases makes the government a major participant in the real estate market. The presence of various government-owned properties can increase or decrease real estate values, depending on what and where they are. A military base, for example, may be desirable because it brings jobs to an area. Conversely, if it attracts undesirable businesses to the area (e.g., bars or adult entertainment), a military base does not enhance surrounding property values.

Numerous governmental subsidy programs have an influence on property values and real estate investment decisions. Some housing programs subsidize rents for lower income groups and may limit rental rates for private properties that participate in the program. Other programs encourage home ownership by offering more favorable terms for mortgage loans than are available in the private sector, in effect competing with it. (Chapter 9 discusses government-subsidized housing in more detail.)

Federal programs are often the key to land development or redevelopment. One such program is *urban renewal,* which opens land in cities to new uses. Urban renewal has both short-term and long-term effects. The short-term effects are often negative because urban renewal displaces the original users to land elsewhere and results in a loss of property value in the sale. When urban renewal eliminates housing, the residents move elsewhere, often to the suburbs. It also encourages the movement of businesses and industries to the suburbs. The displaced owners may have to accept less than market value for their properties because that is all they can get. (The sale price of a property may reflect low values of adjacent, blighted properties.) In the long term, however, urban renewal has many positive aspects, especially as it revitalizes the area. Development of a parcel of land for one use usually attracts development of adjacent land, often for a different use. Industrial development may attract research facilities and offices. Residential development tends to attract retailing and entertainment enterprises. Occasionally the reverse is true.

Different levels of government occasionally impose *rent controls,* usually with the intent of setting upper limits on rental rates to maintain a pool of affordable housing. In general, rent controls interfere with the operation of the laws of supply and demand in the marketplace. In the absence of rent controls, more rents would tend toward the average rate rather than the extreme high (uncontrolled) and low (controlled) rates. Rent controls create an artificial lack of movement in rents at the lower end of the rate range. People tend not to vacate rent-controlled apartments. The stagnation at low and middle rental rates forces those who are moving to go to areas where rents are higher. When controlled rents are substantially lower than market rents, the demand for those units is often disproportionately high, and the demand for units at market rates is consequently low. The reduction in rental income that results when controls are in place means less money is available for maintenance and repairs, so property owners defer maintenance. The lower income and the deferred maintenance contribute to lowering the property's value. In order to sell a property after rent controls have been in place, the owner may have to take a loss. A loss may result anyway through deterioration, which can remove the property from the overall supply and curtail rental income altogether.

Some regulations affect real estate both directly and indirectly. Laws enacted to protect the environment offer a useful example. Concerns about the presence of asbestos in buildings led to demands for containment or removal of the material from certain classes of existing buildings and the use of other materials for fireproofing new buildings. The direct effect was tremendous costs to building owners for containment or removal of asbestos. These demands also had an effect on property value because the presence of asbestos made a building less desirable to prospective buyers. The potential for long-term liability if asbestos was discovered after the sale of the building added to the problem. Although the demand for removal or containment of this potential hazard changed as more research emerged, the effect on the real estate market did not go away. All levels of government can enact environmental regulations, and owners must comply with the most stringent requirements that apply in a given situation. Because of this, the environmental aspects of a property will continue to be a major concern for real estate owners and managers as well as potential investors.

Laws regarding fair housing are of particular interest to real estate managers. All levels of government make *fair housing laws,* and they specifically regulate how houses are sold and how apartments are rented (see chapter 9). Federal income tax laws (discussed earlier in this chapter) specifically affect investment in real estate.

Real Estate Cycles

Just as other businesses have a cyclic nature, so does the real estate market. Statistics regarding real estate sales, new housing starts (single-family and multiple dwellings), mortgage lending, new construction, and absorption rates for rental space show periods of high and low levels of activity. Historically, the total of real estate transactions or sales recorded in real estate markets throughout the United States has operated on a long cycle that averages more than 18 years. However, some cycles have been longer and others have been much shorter. Discrepancies in duration often relate to important historical events (depressions, wars, major technological changes). A short cycle that lasts up to five years also exists. It relates to the availability of mortgage funds, shifts in money markets, and governmental housing programs.

Like the business cycles discussed earlier, the real estate cycle has four components. They generally follow their business counterparts (see exhibit 2.3). As a result of *overbuilding,* demand begins to decline, absorption slows, and rents weaken further just as construction peaks. Overbuilding is a consequence of prosperity, which cannot last forever. It precedes and

Exhibit 2.3
The Business Cycle and the Real Estate Cycle

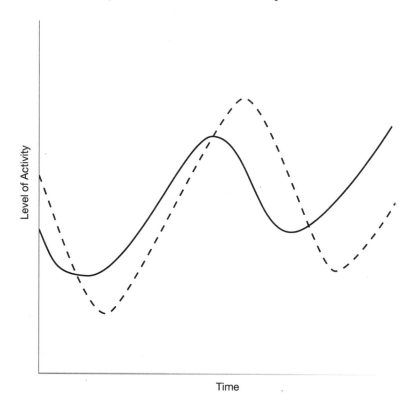

The solid line indicates the business cycle; the broken line shows the real estate cycle, which follows it. Slowing business activity (a downward slope) is characteristic of a period of recession. In the real estate cycle, new construction declines because of overbuilding (a peak) and leads to a period of adjustment during which occupancy declines and rent concessions are widespread. A deep trough indicates depression; occupancy and rents reduce severely. An upward slope signals beginning growth or recovery. In the real estate cycle, this reflects accelerated demand for rental space and increased new construction. The business cycle culminates in prosperity (the peak) which leads to new levels of overbuilding.

then coincides with recession. The real estate market then undergoes an *adjustment*—demand continues to decline, occupancy diminishes further, and rent concessions become widespread. New building slows decidedly during periods of recession and depression. This is followed by *stabilization,* a period in which demand begins to increase despite declining construction starts, making inroads into the excess supply. This coincides with the depths of recession or depression and is the real estate equivalent of

---

The Real Estate Cycle
- Overbuilding
- Adjustment
- Stabilization
- Development

---

recovery. The last stage is *development*. As prosperity returns to the rest of the economy, occupancy is high, rents are rising, and absorption levels are high. Demand accelerates and the market needs new construction to meet the increased demand.

Activity in other sectors of the economy drives real estate demand, which consequently tends to lag behind the upward movements in the general economy. However, real estate demand tends to exceed the heights of the peaks and the depths of the troughs of the general economic cycle. Recovery and prosperity are reflected in high occupancy levels, high rental rates, strong real estate sales, large amounts of money available to lend at acceptable interest rates, and large volumes of new construction. Conversely, during periods of economic recession and depression, vacancies increase, delinquencies in mortgage and rent payments rise, and real estate sales decline in numbers of sales and prices. New construction slows and the numbers of mortgage loans and their dollar values decline.

Many of the factors that influence real estate cycles are inherent in the real estate market itself. Real estate is not always a mirror of the general economy. By its very nature it is local, and local situations have greater impact on the local real estate market. However, conditions outside the immediate market area frequently generate real estate booms and busts. Globalization and institutionalization of investment capital had key roles in the U.S. real estate market in the late 1980s and early 1990s. (The impact on the real estate cycle of the prolonged period of low levels of inflation and high unemployment in the mid- to late 1990s and early 2000s has yet to be measured and is likely to be significant. In particular, the extended period of low interest rates may have ameliorated the effect of higher unemployment to some extent.)

Occupancy levels reflect the relationship between supply and demand at current rent levels. Changes in occupancy levels are of particular concern to real estate managers. However, the public sets the tone of the market. Occupancy levels that are extremely high indicate a probable space shortage and may justify higher rents. High vacancy, on the other hand, suggests a weak market in which renters are likely to resist rent increases.

The rental price level reflects the strength of the current real estate situation. It moves up and down in response to changes in supply and demand.

Consumer Price Index and Rent

The *Consumer Price Index (CPI)* is the most commonly used measure of inflation. The U.S. Department of Labor calculates the current year's cost of a particular array of goods and services consumed by a typical family and reports it as a percentage of the cost of those same goods and services in a *base year* (also set by the Department of Labor; currently 1982–1984 = 100). Among the goods and services "consumed" are food and beverages, housing, apparel, transportation, medical care, and entertainment.

The CPI is computed and published monthly or bimonthly for most of the *metropolitan statistical areas (MSAs)* in the United States. As a measure of inflation, the CPI provides the basis for raising wages and for adjusting Social Security benefits, pension benefits, and income tax schedules. Real estate managers may use it as a guideline for rental rate increases, but this practice has lost favor, especially in commercial real estate where it was once common.

Because existing long-term leases may still include references to the CPI, the following additional information is included here. Upward movement of the CPI favors the real estate manager whose leases include specific provisions for rent increases based on the CPI (*escalation clauses* are discussed in chapter 10). The CPI provides a rationale (measure of inflation) and a rate (the percentage change) for the scheduled rent increases based on a reputable, nonbiased statistic provided by the government. Because the CPI measures inflation over time, annual rent increases based on the change in the CPI are usually realistic. (A rent escalation clause based on the CPI enables the property owner to retain the current value of rent dollars.) However, downward movement of the CPI for any length of time can reduce or cancel the benefit expected. The CPI showed a price decrease in 1955; both before and since, it has always moved upward.

When demand exceeds supply, higher rental rates can be charged, and rent increases at renewal of leases or as automatic adjustments under escalation clauses (in commercial leases) are more readily accepted. Real estate managers must know the prevailing trends in rental rates in their area.

Mortgage lending reflects the lenders' confidence in the safety and desirability of real estate as an investment. Lenders must believe the property is sound, that it will retain its value or increase in value over time, and—most important from their perspective—that it will generate sufficient income to assure repayment of the loan. Real estate managers should keep abreast of current interest rates in their area because rising interest rates adversely affect mortgage lending.

Building activity is a measure of the economic potential of vacant land. Large-scale construction can increase the supply of a specific use and depress the market for that type of space. When a surplus of space exists, construction slows, and that has wide-reaching effects beyond the real estate market itself. Unemployed construction workers may not be able to pay rent. They certainly will not have income to spend for consumer goods, and that will affect other segments of the economy.

Mortgage foreclosures reflect the inability of owners of real property to generate enough income from their properties to pay the debt on them. In general, foreclosures of income-producing real estate are an effect of economic recession or depression. Real estate loses earning power because of reductions in occupancy levels and rental rates. However, the absence of foreclosures does not necessarily signify prosperity. Real estate managers must understand the conditions that lead to foreclosures and be aware of foreclosure activity in the local market.

SUMMARY

The real estate manager's goal is to preserve and increase the value of a property through good management. This can best be done by trying to achieve the highest and best economic use for the property. An evaluation and understanding of economic trends is necessary to the accomplishment of this goal.

Economics covers the activities of production, distribution, and consumption of manufactured goods and agricultural products. Real estate is a part of the economic picture because land is fundamental to economic activity.

Value is attributed to the products of economic activity by agreement to exchange one kind of goods for another. The use of money facilitates exchange because it functions as a standard of value. It allows the measurement and comparison of the value of goods and services that otherwise cannot be readily measured or compared. Money is also a store of value through its purchasing power.

The marketplace is subject to the laws of supply and demand. When supply is less than demand, prices tend to rise; when supply exceeds demand, prices tend to decline. Changes in the supply of money in relation to the volume of goods available for purchase affect the overall economy. More money than goods signals inflation; the opposite signals deflation. Because the federal government can control the supply of money, its actions can lead to inflation and deflation.

In general, business activity is cyclic in nature. Prosperity is a period of economic growth, but economic growth cannot continue forever. Workers who have met their needs and wants tend to save their excess wages. When workers are saving and not spending their income, banks and other financial institutions have capital to lend to businesses for expansion. However, reduced consumer spending reduces business income, and financial institutions that lent freely for expansion become disinclined to lend money for operating capital. The economy slows, and prosperity is followed by a period of recession. Supply exceeds demand, prices drop, and production decreases. Profits fall off and businesses have less income to pay for operating expenses. Wages decrease, and unemployment increases. Borrowing slows, and businesses fail. At its lowest point, the economy may enter a period of depression. Eventually, however, the surviving businesses take stock of their situations. Their inventories are low, and they have to replace equipment. Orders for new merchandise and machinery create demand, which leads to increasing prices, and the economy begins to recover. Recovery soon becomes prosperity, which is a period of high demand in comparison to supply. This is apparent in high profits, high levels of borrowing, and increased production. Unemployment is low, wages are high, and prices for consumer products are high.

Real estate is part of the overall economic picture primarily because of the relationship between land and economic activity. However, the real estate market is itself subject to the laws of supply and demand, and factors in the general economy of the nation and the world can have an impact on it. The real estate market is also affected by governmental actions, both those related specifically to real estate and those that affect the economy at large.

The real estate business is cyclic, and it follows a pattern similar to that of the business cycle. Changes in occupancy levels, rental rates, and mortgage financing are among the specific components of real estate cycles. Often the cycles of real estate are reflections of the state of the general economy, although they tend to follow other trends and to be more extreme.

3

Ownership Forms
and Goals

The purpose of professional real estate management is to achieve the investment goals of the property's owner. People have many reasons for investing in real estate, and ownership can take many forms. The method of purchasing property, the reasons for ownership, and the form of property ownership affect the management of income-producing real estate. To achieve an owner's goals, a real estate manager must first examine how and why a property is owned.

MEANS AND REASONS FOR INVESTING IN REAL ESTATE

Most Americans aspire to invest in real estate at some point in their lives. A principal dwelling is often the largest and most expensive item an average American purchases. Because people normally buy a home or condominium to live in, they may not consider the purchase of their principal dwelling primarily as an investment. A new home owner usually says, "I bought a house," instead of, "I invested in real property." However, purchasing real property is always an investment, regardless of how the owner uses the property.

Means of Investing

An investor or group of investors purchases a property in one of two ways. Either they buy it outright as an all-cash purchase, or they finance part of

---

Liquid Assets

- Savings accounts
- Money market accounts
- Certificates of deposit
- Stocks
- Bonds
- Mutual funds
- Precious metals

---

the purchase price through a loan. Both purchases have specific advantages and disadvantages for the investor.

All-Cash Purchase. An all-cash purchase yields a greater cash return on a periodic basis than a financed purchase because payments for financing (*debt service*) do not consume a substantial portion of the income from the property. Even though an all-cash purchase promises a greater income, this benefit is not without cost. Because the purchase price of income-producing property is commonly quite high, an all-cash purchase may consume most of an investor's assets and limit his or her ability to diversify investments.

The ready availability of large amounts of cash depends on how the cash is held. Savings accounts (including money market accounts and certificates of deposit), stocks, bonds, and/or mutual funds, and precious metals are considered *liquid assets* because the owner can quickly and easily convert them into cash at or near their market value. An investor can withdraw money from a bank account for investment in stocks. The stocks can be converted back into cash and invested in platinum. The investor can then sell the platinum to invest in bonds. The advantage of a liquid asset is the diversity it offers. The investor who owns $100,000 of platinum and decides to purchase $50,000 of stock can simply sell enough platinum to pay for the stock. On the other hand, real property is considered an *illiquid asset*. The owner can only convert real estate into cash in two ways: sell or refinance the property. Neither is quick, and both require agreement on the property's value.

Financing. Borrowing funds to purchase an income-producing property is often necessary or desirable. For real property, when a financial institution approves a loan it drafts an instrument called a *mortgage*. Among other things, a mortgage places a lien on the property in favor of the lender should the borrower fail to repay the loan. (The borrower pledges the property and its deed as *collateral* to secure the mortgage loan. The lender has the right to foreclose the mortgage, sell the property, and apply the proceeds to the

---

Basis of Investment Value

The "value" of an owner's investment in real estate is *equity.* An all-cash purchase gives the owner 100-percent equity. If a real estate purchase is financed, the investor's initial equity is the amount of the cash down payment. When an owner has an amortizing loan and holds a property over time, the owner's equity increases as the principal of the loan decreases. If the owner then sells the property for more than the original purchase price, the increase in the market price is the result of an *appreciation* in value, and the amount of appreciation becomes part of the owner's equity. For example, if an owner pays $10,000 down on a $100,000 real estate purchase and finances the remaining $90,000, the owner's initial equity is $10,000. If the property sells for $120,000 five years later, the seller's equity at that time will be *at least* $30,000 ($10,000 initial equity plus $20,000 in appreciation *plus* whatever equity—if any—has accumulated through amortization).

---

outstanding debt in the event the borrower defaults on the loan.) In essence, the mortgage is the legally binding document that stipulates the loan conditions, but borrowers and lenders alike commonly use the words *mortgage* and *loan* interchangeably. Some states use a *deed of trust* in place of a mortgage. The deed pledges the property as collateral— the buyer holds title to the property as a *warranty deed,* and the financial institution and the buyer execute a note as evidence of the debt. The difference between a mortgage and a deed of trust is that the former requires a court order for foreclosure, but the latter does not.

Mortgages for all real property loans contain three major conditions: (1) They require the repayment of the *principal* (the amount borrowed), (2) they require the payment of interest on the principal, and (3) they require a specific schedule of payments. The process of repayment (*debt service*) addresses all three of these conditions. Borrowers usually pay debt service monthly, and the amount of the payment depends on the interest rate for the loan, the term (duration) of the loan, and whether part of the payment is to pay back principal.

When the purchaser's payments gradually reduce the principal with each succeeding debt service payment over the term of the loan, the loan is fully *amortized.* In the early years of the loan term, the lender allocates most of the borrower's monthly debt service payment to interest and applies only a small portion (initially as little as five percent) to pay down the principal. However, if the payment amount remains the same, the portion the lender allocates to interest gradually decreases as the borrower pays the principal down over time, and the portion the lender allocates to principal slowly increases. The type of loan determines whether the lender uses the debt service payment to amortize the principal and if so, how much it uses for that purpose. In real estate investment, the best loan is usually the one that has the lowest annual debt service because paying less debt service increases the property's cash flow.

In addition to monthly payments, most mortgages have start-up costs such as points and application fees. A *point* is one percent of the total loan amount. If the borrower must pay two points to secure a $100,000 loan, the lender will receive $2,000 at the closing of the purchase (beginning of the loan). Because the acquisition of real estate involves more than the purchase price of the property, some owners consider these additional costs as part of their *initial investment base*. If the purchaser must invest additional funds in the newly purchased property to make it operational (rehabilitation) or to enhance its ability to generate income (installation of new appliances to upgrade apartments and achieve higher rental rates), many investors add the cost of those initial improvements into the investment base as well.

Lenders offer many types of mortgages. Some of the more common types are the fixed-rate, variable-rate, adjustable-rate, and balloon payment mortgages.

Fixed-Rate Mortgage.   In a *fixed-rate mortgage,* the interest rate is constant over the term of the loan. This type of loan was once the industry standard. The individual monthly payments on a loan with a long amortization period (e.g., 30 years) are generally lower than payments on the same loan with a shorter amortization (e.g., 15 years). Lower payments can be beneficial, especially when the income from the property is low. However, a longer amortization period usually has a much higher cumulative cost because the portion of each debt service payment the lender applies to the principal is smaller, and the borrower makes more payments over time.

Variable-Rate Mortgage.   On the other hand, a *variable-rate mortgage* permits the lending institution to raise or lower the interest rate of the loan based on changes in a prescribed index such as the average Treasury bill yield or the prime rate. Interest on most variable-rate mortgages is a few percentage points above the *prime rate,* which is the lowest interest rate available from banks for short-term loans to their most creditworthy customers. The rates are generally lower in the initial years of the loan term than they are for fixed-rate mortgages of comparable dollar amounts.

Adjustable-Rate Mortgage.   An *adjustable-rate mortgage (ARM)* is a type of variable-rate mortgage in which the interest rate is adjusted at fixed intervals (e.g., semiannually or annually) based on changes in the appropriate index. Variable-rate mortgages may have an upper limit or *cap* on the amount of change allowed in a year and over the term of the loan.

Balloon Mortgage.   Lenders sometimes permit repayment of a loan based on an amortization period that is longer than the term of the loan. For example, the fixed debt service payment may be based on a 25-year amortization, but the loan is actually due in 10 years. The monthly payments allocate a small amount to the reduction of principal; the bulk of the payment goes to interest; and the borrower pays a very large *balloon payment* at the end of the term of the loan (i.e., 10 years). The balloon amount pays off the remaining principal balance due. The benefit of this loan structure is that the monthly payment is smaller than that of a 10-year fully amortized loan at the same interest rate. The requirement of a balloon payment compounds the risk inherent in borrowing. If funds are not available for the balloon payment, the borrower must refinance, and the interest rate and monthly payments for the refinancing may be higher. If he or she is unable to refinance, the borrower must sell the property to cover the debt or risk foreclosure.

While financing has many advantages, purchasers must understand that their equity in the property will be less than 100 percent until the principal of the mortgage is fully amortized.

Reasons for Investment

Even though real estate is an illiquid investment, the allure of owning property and the financial rewards of ownership make real estate one of the largest storehouses of wealth. The earnings of liquid investments usually derive from a few sources. Growth in the value of precious metals is based on demand; investors often buy metals to preserve capital. The value of stock can appreciate from both demand for the stock and increasing value (profitability) of the company. Stocks often pay a periodic dividend as well, while the only earnings from a savings account are periodic interest payments. Bonds purchased at less than face value have a fixed maturity date and accrue interest over the period for which they are held. While some bonds are tax free (e.g., municipal bonds), the income from others may be taxable when the bond matures, when the investor converts it to cash, or throughout the holding period as the interest accrues. Real property, on the other hand, can provide all four of the following: capital preservation, capital appreciation, periodic return (regular income), and income tax advantage. While a major consideration in real estate investment is financial return, it has nonfinancial considerations as well. Real estate can also be a means of diversifying an extensive investment portfolio.

Capital Preservation.   Many people believe that investment in real property is a way to preserve capital. Property values tend to rise with the inflation rate if the property is in a good location and the economic environment of the area is healthy. Land and real property are similar to precious metals because they have an *intrinsic value*. They are inherently useful. The intrinsic value of a property should increase at least at the same rate as inflation.

Financial Reasons to Invest in Real Estate
- Capital preservation
- Capital appreciation
- Periodic return (regular income)
- Income tax advantage

Investors interested primarily in the safety of their capital look for property with extremely low risk. Qualities that indicate low risk include the following:

- Prime location
- Durable construction
- Architectural style that will not become outdated
- Excellent potential to increase in value over time
- Established tenancy
- Long-term leases containing *pass-through clauses* (provisions that allow property owners to pass to tenants increases in certain operating expenses and rent escalations)
- Sufficient income from property to pay expenses and debt service (if financed)
- Intrinsic property value nearly equal to purchase price
- Absence of encumbrances (e.g., mechanics' liens or zoning restrictions)

Capital Appreciation.   *Appreciation* is the increase in the value of an asset over time. In real estate investment, capital appreciation is realized when an owner sells a property for more than its original purchase price. Because it does not materialize until the owner sells or refinances the property, capital appreciation can be the ultimate goal of a long-term investment, although appreciation is also possible for a short-term holding.

The manager of real property plays an important role in the capital appreciation of the investment by positioning the property to meet its highest and best use, producing as much income as possible, controlling operating costs as much as possible, and maintaining, preserving, and improving the structure itself. Value can increase for several reasons. If income increases and exceeds any increase in expenses, the property will be more desirable and can sell for a higher price. An improvement in the economy of the area, greater demand for property in the area, rehabilitation of the property, or a change in its use can drive value up as well.

Periodic Return.   The relationship between purchase price and cash flow is a consideration for real estate investors who seek regular, periodic income from their property. (*Cash flow* is the amount remaining after subtracting operating expenses and debt service from gross receipts; see chapter 5). In the same manner that a real estate manager can enhance capital appreciation of the property, he or she can influence the amount of periodic income derived from property operations. However, the amount of income a property can generate is subject to prevailing conditions in the market. (The investor's income can be expressed in dollars—i.e., cash flow—or as a percentage.)

Income Tax Advantage.   Federal and state governments in the United States and elsewhere commonly grant tax incentives for real estate investment. Incentives for property ownership help drive the U.S. economy. To increase the amount of housing stock available, federal and state governments allow income tax deductions for mortgage interest, operating expenses, and depreciation of income-producing residential property. Owners of income-producing commercial properties can take the same kinds of deductions. The deductibility of mortgage interest encourages borrowing, which keeps money in circulation. The demand for loans encourages lending institutions to seek savings and investments, which in turn generate additional tax dollars. The deductibility of operating expenses provides an incentive for the owner to reinvest in the property and keep it well maintained.

Depreciation.   *Depreciation* (also called *cost recovery* for income tax purposes) is particularly enticing because it is a noncash expense that the property owner can take as a deduction from income. The U.S. income tax laws permit an owner to assume that a building has a specific *useful life* in which it will produce income and to recover the cost of the building over a period of years. The depreciation period (or useful life) varies for different types of properties. In theory, if the depreciation period is 39 years, the property owner can deduct 1/39th of the purchase price of the property (excluding the land) each year for 39 years. The calculation of income tax deductions for depreciation is more complicated, however. The tax law sets the periods of useful life for various classes of property. For real estate investments, the depreciation period depends on the type of property (e.g., residential or commercial).

Capital Improvements.   The depreciation deduction also applies to *capital improvements*—investments in equipment or alterations that last for more than one year and increase the value, productivity, or useful life of the property. The number of years the government allows for depreciation of capital improvements varies, and the deduction may be larger during the early years of the depreciation period (*accelerated cost recovery*). The Internal Revenue Service also distinguishes between a capital improvement and a *repair* that preserves the investment in a property but does not lengthen its useful life. As an example, adding new microwave ovens to existing apartments is a capital improvement (added value); fixing a hot water heater is a repair. The cost of a repair is tax deductible as an operating expense for the year in which it is made.

Tax advantages of real estate ownership vary with changes in federal income tax laws. At times, the amount of interest, real estate tax, and depreciation claimed in a given year may result in a taxable loss, which is subject to passive loss limitations. (See chapters 1 and 2 for discussions of the Tax Reform Act of 1986.)

Pride of Ownership.   In addition to the financial reasons to own income-producing property, the real estate manager must understand that investors sometimes own real property because of an inherent pride of possession. Real estate is more tangible than stock certificates or other assets. Property ownership can be a symbol of financial security, wealth, or power. A real property is in a specific location and serves a specific purpose. Those aspects of the property make the owner a contributor to the community, and that alone can give an owner pleasure. In addition, the owner may live on the premises, have an office there, or possibly operate a retail business in the income-producing property he or she owns, so an owner's relationship to the property can have more dimensions than just derivation of income.

Even though pride of ownership cannot be measured in financial terms, those who truly care for their income-producing property usually profit financially from their personal interest in it. Property owners who take extraordinary pride in their holdings may not seek the highest financial return possible; often they prefer to reinvest a portion of the proceeds in repairs, maintenance, and improvements. They respect the need to set aside reserves for future maintenance. Even though such owners may not seek a maximum net income, their pride in the property is likely to increase net income anyway. Attention to maintenance and repairs has the potential to attract tenants. Deductibility of maintenance and improvement costs offers tax incentives, and dedicated care makes capital preservation and capital appreciation more likely outcomes.

PRINCIPAL FORMS OF INCOME-PROPERTY OWNERSHIP

Investors can own an interest in real property in many ways. Each form of ownership provides the investor with different capabilities and limitations in making a profit from the property. (See exhibit 3.1.) No particular

Exhibit 3.1

Characteristics of Ownership Forms

Ownership Form	Taxation Status	Investor Liability	Management
Sole Proprietorship	Single	Unlimited	Personal
General Partnership	Single	Unlimited	All partners
Limited Partnership	Single	Limited	General partner(s)
Limited Liability Company	Single	Limited	Manager member
C Corporation	Double	Limited	No restrictions
S Corporation	Single	Limited	No restrictions
REIT	Modified single*	Limited	Trustees

*Tax losses cannot exceed cash distributions.

form is necessarily ideal; each has certain advantages and disadvantages. Depending on the property and the goals of the investors, one form can be more beneficial than others. The most common forms of income-property ownership are sole proprietorships, partnerships, corporations, real estate investment trusts, and joint ventures.

Sole Proprietorship

The *sole proprietorship* is a mainstay among ownership forms. Most individual owners invest in small buildings—a second house to rent to others or a small storefront or apartment building. The sole proprietor does not often have real estate holdings worth millions or billions of dollars.

A sole proprietor has total control and unlimited liability. Sole proprietors benefit directly from the profits the property produces. They are also directly liable for all financial losses and may be able to take deductions for such losses on their personal income tax. However, deductibility rules vary (passive loss limitations apply). Because of this variability, both the owner and the manager should scrutinize tax provisions and seek the guidance of legal or tax advisors (or both) regarding the deductibility of losses.

A sole proprietor usually takes great pride in owning real estate and generally is more involved in management decisions than he or she might be if more than one person owned the property. The involvement is understandable; such an investment is usually substantial for a single owner.

Because the sole proprietor can take an exceptionally active interest in management, the demand on the manager's time may be disproportionately high. The owner may consider himself or herself the manager's only client. On the other hand, sole proprietors own large numbers of investment properties in the United States, and many of them direct the management of their property in a sophisticated manner. Every sole proprietor is different. By incorporating knowledge of the property and the owner's goals in a detailed management plan, a manager can ensure that the working relationship between the manager and the sole proprietor will be rewarding both financially and personally. (Chapter 4 discusses the development of a management plan.)

Partnerships

Because of the high cost of land and the buildings on it, group ownership is often a more realistic undertaking than individual ownership. A very common association of individual investors is a *partnership,* which is an arrangement that allows each partner to participate in the profits and losses of their mutual investment. The partnership distributes all profits and losses to the partners based on the amount of their investments or as stated in their partnership agreement. Although it must report information on income, gains, losses, etc., annually, the partnership itself pays no income tax. The income (or loss) of the partnership affects the tax reporting of the individual partners based on their shares in the investment.

A partnership (or other form of multiple ownership) may be certified as a legitimate business entity. Depending on state law, a partnership may sue or be sued in the names of the partners or in the firm name. The ownership form does not insulate individual investors from liability. If a partnership is sued and found liable, the general partners would be liable individually and collectively for damages (*joint and several liability*).

Partnerships usually take one of two forms: a general partnership or a limited partnership. The end of this section discusses two special types of partnerships: syndicates and limited liability companies.[1]

General Partnership.   A general partnership involves two or more investors who agree to be associated for business purposes. Title to property is held in the name of the partnership. All partners share in the rights, duties, obligations, and financial rewards to the extent of their own participation or in accordance with the partnership agreement. However, the partners' personal liability for the debts of the partnership is unlimited. Any general partner can commit the other partners to a financial obligation without their consent or knowledge, provided the partner makes the contract for the

1. Two or more investors may own property in joint tenancy or tenancy in common. These forms of ownership usually apply to smaller properties. Under *joint tenancy,* ownership passes to the other joint tenant(s) (owners) upon the death of one of them (right of survivorship). In *tenancy in common,* each tenant (owner) holds an undivided interest in the property, which passes to his or her heirs upon the death of the individual. These forms of ownership are outside the scope of this book.

service or material on behalf of the partnership and not on behalf of the individual. A small number of investors who know each other well and are reasonably certain they can work together cooperatively sometimes enter into a general partnership.

Because general partners are personally and fully liable for the property, they can lose personal assets along with their investment in the partnership if the property faces bankruptcy or a lawsuit. (NOTE: As the name implies, *limited liability general partnerships [LLGPs]* limit the liability of the general partners.) Depending on state laws and the partnership agreement, a general partnership may dissolve if one partner chooses to remove his or her interest. Even if dissolution is not mandatory, it may be unavoidable because selling a partial interest in an established partnership is difficult.

Successfully managing a property for a general partnership can be difficult if all the partners do not agree on an issue and if they do not have a general partnership agreement that defines a decision process. Even among the most cooperative partners, occasional differences of opinion are inevitable. Although the partners may agree that they must take a vote on certain actions and that those who own the majority of the investment must agree to enact a change, one dissenting general partner among five may have equal authority over the manager and the property. The manager is usually in a good position to reconcile any differing points of view, but that consumes time that could be spent more productively. If the manager reports to more than one person, he or she must distribute multiple reports, a process that uses still more time and resources. To avoid financial harm to the property because of or during a dispute, the partners can name one of their number as a managing partner with whom the real estate manager will work exclusively. Such action centralizes the management control and places the obligation for settling differences where it belongs—among the partners.

Limited Partnership.   A more popular form of partnership is the *limited partnership (LP)*. It consists of one or more general partners who supervise the investment, plus a number of limited partners who participate in the arrangement only to the extent of their financial investment. As in a general partnership, the liability of the general partners is unlimited. The limited partners assume no liability beyond their capital investment. (NOTE: A partnership can organize as a *limited liability limited partnership [LLLP]*, which limits the liability of the general partners.)

Two forms of limited partnerships exist. *Private limited partnerships* have thirty-five or fewer investors and usually do not have to register with the Securities and Exchange Commission (SEC), although they may have to file a certificate with state authorities. *Public limited partnerships* have an unlimited number of participants and must register with the SEC when the number of partners and the value of their assets reach certain levels.

Individual investment in a limited partnership does not necessarily require a large amount of capital, so it is attractive to an investor with limited resources who wants to participate in a large venture. As in a general partnership, the tax benefits and obligations pass through to the individual partners based on the provisions in the partnership agreement.

Limited partners have no say in management policies, and they may consider that a disadvantage. The decisions made by the general partners in a limited partnership affect more than their personal investments; the potential exists for all of the partners to lose their investments. If the property requires additional funds because of adverse economic conditions, the general partners are obligated to invest additional capital, but the limited partners are not. Limited partners may make additional contributions to protect their original investment, but they typically do not do so.

The challenges of a limited partnership to management are about the same as those of a general partnership. However, if some limited partners become frustrated with the general partners' decisions, they may try to appeal directly to the manager. If a limited partner is permitted to have direct influence on the management of the property, the Internal Revenue Service can reclassify the partnership as an association that is taxable as a corporation. The IRS could also reclassify the limited partner as a general partner, and he or she would lose the liability protection extended to limited partners.

The real estate manager may be obligated to report to *all* investors in a limited partnership, but such reporting is potentially expensive. To avoid this reporting requirement, the manager should include in the management agreement a clause that clearly delineates the form, frequency, and recipients of reports. To minimize or discourage conferences between the manager and anyone other than the general partners, the agreement should also state an hourly fee for discussion with limited partners, their attorneys, accountants, heirs, executors, or anyone else. In turn, the partnership agreement should provide that the individual who requires special services must pay the charges for them. (See chapter 4 for the contents and purpose of the management agreement.)

Syndicate. A real estate *syndicate* is a special type of partnership formed by any combination of owners who purchase an interest in a property together. The investor may be an individual, a general or limited partnership, a joint venture, an unincorporated association, a corporation, or a group of corporations. Syndication is a way to pool both capital and experience for a property's success. Another advantage of syndication is that people of differing backgrounds can make a formal agreement to accomplish one specific goal. Flexibility of investment is another advantage—the purpose of a syndicate can be to purchase a particular property or the purpose can be to rely on the experience of a *syndicator* to acquire property that appears promising. If more funds are necessary, the syndicate can sell additional partnership interests.

Limited Liability Company.   A *limited liability company (LLC)* is another form of ownership that allows multiple owners to invest in real estate. Its owners are called *members,* and the managing entity may be a participating investor (*manager member*) or a nonparticipant appointed by the members. An LLC is created by state statute, and most states have adopted such laws although the rules and fiduciary responsibilities vary. For federal income tax purposes, the IRS classifies an LLC as a partnership. Unlike the general partners in a partnership, however, *all* LLC members enjoy limited liability; no one member may be held liable for debts or other obligations of the company. In addition, LLCs have lesser tax reporting requirements than do C or S corporations. (The next section discusses C and S corporations.)

Corporations

The difference between a corporation and any other association of investors in the United States is its recognition by federal and state governments. A corporation is chartered by a state, and it is considered to have a legal life of its own. It is an independent legal entity. It can sue and be sued. If a corporation goes bankrupt or loses a lawsuit, the liability of the corporate owners (the stockholders) is limited to the amount of their investment. As an independent legal body, a corporation must pay local, state, and federal income taxes; it cannot transfer its tax deductions to its shareholders. Depending on the structure of the corporation, corporate profits may be subject to *double taxation*—at the corporate level and again at the individual shareholder level when dividend distributions are made.

Income tax law in the United States recognizes two types of corporations for tax purposes: C corporations and S corporations. The government legally defines most corporations as *C corporations.* These entities pay income tax and have no restrictions on the number of shareholders they have or the types of stock they issue. The obligation of a C corporation to pay income tax is the main limitation on its ownership of real estate as a primary business endeavor. Even so, the attraction of limited liability for all participants (directors as well as shareholders) is a positive feature for some real estate investors.

Unlike a C corporation, an *S corporation* combines the ownership features of a corporation with those of a partnership. It does not pay federal income tax, so it does not incur double taxation; profits (and losses) pass directly to the shareholders. Because the investors are shareholders and not partners, their individual liability is limited to the value of the stock they

---

Corporations as Real Estate Owners

While a group of investors may form a corporation specifically to purchase and operate one or more income-producing properties, corporations created for purposes other than real estate investment also become real estate owners. Such a corporation may own the building in which it conducts its business and derive additional income from the property by leasing any excess space. For example, one of the major department stores that anchors a shopping mall may own all or part of the mall. A manufacturing company may develop land around its factory into an industrial park. A bank, advertising firm, or other service company may build or purchase a premier office building for its business operations and rent out the space it does not use. Such rental income is generally secondary to the income generated by the main business operation of the corporation (e.g., retail sales, manufacturing). The managers of corporate-owned real estate may have broad responsibilities that include acquisition and disposition in addition to real estate management specifics (e.g., property maintenance, record keeping, and reporting).

---

own. Stock ownership inherently provides for the election of a board of directors, a factor that ensures centralized management. In addition, ownership of the investment is more easily transferred through stock shares than it is in a limited or general partnership.

The eligibility requirements for classification as an S corporation are strict. To be eligible, the corporation may have no more than 75 shareholders and can offer only one class of stock. All shareholders must be individuals or estates; other corporations or business ventures cannot hold stock in an S corporation. Classification as an S corporation is by choice; otherwise, a corporation is classified as a C corporation. Some states may not recognize S corporation status and may impose state corporate taxes in spite of the designation.

Working as a real estate manager for a corporation may involve more administrative procedures than working for a sole proprietor or a partnership because of corporate reporting to the government, its directors, and its shareholders. The board of directors may be the authority for management decisions, although the manager's contact may be someone other than a board member whose primary responsibility is unrelated to real estate. Decisions involving the property may require formal documentation and board approval. Budgets and financial statements for the property may have to conform to the accounting standards of the corporation, even though such standards may not be suited to real estate management. The corporation may require one budget for the calendar year and another for the fiscal year if the two are different, and it may require both cash and accrual-basis accounting. The manager's duties may include annual audits and filings with the SEC. Because working with a corporation can create the potential for uncomfortable compromises between confidentiality and mandatory public disclosure, the manager must maintain all information in the strictest confidence. Only the corporation should release corporate information.

Real Estate Investment Trusts

Another vehicle that permits small investors to engage in large real estate ventures is a *real estate investment trust (REIT)*. A REIT is a specialized trust fund that invests exclusively in real estate. Investment in a REIT can take one of three paths: direct investment, investment through mortgage lending, or both. A REIT issues *shares of beneficial interest* that can be traded publicly, and its passive losses cannot exceed the cash distributions to the trust beneficiaries. For a REIT to avoid double taxation, it must distribute at least 95 percent of its taxable income to the shareholders (if a REIT has any retained income, corporate taxation rules may apply), and it must meet several requirements to ensure that most of its income is derived from real estate. Investors in a REIT are liable only to the extent of their investment.

Because REITs operate through shares, they can offer greater security than limited partnerships by diversifying their assets among properties in several locations (provided the trust is astutely managed and the REIT is significantly large). If shares of the REIT are publicly traded, the beneficiaries have two distinct advantages—they profit from real estate investment and their funds remain liquid. However, REITs must distribute most of their earnings, and adequate reserves may not be available for capital improvements to or additional investments in a property owned by a REIT. Likewise, a REIT has few options for preserving its capital. If the real estate market becomes unfavorable, most owners of real property can liquidate their assets, possibly taking a one-time loss, and invest the remaining capital in something else. A REIT, by definition, must keep its money in real estate.

The challenges of managing a property owned by a REIT are similar to those posed by corporate ownership.

Joint Venture

Investors can use any combination of the ownership forms previously described to establish a *joint venture*. The purpose of joint venture ownership is to share the risks and the rewards jointly by contributing the appropriate knowledge, skill, or asset. The advantages, disadvantages, and tax obligations depend on the type of business entity selected for the joint venture. Some of the most common joint venture relationships are between a developer and an institutional investor or lender who undertake a new project. The lender invests capital, land, or both, and the developer contributes knowledge to make the project succeed. Foreign capital is often invested in real property in the United States via joint ventures. In that case, a domestic entity nurtures the development and the foreign investor provides the capital.

The challenges of managing real estate owned by a joint venture depend on the type of business entity the joint venture chooses.

SUMMARY

A comparison of investment options reveals that real estate is highly illiquid when compared to stocks, bonds, and other investment vehicles that an investor can convert to cash relatively quickly and easily. However, the various forms of real estate ownership and the many advantages of that ownership sustain real estate's popularity as an investment.

Investors can purchase real estate with cash or a combination of cash and financing. Mortgage loans commonly have a fixed maturity and interest rate, but some mortgages have flexible terms that take advantage of market fluctuations. The terms of the loan can have a profound impact on the property's success based on changes in the property's income, the overall economy, and the owner's expectations from the investment.

The reasons for owning real estate include capital preservation, capital appreciation, periodic return (cash flow), income tax advantages, and pride of ownership. Any of these reasons alone may be sufficient for an investor to purchase a property. However, the investor usually considers a combination of these factors before making a purchase.

The principal forms of property ownership are sole proprietorships, partnerships (including limited liability companies), corporations, real estate investment trusts (REITs), and joint ventures. Each ownership form has advantages and disadvantages, and no single form is necessarily ideal. Each has different effects on income from the property, payment to the investor, tax obligations, and the relationship between the owner and the manager. Understanding the subtleties of the owner's reasons for investing in a property and knowing the form of ownership gives the real estate manger the basis for determining how to manage the property and how to improve its productivity.

4

Establishing Management Direction

The reasons to own income-producing property are often multifaceted and encompass more than production of a favorable financial return on the investment. When an owner contracts with a real estate manager, the owner's goals for the property become the real estate manager's goals. These goals and the methods for their achievement are the basis of two documents—a management plan and a management agreement.

THE MANAGEMENT PLAN

An important element in the management of real property is a specific *management plan*—an analysis of the current physical, fiscal, competitive, and operational conditions of a property expressed in relation to the owner's goals. If the conditions are not suitable for attaining the owner's goals, the real estate manager commonly uses the management plan to recommend and support physical, financial, or operational changes. A management plan may also evaluate the feasibility or practicality of plans the owner has for the property.

Because of the unique aspects of each property, each real estate manager's management style, and each owner's expectations, no definitive form of management plan exists. For some properties, an operating budget and a list of the manager's observations may suffice. For others, a document that is hundreds of pages long may be necessary to give a complete perspective on the current condition of the property and the programs required to

---

Real Estate Management Documents

Management Plan A logical, deductive, intensive analysis of all factors related to a property, such as its location, physical condition, financial status, competitive position, and highest and best use.

Management Agreement A formal contract that defines and explains the duties and responsibilities of the owner and the real estate manager and establishes their business relationship and the manager's compensation.

---

make its operation effective. Regardless of the size or form of the plan, its appearance and presentation are always important. Logical assertions and conclusions and clear statements of the facts exemplify the preparer's real estate management skills and his or her ability to communicate effectively.

The usual starting point for a management plan is a definition of the owner's goals for investment in the property. (See chapter 3 for forms of ownership and types of goals.) The owner's goals narrow the scope of the manager's research and the recommendations in the management plan. If the owner expects rapid capital appreciation from a property, the management plan may center on improvements that require a short time. Ways to increase the net operating income (NOI) are another important inclusion because a higher return from a property increases its value. For owners who want a consistent return from their investment, a real estate manager may create a schedule of gradual improvements that will maintain a high occupancy rate and create the potential for steadily increasing cash flow. (Chapter 5 describes net operating income and cash flow in detail.)

The goal of the manager, as exhibited throughout the management plan and the actual management of the property, should agree with and complement the goal of the owner. That goal is usually for the property to reach its *highest and best use,* meaning that it generates the highest NOI possible and attains the best possible use based on its location, size, and design.

When developing a specific management plan, real estate managers usually perform the following evaluations:

- Regional analysis
- Neighborhood analysis
- Property analysis
- Market analysis
- Analysis of alternatives
- Cost-benefit analysis
- Conclusion and recommendations

The most important aspect of a property's value is its location. To gain a clear understanding of the effects supply, demand, and location have on

---

Components of a Management Plan

- Regional analysis
- Neighborhood analysis
- Property analysis
- Market analysis
- Analysis of alternatives
- Operational changes
- Structural changes
- Changes in use
- Cost-benefit analysis
- Conclusion and recommendations

---

a property, a real estate manager must define and thoroughly describe its surroundings. Two identical buildings, one located on Wall Street in Manhattan and the other in a small rural town, obviously will have different dollar values even though their designs and structures may be the same. A building is not easy to move, nor is its inventory of space easy to change. The demand for space in any income-producing property affects its value. The amount of income it can produce depends on the number and quality of the rental spaces of that type available locally and their proximity to the subject property.

Because value is dependent on location, the real estate manager must understand the economic, governmental, and physical conditions that affect a property. After the real estate manager outlines major national concerns, the most logical place to begin the evaluation is with the region.

Regional Analysis

A *regional analysis* outlines general economic and demographic conditions as well as geographic features of the area surrounding the property. Those conditions affect tenancy and the demand for space in a particular property.

Demand ultimately gives value to real estate. People and their economic means create demand. To understand the level of demand for a property, the real estate manager investigates pertinent information about the general characteristics of the region by collecting historical data and growth projections for all facets of the region. The information collected includes the people who live there *(demographic profile)*, business and industry, tourism and recreation, public improvements and facilities, transportation and traffic conditions, the educational system, and the local economy. The manager then evaluates these data, seeking trends that signal (1) future growth and opportunity, (2) little or no change from the current conditions, or (3) eventual decline. The government and social climate of a region also greatly

Sources for Demographic and Related Information

Demographics is the statistical analysis of populations. The primary source for most demographic data about the United States is the census the federal government conducts every 10 years in years ending in zero. The census data are sorted and tabulated in numerous ways to show specific relationships. Although the tabulations themselves are objective, extrapolation of trends from the statistics is somewhat subjective. By themselves, numbers do not indicate whether a property will attract enough tenants from a region or neighborhood to succeed. That must be projected from evaluation of the data.

In addition to publishing decennial census results, the United States Department of Commerce, Bureau of the Census, produces many other statistical profiles on its own and in conjunction with federal departments and agencies. *The Census Catalog and Guide* lists the reports available and their publication dates. A few publications that are especially valuable to real estate managers are the *American Housing Survey,* conducted every other year in odd-numbered years, and the *Economic Census,* conducted at five-year intervals in years ending in two and seven. The annual *Statistical Abstract of the United States* is a compilation of more recent information added to the census data. It is an easy-to-read, compact resource. Information from all three of these publications is available on the Internet at www.census.gov under American FactFinder.

Numerous private companies compile and publish demographic data in both print and electronic formats. Many of these firms are subsidiaries of companies that already maintain vast databases (e.g., insurance companies, savings associations, mailing houses, phone companies). They may combine their data with census results or just compare their results with correlative census figures to verify accuracy. These companies specialize in analyses of very small geographic areas. They sort data on the basis of census tracts, city blocks, zip codes, area codes, phone prefixes, or any other specific boundaries the customer identifies. Such reports are economical in consideration of the time necessary for compilation. A further convenience is that many research companies promise delivery of the reports within a few days' time.

affect the value of its real estate, so a manager must carefully analyze these regional components as well.

Most of the data for a regional analysis in the United States come from statistical compilations available from many sources, including the federal government (Department of Commerce, Bureau of the Census, Department of Labor, Bureau of Labor Statistics, and Department of Housing and Urban Development). Statistics compiled by the U.S. government are available via the Internet. Commercial firms also localize such statistics. Professional associations—Institute of Real Estate Management (IREM®), Building Owners and Managers Association International (BOMA), International Council of Shopping Centers (ICSC), National Association of Industrial and Office Prop-

---

Sources for Demographic and Related Information (*concluded*)

A number of companies offer geographic information system (GIS) software that can analyze census and related data for a defined area; the software often includes mapping capabilities. These programs allow the user to perform a demographic analysis for a specific area. Access to well-maintained, current databases ensures that such analyses are accurate.

Demographic reports about specific regions and neighborhoods may be available through state information departments, local civic groups, REALTOR® boards, and business councils. The chamber of commerce is often the best starting point for any demographic research. It may have specific data on hand, or it may have information concerning the location of local data.

For real estate management purposes, the manager must view demographic data in the context of local property values, rents, and expenses. Sources for this information are the Institute of Real Estate Management's annual income and expense analyses for specific property types (office buildings, shopping centers, federally assisted apartments, conventional apartments, condominiums, co-ops, and PUDs). These reports contain national summaries, metropolitan area reports, and regional compilations. Operational statistics for office buildings are also available from the Building Owners and Managers Association International (BOMA); similar data on industrial properties is available from the National Association of Industrial and Office Properties (NAIOP); ULI (The Urban Land Institute) publishes comparison data on shopping centers and multifamily housing, and the National Apartment Association (NAA) compiles statistics on rental apartments.

---

erties (NAIOP), National Apartment Association (NAA)—publish property-type-specific reports for regional and national comparisons. However, the most valuable information is available within the region itself through state and local governmental agencies, utilities, local industries, financial institutions, chambers of commerce, and local economic development agencies.

Neighborhood Analysis

The next step is an in-depth study of the immediate neighborhood. The *neighborhood analysis* is a detailed look at the population and real estate near the subject property. Similar to the regional study in content but more narrowly focused, the neighborhood analysis is an evaluation of data related to nearby sites and the competition. (A *neighborhood* is a geographic area within which a property competes for residents.) Because the neighborhood analysis centers on the immediate surroundings, this study may seem more important than the regional analysis. Without a thorough regional analysis, however, the neighborhood analysis can be too optimistic or too pessimistic. Just as changes in the neighborhood affect a property, changes in the region affect the neighborhood.

Boundary Definition.   Analyzing a neighborhood first requires a definition of boundaries. The neighborhood of a particular property may consist of a few adjacent buildings or it may comprise an area of many square blocks. Often the neighborhood boundaries are natural or constructed barriers (rivers, lakes, ravines, railroad tracks, parks, streets) that separate discrete areas that have common characteristics in population or land use. Sometimes neighborhood boundaries are not visually discernible; the manager may have to compile information from such sources as the United States census, municipal and county governments, local government offices, local utility companies, newspaper reports, the local library, the school board, and social agencies to map a neighborhood precisely.

The objective of analyzing the neighborhood is to characterize the population, economic elements, and property types that are dominant. Considerations such as age, education, ethnic group, income levels, and institutions (e.g., colleges, hospitals) are part of the characterization of a residential neighborhood. The types of businesses (complementary and competitive) and their clientele and employees differentiate the neighborhood of a commercial property.

Physical Inspection.   A physical inspection of the neighborhood is also essential. The manager wants to know whether the neighborhood is well maintained. General cleanliness and neatness, so-called *curb appeal,* is very important for all types of properties. In reporting the analysis, the real estate manager may single out particular features in the neighborhood that favor the subject property. In the neighborhood analysis for an apartment building, the manager may comment on the location and quality of schools, accessibility to stores, and the level of public transportation service. Important components of the neighborhood analysis for an office building would be transportation, restaurants, and types of business services. The neighborhood of an office building is often called a *micro-market.* Merchandise categories and price lines of retail operations and the numbers of similar businesses—or their absence—along with a demographic profile of shoppers define the *trade area* (neighborhood) of a shopping center.

Data Evaluation.   Once the real estate manager has defined the boundaries and made a physical inspection of the neighborhood, he or she can evaluate the collected data. A neighborhood is not a static environment; it changes continually and its changes affect the property. Therefore, the manager examines the changing neighborhood conditions, includes definitions of those trends in the neighborhood analysis, and explains why he or she thinks they are occurring.

Changing numbers of individuals in different age and income groups and changes in household sizes indicate *population shifts*. Fluctuating real estate sales prices and rental rates reflect *economic shifts*. Differences in types of property development (new versus renovated), changes in land value and use, rental rates, and vacancy rates are other indicators of specific trends.

If results of the neighborhood analysis seem incomplete or uncertain, the manager should investigate further. A complete and fair perspective is essential to an accurate market analysis. For instance, population growth often indicates prosperity for a neighborhood; it can also signal the reverse. A population increase because some older homes in the neighborhood have become rooming houses usually indicates deterioration. Likewise, an excess of vacant commercial space may be the result of new development in response to increased demand. In established properties, vacancies can signal an inability to support retail and other businesses. A manager would be unwise to predict a change in land value from a single statistic. Evaluation of its cause in the context of other specific statistics is essential to understanding a particular trend and its impact.

The more a real estate manager knows about a neighborhood, the better. The best neighborhood study is one that is always up-to-date. The manager must monitor current trends to know whether conditions are improving, staying the same, or declining.

Property Analysis

The real estate manager next applies the same analytical method to the property itself. A *property analysis* includes the results of a careful inspection of the building along with a description of its rental space and common areas, its basic architectural design, its overall physical condition, and factors related to its recent operation. The following are some of the questions a real estate manager should be able to answer from a property analysis.

- *Building size.* How many units or leasable square feet does the building contain? What size are the spaces (the number of rooms and square feet in each apartment; configuration and method of measuring commercial space)?

- *Condition.* What is the physical condition of the building structurally and with regard to maintenance (roof, masonry, elevators, HVAC, other mechanical equipment, cable and wiring, windows and trim, doors, other hardware)? Is obsolescence correctable? How can functional inadequacies be corrected? Should the real estate manager consult a structural engineer or other professional about the condition of any elements of the building?

- *Common areas.* What is the condition of the most heavily used elements (floors, floor coverings, lobbies, entrance halls, elevator cabs, escalators, hallways, stairways, storage areas, amenities such as fitness centers)?

- *Residents' individual spaces.* How attractive is the rentable space (layout, exposure, view, features, and resident finish)?

- *Occupancy.* What is the current occupancy level and what has it been historically? What is the composition (and character) of the tenancy (two adult roommates with no children in apartment 101; a law office with 100 employees in suite 1800; a convenience store in unit 3)?

- *Curb appeal.* How desirable is the property (visual impression, age, architectural style, grounds, layout, approaches, public space, signage)?

- *Building-to-land ratio* or *floor area ratio (FAR).* What is the relationship between the building and the land on which it is located (current zoning, parking)? Can the owner use the building or the land more efficiently?

- *Compliance status.* What, if any, evidence of violations of health, safety, or environmental standards is present? Is the building compliant with the Americans with Disabilities Act?

- *Current management.* What are the current standards of building management? What policies and procedures are in effect for selecting residents, hiring and training staff, maintaining the building and grounds, collecting rents, controlling purchases, and administering the policies and procedures? Are they documented in an operations manual?

- *Staff.* How is the property currently staffed? What are staff attitudes, capabilities, training, and goals?

- *Financial integrity.* What is the status of the property with respect to NOI? What is its level of debt? Are expenses high or low compared to competing properties?

The real estate manager must review the status of existing leases, which are the basis of the property's revenue stream. At commercial properties, lease negotiations in progress may be a consideration. The question of economic depreciation may also require examination. Does an exterior condition have a negative impact on the property (e.g., traffic noise from a freeway built next to an existing residential property)? The unique features of each property will suggest additional considerations.

In the examination of the property and analysis of the information obtained, the manager should keep in mind that the owner's ultimate goal is usually to achieve the greatest return on his or her investment by putting the property to its highest and best use. So far, the manager has seen only part of the picture. The information gathered in the regional, neighborhood, and property analyses is essential to the market analysis.

Market Analysis

The term *real estate market* has different meanings in relation to such diverse aspects of real estate as mortgage interest rates, development, property cost, property value, and even rental rates. All of these except mortgage interest rates relate in some way to the level of competition and the demand for rental space in a particular property. A *market analysis* determines the level of demand for rental space in a specific building in comparison to the demand for space in competitive buildings. The analysis entails gathering information about specific comparable properties and comparing their features to those of the subject property.

Once the real estate manager learns what other buildings offer, he or she can evaluate the advantages and disadvantages of the subject property accordingly. Most important, the market analysis must only account for competing buildings within the neighborhood and the region in which the neighborhood itself is located, based on the information derived from the regional, neighborhood, and property analyses. After comparing the property to its competitors, the manager analyzes regional and neighborhood factors that affect, or could affect, the performance of the subject property. The manager conducts this study based on the current condition of the property. Speculation on how the property would fare in the market if it were remodeled or improved is premature at this point. Examining the property in its current condition establishes a point of reference to measure whether a projected change will make a difference and, if so, how much. The principles of conducting the market analysis are essentially the same for all types of properties: (1) determine which properties are competitors, (2) complete a comparison grid analysis to compare the subject property to the competition, (3) set rents based on the comparison, and (4) write a narrative report.

Define the Competition.   The real estate manager first singles out the buildings that are in competition with the subject property. To determine which buildings are legitimate competitors, the manager examines the subject property at the submarket level. A *submarket* is a segment of the overall market that is limited by a particular market influence. The individual markets include office, retail, industrial, apartment, and single-family home markets. This categorization reduces the number of potential residents and potential competitors.

Other factors narrow the field even further. Prospective residents usually prefer to locate in one portion of the region, so they limit their search to the part of town they prefer. They also commonly search for a particular type of rental space—households of three or more people do not look at studio apartments; convenience store owners do not seek supermarket-sized spaces; image-conscious corporations do not establish their head-quarters in warehouse space. Because prospects narrow their focus, the real estate manager should narrow the focus of the market analysis to determine the true competition. The subject property is compared to similar properties in the neighborhood or general vicinity, not to property across town or in another region (unless the manager concludes that the neighborhood of the property includes those areas). However, even if property across town is not in direct competition with the subject property, its standing in the market will have an influence because it is a part of the market as a whole. The narrative description of the market accounts for this influence.

Facts learned in the regional and neighborhood analyses should indicate which buildings are in competition with the subject property. Generally they are of comparable size and have apartments or commercial spaces of similar size at similar rental rates. Once the manager identifies those properties, he or she can compare their features and amenities with those of the subject property and rate them appropriately. Real estate managers gather different information for residential properties than they do for commercial properties.

Residential Markets. Prospective residents usually assign a dollar value to amenities based on perceived benefit. For this reason, when comparing the subject property to the competition, a real estate manager should list those features and amenities that may influence a prospective resident to sign a lease. The following considerations pertain to most residential markets:

- Number and types of apartment units available within the area

- Average age and character of the building in which they are located

- Features that are similar in most units within the market—size, layout, equipment, amenities (what defines a typical unit)

- Current rent for an average unit on a monthly (and square-foot) basis

- Cost of utilities (gas, electricity, water, sewer) and parking; and who pays for them (property owner or resident)

- Availability of public transportation or access to major highways or arterial streets

- Occupancy level of all units of a given type; occupancy level of units of the specific type in the market that are superior, average, and inferior

- Rental rates and occupancy levels in recent years (the trend for each)

Commercial Markets.   For commercial space, the manager compiles data on the following types of property characteristics:

- Square footage of a particular type of space (office, retail, industrial) available within the area

- Average age, character, and condition of the building in which the space is located

- Types of commercial tenants who use a particular commercial space (major space users or professionals in private practice—e.g., doctors, lawyers; direct retail sales or service versus intermediaries; manufacturers of finished goods, or suppliers of component parts)

- Mix of commercial tenants in a building

- Accessibility via public transportation or arterial roads

- Availability and cost of parking (especially in a central business district)

- Presence of amenities that serve commercial tenants' employees (e.g., restaurants)

- Current rent (base rate) per square foot for a typical space of the type and how quoted (monthly or annually)

- Whether and how the common area is included in the rent (add-on factor)

- Types of concessions negotiated in leasing space of the type (free rent, moving allowance, etc.)

- Typical lease terms (numbers of years) and provisions for rent escalations (flat rate; consumer price index [CPI], or other index or calculation)

- Types of operating expenses passed through to commercial tenants pro rata

- Whether retailers pay percentage rents (percent rates)

- Occupancy level of the type of space (office, retail, industrial); occupancy level of the type of space in the market that is superior, average, and inferior

- Rental rates and occupancy levels in recent years (trends)

The manager should pose many questions. How do the rent and occupancy trends compare with real estate market trends in general? How do vacant

Exhibit 4.1
Sample Comparison Grid (Residential Property)

	Subject	Comparable #1		Comparable #2		Comparable #3	
Name/Address							
Type of Unit							
Square Feet in Unit							
Rental Rate							
Rate/Square Foot							
Categories	**Description**	**Descrip.**	**Adj.**	**Descrip.**	**Adj.**	**Descrip.**	**Adj.**
Location							
Age							
BUILDING CONDITION							
Exterior							
Grounds							
Common Areas							
PARKING							
Condition							
Open/Covered/Garage							
Ratio							
Other							
APARTMENT INTERIOR							
Floor/Carpet							
Drapes/Blinds							
Stove/Refrigerator							
Dishwasher							
Washer/Dryer							
Closets/Storage							
Air Conditioning							
Other							

Exhibit 4.1 (*concluded*)

AMENITIES							
Laundry Room(s)							
Swimming Pool(s)							
Other							
Owner-Paid Utilities							
Pets Allowed							
Other							
Total Rent Adjustments							
Adjusted Rent/Unit							
Adjusted Rent/Sq. Ft.							

If the feature in the subject property is better than that in a comparable property, the rent for the comparable is adjusted upward; if the subject property's feature is not as good as the comparable's, the rent for the comparable is adjusted downward. The adjustments for each comparable property are totaled, and its rental rate is changed—increased or decreased—based on the net adjustments (see accompanying narrative).

apartments or commercial spaces in the area compare to those in the subject property with regard to size, age, condition, amenities, and rents? Based on the results of the neighborhood analysis, is the number of prospective tenants for the subject property increasing or decreasing? Is the absorption rate positive or negative?

Complete a Comparison Grid. To make an effective comparison, the real estate manager categorizes the features of the competitive properties with respect to the subject property using a *comparison grid* (exhibits 4.1 and 4.2). Specific features are listed at the left, and the comparable properties are indicated as column headings. Some categories are straightforward (age of the building, for example); others (location, condition, and appeal) are subject to interpretation. Still others may require additional explanation. A "pets allowed" category may be listed as a straight yes or no for most residential properties, but some apartments may have very specific provisions (separate pet agreement, additional rent or fees). For commercial properties, rental rates account for additions to base rent (e.g., pass-through expenses, percentage rent), and a comparison of major and minor space users (anchor and ancillary tenants at shopping centers) is included.

Exhibit 4.2

Sample Comparison Grid (Commercial Property)

	Subject	Comparable #1		Comparable #2		Comparable #3	
Property Name							
Base Rental Rate							
− Concessions							
+ Expense Pass-Throughs							
+ Tenant Improvements							
+ Tenant Effective Rent							
Categories	**Description**	**Descrip.**	**Adj.**	**Descrip.**	**Adj.**	**Descrip.**	**Adj.**
Location/Accessibility							
BUILDING CONDITION							
Age							
Exterior							
Grounds							
Common Areas							
Commercial Space							
Other							
BUILDING SYSTEMS							
Elevators							
HVAC Efficiency							
After-Hours Charges							
Life Safety							
Other							
AVAILABLE SPACE							
Location							
Floor Plate							
Storage							
Telecommunications							

Exhibit 4.2 (*concluded*)

Other								
PARKING								
Open/Covered/Garage								
Visitor Spaces								
Parking Ratio								
Cost to Tenant								
Other								
AMENITIES/FEATURES								
Vacancy Rate								
Total Rent Adjustments								
Adjusted Effective Rent/ Rentable Square Foot								
× R/U Ratio								
Adjusted Effective Rent/ Usable Square Foot								

This form is typical of those used to evaluate office buildings. Concessions and tenant-paid improvements are prorated based on the R/U (rentable area/usable area) ratio (see chapter 10). Comparison data for a shopping center would emphasize anchor draw, tenant mix synergy, visibility from the street, signage, and the amount of drive-by traffic. Information about deal-making rents, percentage rates, and specific pass-throughs might also be included.

Consistency in rating or ranking is most important. In preparation of the comparison grid, the real estate manager must use the same rules of assessment for each category of analysis for all properties. Describing and rating "location" on the comparison grid can be difficult, yet the location of a property within the neighborhood is its prime marketable feature. For instance, being a block from a supermarket or a mass transit stop would ordinarily be a promotable feature for a residential property; being next door to the bus depot or to the parking lot of the supermarket would not. On the other hand, being next door may be more attractive than being three miles away from those amenities. Location next door to a hospital is a selling point for offices designed for physicians and allied health professionals, but it is a detriment for industrial space with heavy incoming and outgoing truck traffic. Being near a courthouse is a desirable feature for space usable as law offices, but that location is not a selling point for stores seeking high-end retail tenants.

Because most factors involving location are relative and complex, a separate location analysis can help the real estate manager evaluate how the property's location affects demand. Exhibit 4.3 lists some of the factors that influence location quality perceptions for prospective tenants.

Comparison grid analysis allows the real estate manager to determine how the rental space in the subject property compares to similar space in the market on a feature-by-feature basis. The purpose of the exercise is to show whether a particular feature at a comparable property is better than or not as good as the same feature in the subject property and how the total of these features affects quoted rents. By attributing a dollar value to each feature, a market-level rent can be determined for the subject property based on the comparison. If the feature in the subject property is better than in a comparable property, the rent for the comparable is adjusted *upward*; if the feature in the subject property is not as good, the rent for the comparable is adjusted *downward*. The adjustment amount (negative or positive) is based on what the manager estimates a resident would pay for the feature or would not pay because of its absence. For each property, the real estate manager totals the adjustments and changes its rental rate to reflect the net adjustments. The manager then analyzes the rents for the comparable properties to determine a market rent on a per-unit or a per-square-foot basis. (Typically, a comparison grid analysis is completed for each type of apartment unit in a residential property.)

Set Rents.   The real estate manager evaluates quoted rents and occupancy levels of the competing rental apartments or commercial spaces to determine the rent that the owner can charge for the subject property based on quality, services, amenities, and other attractions (e.g., a view). The comparison grid indicates whether the rent for the type of space in the subject property is below, at, or above market rates. Based on this information, the manager can evaluate the current *rental schedule* of the subject property and compare it to the rental schedules of other properties on the comparison grid.

To determine whether to adjust the current rental schedule of the subject property, the real estate manager searches for an optimum balance between vacancy and maximum income. While the ideal is maximum rent and maximum occupancy, reality dictates that vacancies will be present. In fact, an increase in rent may initially increase vacancies. With this in mind, the manager strives for a realistic maximum rent that will minimize the impact on the occupancy rate. Rents and vacancies are important considerations

Exhibit 4.3
Some Factors That Influence Location Quality

Access to Transportation
Proximity to major roads
Proximity to interstate highway(s)
Proximity of mass transit stops

Personal and Property Safety
Crime against people
Crime against property
Access to police, fire, and emergency medical services

Neighborhood and Surroundings
Reputation and acceptance level of the neighborhood
Conditions and reputations of areas traversed to reach local facilities

RESIDENTIAL PROPERTY
For a residential property, relative convenience of different modes of transportation are important along with the following:

Convenience of Local Facilities
Central business district (CBD)
Convenience store or center
Neighborhood shopping center/supermarket
Regional mall or larger shopping center
Major employment locations (if different from CBD)
Schools and colleges
Parks, sports and fitness centers, and other recreational facilities
Cultural/entertainment centers
Social services (government and human services centers)

OFFICE BUILDING
For an office building, a prospective tenant will want access to a pool of qualified workers (office and technical skills) along with a suitable client base and some or all of the following:

Availability of Business Services
Adequate to cutting-edge communications facilities, services, and support
Printing and related services
Delivery/shipping services and messengers
Office, computer, and photocopying supplies and support
Industry-specific support services and suppliers
Temporary staffing agencies
Professional consultation (accounting, legal)

Availability of Services for Employees
Restaurants and other food outlets
Day care facilities
Fitness facilities
Dry cleaning, shoe repairs, valet services
Drug sundry stores

(Continued)

Exhibit 4.3 (*concluded*)

RETAIL

Retail tenants look for complementary businesses that attract similar customers and a shopper profile that matches their merchandise categories and price lines. They also look for the following:

Retail Property Attributes

Amount of traffic passing the property (vehicular and/or pedestrian)
Visibility from the street
Signage possibilities
Ease of ingress and egress (no one-way streets or limitations on turns)
Nearby streets, highways, and thoroughfares
Amount and configuration of parking

---

in estimating changes in gross receipts and NOI that will result from an increase in rents. Finally the manager prices each unit or space according to its location, view, amenities, etc.

Write a Narrative Report.   The market analysis generally includes a narrative overview of market trends and observations. The absorption rate in the neighborhood or region usually warrants discussion. The *absorption rate* of a property type is the amount of space leased compared to the amount of space available for lease over a given period, usually a year. The rate relates to both construction of new space and demolition or removal from the market of old space. Different property types within the same region have different absorption rates.

If demand exceeds supply, the absorption rate is favorable because overall vacancy decreases. If supply exceeds demand, the absorption rate is unfavorable, and lenders tend to curtail their financing of the development of similar properties, which eventually causes a slowdown of growth. A negative absorption rate can also result from other changes in a market. If a major industry closes and not enough jobs are available, people will move away from the area, and the lack of jobs will discourage others from moving in. The amount of residential space available for lease will quickly exceed demand, irrespective of any new construction. The commercial sector may also slow based on this major change. However, the effect of reduced demand is not always immediately apparent. Construction may simply continue because the financing is in place. If the developer obtained financing when the level of demand was high, market trends may be unfavorable when construction starts, and stopping construction may cost more than completing the project. As the new space fills over time, demand will again exceed supply and the absorption rate will again be favorable, encouraging new construction and causing the cycle to repeat.

In addition, the narrative portion of the market analysis includes trends observed in the regional and neighborhood analyses that can affect the sub-ject property. For a residential property, a shift in the demographic profile of the neighborhood (e.g., from families to empty nesters) would be noted here, along with the manager's conclusions regarding the favorable or unfa-vorable effects that shift may have on the demand for rental apartments. If the regional analysis showed that a nearby company (Boeing or Microsoft) would be expanding its operations and hiring more people, the manager might reason that demand for rental space will increase. The manager may further reason (from the comparison grid) that the competing buildings in the neighborhood are better suited to profit from the anticipated population growth.

Population changes also affect the leasing of commercial space. Edu-cation levels and technical skills determine the caliber of potential office workers. Household income levels indicate the price levels of merchandise that will sell in a particular area—Bloomingdale's and Nordstrom offer dif-ferent price lines than do Target and Wal-Mart. These considerations should guide the development of a marketing program for the property that will capitalize on any positive trends and insulate the property from the impact of negative trends. (Chapter 8 discusses marketing.)

Many management plans conclude with the market analysis. The re-search to this point can substantiate a need for a new rental schedule and indicate the increase that the property can attain without compromising its competitive strength. In other words, if implementation of a new rental schedule alone will place the property in a condition of highest and best use, enough said. However, many properties—particularly commercial properties—demand a more comprehensive examination of their future prospects.

Analysis of Alternatives

Some properties require changes in operations or some form of physical change to justify a rent increase, elevate the occupancy level, control ex-penses, and subsequently bring them to their highest and best use. In the effort to improve the performance of a property, the real estate manager should investigate the range of possible changes and evaluate their an-ticipated effects—in other words, conduct an *analysis of alternatives.* The intent of the changes proposed in this section of a management plan is to increase NOI—which is the tangible and measurable benefit of the in-vestment in the property—and thereby increase the property's value. Each proposed change also carries with it a cost, so the manager must conduct an analysis that compares the costs and the benefits of each proposal or combination of proposals made in the analysis of alternatives.

In some instances, improvements to real property may preserve value rather than increasing income—upgrading an HVAC system and replacing a roof are examples. Ignoring the needed improvement could result in decreased rents, lower occupancy, increased operating expenses, and a lower value. Preserving value and the capital invested in the real estate are important to every investor. Such investments in capital improvements also warrant a cost-benefit analysis because their costs may be factored into the residents' rents or result in operating expense reductions, and the owners will need to know how long the *payback period* will be until they recoup their investment.

In analyzing alternatives, the real estate manager considers operational and physical changes. Operational changes are procedural. Physical changes can range from rehabilitation or modernization of the current building to outright change in the use of the building or the site.

Operational Changes.   These changes affect procedural methods or efficiency but not the physical makeup of the property. The net effect is to increase income or reduce operating expenses and thereby increase NOI. Operational changes range from adopting a new rental schedule based on the market analysis to using low-wattage bulbs in common-area lighting. The manager may consider reducing staff or charging back to residents some common-area expenses such as heating. Strategies to reduce outside service expenses include renegotiating contract terms with certain service providers (e.g., elevator maintenance) or calling for bids on recurring services that are not under contract (e.g., landscaping, parking lot sweeping).

Even though the intent of operational changes may be to reduce operating expenses, the real estate manager must be sure to maintain the property's quality. After completing the market analysis, the manager should be keenly aware of the services provided at competing properties. Any recommendation that sacrifices any similar services may be more costly than the savings achieved. However, examination of the competition may lead to the discovery of new methods that will reduce operating costs yet preserve or enhance service standards.

Structural Changes.   Rehabilitation and modernization can lengthen the economic life of a property. *Rehabilitation* is the process of renewing the equipment and materials in the building. It entails correcting deferred maintenance. *Modernization* (correction of functional obsolescence) is inherent in the rehabilitation process. To make the property competitive, similar equipment of more modern design will replace the original equipment. New carpeting, upgraded electrical service, equipment that is more energy efficient, or any other physical improvement that does not affect the use of the property can be rehabilitative. The list of possibilities in this arena is virtually endless. When a real estate manager proposes physical changes, the management plan must include an expense budget and/or a capital budget showing the allocation of funds for the changes and the anticipated impact on NOI, cash flow, and property value. The owner may also require an analysis of debt service (if the funds are borrowed) and cash flow.

Changes in Use. A recommendation to change the use of a property must be well-founded. Such a procedure is complex, expensive, and therefore not usual. However, the rewards of a successful change in use are often substantial. Once a change of use is implemented, reverting to the original condition is difficult. The property owner and manager must always carefully weigh the anticipated improvement in performance expected from a change in use against the risks of that change. The most common changes include adaptive use, condominium conversion, and demolition for new development.

Adaptive Use.   *Adaptive use* (recycling) of existing structures is usually more economical than building new structures. Capitalizing on an existing shell and foundation eliminates the cost of demolition and part of the cost of new materials. In the United States, old factories, warehouses, train stations, and post offices have gained new life as offices, shopping centers, apartments, and entertainment complexes. Office buildings have become hotels and condominiums.

Adaptive use is a way to reduce development costs, convert obsolete property to meet new market demands, preserve historical architecture, or revive a location that is not achieving its highest and best use. A recycled building may not achieve the same rent per square foot as a new one, but the start-up costs are lower and the debt service requirements are usually less. Adaptive use projects make sense when cash flow per square foot will be greater than the original use cash flow. Old buildings, whole city blocks, and even sections of towns have been preserved and made profitable through adaptive use. As an example, Ghirardelli Square in San Francisco, a charming, multilevel, brick complex of specialty shops, restaurants, and theaters, was originally a chocolate factory.

Condominium Conversion. The primary advantage of *condominium conversion* is the potential to achieve a high profit in a short time. The appeal is even greater when high financing costs reduce cash flow. Converting a rental property to condominium ownership allows the original owner to recapture his or her investment, pay off the mortgage, and keep any excess funds as profit. If rent control restricts a property owner's ability to increase rents to market levels, condominium conversion may circumvent the potential loss of income, although current renters may have the right to remain despite the conversion. Review of state and local laws regarding condominium formation and conversion is essential to determine the feasibility of a particular conversion.

Although condominium conversion was once limited to apartment

---

Redevelopment and the New Urbanism

In both urban and suburban areas, redevelopment may no longer simply take down one structure and replace it with another as the concept of the *mixed-use development (MXD)* expands. A parcel of land that was previously home to an industrial use or an apartment complex is likely to be redeveloped to incorporate a variety of residential uses (affordable as well as upscale rental apartments plus single-family homes, condominiums, townhomes, and senior citizen housing) and commercial uses (retail, entertainment, storefronts) into a "pedestrian-friendly" neighborhood. This phenomenon, called *new urbanism,* includes higher-density development with narrow streets complemented by wide sidewalks. Emphasis is on walking rather than driving, and shops are within walking distance of homes. The goal is to develop true neighborhoods with public green spaces, businesses that serve the people who live there, and a mix of housing styles and prices. This *urban village* strategy is revitalizing urban areas and creating an identifiable downtown in suburbs that do not have one.

---

buildings, the concept has now extended to other property types—even parking lots in congested metropolitan areas are sold by the parking space. Commercial condominium ownership is not very common, but it does exist. However, businesses usually require space for growth, and owning only a portion of a building limits the potential for expansion. In addition, the financial obligations that are part of such ownership make subsequent relocation difficult. Consequently, conversion of a commercial property to condominium ownership is less likely to be practical or successful.

The success of a condominium conversion depends on the adaptability of the building to the form of ownership. In most cases, the building and all of its components must be in the best possible condition for the property owner who is doing the conversion to achieve the greatest possible return on his or her investment. The property owners must also consider the fact that a condominium is a long-term financial commitment for the buyer—a prospective owner is usually more selective than a prospective renter.

Demolition for New Development.   Demolition may seem to be an easy alternative, but it can be very expensive. The cost of razing a building combined with the cost of erecting a new one increases the necessity for the new structure to generate a high level of income. A proposal to tear down a building, even if it is in serious disrepair, can lead to a public outcry and tarnish the image of the new structure. If a site is listed in the National Register of Historic Places, demolition of the building is prohibited. The decision to demolish an old building and replace it with something new requires thorough review of more than the financial aspects. The impact on the neighborhood and the possible loss of goodwill are also important considerations.

If demolition is the most feasible alternative, replacing the existing structure with a mixed-use development may be a possibility, especially in an urban area. A *mixed-use development (MXD)* commonly has three or more significant income-generating uses and conforms to a coherent plan. It represents a more intensive use of urban land than a single-use building on the same site. Examples are the MCI Center (formerly Broadway Plaza) in Los Angeles, which includes offices, a hotel, retail space, and a large parking garage, and Water Tower Place in Chicago, which has a similar complement of uses and condominium residences. Such MXDs require superb locations and complicated financing. However, smaller- to medium-sized buildings can become MXDs. In urban neighborhoods, MXDs with residences above ground floor retail stores have become popular. Because such projects derive income from several uses, they are less likely to falter if income from one of those uses decreases.

Cost-Benefit Analysis

Changing a property always involves costs. The amount and extent of the costs depend on the scope of the changes. Establishing a new accounting procedure (an operational change) may only require training of staff and replacement of a current paper form or computerized document, but these have measurable costs. Rehabilitation and other structural changes are costly and can cause interruption of part or all of the rental income while the work is done. Even a recommendation to maintain the status quo has to be justified financially.

In order to determine whether a specific recommendation will improve the property's income, the real estate manager does a *cost-benefit analysis*. The manager must evaluate each alternative to ascertain that it will indeed yield higher levels of NOI and cash flow than the property will yield if left unchanged. Recovering the costs of making the change (plus any financing) is also an issue. Clearly the benefit (increased NOI—and therefore property value) must outweigh the cost if a recommendation is to be feasible. This means evaluating the *payback period*—the amount of time for the change to pay for itself. The cost-benefit analysis should also show the potential increase in property value from the improvement. Exhibit 4.4 shows an example of a cost-benefit analysis.

Conclusions and Recommendations

Management plans can be long and complex. A recapitulation of the major conditions that affect the property and a summary of the primary recom-

Exhibit 4.4

Sample Cost-Benefit Analysis Calculation

The manager of a 30-year-old apartment building discovers that residents in the neighborhood tend to pay higher rent for apartments with new kitchen appliances. While the refrigerators and ovens in the 50 units at the subject property are as old as the building, they still operate well. However, new appliances and built-in microwave ovens are standard equipment in comparable buildings nearby. Suppose the manager calculates that replacing appliances will cost $2,000 per apartment, or $100,000 for the entire building. Suppose further that the improvement will allow an increase in rent of $50 per apartment per month and that the property historically has had 90% occupancy (45 leased units out of 50). The manager would calculate the payback period, return on investment (ROI), and increase in property value as follows:

$2,000/apartment × 50 apartments = $100,000 total cost of improvements
$50 additional rent × 45 leased units = $2,250/month additional income
$100,000 total cost ÷ $2,250 per month
  = approximately 44 months (payback period)

$2,250/month × 12 months = $27,000 additional annual income as NOI
$27,000 increase in NOI ÷ $100,000 improvement cost
  = 27% return on investment (ROI)

$27,000 increase in NOI ÷ 0.10 (cap rate) = $270,000 increase in property value
$270,000 increased value − $100,000 improvement cost
  = $170,000 net increase in value

The calculation assumes the improvement cost is paid in full by the owner or from reserve funds accumulated for the purpose. Whether a 44-month payback period is reasonable or feasible for such an undertaking depends on the owner's expectations of the property. The possibility of a higher occupancy rate because of enhanced desirability of the apartments may reduce the payback period to less than 44 months. Operating expenses may also decrease because of lower repair expenses, which may reduce the payback period even more. The owner also benefits from a cost recovery deduction for the improvement (depreciation), which reduces the owner's tax liability on the income from the property.

On the other hand, if the owner financed the improvement cost, the debt service on the loan would reduce the total annual revenue, the increase in property value, and the owner's return on investment. The payback period would increase.

mendations can make the document easier to follow. This section should also include the rationale for specific changes and the expected results. A statement of the anticipated long-term financial performance—the effect on the bottom line—usually helps the owner understand the reasoning behind the management plan. Highlighting this information in an *executive summary* at the beginning of the document may help guide the owner through the document better than if that information only appears at the end of the report. Recommendations that relate to only one area of the property's operation may not require a very complex management plan. A market analysis may be all that is necessary to assess the condition of a property and recommend maintaining status quo. However, any proposed change, including a change in rental rates, requires a cost-benefit analysis.

THE MANAGEMENT AGREEMENT

In many ways, the real estate manager assumes the role of the owner in conducting the day-to-day business of the property. Residents often do not know who actually owns the property; many residents regard the manager as the property owner. The residents are correct in thinking that way because the manager often has the legal authority to establish leases, set rents, and safeguard the property. The manager operates the property on the owner's behalf and represents the owner to residents and others who have business with the property. To formalize this relationship, the owner and manager must agree on a variety of terms and responsibilities.

A *management agreement* is a formal and binding document that establishes the manager's legal authority over the operation of the property. The manager usually is an *agent* of the owner and serves as the owner's *fiduciary* or trustee of the owner's funds and assets associated with the property.[1] The management agreement is a legal contract that should be written by or prepared in consultation with a lawyer. The agreement establishes the relationship between the owner and the manager for a fixed period, defines the manager's authority and compensation for services provided, outlines procedures, specifies limits of the manager's authority and actions, and states financial and other obligations of the property owner. The contents of a management agreement generally include:

- Full names and identification of the property owner and the real estate manager
- Description of the property
- Term (duration) of the agreement
- Responsibilities of the manager
- Obligations of the owner
- Compensation for management services

A good management agreement also includes provisions for termination of the arrangement under specific conditions as well as numerous clauses

1. Many institutional investors prefer the real estate manager to be an *independent contractor* rather than an agent. The status and liability of an independent contractor are very different from those of an agent, and the manager should consult an attorney before agreeing to such an arrangement.

The Manager as the Owner's Agent

The *management agreement* establishes a relationship in which the real estate manager *(agent)* is authorized to act on behalf of the owner *(principal)*. The agent's words and actions are binding on the owner. In the role of agent, the real estate manager must exercise a standard of care in managing money and property for the owner *(fiduciary capacity)*. Being a fiduciary creates certain legal obligations. The manager must be loyal to the interests of the client and not engage in activities contrary to that loyalty. This means paying scrupulous attention to handling the owner's funds and not accepting any fee, commission, discount, gift, or other benefit that has not been disclosed to and approved by the owner-client.

Real estate managers who achieve the CERTIFIED PROPERTY MANAGER® (CPM®) designation subscribe to a specific code of ethics. In addition to the fiduciary obligation noted here, the CPM® Code of Ethics requires managers to hold proprietary information in confidence, to maintain accurate financial and business records for the managed property, and to protect the owner's funds. The Code also outlines duties to one's employer, to former clients and employers, and to tenants and others. It sets forth requirements for contracting management and managing the client's property and addresses relations with other members of the profession and compliance with laws and regulations. Ethical practices are an important part of professionalism in real estate management.

---

related to general legalities. (The Institute of Real Estate Management offers a Management Agreement form that includes an explanation of the typical components of an agreement along with possible variations and additions.)

Basic Components of an Agreement

Fundamental to every contract are the names of those entering into it, the purpose of the agreement, and the length of time it is to be in effect. In a management agreement, these elements are the parties, management of the property, and the term (or duration). The parties to a management agreement (the property owner and the management company or an independent real estate manager) must establish their authority to negotiate and sign such an agreement. In particular, individuals who represent a partnership or a corporation must have specific authorization to sign contracts. The street address may uniquely identify the property; however, including the legal description of the property according to its title documentation may be appropriate. If the property has a special name, the agreement usually lists that name as well. The term of the agreement is the period for which it will be in effect—usually stated as a specific number of years and including beginning and ending dates. The agreement often contains a provision

---

Contents of a Management Agreement

- Parties to the agreement
- Description of the property
- Term of the agreement
- Responsibilities of the manager
- Financial management
- Reports to ownership
- General property management
- Obligations of the owner
- Insurance
- Operating and reserve funds
- Liability
- Legal and regulatory compliance
- Compensation for management services
- Provision for termination

---

for automatic renewal on an annual basis when the initial term expires, provided it is not otherwise officially terminated. The duration of the agreement and its renewability are negotiable, as are all of the other terms and conditions.

Responsibilities of the Manager

Financial management, reporting, and general property management activities are among the real estate manager's normal duties. Much of this work is interrelated; reporting and record keeping are natural functions of both financial management and general property management. The management agreement formalizes these functions of the manager, often providing specific procedures to follow and sometimes stating intervals of time (monthly, annually) for performing various duties.

Financial Management. The management agreement details the financial arrangements between the owner and the real estate manager. These agreements include the treatment of bank accounts, owner's and manager's funds, income, expenses, lending, and audits.

Establishment of Bank Accounts. The establishment of an *operating account* is an important provision of the management agreement. The manager usually chooses the financial institution and establishes the account, although the owner may participate in the decision. Receipts and expenditures flow through the operating account. The management agreement may require that a minimum balance remain in the operating account at all times. It may also call for the owner to advance to the manager an amount equal to the first month's expenses. Apart from the necessity of having adequate funds to pay the operating expenses of the property, the bank may require a minimum balance. The operating account can simply be a commercial checking account.

The manager and the owner may agree to maintain more than one bank account. Security deposits and reserve funds should be separate from operating funds. In addition to protecting the funds, this measure often makes accounting for security deposits and reserves easier for the manager. The laws of many states require that security deposit funds be in a separate account. Regardless of the number of accounts necessary to maintain the property's funds, the management agreement usually mandates that deposits be in federally insured accounts. The agreement obligates the manager to inform the owner if the balance in any account for the property exceeds the federally insured amount.

Separation of Funds.   The management agreement should clearly state that the owner's and manager's funds should not be mixed *(commingled)*. This is not just a legal requirement. It is also a matter of professional ethics and good business practice. All funds the property earns—directly or indirectly—belong to the owner. The manager is entitled to compensation from the property's income and, as the owner's agent (or fiduciary), often has the authority to make those payments to himself or herself. The real estate manager must fully disclose all financial transactions to the owner.

Collection of Income.   The management agreement authorizes the manager to collect rent and any other income due the property. The manager can also charge fees for late payments, checks returned for non-sufficient funds (NSF), credit checks, and other administrative work. Some managers retain fees collected from residents for these services as compensation for these exceptions to regular practices, others receive separate management compensation on the fees collected. Unless state law prohibits it, the manager and the owner negotiate the compensation for such collections, and the management agreement specifically states their arrangement.

Payment of Expenses.   Payment of expenses is another of the manager's duties. Expenses may include debt service in addition to normal operating expenses. The remainder after all income has been collected and expenses have been paid (i.e., cash flow) is sent to the owner on a schedule established in the management agreement. (Major investors are likely to arrange for electronic transfer of funds out of their properties' operating accounts on a regular schedule.) If the property has more than one owner, the management agreement should state the proportionate distribution of the funds.

Treatment of Loans.   The manager usually seeks prohibition from lending funds to the property for any reason. In the event of an operating deficit, the owner must make up any difference immediately. However, the owner may ask the manager to make up the deficit temporarily with management funds (if permitted by local law), and the manager may elect to do so. To allow for that situation, the management agreement should state that such an amount would constitute a loan at a specified interest rate. The agreement usually obligates the property owner to maintain a minimum balance in the property's operating account to avoid such deficits.

Provision for Audits.   The owner usually has the right to audit the accounts of the property at any time, although the owner and manager may agree to a routine schedule for this procedure and state the schedule in the contract. Audits are at the owner's expense unless discrepancies in excess of a predetermined percentage are found. If the manager has erred and a discrepancy greater than the limit has resulted, the manager may be financially responsible for the audit. The management agreement may also state that all ledgers, receipts, and other records pertaining to the property belong to the owner even though they are usually in the manager's possession. When the agreement ends, the real estate manager must turn the records over to the owner.

Reports to the Owner.   Property managers send owners a monthly management report that often consists of several parts, including a statement of operations, a record of income, a record of disbursements, and a narrative report of operations. The narrative is a great way to communicate with the owner. Budget variances and their causes are important information for owner and manager. The manager must usually prepare an annual budget for operating the property, and the agreement usually states how and when that is to be done. Although preparation of these reports requires significant time, the use of computers permits rapid arrangement of data to satisfy both parties and expedites report preparation.

The number of written reports and their respective formats are negotiable items. Institutional owners often require that managers' reports conform to the institution's forms (or utilize the same computer software), a process that can involve considerable time and expense. Because of this, the owner and the real estate manager should consider the reporting requirements before they negotiate the management fee.

Apart from the financial reports required by the agreement, many situations arise in which a telephone call or personal visit with the owner may be necessary or appropriate. The level and frequency of personal contact depends in part on the owner's personality and requirements. Some owners request frequent consultation; others prefer to distance themselves from the relationship.

The real estate manager is a professional contracted to maintain the property, and he or she generally has the authority to handle any crisis. If disaster strikes, however, the owner must know what has happened. The manager's priority in any crisis is to gain control of the situation—inform the proper authorities, notify the insurance agent if warranted, and consult with contractors as appropriate. Then, as soon as possible, the manager should speak with the owner and describe what he or she is doing to rectify the situation.

General Property Management.   The real estate manager is not an employee of the owner, and the management agreement should clearly state that fact. A real estate manager provides a service and is either self-employed or an employee of a management company. The management agreement details the manager's authority to manage the property, including promoting the property, executing leases, hiring and supervising staff, administering the payroll, and overseeing maintenance.

Advertising the Property.   The manager of a residential property has the authority to advertise apartments available for lease; such advertising is at the owner's expense. The manager and owner should establish objectives for advertising and state them in the management agreement. A real estate manager might promote space for lease in a small office building or a strip shopping center the way he or she would promote a residential property. However, prospecting for commercial tenants is an integral part of the leasing activity at large properties.

Executing Leases.   The manager may have the authority to execute leases. For residential properties, this usually includes authorization to select residents, set rents, and enforce lease terms, in which case, the owner and manager should agree in advance on the lease form, financial requirements for tenancy, and rental rates.

Commercial property managers usually execute lease renewals, and they often execute new leases in buildings that have few vacant spaces. For larger commercial properties, a separate leasing agent handles most of the leasing, and the manager's participation in leasing activities is usually less direct. The complexity of the leases and the rents for commercial space may dictate the manager's role. *Leasing agents* may be employees of a property, but because of their specialized role, they often have separate contracts and receive commissions based on the value of the negotiated leases. For a new property, the manager may supervise the initial lease-up and then be directly responsible for renewing leases as they expire. Regardless of a particular leasing role, the manager must understand the particulars of each lease because he or she will ultimately administer its terms (collect the rents and provide services to the resident or the commercial tenant).

Hiring Staff and Administering Payroll.   The manager usually hires and supervises staff and administers payroll, but the owner is frequently the employer of the property's staff. The staff may include maintenance personnel, site managers, and anyone else who works full- or part-time on the property or in its behalf. The expenses of employment, including salaries, benefits, employment taxes (Social Security, Medicare, and unemployment), and workers' compensation insurance premiums, are the responsibility of the owner and are paid out of the property's operating funds.

Managing Maintenance.   The manager has the authority to perform all necessary and ordinary repairs and replacements to preserve the property and to make all alterations that are required to comply with lease agreements, governmental regulations, and insurance requirements. Apart from specific budgeted expenditures, the management agreement usually states a maximum dollar amount the manager can spend for individual items of maintenance without obtaining prior approval from the owner—except in the event of an emergency. Because of the manager's authority over the owner's finances, the management agreement may include a provision that requires the manager and others who handle the owner's funds under the manager's supervision to be bonded and that states the amount of liability involved.

Obligations of the Owner

The owner is responsible for insuring the property, and the agreement should require that the manager be identified on all policies as an additional named insured party. (If the owner is the employer of record, the real estate manager or the management company should be listed as an alternate employer on the owner's workers' compensation insurance policy.) Premiums and deductibles are expenses of the owner, although the manager may pay them out of the operating funds. The types of insurance required depend on the specific property and local practice. The owner and the manager should both consult their insurance agents to determine the most complete coverage for the property.

An important issue to negotiate for the management agreement is whether to establish and maintain a reserve fund. For residential properties, the reserve fund is usually a percentage of the property's gross receipts or NOI to be set aside on a regular basis. For commercial properties, a specific amount per square foot of building area is sometimes set aside.

The agreement should state the owner's responsibility for the property's compliance with applicable governmental regulations (e.g., environmental laws, building codes) and for any associated insurance requirements. It should also indemnify the agent against liability for noncompliance. If the owner does not cure any discovered noncompliance, the manager—as the owner's agent—could become liable. However, the agreement should require the manager to advise the owner of any known noncompliance. The owner must then decide to implement changes or corrections and authorize the manager to do so.

Compensation for Management Services

The usual compensation for real estate management services—the *management fee*—can be a fixed fee, but it is usually the greater of a minimum fixed fee or a percentage of the gross receipts (effective gross income) of the managed property. The owner and the real estate manager always negotiate the specific percentage, and they should negotiate a minimum monthly fee and state it in the agreement to assure the manager of compensation in case of a shortfall in collections. (Management for home-owners' associations—e.g., condominiums—is compensated by a flat fee; see also chapter 5.) In setting a fee, the manager should take care to be certain of adequate compensation for the full range of services provided. Negotiating separate fees or commissions may be appropriate for services the manager might provide that are not generally part of the regular management duties, such as leasing a new building, executing commercial lease renewals, or overseeing construction, rehabilitation, or remodeling.

SUMMARY

The management objectives of each property are unique. Two documents spell them out: a management plan and a management agreement.

A real estate manager must know how to assess a property's potential and how to explain that assessment through a management plan. Evaluation of data on the region, the neighborhood, and the property itself forms the basis for an analysis of the property's current market position. Assessment of the property's structural integrity, operating history, rent levels, and other factors indicates whether change is necessary to bring the property in line with market demand. Every change proposed to improve profitability involves a cost, and the manager must evaluate the proposed benefit in terms of its cost.

A management agreement is a formal contract between an owner and a real estate manager. It outlines the responsibilities of the manager and the obligations of the owner and authorizes the manager to operate the property on the owner's behalf. Even though the manager has extensive authority, the owner is ultimately responsible for the property.

5

Financial
Management

Most income-producing properties have multiple sources of income they must receive and a variety of expenses they must pay in a timely manner. The real estate manager must accurately record the nature of the income and expenses to maximize income for the owner and precisely reflect the financial status of the property. For most rental properties, cash receipts and expenditures relate to one of three categories: normal day-to-day operations, reserves (which may include capital improvement costs), or security deposits. Managers record funds they receive and pay out in an accounting system that is the basis for regular reports to the owner. However, financial management goes beyond recording and reporting. It includes specific projections of income and expenses in the form of budgets. It also serves as a basis for analyzing the efficiency of operations.

Effective financial management of real estate is not complicated. To achieve a positive balance of accounts over time, the level of income must be greater than the level of expense. The key to maximizing net income for an income-producing property is evaluation of the disposition of funds—both receipts and disbursements.

EVALUATION OF OPERATING FUNDS

For any income-producing investment, the measure of its profitability is the amount of return to the investor. For rental real estate, the most important measures are net operating income (NOI) and the cash flow that results from efficient operation.

The Cash Flow Chart

The real estate management profession has adopted specific terms to identify the various types of income and expense related to cash flow. The chart that follows shows the relationships of the income and expenses to each other.

CASH FLOW CHART

	Gross Potential Rental Income
minus	Vacancy and Collection Loss
plus	Miscellaneous Income
equals	Effective Gross Income
minus	Operating Expenses
equals	Net Operating Income (NOI)
minus	Debt Service (Interest and Principal)
equals	Pretax Cash Flow
minus	Income Tax
equals	After-Tax Cash Flow

The real estate manager's involvement with financial management often ends with the production of NOI. However, the owner's assessment of the property's investment return is usually based on pretax or after-tax cash flow. Although the manager may have no control over these outcomes, he or she must be aware of how to calculate them and how the owner evaluates them. The following sections define the components of cash flow.

Gross Potential Rental Income.   The maximum income the property can earn from rent is its *gross potential rental income*. This component of cash flow is a financial inventory of all the leasable spaces in a building at their current rental rates—if occupied. Once established, this figure remains fairly constant from month to month. The only factors that can change gross potential rental income are changes in rental rates or changes in the space available for rent. Gross potential rental income does not indicate income actually received. It is a statement of the amount of income that the owner would receive if the building were fully leased and all tenants paid their rents in full and on time.

Changes in rental rates occur most commonly when leases are renewed or when new residents or commercial tenants move in. Changes in the leasable space are more complex. Older buildings may have storage and

---

Two Types of Vacancy

Physical vacancy means the percentage of units (apartments, office suites, store spaces) that are unoccupied and available for lease.

Economic vacancy indicates the percentage of units that are not producing income. In addition to unoccupied units that are available for lease (physical vacancy), this includes the following:

- *Space that is leased but does not yet produce income.* A resident may rent an apartment in August that has a lease term beginning in October. Commercial space is often leased in an unfinished condition; rent payment (which may include reimbursement of tenant improvement costs) begins after construction is complete and the tenant moves in.
- *Delinquencies.* If a resident or commercial tenant is behind in rent payments, the unit or space is classified as occupied, but it is not producing income.
- *Leasable space that is used for other purposes or is otherwise unleasable.* Examples are spaces used as models for leasing purposes, for property offices, or for storage space; apartments provided as compensation to staff members who live on-site; and apartments or commercial spaces that are not in fit condition to be leased or occupied.

---

other areas that arc unleasable. Yet if those areas can be made leasable, the income they generate may be listed as additional rental income.

In an older office building, for example, the building maintenance department may currently store supplies and equipment in space in the basement that originally contained offices. While the space may no longer be usable for offices, it may be leasable to current tenants as space for storage of supplies and records. If the manager decides to use the space that way, he or she should itemize the scheduled rental income for the space as additional rental income or include it in miscellaneous income.

On the other hand, conversion of a basement apartment into a laundry room makes it part of the common area and therefore unleasable for occupancy. However, card- or coin-operated washers and dryers produce revenue that should be reported as miscellaneous income.

New developments commonly have model units, which managers often consider unleasable. However, such models are usually in perfect condition and could command a higher rent than similar units available for lease. Setting a rent for the model unit and including it in the gross potential rental income category reminds both manager and owner that if a prospect wanted to lease the model, it would be available for that purpose.

Vacancy and Collection Loss.   The actual rent received is rarely equal to the gross potential rental income. Vacant space produces no income, and rents not collected represent lost income. Both reduce the rent collected.

In the flow chart, *vacancy and collection loss* is subtracted from gross potential rental income to indicate the actual amount of rental income for a given reporting period (usually a month). Managers usually list delinquent rents and losses because of vacancies separately. When finally paid, delinquent rent is added to the income category, therefore nonpayment of rent is a true loss of income. On the other hand, vacancies simply reduce gross potential rental income; they do not represent a loss. The real estate manager has a duty to pursue collection of unpaid rent. If the nonpayment persists, however, the manager should refer the matter to a professional collection agency or an attorney for aggressive reinforcement of the obligation owed to the owner.

Miscellaneous Income.   Income derived from sources other than scheduled rent—e.g., coin-operated laundry equipment, pay phones, vending machines, late fees—is called *miscellaneous income* (or *unscheduled income*). Other related sources of income include telecommunications installations (rooftop satellite dishes, interior cable risers), automated teller machines (ATMs), leased storage space, and express shipment drop boxes (UPS, FedEx). Unscheduled income may also include previously unpaid rent that is recovered after a tenant no longer occupies the rental space, usually after the manager has turned the matter over to a collection agency or an attorney. *Pass-through operating expenses* (costs such as common area maintenance and taxes that the owner charges to the tenants) may be accounted for here as well. However, commercial property managers usually include them in the scheduled income, often as a separate line item, because these expenses are estimated in the budget and paid by tenants as additional rent.

Effective Gross Income.   Subtracting the vacancy and collection loss amount from the gross potential rental income and then adding to it the miscellaneous income yields the *effective gross income* of the property. This figure should match the total amount collected (gross receipts) during the reporting period. In this respect, the effective gross income total can help verify the accounting for the rent and other receipts during the reporting period. Effective gross income, which can vary substantially from the gross potential rental income for the property, is the amount that is available to pay building expenses, debt service, and a return on the owner's investment.

Operating Expenses.   The *operating expenses* of income-producing real estate include the costs of operating a business (payroll, office supplies) in addition to the costs of maintaining the condition of the property (maintenance, repairs, groundskeeping) and providing services to its occupants (utilities, decorating, security)—in other words, all of the regular expenses of operating the property with the exception of debt service. Insurance, real

---

Calculating Cash Flow

The cash flow chart may also be presented as shown here. This more detailed format lists loss items separately and accounts for pass-through expense reimbursements (typical for commercial properties) and reserve funds. Net operating income is also called *net income before debt service.*

    Gross Potential Rental Income
−   Vacancy
−   Collection Loss
=   Net Rent Revenue
+   Total Miscellaneous Income
+   Expense Reimbursements (pass-throughs)
=   Effective Gross Income
−   Total Operating Expenses
=   Net Operating Income (NOI)
−   Debt Service (interest and principal)
−   Reserves for Replacement and Capital Expenditures
=   Pretax Cash Flow
−   Income Tax
=   After-Tax Cash Flow

NOTE. *Reserve funds* are monies set aside to accumulate for future use; *capital expenditures* are amounts paid out of NOI for capital items (without regard for prior accumulation of reserves). The owner's requirements and the property's tax situation determine these items: Home-owners' associations (e.g., in condominiums) are required by law to maintain replacement reserves; institutional owners typically do not accumulate reserves.

---

estate taxes, and fees for legal and accounting services and management are also operating expenses. (The accounting section later in this chapter discusses specific categories of expense.) One objective of tracking operating expenses is to calculate how much of the effective gross income remains after payment of the bills. An even more important objective is to keep that remainder at a consistently high level. The owner and manager can compare operating expenses as a percent of effective gross income to industry statistics as a measure of the effectiveness of the financial management of the property.

Net Operating Income. What remains after deducting operating expenses from effective gross income is *net operating income (NOI).* This amount is an objective measure of the real estate manager's success. The manager strives to attain the highest possible level of income while controlling expenses in order to maximize NOI for the owner. Any variance in effective gross income, operating expenses, or both will cause NOI to vary. Depending on the agreement between the manager and the owner,

---

Return on Investment

Investment return may be expressed in dollars (cash flow) or as a percentage. The percentage rate is often referred to as *return on investment (ROI)* or *cash-on-cash return*. The percentage of ROI is calculated by relating the annual NOI from the property to the dollar amount of the owner's initial cash investment. The formula follows: NOI ÷ initial cash investment = percent return. For example, if an investor purchases a property with $100,000 down and the property produces an annual NOI of $10,000, the result is a 10 percent return.

$$\frac{\$10,000\ (NOI)}{\$100,000\ (initial\ cash\ investment)} = 10\%\ (return)$$

The same formula can be used to calculate ROI based on pretax or aftertax cash flow. This is a very basic description of the calculation of ROI; for many real estate owners, the calculation is more complicated.

---

financial management of the operating funds may end with the manager's submission of the NOI to the owner, but other expenses are customarily paid from NOI as well.

Debt Service.   An owner's personal evaluation of a property will not stop at NOI. The *debt service* obligation of a property—the amount required to repay the mortgage—is deducted from NOI. Although this amount is a recurring expense, it is not an operating expense. An owner will want to know if a property will generate enough cash to service the debt and provide a satisfactory return on his or her investment. In some instances, the real estate manager handles the payment of debt service for the owner; other owners prefer to make those payments themselves. Who will make the debt service payments is subject to negotiation in developing the management agreement (see chapter 4).

Cash Flow.   The amount remaining after subtracting debt service from NOI is the *cash flow*. (When the required debt service payment exceeds the amount of NOI, the cash flow is negative.) Cash flow is the owner's pretax income and one measure of *return on investment (ROI)*.

Two important payments are made from the cash flow of the property. These are contributions to the *reserve fund* (discussed later in this chapter) and personal *income taxes*. Although reserve funds come from the cash flow, the real estate manager sometimes deducts the reserve amount directly from NOI and accumulates it for future use. The owner generally calculates and pays his or her own income tax. Depending on the arrangement between the owner and the manager, the actual amount the owner receives from the real estate manager may be the same amount as the cash

---

Managing Financially Distressed Property

Property has undergone a downturn in its financial management if it is in *receivership* (turned over to an impartial third party who controls and pre-serves the asset for the benefit of the parties affected) or *foreclosure* (re-possessed by the lending institution to satisfy a loan that is in default) or if the owner is *bankrupt.* When income falls short of meeting debt service, the real estate manager or the owner may reduce some services or offer less-expensive services. If tenants become dissatisfied, they may move out at the end of their lease terms, increasing the financial burden on the property. The loss of income forces the owner or manager to reduce services further, and more tenants may leave as their leases expire. Those who remain may not pay rent regularly because they are in financial distress themselves. When a new manager takes over, he or she may find the property to be entirely vacant and in need of repair.

In order to manage such property appropriately, the real estate manager must know the owner's objectives and time frame. A lending institution may require only that the manager maintain the status quo because it may want to sell the property quickly to avoid additional losses. However, when the objective is to make the property profitable, the manager generally lists the conditions that require immediate attention and those that can be ad-dressed in stages. The conditions may involve rehabilitative work, collec-tions from tenants whose rent is past due, and evictions. These lists of items and their priority rankings can be the basis for a budget that indicates how much additional capital the owner must invest in the property to re-establish it in the marketplace.

---

flow. In fact, if the owner has no loan on the property or if the owner makes the mortgage payments and does not maintain a reserve fund, cash flow can be equivalent to net operating income.

Other Considerations

The amount of the debt service payment depends on how much cash the owner used to purchase the property and the terms of the mortgage loan. The property owner may ask the real estate manager to consider whether the owner or the property could benefit from refinancing the debt and to make recommendations accordingly. Refinancing can provide extra cash by reducing the owner's equity in the property. Depending on the current market, the owner may be able to refinance an existing loan for a lower interest rate, a longer term, or a larger or smaller principal amount. Some-times refinancing lowers the amount of the periodic debt service payments, thereby increasing the pretax cash flow and producing a higher return on the owner's investment.

The NOI of a property will be the same regardless of whether the owner purchased the property with cash or financed most of the purchase price. The constancy of the NOI of an income-producing property makes that sum a definitive measure of a property's market value.

Property Valuation.   From the perspective of a real estate manager, the importance of maximizing NOI is obvious. Although several criteria determine whether a property owner will renew a management agreement, a manager who can produce enough NOI so the owner can pay debt service and receive a satisfactory return on the investment is more likely to have his or her agreement renewed. The level of NOI represents more than the owner's return on investment; it also directly affects the *value* of the property.

One method of calculating the estimated market value of income-producing real estate is the *income capitalization approach*. Appraisers also use other methods to determine the value of real property. (Chapter 12 describes those methods.)

Using the income capitalization approach, estimated market value (V) is calculated by dividing the annual net operating income (I) by a *capitalization rate* (R) as indicated in the equation that follows. (The capitalization rate or *cap rate* is a decimal constant.)

$$\frac{I}{R} = V, \text{ or } \frac{\text{Net Operating Income (NOI)}}{\text{Capitalization Rate}} = \text{Estimated Market Value}$$

As an example, if the cap rate is 10 percent (.10 as a decimal) and the annual NOI of a property is $100,000, the property's estimated market value is $1 million ($100,000 ÷ .10 = $1,000,000). The same property valued with an 8.5 percent cap rate ($100,000 ÷ .085) has an estimated value of $1,176,471. The lower the cap rate, the higher the value. The higher the cap rate, the lower the value.

Investors use a cap rate to determine the potential return that a property will produce. An owner whose goal is to preserve value has a much different (usually lower) expectation of a return on investment than one whose goal is capital appreciation. The cap rate for a specific property depends on the property type, the cap rates on recent sales of comparable properties in the area, and market conditions, including interest rates. Variations in the cap rate have major effects on value—value declines as the cap rate rises.

When the same cap rate is used in a comparison of similar properties in a market area, the property with the highest annual NOI will have the highest estimated market value. If the NOI of a property decreases and the cap rate does not change, the property value will decrease. This is in addition to the reduction in periodic income resulting from the lower NOI. On the other hand, any factor that helps to increase NOI also increases property value. For example, a rent increase of $100 per month on one leased space adds $1,200 to NOI; at a 10-percent cap rate, that rent increase improves the property's estimated market value by $12,000 ($100 × 12 months = $1,200 ÷ .10 = $12,000).

Income Tax.   A manager may have no involvement whatsoever in the tax paid on the income generated by the property he or she manages, but the growing complexity of income taxation and its effect on real estate owner-ship increase the manager's need to understand these taxes. Income taxes on profits from real property ownership usually are levied against the indi-vidual investor's personal income. Stated very simply, if an owner's taxable income from a property is $10,000 and that amount is subject to tax at a 28-percent rate, the amount of tax owed is $2,800 ($10,000 × .28). Assum-ing a pretax cash flow of $15,000, the after-tax cash flow would be $12,200 ($15,000 − $2,800). Because each individual's tax obligations are different, the real estate manager can only estimate *pretax cash flow*. Professional tax accountants and attorneys can best advise an owner regarding the taxes on investment income and the resulting after-tax cash flow.

Reserve and Security Deposit Funds.   The operating funds of a prop-erty are usually the most extensive and require the most attention, but reserves and security deposits also need continual monitoring. While oper-ating funds may not always be in an interest-bearing account, reserve funds depend on regular earnings for part of their value. Security deposits must be maintained and accounted for separately.

Reserve Fund.   A *reserve fund* is money regularly set aside to pay future expenses. If this money comes from the income of the property, it is de-ducted from NOI. A reserve fund is commonly used to pay for major capital expenditures (e.g., boiler or roof replacement); regular operating expenses are generally paid from monthly receipts.

The reserve fund is usually kept in an interest-bearing checking or money market account. Because the reserve fund generally earns interest, some managers use it to accumulate funds for operating expenses that are not paid monthly. Real estate taxes and insurance premiums are often due only once or twice a year. Prorating the amounts and accumulating funds on a monthly basis means the money will be available when the payments are due, and cash flow will remain fairly constant from month to month. When the funds for these infrequently paid operating expenses accumulate in the reserve account, the manager must be sure to record the payments as operating expenses when they are made.

Specific amounts deposited into the reserve fund for *capital improve-ments* can be a set percentage of effective gross income or NOI. Because deposits to the reserve account are usually for a predetermined purpose (such as replacing major equipment in five years or remodeling apartments according to an established schedule), the periodic payments into this account can be budgeted as a set amount.

Developing a reserve for *capital expenditures* usually requires accounting for the funds on a capital expenditure report and a ledger. The expenditure is paid as a check drawn on the reserve account. It is important to note that the accumulation of reserve funds reduces the amount of cash available to the owner from the income of the property. Because of this, an owner may be reluctant to allow the accumulation of such funds. The owner and manager may also have different perspectives on the adequacy of reserve funds and their disposition. The availability of reserve funds is extremely important and is subject to negotiation in establishing the management agreement.

Security Deposits.   Residents and commercial tenants usually pay a security deposit as a guarantee of their performance of the terms of the lease (payment of rent, preservation of the property, etc.). Many states regulate the maintenance of security deposits. Some require property owners to hold the deposits in trust or in a separate bank account that is established and maintained exclusively for security deposits. Many states and municipalities require property owners to pay interest on the amount held and may require that security deposit funds be held in an interest-bearing account. Such laws also commonly stipulate the rate of interest to be paid, but that rate is usually low enough that earnings on the security deposit account may exceed what the owner owes to the residents or commercial tenants, providing a small amount of additional income. However, the amount of that extra income probably will not pay for the process of accounting for security deposit interest and maintaining the account. The real estate manager must know and follow the applicable laws relating to security deposit collection and maintenance and any requirements regarding the payment of interest. In some states, residential properties incur stiff penalties when they do not scrupulously observe these requirements.

For tax purposes, the interest the account earns is reported as income to the owner if it is not distributed to the tenants. To reduce (or eliminate) the owner's tax obligation on the interest, the manager may need to issue checks to the residents or commercial tenants annually and report the distribution to the Internal Revenue Service and to the tenants on the appropriate income tax forms. The real estate manager should be aware of the current tax laws and their application to such funds. Even if the amount of interest owed to each resident or commercial tenant is relatively small, the cumulative amount owed to all tenants could require the owner to pay much higher income taxes if the account is not properly maintained.

If the resident or commercial tenant meets all of the lease obligations, the security deposit is ultimately returned. If not, part or all of a security deposit may be retained to pay for damage to the leased space (wear and tear that exceeds normal standards) or to compensate the owner for any debts the tenant owes (late fees, past-due rent, etc.). Many states require specific written notice to residents of the amounts withheld from the security deposit and the reasons for withholding them.

ACCOUNTING FOR INCOME AND EXPENSES

The real estate manager commonly deposits rents and other regular income of the property (excluding security deposits and monies intended for reserves) into a checking account that is exclusively for the payment of expenses of operating the property. Records of income and expense must be accurate because these records are the basis for disbursing funds to the owner and filing income taxes. They must also be consistent to avoid duplications and omissions and to verify budget projections.

Accounting Systems

The property owner and the real estate manager must agree on the basic accounting systems they will use for the property. Based on their agreements, the manager can set up a chart of accounts and journals to document receipts and disbursements. The owner and manager must also agree on which method of accounting they will use.

Chart of Accounts.   The best way to ensure accuracy and consistency in accounting is to establish a *chart of accounts* (exhibit 5.1), which usually has account numbers or codes for specific categories of income and expense. No chart of accounts is definitive; most buildings have unique features that require separate categories, entries, or subentries. The type of property and its size affect the scope of a chart of accounts.

Depending on the level of detail desired, the manager can group income and expense categories under general headings or subdivide them further. A detailed chart of accounts usually provides account codes for security deposits, reserve funds, and debt service payments. Specific capital expenditures may also have account codes. In this way, the chart of accounts can identify *all* income and expense items for a property.

The real estate manager uses this information not only for purposes of accounting but also for reporting to the owner and others as well as for preparing accurate budgets. The manager who must develop a chart of accounts for a new property or for new management of an existing property can seek advice from a professional accountant so he or she can be sure to identify all of the separate accounts a specific property needs.

Exhibit 5.1
Common Categories for a Chart of Accounts

Operating Income
Rents
Miscellaneous Income

Operating Expenses
Management Fee and Administrative Costs
Payroll and Related Expenses
Utilities (Gas, Electricity, Telephone)
Cleaning
Maintenance and Repairs
Supplies
Miscellaneous Services
Security
Legal Expense
Groundskeeping
Water and Sewer
Rubbish Removal
Interior Painting and Decorating
Recreational Amenities
Real Estate Tax
Advertising and Promotion
Insurance

These major categories are usually divided into subaccounts to facilitate tracking of specific income and expense items.

Journals.   Accounting records may be documented in a general journal that shows receipts and disbursements as well as the separate accounts to which the individual items relate. However, real estate managers usually record income received in a *cash receipts journal* and payments in a *cash disbursements journal*. A separate *general ledger* shows the current balance of the owner's account. Some computer software programs contain charts of accounts that allow the user to add accounts as needed.

Accounting Methods.   The owner and manager must agree on the method of accounting so financial records and reports will be consistent, accurate, and easily understood. *Cash-basis accounting* records income when it is received and payments as they are made. *Accrual-basis accounting* records income when it is due and expenses when they are incurred, and the records may not reflect actual receipts and disbursements. The entire accounting and reporting system should conform to one of these two methods. Some managers use a modified cash system in which expenses that are not due monthly (insurance, taxes) are accounted on an accrual basis. When using such a mixed system, the manager must adjust the records of net operating income to reflect the partial accruals.

Major Sources of Income at Commercial Properties

- Base rent
- Operating expense pass-throughs—utilities, common area maintenance (CAM) charges, extra services
- Paid parking
- Reimbursement of tenant improvement costs
- Miscellaneous revenue sources

Retail properties may also collect percentage rent and contributions to a marketing fund or merchants' association.

All transactions, no matter how inconsequential, should be recorded on the day they are made, especially those involving petty cash. Use of a *purchase order* or other written record for every purchase over a set amount ensures that the merchandise or service received is acceptable and matches the order.

Income Categories

In residential properties, the only distinction between income sources may be rents, utilities (billed to residents), and miscellaneous income (discussed earlier in this chapter.) At commercial properties, however, commercial tenants often pay one or more amounts in addition to *base rent* each month. If the owner passes all or part of the real estate taxes, property insurance, and common area maintenance (CAM) costs through to the tenants, those charges may be categorized as *additional rent*. Improvements to a commercial tenant's leased space that are charged back to the tenant (sometimes with interest) may also be categorized as additional rent. Where leases for retail space require payment of *percentage rent,* such income would be accounted separately from the base rent. Regardless of the property type, if tenants are charged for parking, a separate income category may be warranted; this is especially true if parking space is leased to nonoccupants of the building. Some items discussed earlier as sources of miscellaneous income (e.g., rents or fees from telecommunications installations or storage spaces) may be itemized separately, especially when the amounts are substantial.

Expense Categories

Although amounts and types of expenses vary by property, the real estate management profession recognizes some common expense categories (see exhibit 5.1). Every real estate management company defines expenses its own way. Managers may subdivide some major categories to adequately account for the operating expenses of a specific property. In addition, property owners sometimes request unique expense categorizations. The real estate manager must understand and consistently apply the management firm's categorization of expenses as well as the owner's.

Management Fee and Administrative Costs.   The compensation paid to the managing agent may be a percentage of the effective gross income of the property, a flat fee, or a combination of the two. When a combination fee is used, the flat fee is usually a stated minimum, and the actual fee paid is the greater of the two amounts. (The minimum fee assures compensation for management if the effective gross income is below expectations.)

Administrative costs is the heading for supplies, postage, photocopies, fax charges, and other common expenses associated with operating an on-site office if a separate account for *office expenses* does not exist. At times, nonstandard charges such as fees for tax preparation may be listed as administrative costs.

Payroll and Related Expenses.   Payroll and benefits may be listed as a single item, but the various deductions and distributions usually require separate accounting for wages or salaries, withholding taxes, benefits, and the various employer contributions required by state and federal governments for Social Security, Medicare, and unemployment taxes. Because of the complex accounting, the manager may prefer to list each of these items as a subaccount under payroll. As an alternative, payroll may be established as a subaccount in the appropriate operating expense category on the basis of the employees' duties (e.g., administration, maintenance, grounds-keeping). In such a case, subentries would be made for salaries, benefits, and taxes. How payroll is listed depends on the preferences of the owner and the manager. The most important point is to be consistent.

The payroll schedule can skew monthly reports and the monthly flow of cash through the accounts of the property. Management firms generally receive rental income twelve times a year, on the first of every month, but they rarely use a monthly payroll, and a weekly payroll is often impractical. Paying employees biweekly (twenty-six times a year) yields ten months with two pay periods and two with three pay periods. To avoid such variations, real estate managers commonly use a semimonthly payroll system.

A *semimonthly payroll system* pays employees twice a month (usually on the fifteenth and the last day of the month). That system balances payroll distribution against rental income. Because rent is commonly collected on the first of the month, activities during the first week of the month usually center on processing incoming checks and issuing late notices for unpaid rents. The middle of the month is usually less active from an accounting standpoint, so a semimonthly payroll system can help to ensure steady bank balances, a monthly payment to the owner that is fairly constant, and a manageable schedule of activities in the accounting department. A semi-monthly payroll may require additional computations for employees paid by the hour because the number of workdays per pay period varies, but the savings that result from preparing payroll only twenty-four times a year instead of twenty-six may offset the additional work. No matter how payroll distribution is scheduled, additional accounting is required for hourly employees who receive overtime compensation.

Utilities.   This category of expense may require several subaccounts to provide accurate and appropriate records. Bills for gas and electricity are usually issued and payable on a monthly basis, although the number of days in the billing period may vary without regard to the number of days in the month. In addition, the price of production and delivery may increase or decrease monthly or rates may vary seasonally. These differences can cause variances in the monthly utility expenses for a property even though consumption may remain constant. Some utility companies, especially those whose rate structures vary based on the season of the year, offer programs to equalize bill payments. If utility costs are passed through to the tenants (as is commonly done at commercial properties and may be done at residential properties), additional accounting is required to prorate and collect the utility charges.

Although telephone costs may be listed as an office expense for the property (if such a category is established), they may be more appropriately recorded in a subaccount under utilities if telephone and related services are provided as a property amenity and charged to tenants. *Telephone expense* includes facsimile (fax) machines, Internet access, usage charges, toll-free numbers, voice mail, and other related services. Different companies may provide local and long-distance telephone services. This same utilities subaccount might also be the place to record cable or satellite communications expenses unless they warrant separate subaccounts.

Cleaning.   This category applies primarily to office buildings. If the management company provides this service for commercial tenants, daily cleaning is a significant expense that requires a subaccount.

Maintenance and Repairs.   This category accounts for all general maintenance and repairs, both interior and exterior. It commonly includes expenses incurred for exterior painting and cleaning, elevator maintenance contracts, boiler inspection and repair contracts, air-conditioning service contracts, parts, small hand tools, and fire protection systems and equipment. Other related expenses include plumbing, electrical, plastering, tuck-pointing, and carpentry services. If the management company employs staff to perform some or all of this work, this category may include their payroll expenses. Fees for maintenance contractors, however, should be a separate item in the maintenance category and should not be payroll expenses.

Because so many operating expenses may seem related to maintenance or repairs, this category has the potential to become too broad. To avoid this, real estate managers may list certain types of maintenance or repairs as separate subaccounts because of their recurrent nature, because of the amount of expense they represent, or both. Groundskeeping expenses may be included in maintenance, although they are often substantial enough to merit their own category. Interior painting and decorating costs are usually separate, in part because owners and managers may have that work done for purposes of marketing and not just to maintain the leased premises.

Supplies.   The supplies category accounts for regularly replaced items. However, office supplies may be listed under administrative costs and cleaning materials may be included under cleaning or maintenance and repairs accounts. The real estate manager may use this category to record replaceable goods that are purchased in large quantities or that are particularly expensive. Irregular purchases or materials that are replenished infrequently may also be accounted for in the supplies category. Except for specific recurring expenses, the supplies category may not need subaccounts.

Because price reductions are common for volume or bulk purchases, the manager should consider the frequency of replacement and the cost of holding inventory compared to the discount offered. A sale on light bulbs may offer a 10-percent discount on bulbs purchased in a lot of 100 or more. If the property replaces that number of bulbs annually and has ample storage space, such a discount may be worthwhile. However, if the property only uses 20 bulbs annually, the initial investment and the storage costs done for the larger quantity may cancel the value of the discounted bulk purchase.

Miscellaneous Services.   This category is for expenses related to upkeep of the property that are infrequent or of too small a dollar value to itemize into subaccounts. Having keys made and repair or repainting of signs on the property are likely expenses for this category. Seasonal and regional considerations may also apply. In the northern United States, pest control may be in this category; in the South, however, this expense is often a separate subaccount. Conversely, snow removal would be a subaccount in the North but managers might omit it in extreme southern regions where snow is rare. At commercial properties, this category may be called *building services*.

Security.   Because of the inherent liability risks, many properties that provide a security force contract that service from an agency. Managers usually list other security-related expenses in the category that reflects their direct cost—e.g., nighttime lighting of parking lots and common areas would be included in the electricity expense under utilities. Although the presence of a door attendant or a building concierge may deter criminal activity, real estate managers usually regard the service provided by that staff member as a convenience to tenants and visitors rather than security as such, so the salary involved is a payroll expense.

Legal Expense.   Charges frequently arising in this category include the costs of prosecuting tenants for unpaid rents and evictions, protesting real estate tax assessments, and periodically reviewing legal documents (leases, contracts). Depending on the size of the property and the frequency of legal consultation, a retainer may be a regular expense in this category.

Groundskeeping.   The extent of this cost depends on the size of the area maintained. Landscaping maintenance, fuel for power equipment, and similar recurring expenses fall into this category. Regular expenses, including parking lot sweeping, might be separate subaccounts.

Water and Sewer.   This expense fluctuates seasonally. Most communities bill water and sewer charges together (sewer may be charged as an added percentage of the water cost—presuming that water intake at a property determines how much sewage it produces—or as an additional flat fee). Often this is a subaccount in a utilities category that includes energy (gas, electricity) expenses and rubbish removal. However, related specifics such as faucet and pipe replacement are categorized as maintenance or plumbing expenses.

Rubbish Removal.   Large properties usually contract with a private, licensed waste hauler to have trash removed from their sites. The charge is often based on the number of pickups at the site each month and the number and size of containers, although it may be based on the weight or volume (cubic yards) of material removed or a combination of volume and number of pickups. Many states and municipalities have mandatory recycling laws that require separation of recyclable materials (paper, glass, plastic, and metal items) from organic waste and other forms of trash. In some areas, recyclables may be collected separately. A separate contract for removal of recyclables may be necessary for commercial properties. Management records may list rubbish removal as a subaccount under utilities if a separate category is not necessary.

Interior Painting and Decorating.   Painting and decorating of interior areas can be a large and frequently recurring expense, especially in residential properties, so it is often a separate category from maintenance and repairs. In addition, the purpose of the work may be solely to improve the appeal of the property, not strictly to maintain it. The interior painting and decorating category also covers charges for such items as wallpaper, painting equipment, and contractors. If the property or the management firm employs full-time decorators, their wages and benefits may be listed here or as a payroll expense. At commercial properties, tenants may be responsible for painting and other improvements to their leased premises, and if the property owner contracts for the work, the commercial tenant may pay the costs as prorated additional rent.

Recreational Amenities.   Recreational amenities were once limited to residential property, but many office buildings now offer such facilities for tenants' employees to use. The maintenance and servicing of exercise equipment, swimming pools, and other recreational facilities are in this category, with subaccounts for each amenity as appropriate. If utilities for the amenities are metered separately, the charges may be listed here as well so the full cost of operating the recreational facilities can be seen at once. Otherwise, such charges belong in the utilities category. Salaries for staff members dedicated solely to recreational services—e.g., exercise instructors—may be accounted here (for the same reason that utilities would be) or under payroll expenses.

Real Estate Tax.   Many municipalities levy a tax on the assessed value of real property. The tax may be payable quarterly, semiannually, or annually; however, some managers budget for this expense on a monthly basis to ensure that the full amount is available when the tax becomes due. If the owner financed the property, the lending institution may require cumulative payment into an escrow account for the real estate tax. Under some types of office, industrial, and retail leases, the owner passes this tax through to the commercial tenants on a pro-rated basis. The pass-throughs are estimated and collected monthly (in advance), and the manager may hold these funds in a reserve account until the tax is due.

Advertising and Promotion.   The frequency and amount of expenses incurred for advertising and promotion depend on the property type, the vacancy level, response to market demand, and the age of the building. Advertising to lease space is most common in residential properties. New developments require more promotion than buildings established in the marketplace. For established properties, a twenty-word advertisement in the classified section of the newspaper may be sufficient. A new property may buy a half-page display ad in a local magazine for a year, or it may use another type of major promotion. Because of this variance, the manager and the owner may decide to budget a fixed amount per reporting period and to monitor these expenses separately.

At commercial properties, prospecting for tenants usually takes a different approach. Managers or leasing agents often seek out prospects rather than waiting for them to contact the property. In such situations, advertising and promotion is part of a larger process and may be identified as a subaccount or listed as a related expense in a separate category for leasing.

Insurance. Insurance premiums come due on varying schedules, although semiannual and annual payments are most common. This category is usually limited to insurance relating to the property. Employee medical coverage, workers' compensation, and employment insurance taxes (Social Security, Medicare, unemployment) are accounted as payroll expenses. The types of insurance usually accounted in this category follow:

- *Fire insurance* protects the policyholder against all direct loss or damage to the insured property from fire.

- *Extended coverage (EC),* usually purchased as an addition to fire insurance, covers loss from specific perils (windstorm, hail, explosion, riots and civil commotion, aircraft, vehicles, smoke, and water damage from fire fighting).

- *Boiler insurance* pays for any damage resulting from a boiler malfunction.

- *Property damage insurance* protects against liability for damage to the property of others that occurs on the insured property.

- *Bodily injury insurance* protects against liability for damages arising out of injury or death occurring on the property.

- *Special form insurance* (previously referred to as *all-risk insurance*) covers damage from any cause that is not specifically excluded from the policy. This type of policy includes most property and liability coverages that are offered as separate policies. (Some states require that liability coverage be a separate policy.)

- *Rent loss insurance* protects the owner from loss of income resulting from damage that makes all or part of the property unleasable.

- *Owner, landlord, and tenant (OLT) liability insurance* covers claims against a property owner, a landlord, or a tenant arising out of injury to a person or persons on the property.

- *Umbrella liability insurance* provides additional liability coverage beyond the limits of the basic liability policy.

- *Automobile insurance* is purchased for service vehicles owned by and operated for the property and to protect the property owner from liability incurred as a result of operating these vehicles.

- *Fidelity bonding* protects one individual against financial loss that might result from dishonest acts of another specific individual. Though usually obtained from an insurance company, this is not an insurance policy as such. It is a three-party arrangement called a *surety*. A management firm usually purchases fidelity bonds for its employees (specifically, those who handle money); the bonds would not be an operating expense for the property unless they were maintained for site staff the property owner employed.

Some properties may need additional insurance coverage because of special conditions, and real estate managers may obtain more favorable premiums by insuring several properties under one *blanket policy*. The best practice is to consult with an insurance agent who specializes in the type of property in question. (Chapters 9, 10, and 11 describe insurance requirements for specific types of properties.)

REPORTING ON INCOME AND EXPENSES

The documentation of all financial transactions that pertain to the property is an important aspect of the real estate manager's responsibility. In addition to recording these transactions in the accounting records when they occur, the manager is custodian of the records of all the property's financial transactions. The manager uses those records as the basis for the preparation of regular reports to the property owner and sometimes to the residents or commercial tenants. In real estate management, the reporting process is increasingly computerized.

Accounting Software

While some records may be maintained temporarily or permanently as paper copies (e.g., bank statements, rent receipts), most financial information related to the management of real estate today is ultimately entered into accounting software programs. These generally have template forms into which specific data are entered. The software automatically calculates results for rows, columns, or select groups of information. It will also merge individual records into a report for the owner. Such accounting software programs can be expensive.

Inexpensive software packages designed for small business owners can satisfy the accounting and form requirements of an owner of a single, moderate-sized property or several small properties. Creating specific reporting forms and formats in a straightforward spreadsheet program may adequately address some owners' information needs.

Record keeping and reporting with respect to the individual tenant and the property as a whole as well as data analysis are routine functions of software accounting and spreadsheet programs. Reports include year-

Reports to Owners

• Statement of Operations
• Rent Roll
• Vacancy Report
• Delinquency Report
• Lease Expirations
• Leasing Report
• Cash Disbursements
• Statement of Receipts
• Reserve Account Transactions
• Explanation of Budget Variances (narrative summary)
• Budget

Advertising and promotion might be a separate report or might be included in the leasing report. When commercial tenants pay percentage rent, reports for retail properties include a tenant sales analysis report. The real estate manager may report other on-site activities (e.g., construction progress) separately as necessary or appropriate.

to-date (cumulative) results, comparison to the current-year budget, and comparison with performance from the preceding year.

Whatever software program a real estate manager uses, the importance of a file backup system cannot be overemphasized. The manager must also maintain backup copies of all essential information in a secure location off-site to avoid potential loss in the event of fire or other damage to the management office or its computers.

Management Reports

The real estate manager must keep records and issue reports on the property as a whole and each leasable space, both occupied and vacant. The manager maintains all receipts, bank statements, canceled checks (or microfilm check image statements), copies of purchase orders, and copies of receipts issued for payments made to the property. He or she reports information from these records to the property owner on a regular schedule, usually once a month. Clients who own several properties managed by the same firm may request comprehensive portfolio reports as well.

In addition, the real estate manager may make reports to residents or commercial tenants in the form of bills, receipts for payments, statements of interest earned on security deposits, damage assessments, and other financial transactions related to their occupancy of leased space in the property. The sections that follow describe some of the types of reports a real estate manager makes.

Rent Roll. The principal record of income for a rental property is the *rent roll*. This is a record of the residents or commercial tenants, their unit or suite numbers, and their specific rental rates and lease terms as well as whether rent is paid or is past due. If certain operating expenses are pro-rated and passed through (as in commercial leases), the amounts due and paid are also recorded in the rent roll.

Computerized rent roll information can be sorted based on various parameters, which permits convenient production of vacancy reports, delinquency reports, and reports on lease expiration. The real estate manager regularly sends those reports to the property owner.

Rental Ledger. The manager usually maintains a *rental ledger* for each rental unit or space. The ledger lists the resident's or commercial tenant's name, phone number, unit identification, rental rate, late charges, security deposit amount, move-in date, lease terms, recurring charges, pass-through charges, and other pertinent facts about the leasing arrangement. The rental ledger records all payments the resident or commercial tenant makes, including late charges, reimbursements for damage or tenant improvements, and receipt and disposition of the security deposit.

Rent Bills and Receipts. Commercial tenants may receive a monthly rent bill (statement of rent due) because their leases usually include requirements to pay prorated pass-through charges (see chapter 11). When the rent is a flat rate (as in residential properties), a bill is rarely issued. Issuing receipts may be necessary (or appropriate)—especially when a lease agreement is initially set up—if the tenant pays in cash or makes a partial payment. Copies of dated rent bills marked "paid" are an effective verification of the monthly income records.

Operating Expenses and Receipts Reports. Payments for operating expenses are recorded chronologically on a *cash disbursements report* (also called *check vouchers*) that lists the vendor, the amount, and the check number for all payments and includes items that are not operating expenses (debt service, payment for capital expenditures).

Rents and other sources of income are likewise recorded chronologically on a *statement of receipts report* that identifies the source and amount of all monies received from concessions (e.g., vending machines, coin laundry equipment), storage space rental, parking fees, late charges, etc. Some firms have a separate report for other or miscellaneous income that is known as *miscellaneous cash receipts, miscellaneous income,* or *miscellaneous receipts*. A *reserve account transactions report* lists deposits to and withdrawals from the reserve fund.

Bank Account Records.   The real estate manager maintains the property's bank accounts and reconciles the bank statement with property records of checking account deposits and payments. Traditionally, checks, money orders, and cash have been the accepted forms of payment. However, payment via credit cards, debit cards, and electronic transfer of funds is also widely accepted, and such payments are becoming increasingly common in the real estate management industry. Businesses and banks encourage people to pay bills electronically, and they will arrange to make regular payments automatically. If the manager uses electronic transfer of funds to pay property expenses or to receive rents and other income, the direct deposits and payouts show on the bank statement. While a checking account reconciliation report may be included with the monthly report to the owner, it is not always a requirement.

Statement of Operations.   A *statement of operations* (also called an *income statement*) is an at-a-glance view of the property's gross amounts of income and expenses for the period. It emphasizes the cash flow paid to the owner. For small enterprises, the statement of operations may be the only financial report. For large properties, this statement usually accompanies more detailed reports such as the rent roll, the vacancy and delinquency reports, and the leasing report.

Narrative Report of Operations.   The owner should also receive a *narrative report of operations*. This report explains any differences or *variances* between the actual income and expenses and the amounts projected for them in the budget. If an extreme variance occurs in either income or expenses, a personal meeting with the owner usually provides a better setting for such explanations. When the variations are minimal, a narrative report may not be required.

BUDGETING

Budgeting is not an exact science. The actual income and expenses of a property rarely (if ever) conform precisely to budget projections. A budget is a tool. The real estate manager uses it to establish the priority of spending based on the amount of income the property produces and the expenses incurred as well as to estimate cash flow. The budget helps the manager minimize the variance of the property's NOI and assess the property's cash position at a given time. When an unexpected expense creates a cash shortage, the budget can guide the manager's evaluation of alternatives for meeting the expense.

Types of Budgets

• Operating (annual)
• Capital
• Long-range

The real estate manager should also prepare a separate *marketing budget* each year (as an extension of the annual operating budget) as well as during lease-up of a new property or following rehabilitation.

Several types of budgets exist. Real estate management commonly uses three: operating budgets, capital budgets, and long-range budgets.

Operating Budget

The most commonly used budget is an *operating budget* that lists the principal (or regular) sources of income and expenses for the property, usually on a monthly basis. The amount listed as gross potential rental income in the income and expense reports for the property should be fairly constant from month to month. Every other item of income or expense for the property is added to or subtracted from the gross potential rental income to calculate NOI. The NOI reflects any variance in individual entries. Therefore, even though gross potential rental income may be a fixed amount, the NOI and cash flow can vary substantially. A budget permits better projection and monitoring of income and expenses.

Aside from indicating the sources of income and expenses for a property, a budget indicates *when the transactions are expected to occur.* Differing monthly amounts allocated for heat and air conditioning over the course of the year reflect seasonal variations in energy consumption. Advertising expenditures for an established apartment building may be minimal for most months, so the greatest part of funds allocated for this expense are divided among the months of highest expected leasing activity. On the other hand, a new development or a property that is undergoing extensive rehabilitation may require a large advertising budget divided equally over the year to reflect the intensity of the leasing activity.

The budget is also the starting point for considering alternatives for paying unanticipated expenses. If winter weather is exceptionally cold and snowy, higher fuel consumption generally increases the fuel expense for the property. Greater demand for fuel usually leads to price increases, and that, coupled with increased consumption, can devastate a fuel budget. Other increases in season-related expenses, such as snow removal, can have a significant effect on cash flow. When such extra expenses conflict with projections made in the budget, the manager can review other projected expenses. If another budgeted expense can be postponed temporarily (or omitted altogether for the year), that change may offer a way to offset part or all of the extra weather-related expenses. Regardless of the alternatives considered, the manager should notify the owner of any action taken—in accordance with the terms outlined in the management agreement.

Annual Budget.   The *annual budget* is the most common form of operating budget. There are two kinds of annual budgets: historical and zero based. To prepare a *historical budget,* the manager generally reviews income and expenses from previous years. A *zero-based budget* consists solely of projections; it ignores past operating expenses. The annual budget projects the whole year's income and expenses for each account (exhibit 5.2). If the real estate manager anticipates any departures from normal operations for the upcoming year (e.g., temporarily high vacancies because of remodeling), the budget should account for them as well.

Possibly one of the most valuable aspects of this annual exercise is the presentation of the new budget to the owner. It offers a natural opportunity for the owner and the manager to discuss the past performance of the property and to adjust individual budget items as they preview the coming year. By reviewing each item in the budget, the manager can explain how anticipated income and expenses may affect the property's performance. Gross potential rental income, vacancy and collection loss, and effective gross income categories will reflect planned increases in rents. An increase in staff size or wage adjustments will affect payroll expenses. The owner and the manager must agree on the budget before it is implemented, so they should review each line item in detail.

Monthly Planning.   Monthly planning is particularly useful when the manager reports to the owner monthly. An annual budget is often developed in greater detail by allocating an amount for each line item on a month-by-month basis. Some items divide easily into twelve equal parts because they do not change from one month to another; others vary substantially from month to month based on seasonal and other factors. Projecting income *when it is expected to be received* and expenses *when they are expected to be paid* is important. If a property normally incurs an expense in March and pays it in May, budgeting for that expense in March will result in variances for both months, and the variances will require explanation.

Quarterly Budget Updates.   The annual budget serves as a point of reference for the manager and the owner. However, actual income and expenses can differ significantly from such a budget as the year progresses. To compensate for such differences, real estate managers sometimes prepare *quarterly budget updates* that reflect adjustments to the original projections made in the annual budget. These modified budgets can be more accurate

Exhibit 5.2
Items Common to an Annual Operating Budget

INCOME
Gross Potential Rental Income
Less: Vacancy and Collection Loss
Miscellaneous Income
Effective Gross Income

EXPENSES
Management Fee
Administrative Costs
Payroll
Payroll-Related Expenses
Electricity
Gas
Telephone
Cleaning
Maintenance and Repair
Supplies
Miscellaneous Services
Security
Legal Expenses
Groundskeeping
Water and Sewer
Rubbish Removal
Interior Painting
Interior Decorating
Recreational Amenities
Real Estate Tax
Advertising and Promotion
Insurance
Other Expenses
Total Expenses

Net Operating Income
Less: Debt Service
Cash Flow

than the annual budget because the projections are not so far into the future. In addition, such quarterly budgets cover the approximate time of one season, so their projections of seasonally affected income and expenses can be more accurate. Occasionally new or adjusted monthly budgets may be necessary or appropriate for the same reasons.

Capital Budget

Because one purpose of a reserve fund is to accumulate capital for improvements, a *capital budget* is prepared to show how much to set aside in the reserve fund on a regular basis. In principle, this simply requires calculating the cost of the improvement and dividing the total by the number of months before the change is to be implemented, then factoring in interest income that the account will earn.

However, if funds are to be accumulated over a period of years, the manager must also consider inflation. If the interest earned on the accumulating reserve is not substantially higher than the rate of inflation, the anticipated total accumulation will not meet the actual cost of the improvement. Furthermore, the cost of materials may rise faster than the inflation rate, so a larger monthly allocation will be necessary to assure a reasonable match between the amount of reserve funds and their anticipated use. Capital budgets include leasing commissions, tenant improvements, major maintenance, and improvements or additions to the property.

Managers who work for institutional owners approach a capital budget differently. These owners rarely accumulate reserve funds. Rather, their capital budgets reflect anticipated expenditures for specific capital improvement projects, tenant improvements, and leasing commissions.

Long-Range Budget

Use of a capital budget often leads the manager and the owner to develop a *long-range budget* that illustrates the relationship between operating income and expenses over five or more years in the life of a property. The level of detail and precision is less in this type of budget than in an annual budget because projections cannot be as accurate for the longer time involved.

A long-range budget can show the owner what to expect over the time he or she plans to hold the investment. It can illustrate the anticipated financial gain from a rehabilitation program, a new marketing campaign, or a change in market conditions. Long-range budgets illustrate expected income, expenses, and sources of funding. Long, major projects may require the owner to make extraordinary cash contributions or financing arrangements in the early years of the holding period. Ideally, the owner will recover these extra contributions in the later years of the holding period, after the income from the property stabilizes at an amount greater than it was when the property was purchased or when the changes were implemented.

SUMMARY

The success of an income-producing property is measured by the amount of money it generates. Gross potential rental income is adjusted for vacancy and collection losses and for receipts from sources other than rent (miscellaneous or unscheduled income) to determine the effective gross income of the property. Operating expenses are deducted from that amount to find the NOI of the property. For some types of operations, NOI is the bottom line.

For most real estate investments, however, NOI is adjusted by deducting the expense of the loan (debt service) and money set aside as reserve funds to yield cash flow. This amount is usually paid to the owner who is then responsible for any tax liability resulting from the real estate operation.

Financial management of a property involves establishing and maintaining thorough and accurate financial records for the property as a whole and for individual units, residents, or commercial tenants. Every dollar of income or expense must be accounted and categorized based on its source or destination as identified in a chart of accounts. The accounting records are the basis of the financial reports the manager sends to the owner each month. The real estate manager also uses them to develop budgets to project future income and expenses. The manager's objective is to maximize NOI and minimize variances between actual and budgeted income and expenses.

6

Staffing

The real estate manager is responsible for a wide array of duties. Rarely does a single manager[1] perform all of the tasks inherent in these responsibilities, nevertheless, it is the manager's duty to ensure that all of the following work is accomplished:

- Conduct a security and safety audit.
- Develop a maintenance management program.
- Develop an emergency procedure plan.
- Establish rents that make the units or spaces marketable; know the competition.
- Market and prospect for tenants for vacant premises; retain existing tenants.
- Develop and implement a resident or commercial tenant retention program.
- Collect rent and other fees; properly account for these funds; prepare long- and short-term budgets.
- If authorized, pay any expenses the property incurs.
- Manage employees of the management firm and staff at the site.

---

1. This text assumes that the real estate manager is employed by a management firm rather than directly by an owner.

- Develop the property management plan.
- Communicate with the property owner.

The real estate manager can accomplish these responsibilities in three ways: (1) hire staff to work on the site, (2) assign employees of the management firm to work at the site, or (3) contract with others to provide the necessary workforce. The manager of the property may serve as a bridge between the site personnel (maintenance, on-site leasing, and site administration) and the employees of the management firm (accounting, marketing and leasing, and clerical workers). He or she may be the supervisor of all of these individuals and report to a senior or executive property manager in the management firm.

In order to hire, develop, and retain qualified staff, principals of real estate management firms should consider the reasons they are managing a client's property or portfolio. The relationship between the goals of the property owner and those of the real estate manager is the foundation of the relationship between the manager and the staff. The employees must understand the owner's and the manager's goals and work toward fulfilling them by cooperatively applying their abilities. They must believe that meeting these goals is a worthy endeavor and that they are treated fairly. In fact, the employees must recognize the relationship between the manager and the owner, understand how the goals of these two entities relate to each other, and appreciate how individual efforts contribute to the success of the enterprise and increase the value of the property. The owner, the manager, the staff, the residents or commercial tenants, and the property itself should all benefit from the relationship.

STAFF REQUIREMENTS

On-site staff are usually hired to work at a single property. Employees of a management firm may provide services to more than one property; their services to a particular property are part of the contractual arrangement with the property's owner. Outside contractors may perform all types of work, but they most often do work that requires specialized skills or equipment or specific licensing. The execution of the tasks necessary to manage a property requires cooperation among on-site staff, management firm employees, and contractors. The real estate manager must assign each specific task to one of these groups.

On-Site Staff

The type of property, its size and layout, and the number of residents or commercial tenants determine how much work is done on-site and how large a staff is needed. Managers of residential properties may have to

The Employer of On-Site Staff

On-site staff members may technically be employees of the property owner rather than of the property manager. (That is often the arrangement when an individual real estate manager contracts directly with an owner to manage a single property.) However, the real estate manager or other employees of the management firm may actually hire, train, supervise, and terminate the on-site staff in addition to processing their payroll. This sometimes raises a question as to who is the true employer of on-site staff—the property owner or the management firm. Even though a management agreement may stipulate that the owner is the employer of the on-site staff, the U.S. Department of Labor may take the position that they are employees of the management firm because of the circumstances of their employment. Regardless of who employs the on-site staff, their wages are paid out of the operating funds of the property.

On-site staff members normally work only at one site. However, if a property owner or a management company has several buildings that are near each other, staff members may be assigned to all of their buildings and not just one of them. In such situations, the labor cost of work performed may be charged to the respective properties on an hourly basis, or a worker's total compensation (per month or per year, including both wages and benefits) may be allocated on a percentage basis to each property to account for all hours worked.

Whether the owner or the management company is the employer of on-site staff is an important question that relates to the assignment of risk, hold-harmless provisions in contracts, etc. The issue should be negotiated beforehand and should be documented in the management agreement.

respond to residents around the clock. Office building managers provide services to tenants and their employees during business hours while cleaning and other custodial tasks are typically done after hours, usually in the early evening. Large shopping centers require staffing not only while stores are open for business but also during off-hours (security, custodial maintenance).

While all properties require on-site work, many are too small to justify a regular part-time or full-time staff member. The real estate manager must weigh the cost of hiring a staff member against the cost of leaving the work undone or having a contractor do it. Leaving the work undone is usually the most expensive alternative because the property's competitive strength and value will diminish as a result. In actuality, the manager must determine how to have the work completed for the least cost.

If a property requires sufficient maintenance and repair work to occupy one or more people full time, hiring skilled staff is usually the most economical approach. However, an individual with a single skill (e.g., carpentry, plumbing) usually is not hired on a full-time basis. Large properties that include complex operating systems are more likely to employ skilled personnel to maintain these systems. Having one or more contracts for skilled labor as needed is generally a better choice for a small property that requires only occasional repairs amounting to less than a day's work every week or so. A contract laborer usually earns a higher hourly wage than a full-time employee; however, a *contract for labor as needed* means that money paid is for specific work done and actual hours worked and payroll taxes and forms are not necessary.

The most common on-site work is maintenance, but many other duties at a property may require part-time or full-time staff. If the property has its own office, it may warrant an office manager or full-time clerical worker. Front desks in large properties must employ staff during times the building is open—if not around the clock. Large luxury apartment buildings may have door attendants and concierges. High-rise office buildings may have lobby attendants, day porters, and security guards. Major shopping centers and enclosed malls may offer services to customers (information, stroller rentals) in addition to providing personnel to clean the common areas and security for the commercial tenants, their employees, and their customers. Having a large staff may also necessitate employing supervisory personnel (director of operations, services manager), all of whom report to the manager of the property. (Chapters 7, 9, and 10 discuss other on-site duties.)

Employees of the Management Firm

The size of a management firm and the range of services it offers depend on the extent of its portfolio. Management firms often begin as two-person enterprises: A real estate manager starts an independent management business with one or a few clients and most likely hires a second person to do clerical work. This employee may only work part time; the work may not be sufficient to warrant full-time employment at first. The clerical employee of a new management firm may be responsible for several office activities, such as processing correspondence, answering the telephone, accounting and record keeping, balancing bank accounts, and making bank deposits. As the firm secures more management contracts, additional employees may be hired—a full-time administrative assistant and then, perhaps, a property accountant. As the size of the firm's portfolio increases, greater specialization of staff members' roles becomes necessary. Specialization reduces the number of daily interruptions of one specific assignment by an unrelated task that has the same or greater priority. However, one individual must often perform numerous unrelated tasks, especially in small firms with limited economic means.

A real estate manager in charge of a management firm must continually ask two questions regarding the size of the management firm's staff: (1) Is it the right size to give every client timely and accurate service? (2) Is it adequate to perform its own administrative tasks? When a firm's portfolio

Factors That Determine Management Firm Staffing

- Number of properties managed
- Types of properties managed
- Size and tenancy of managed properties
- Number of clients (property owners) served
- Level of service required
- Location of managed properties
- Size of on-site staff at managed properties
- Size and experience of property manager's support staff

is rather small, one or two employees in addition to the real estate manager may be able to provide tenant services, client services, and routine office administration. However, if the management firm is to expand, or if clients require additional services at some point, the manager must compare the cost of additional staff with both the service requirements of the firm's clients and the needs of the management firm. The number of staff members and their level of specialization within the management firm depend on eight factors.

1. *Number of properties the firm manages.* A fledgling management firm usually has very few accounts, so the expense of a management support staff may be neither justified nor feasible. The founding real estate manager initially does most of the work. With more accounts, however, the real estate manager may need to hire additional managers to handle the day-to-day management of individual properties. These managers can be assigned by property type, by owner, by geographic proximity, or by number of residential units or square feet of commercial space. This level of specialization allows the founding manager more time to seek new clients. The central office may employ an administrative staff to relieve the managers of some of their administrative functions.

2. *Types of properties in the portfolio.* Some management firms specialize in office, retail, or residential property, although many manage any type of property with equal ability. A firm with a large number of diverse property types in its portfolio may have divisions for each property type; in which case, each division is likely to have its own leasing and marketing personnel.

3. *Size and tenancy of managed property.* Dealing with tenants in each phase of the cycle of tenancy (see chapter 8) requires significant work, so actual and potential numbers of tenants affect the size of

the firm's administrative and support staff. The potential number of tenants is based on the number of existing units in each property that is managed or the capacity for its square footage to be subdivided into leasable spaces. The total number of units or square footage involved and the frequency of turnover influence the size of the marketing and leasing staff. The number of tenants affects accounting requirements, and that is reflected in the size of the accounting department staff. A property of substantial size may require the assignment of full-time firm employees to that property alone, even though they may perform their duties at the management firm office and not on-site.

4. *Number of clients the firm has.* Just as the potential and actual tenant population influences the size of the firm's staff, the number of owners served influences the management firm's reporting, accounting, and administrative workload. A firm usually keeps a separate accounting file (subdivided for specific properties) for each client.

5. *Level of service required.* Clients may have unique needs for which the management firm must allot time. Some property owners—institutional owners in particular—may request or require that their reports conform to their standard formats, and the management firm may have to send multiple reports to various investors or partners.

6. *Proximity of the managed properties to each other.* A management firm that specializes in super regional shopping centers is more likely to have a multistate or nationwide clientele than one that exclusively manages residential property. Each property may require a site manager and support staff if the properties are located in different counties or states. However, with advances in telecommunications, many functions may be completed efficiently and quickly at the management firm's headquarters. In an urban area where several properties are close to each other, a single manager may be able to manage several properties because of reduced travel time.

7. *Size of on-site staff.* The size of the on-site staff may influence the amount of involvement a manager has with the property. When a large staff works on-site, the manager may have to devote more time to that property alone, thus limiting his or her availability to manage other properties.

8. *Size and experience of property manger's support staff.* Whether a property manager has administrative assistants and property accountants to perform some of the management duties will determine the number of properties he or she can manage.

The staff requirements of a management firm can grow for many reasons, particularly in areas of responsibility not directly related to managing properties. So much mail may flow through a large firm that a mailroom supervisor is necessary. Data entry and retrieval may demand a management information systems (MIS) specialist. While these personnel are not directly involved with real estate management, their presence means the real estate manager can do his or her job without distraction. The potential for the business of a management firm to expand is great, and the number of people it employs will grow accordingly. In contrast, the potential for an on-site staff to expand is small—the number of people employed directly at a property rarely increases because changes made to a property are usually not significant enough to alter the size or organization of the staff. (Addition of leasable space or changing from gross leases to net leases would be the exceptions.) Actually, on-site staff may decrease as technology lessens the need for specific skills or eliminates jobs altogether—e.g., elevator operators were once essential but are now rare.

Contractors

Because hiring employees is expensive, contracting labor for temporary or intermittent tasks can be economical. The management firm usually hires contractors (the owner may occasionally hire them), depending on whether the work is limited to one property or is needed by the firm's central office. Managers may hire contract workers to work on-site at the property or at the management office, or they may outsource the work.

On-site Contract Workers. Contract workers at a site perform a variety of tasks. They often do maintenance tasks that require special equipment or training (elevator maintenance, roof repair) or licensing (pest control). Managers often contract seasonal services (lawn care, snow removal, decorating, exterior painting, window washing) and even daily maintenance (janitorial). If the property needs security on-site, contracting for this service can reduce the property owner's liability (shift it to a third-party contractor) in the event of a crime or other incident. (Chapter 7 outlines maintenance contracting procedures.)

The management office may employ part-time or temporary workers, especially for administrative work such as filing or accounting. Temporary employees can be contracted for a day, a week, or longer for specific assignments. Companies that specialize in providing skilled labor for maintenance, clerical, or administrative duties are common in large cities.

On-site or in a small firm, the property manager, a full-time leasing employee of the owner, or a leasing company is in charge of leasing. However, very large properties or those with high vacancy rates or frequent turnovers

may benefit from a full-time leasing agent. Initial lease-up of a new or renovated property also demands full-time attention. Leasing is one real estate
management task that real estate managers can often successfully contract.
A leasing agent provides specialized expertise. For each successfully negotiated lease, a leasing agent on contract usually receives a commission based
on a dollar per square foot of space leased or a percentage of the rental
income over the term of the lease.

Outsourcing.   Another approach to contracting is to *outsource* an entire
function. For example, a small management firm that does not have a staff
member to recruit and process job applicants may contract an outside service on an as-needed basis to perform these tasks. Management company
personnel still interview and hire the individual, but the contractor pre-
screens applicants' résumés, narrows the field of prospects to interview, and
handles all the paperwork, including the reference checks.

Other firms will take over management of all personnel operations,
from the hiring process through preparation of payroll and administration
of benefits, which the contracted firm provides. For a small company, the
outside source can relieve an administrative burden and may expand the
benefits the firm can offer its employees (e.g., medical insurance coverage)
when the total number of employees is too small to form a group acceptable to an insurance carrier.

Management firms may also outsource accounting. This can be very
helpful if the small firm does not have sophisticated accounting software
programs that create reports automatically once data are entered into the
program's forms or formats.

Leasing is another function that a firm may outsource effectively. Contracting with leasing professionals can ensure timely completion of this
activity. If the management firm does not have skilled leasing personnel,
outsourcing can ensure that all contacts with prospective tenants meet the
firm's requirements—and comply with fair housing laws for residential
marketing and leasing. Sometimes a management firm benefits from outsourcing activities such as marketing, advertising, and public relations, including the preparation of newsletters to tenants, rather than performing
them in-house.

Determining Adequate Staff Size

Providing an adequate staff for a property or a management firm—or
both—requires careful planning and close examination of resources. The
first step in this process is to list the essential tasks and estimate the time
each requires on a weekly or monthly basis. The initial assessment may be
very detailed, accounting for everything from the time necessary to mow
the lawn to the time required to collect rent. The final compilation might

resemble a budget, except that hours of work per week or per month are the primary quantitative measures rather than dollars and cents. Analysis of the resulting list should indicate how many workers are necessary for efficient operation and adequate service to the tenants and the property owner.

The size and type of the property as well as particular tenant requirements understandably influence the preparation of this list. Once all functions are noted and the average amount of time for each is calculated, the various duties can be grouped together by category. These groupings may be the basis for job descriptions or for setting up departments (e.g., maintenance, administration). The manager can also use the groupings to decide how many full-time and part-time workers the property needs, as well as which tasks outside contractors may complete most economically. To be accurate, any estimate of the number of workers required must also allow for days off (sick time, vacations). Such time budgets may be prepared for each property as well as for the management firm. When duties are duplicated, the real estate manager should evaluate further to decide whether the duplication is necessary or if consolidation is possible.

HIRING QUALIFIED PERSONNEL

One of the largest ongoing investments of property owners and real estate managers is in the staff they employ. To build a capable, dedicated staff, managers must pay careful attention to the recruitment and selection processes. Beyond that, they must invest many hours and dollars in continual training and development of the staff.

Recruiting Applicants

A real estate management firm can find qualified candidates for specific positions in several ways, including promotion of current employees, help-wanted advertisements in newspapers or on the Internet, employment agencies, and personal referrals.

Internal Promotion. Promotion is an effective way to retain and increase the value of excellent employees. Some believe that promotion from within doubles the cost of training because the person who is promoted and the successor to that person's former position must be trained simultaneously. The initial training expense may be slightly higher, but promotion can be highly rewarding and is often more efficient. It is also excellent for morale. The promoted employee is already familiar with the company and may even understand the new position quite well. If time allows, the person promoted may be able to train his or her successor, thus reducing the demands on the trainee's supervisor. In addition, the newcomer enters a

---

Contents of a Job Description

- Position title
- Position that supervises the work
- Duties and responsibilities of the position; level of authority
- Requisite skills and education
- Other qualification requirements (specialized training, licensure or certification, years of experience or level of expertise)

The job description should also include a statement referring to "other duties as may be assigned by the supervisor" or the like so the real estate manager can allocate tasks to staff members on an as-needed basis. (NOTE: Collective bargaining agreements are very specific; job descriptions for positions held by union workers cannot include such a reference to other duties.)

Job descriptions should *not* include any reference to race, religion, national origin, gender, age, disability, or any other characteristics that could be interpreted as discriminatory. Title VII of the Civil Rights Act prohibits discrimination in employment practices (Equal Employment Opportunity— EEO), and the Americans with Disabilities Act (ADA) limits job descriptions and hiring decisions to a position's essential functions.

---

lower-level position, a situation that provides room for his or her individual growth within the company rather than fostering a need to seek opportunities outside of it.

Help-Wanted Advertisements.   Help-wanted advertisements in newspapers, in trade magazines, and on the Internet generate quick responses. Such advertisements can yield hundreds of candidates, but many of them will be overqualified or underqualified for the position. Filtering out the most-qualified candidates is often burdensome. To facilitate the screening process, the help-wanted advertisement should describe the duties of the job and the required qualifications and instruct respondents to submit a résumé, work history, or other pertinent information that matches them to the position's requirements. Newspapers commonly offer the opportunity to use a box number rather than the employer's address and phone number. Such box numbers preclude receiving a deluge of phone calls and letters from hopeful candidates, which require staff time and other expenses for direct responses and follow-up by the employers.

Employment Agencies.   Employment agencies can also be useful for finding qualified candidates for a position. The real estate manager must give the agency a detailed *job description* and a list of minimum job specifications so it can screen candidates for the skills or experience necessary for the available position. The agency spares the employer the time required for

---

Contents of an Employment Application Form

- Applicant's name, address, and telephone number
- Applicant's Social Security number and citizenship status
- Educational background, specific skills, and relevant training
- Current and previous jobs and their respective responsibilities
- Current and previous employers' names, addresses, and telephone numbers
- Duration of employment, rate of pay, and supervisor's name for each job
- Reasons for changing jobs
- Professional and personal references
- Authorization to contact former employers to verify employment information, to contact personal (character) references, and to run credit and criminal background checks (including agreement to submit to drug testing).

Information that could be interpreted as discriminatory, such as the applicant's age (birth date), marital or family status, physical or mental disability, or religious affiliation, should not be requested on an employment application (or in a job interview).

---

such screening; the employer interviews only the most qualified candidates. Such time and work savings can be substantial, especially if the employer's staff does not include a personnel recruiter or if the position to be filled requires specialized skills. A consideration, however, is the agency's fee, which is often a percentage of the annual salary for the position filled.

Personal Referrals.   Personal referrals from current employees of the company or from acquaintances of the real estate manager can be very valuable. Such prospects usually know something about the company, and they are most likely capable individuals or they would not have been referred. Another source for referrals is through professional activities. Membership in professional organizations can provide many contacts that allow managers and other real estate professionals to keep up-to-date on local business activities, including who is working for what companies and how well those people are doing. Established professional relationships can help a real estate manager locate the right person for a position and quickly check his or her credentials.

Unsolicited Applications.   In addition to a company's active recruiting, the property or the management firm may occasionally receive unsolicited résumés and applications. The manager should examine these applications when they arrive even if no positions are available. Information sent in this manner is often evidence of an applicant who has sound qualifications and

a sincere interest in working for the property or the firm. If such an applicant appears to have the proper credentials, the manager should keep his
or her résumé or application on file.

All who inquire about possible employment should receive a letter in
response, regardless of whether the manger will retain their inquiry. The
reputation of a company is one of its greatest assets, and even a letter of
rejection can favorably impress its recipient. Such goodwill is especially
important in real estate management. At some point, the rejected candidate
may be in a position to affect something the management company wants
(e.g., a lease), or the company and the applicant may consider each other
for a career opportunity again in the future.

Selecting Employees

Regardless of how a prospective employee is recruited, all candidates
should complete an *employment application form*. Such a form organizes
and standardizes the information needed to make the hiring decision. A
personal interview is generally necessary before the manager can make a
final decision on employment. In addition to finding out if the candidate is
capable, interviews help managers ascertain if the applicant is compatible
with the requirements of the job and willing to work toward the goals of the
property owner or the management firm. Individual applicants should be
evaluated based on the requirements for the particular position.

Before making a formal offer, the real estate manager should verify
the employment application information. To acquire all the information
needed, the manager should have applicants sign a separate waiver (to
be copied and sent to former employers) that releases previous employers from liability for information given in references. The manager should
request a copy of the applicant's driving license and obtain a copy of his or
her driving record. The driving record may include information about reck-
less behavior or substance abuse that might not otherwise be available. The
manager should verify that educational institutions or professional organizations referenced in the application in fact granted the applicant's academic
degrees or certifications.

The real estate manager should obtain fiduciary bonds on all employees who will handle money. Bonding companies typically require credit
checks and police reports on applicants for bonds. Because of the potential
liability in the event of a crime against a tenant's property (theft) or person
(assault), the manager would be prudent to run credit and criminal background checks on all prospective employees—regardless of whether they
will handle money. The applicant's written authorization is required to secure credit and criminal activity information.

Drug testing with negative findings is often a requirement of employment and is another way to reduce potential liability for the owner and
manager. Employers should use a written agreement regarding their drug

---

Employment Contracts

The property owner and the management firm or an independent real estate manager typically contract real estate management services under a
specific management agreement. In situations in which a property has a
large staff, an employment contract for certain types of supervisory and
management staff positions may be appropriate, especially if the position
will require the individual to work with company- and/or client-confidential
information. Employees do move on to other positions as better opportunities arise, and they are likely to be in positions where they may compete
with the former employer. Employers are well advised to have such employees sign an employment agreement that includes a noncompete clause
that is fair and equitable to both parties as well as confidentiality provisions.
In particular, this might apply to real estate managers who are employees
of a management company.

---

testing policy. Prospective employees should only be required to take a
drug test after receiving a conditional offer of employment. However, the
real estate manager should seek the advice of legal counsel before imple
menting such practices.

Verifying information provided on job applications can be a time-
consuming activity, and the information gathered may be incomplete or
inaccurate. Privacy laws require employers to safeguard personal information that applicants supply. Using an employee-screening service, which
will have more resources available to it, has the advantage of distancing the
employer from liability related to the screening process. (NOTE: Tenant-
screening services may also screen job applicants.)

The formal offer of employment should always be in writing, even after
an offer is made and accepted over the telephone or in person. Generally,
within three days of hiring, the new employee and the employer must complete an *Employment Eligibility Verification form (Form I-9),* which verifies
the employee's identity and right to work in the United States. Employees
can present a number of documents to verify their identity and right to
work. Employers should retain I-9 forms in the employee's personnel file
for at least three years.

Applicants who are not offered the job should promptly receive rejection letters as a matter of business goodwill, but not until after the selected
candidate is employed and performing the job.

Although some reasons for selecting one candidate over another are
subjective, the promise of capability combined with demonstrated reliability are usually the main factors in selecting a new employee. Gender, race,
age, religion, national origin, or physical ability (and in some locales, sexual
orientation and other protected classes) should not enter the decision. Nor
should such factors ever influence the compensation offered to an applicant, the compensation of a current employee, or any other decision that

---

Contents of an Employee Manual

- Company description and history
- Company policies and procedures
- Employment rules
- Employee benefits
- Department and company organization

Employers should require employees to sign a statement acknowledging receipt of the manual; they should also require the employee to return the manual when leaving the company.

---

affects an applicant or employee. Title VII of the *Civil Rights Act,* which is enforced by the United States *Equal Employment Opportunity Commission (EEOC),* prohibits discrimination against employees and applicants for employment. Various state and local laws may also prohibit discrimination in employment, and their requirements may be more stringent.

The importance of nondiscrimination in the workplace goes beyond legal compliance. The population of the United States is extremely varied. People of all races and creeds own and rent property. To provide owners and renters with superior service, the staff of the property and the management firm should reflect the diversity of the community. The owner and the management firm should provide diversity training to the property staff. The ability to work with, and for, people whose backgrounds are varied is an asset of incalculable worth.

ORIENTATION OF NEW PERSONNEL

All new employees should receive training and orientation regardless of their competence or familiarity with their new duties. Every company has a unique culture and particular procedures. New employees must be properly introduced to the work environment to make them fully productive as quickly as possible. Each employee should have a copy of his or her job description, and all employees may benefit from knowing the functions of the various departments. An *employee manual* that states company policies can reinforce an orientation program. An employee manual should include the following:

- The general rules of employment—hours of work, paydays, holidays, sick leave, vacations, etc.

- The company's policies affecting internal and external activities—public relations, ethics, employee attitudes, promotion from within, discrimination, sexual harassment, etc.

- Information about the company—a brief history, a statement of objectives, and an organizational chart.

Once employees are established in the job, the manager should schedule regular *performance reviews* and he or she should conduct them as promised. These sessions should be structured to help employees increase their value to the firm.

Businesses commonly review employees' performance at least once a year. In addition, new employees may receive employment reviews after the first three months. This review early in the period of employment can be an opportunity for both employer and employee to reaffirm their employment decisions—or to agree that the decision was not right and go their separate ways. Employees adapt to their new work surroundings and obligations at their own pace. Depending on the job and the individual, some employees require as much as a year on the job before their productivity reaches the level the employer expects. Conversely, the employer may realize early that an employee is incapable of doing the job assigned. A comprehensive review of the employee's performance may indicate that his or her talents lie elsewhere. Review of the job description may reveal that the work is too much for one person to do. Additional training or a transfer may be a way to retain an employee who shows promise but is not qualified for the job he or she was hired to do.

RETAINING VALUABLE EMPLOYEES

A talented and dedicated staff is an employer's most valuable resource. Developing qualified staff requires great effort, and continually rebuilding a staff because of turnover is extremely expensive. An employer can minimize personnel costs and increase the value of individual employees by retaining responsible, dedicated people. Appropriate compensation, open communication with employees, and consistent encouragement of individuals to grow in their jobs facilitate employee retention.

Compensation

Pay and benefits are the tangible rewards of dedicated service. Compensation must meet market levels to keep employees satisfied. It must also offer employees security and incentives to strive for greater rewards.

Wages. The federal *Fair Labor Standards Act (FLSA),* which the government revises from time to time, regulates the minimum wage per hour and the maximum number of hours employees can work per day and per week in positions that are paid an hourly wage. If the maximum number of hours per day or cumulative hours per week exceeds those prescribed, the employer is required to pay overtime—standard wage plus 50 percent. In addition, employers are required to pay employees for *all* hours worked in a workweek, including time worked in the workplace, time spent traveling as part of the job, training, and work performed at home at the employer's request or with the employer's permission. While employers must follow the minimum wage law, market demands generally require a higher wage rate to recruit qualified employees. Other incentives such as double-time pay for working on holidays may also be necessary.

To be *exempt* from the Wage and Hour Regulations of the FLSA, a position must meet several specific tests. Among them are supervision of others and performance of office work directly related to business operations. Determining whether an employee is exempt from overtime requirements under the FLSA has long been problematic because the rules were confusing. Under new rules put into effect in August 2004, the U.S. Department of Labor (DOL) issued specific guidelines for determining exempt status, including salary level: In addition to hourly workers, white-collar employees whose annual salary is less than a certain dollar amount ($23,660 in 2005) must be paid overtime when they work more than 40 hours in a workweek. (Previously, the hours per day or per week maximum did not affect exempt employees.) The new rules also spell out the duties that define the roles of exempt employees.

Employers should schedule salary adjustments regularly, budget them routinely, and administer them fairly. Reliable, dedicated employees will continue to provide quality service if their good performance is noted and compensated. One incentive to excellent performance—and cost-consciousness—is to link a portion of the employees' compensation directly to the employer's annual profit.

Benefits.   Life insurance, employee and dependent health insurance, dental insurance, disability insurance, retirement plans, car allowances or company cars, stock options, savings programs, and paid vacations and holidays are common benefits. Many of these benefits are based on seniority or level of responsibility, and their distribution is often complicated by the effort to avoid or defer tax payments on them. If the employer's goal is to retain employees, these benefit plans must be carefully explained so the employees can comprehend their value.

Federal Programs.   The United States government requires employers to participate in federal programs that provide for workers if they are terminated, retire, or become disabled.

FUTA.   The *Federal Unemployment Tax Act (FUTA)* and various state unemployment programs are intended to ensure compensation if an employee is laid off or terminated. The employer alone makes the contributions, and the amount or rate is based on the number of employees and the number of claims made. Usually minimum and maximum amounts are paid—on a per-employee basis and related to the employer's history of layoffs. The federal government collects the FUTA taxes, but the state usually administers the unemployment compensation.

Worker's Compensation.   Employers must also provide *workers' compensation insurance* to compensate employees in the event of a work-related illness or injury. Employers purchase the insurance through the state or from a private insurance company. Privately purchased workers' compensation insurance is commonly associated with a short-term disability plan.

Social Security/Medicare.   In addition to these employer-paid programs, workers collect Social Security and they may collect Medicare benefits when they retire. Funds for these benefits are collected and administered under the *Federal Insurance Contributions Act (FICA),* and the employer and employee contribute funds equally based on the employee's income.

Communications

Employees are genuinely interested in the company they work for, and they want to know about the successes, failures, and general activities of the business. Clear communication with employees is a valuable retention tool. Many employees' only source of information about their company is their coworkers. Their reliance on this news source creates the potential for damaging rumors to spread. To avoid such rumors and their consequences, employers should disseminate information that affects the business in a timely manner and explain it fully. News of particular significance (i.e., items that the press may publicize favorably or unfavorably) should be released to all employees at the same time to avert speculation.

Many companies use a newsletter to communicate with their staff. Employees welcome recognition of service anniversaries, promotions, and personal news items about their fellow workers along with news about the company's activities. Management most often publishes and controls the newsletter. However, it should be directed to all employees, and the writing style should be friendly and personal. Its copy and design should reflect the company's image and standards. Employees who work for a company that emphasizes superior quality expect a publication that has an appealing design and is free of typographical and grammatical errors.

Central to the communication program of any company is the policy manual or manuals. This material gives all employees a reference to consult for information on company benefits, work hours, and minimum performance standards for particular procedures. Individual departments may institute policy or procedure manuals for the tasks they perform, but all employees should receive some definitive source of information regarding their relationship with the company as a whole (e.g., an employee handbook).

Another form of written communication from an employer to an employee is a *job description*. This document outlines the responsibilities and duties of an individual's job. It may also indicate the direct supervisor and any subordinates.

Grievances are a natural part of life and work. Misunderstandings that arise can result in the loss or dissatisfaction of reliable employees if the employer does not address their concerns promptly and sincerely. An open-door policy for airing work-related problems that prohibits recriminations against those who use it can preserve an excellent working relationship. An open-door policy allows employers to examine their working relationship with their employees. If employees belong to a union, the contract usually outlines specific grievance procedures. Maintaining good relations with the union can make the process more workable.

Managers should expect all workers to use their skills and talents to the maximum in their work. They should treat all coworkers with respect regardless of the tasks they perform or whether their position is that of a supervisor or a subordinate.

Promoting Morale

Effective communications are only part of an overall program to maintain employee morale. Recreational activities among coworkers should also be encouraged. Employees who are dedicated to their jobs yet balance their hard work with recreational activities—and can differentiate between the appropriate times for each—usually have a positive attitude about their careers. Company-sponsored baseball teams, golf outings, and bowling leagues are common pastimes among coworkers. The cost of such sponsorship may be very little—a set of matching T-shirts is a nominal investment in employee enthusiasm.

Managers should expect excellent performance of every employee, and they should compensate their employees for such performance. However, occasional thanks for a job well done are also important to an employee. Dedicated employees want to know that their employer appreciates their work and that it contributes to the organization's success. An expression of gratitude, whether oral or written, can add greatly to good morale.

Continual Training

In the normal pace of business and family life, time is rarely available for additional training or education. As a result, formal education for many employees ends with high school, trade school, or college. As an incentive to continue learning, many employers institute education reimbursement programs for their employees. The rules and incentives for these programs vary greatly, but the benefits to the employer can be substantial.

In addition to formal course work, many associations and corporations sponsor seminars and courses in aspects of real estate management as well as other disciplines such as accounting, maintenance, and human relations. Seminars that teach management and interpersonal skills foster both personal and professional development. Before sending employees to any workshops or seminars, the employer should investigate the cost and quality of such programs. If the seminar is to take place in a distant city, a phone call to the sponsor may find a closer location or another date that can save considerable expense and time away from work. Sometimes employers can bring such programs into the workplace for the benefit of all employees. The size of a company and the resources available to it determine the extent to which it can offer such educational programs.

Developing Talents

While a job description is a valuable reference for both employer and employee, it can hinder the employee's progress if interpreted too narrowly. The job description should define the basic functions of a position but should not set limits on what the person in it can do. Employees commonly desire definite boundaries to their duties. However, boundaries can limit more than the number of hours that an employee must work; they also permit employees to concentrate only on the minimum the employer expects them to do. While boundaries help create a sense of security, they can also be stifling—people begin to think they are in a rut at work. In establishing boundaries, balance is important. If workers resist change too much, their department can stagnate and hinder a thriving business. If they pursue every new opportunity and ignore fundamental procedures, the department or company can founder from lack of direction.

Most job descriptions gradually change in the course of an evolving business, so workers must increase their knowledge to be able to keep up the pace. Communication and training enable workers to grow with the demands placed on the business; so does encouragement. If an employer encourages employees to undertake new tasks, and if they are legitimately capable of mastering the work, they will be productive workers. In such cases, the employer may not have to hire additional staff in order to expand its operations. The employees also gain if they develop more self-confidence and can base their sense of security on their own growing abilities rather than the minimum their jobs require of them.

EMPLOYEE DISCIPLINE

In spite of the efforts an employer may make to retain valuable employees and to develop their talents, situations unfortunately may occur in which employee discipline becomes necessary. When an employee disobeys a firm's policies, the employer has two choices: discipline or dismissal. These alternatives are substantially different. *Discipline* implies reform; *dismissal* precludes the possibility of reform. Which action to take depends on the infraction involved. The desired result is the same regardless—the employer hopes to remedy or undo any damage from the employee's actions and prevent any recurrence.

Employment Policies

The *employee manual* (discussed earlier in this chapter) should state company policies regarding employee behavior, discipline, and termination. In small companies that do not have an employee manual, the orientation program should cover those issues. Employees should sign a statement that they have received and understood the company's policies. The signed statement should be kept in the employee's file.

Most work rules are absolutes. They should be easy to enforce because of that. Employees should not lie; they should not steal—either time or supplies. They should not be hostile toward others. They should respect the instructions they receive from their supervisors. In addition, they should not abuse drugs or alcohol in the workplace (or come to work unfit to perform their duties because of such abuse), commit acts of violence, or interact with their coworkers (or tenants of the property) in a manner that could be interpreted as sexual harassment or otherwise abusive.

Progressive Discipline

Some of the most vexing disciplinary problems are a result of minor disobedience. The circumstances that require discipline can provoke anger, but employers must restrain their anger. It is important to preserve impartiality and respect for the employee.

When a supervisor learns about or witnesses an infraction, he or she should write down what is known about the incident and interview the employee regarding the matter. Any required disciplinary action should take place as soon as possible after the offense, and the matter should be discussed in privacy and in confidence. Accusing an employee of wrongdoing in the presence of coworkers neither rectifies the problem nor serves to rehabilitate the offending employee. Moreover, other employees who witness the exchange between supervisor and subordinate may lose their respect for the employer.

Although the employer should establish a thorough and impartial system of discipline, writing a comprehensive set of disciplinary measures to cover every possible circumstance is impossible. Regardless, the employer must deal with all employees individually and fairly, based on the nature of the incident. To ensure fair treatment, all similar incidents should be handled similarly—i.e., disciplinary measures should be applied consistently.

The employer should establish a system of *progressive discipline* to provide ample opportunity for the employee to change or correct his or her behavior. Such a system usually involves verbal warnings, written warnings, probation, and termination. The first three steps are discussed below. Since termination can be complex, it is discussed in the next section. The employer should carefully document any disciplinary action against an employee—even a verbal action.

Verbal Warnings.   The number of notices (warnings) given to an employee regarding a particular problem depends on the type of infraction. One or more conversations calling attention to the company policy and asking for the employee's commitment to eliminating the problem may be all that is necessary if an employee is repeatedly late for work or regularly extends his or her lunch period beyond the allowed time.

Written Warnings.   A written memorandum copied to the employee's personnel file would be the next step. Some undesirable behavior may require a written notice from the beginning. This is particularly appropriate if an employee is not following company procedure properly, and that is causing problems for others on the staff.

For more serious infractions, a disciplinary meeting should be attended by a third party—preferably a member of management. This person can attest to the conversation held, agreements reached, and the accuracy of any memorandum placed in the employee's file.

Probation.   Sometimes a period of *probation* is necessary. Probation gives the employee a fixed amount of time to overcome his or her work-related problem. It allows an employer to monitor and report on the employee's improvement. During probation, the supervisor should remind the employee that being on probation might affect his or her next performance review. If the employee corrects the problem before the next performance review, canceling the probation officially (in writing) may be appropriate. The supervisor should inform the employee that if the problem is not corrected, his or her employment will be terminated. Regardless of how the disciplinary action is set up, pay and benefits should remain intact during a period of probation.

EMPLOYEE TERMINATION

The typical American employee no longer makes one place of business his or her lifelong workplace. Seven to ten company changes and four or

---

Some Federal Laws That Affect Employment

Immigration Reform and Control Act (IRCA) requires the employer to verify an employee's identity and eligibility to work in the United States. Employees must complete Immigration and Nationalization Service (INS) form I-9.

Civil Rights Act (Title VII) prohibits discrimination in employment—hiring, compensation, promotion, termination.

Americans with Disabilities Act (ADA) prohibits discrimination in employment based on physical or mental disability. Employers must make *reasonable accommodations* for qualified applicants or employees who have a disability by improving access, restructuring jobs, adjusting work schedules, and the like.

Age Discrimination in Employment Act (ADEA) prohibits discrimination against older workers.

Fair Labor Standards Act (FLSA), also called Federal Wage and Hour Law, regulates hourly workers' wage rates and the number of hours worked and requires overtime compensation for time worked in excess of 40 hours per week. Employers must pay workers for all hours worked, including work performed at home and travel as part of the job. New rules issued in 2004 require employers to pay some formerly exempt employees overtime based on a minimum salary requirement and definitions of specific duties of exempt positions.

Federal Insurance Contributions Act (FICA) requires employer and employee to contribute equally to the Social Security fund and Medicare.

Federal Unemployment Tax Act (FUTA) requires employers to contribute funds to compensate employees who are laid off or terminated.

Family and Medical Leave Act (FMLA) requires employers to grant eligible employees up to 12 weeks of unpaid job-protected leave in the event of a serious health condition or to care for a family member. This is more likely to affect a management firm than a single property. To be required to participate, the firm must have at least 50 employees within 75 miles.

---

five career paths are common. Turnover is a way of life because of resignations, corporate takeovers, layoffs, and changing client needs. When change occurs, employees should never feel they are just another commodity. Whether an employee retires or resigns or whether the employer must lay off or terminate the employee, such a departure is always stressful. Nevertheless, dealing with such matters is a natural part of managerial responsibilities.

Facing a Layoff

When income decreases or expenses increase, or if tenants or clients are lost, a layoff may be the only way to counter the financial shortfall. Whether

> **Some Federal Laws That Affect Employment (*concluded*)**
>
> **Occupational Safety and Health Act (OSHA)** regulates safety conditions in the workplace. It mandates use of protective clothing and devices for certain types of tasks.
>
> **Drug-Free Workplace Act** requires employers who contract with the U.S. government to certify that they maintain a drug-free workplace and have a published statement notifying employees that drug activity is prohibited in their workplace and specifying the actions that will be taken against those who violate the prohibition. Employees must abide by the terms of the employer's drug-free workplace policy as a condition of their employment.
>
> **Employee Polygraph Protection Act (EPPA)** prohibits the use of lie detector tests in most business situations. However, in the event of an economic loss, polygraph tests may be used subject to notification and other restrictions.
>
> **Worker Adjustment and Retraining Notification (WARN) Act** requires employers of large numbers of workers to give affected workers 60 days' notice if a mass layoff or business closure is planned. (The number of workers the company employs determines whether WARN applies.)
>
> **Consolidated Omnibus Budget Reconciliation Act (COBRA)** requires employers to offer employees an opportunity to continue their group health care coverage for a time by paying the premiums themselves when they are terminated or leave their jobs.
>
> **Employee Retirement Income Security Act (ERISA)** safeguards employees' rights to benefits under a company's pension.
>
> State and local laws may expand on the requirements of federal laws. For example, some locales prohibit discrimination in employment based on sexual orientation. Real estate managers must understand the laws that govern employment at all levels, and they must follow the requirements of the most stringent ones.

permanent or temporary, a layoff can be devastating to the employees and their families. The stress on those who remain will increase. They will be concerned about their job security, and because of the staff shortage, they may have to perform additional work without additional pay. The manager also endures strain in this situation. The personal feeling of responsibility and the work to salvage the business exact a high toll.

The employer who must resort to a layoff has very few options for assisting the terminated employees, especially with finances. However, the manager may have some means for providing assistance if strong training and communications programs are in place. Training in financial management can help develop habits of frugality the individual can use on his or her own. Programs that help employees define and expand their job skills can lead to less time without a job in the event of a layoff because the individual has more and better job skills and therefore more to offer potential employers. Business associates of the employer may have positions available, and job-seeker services and résumé consultants may be able to help. The most valuable assistance involves being direct with employees about the condition of the business and giving them as much warning as possible about its future. (Sale of a building or closing of a management company may be subject to the *Worker Adjustment and Retraining Notification [WARN] Act,* which requires 60 days' advance notice of a layoff if it impacts 33 percent of the employer's workforce, provided that at least 50 employees are to be laid off.)

Providing employees with proper notice of an impending layoff and helping them with the unemployment application forms are a few steps that an employer can take if a layoff becomes inevitable. Before notifying any employees, however, the employer must review the personnel list to preclude discrimination against any group because of the layoff. In real estate management, layoffs usually begin in the departments that are not directly involved in providing service to tenants or property owners, and seniority often determines which employees will remain.

Dismissing an Employee

The most extreme action an employer can take against an employee is *termination*. In many states, employment is *at will,* and either the employee or the employer may terminate the relationship at any time for any reason (with or without cause). Exceptions to this are antidiscrimination (protected classes), antiretaliation (whistle-blower) statutes, and specific contractual arrangements, including collective bargaining agreements.

A primary concern for the employer is protection from an unjust termination suit, so termination is usually a last resort. Employers should seek advice of legal counsel before adopting specific employment policies, especially those regarding unacceptable (i.e., dangerous) behaviors and their consequences. Grounds for immediate dismissal, though widespread, often have legal or social ramifications.

In implementing discipline and termination procedures, the employer must be sure to administer its system consistently. Discrimination claims are based on disparate treatment of differently situated individuals. To avoid susceptibility to such claims, the employer must carefully document all disciplinary actions and terminations. Prior to taking any action under its policy, the employer should review its files for any past instances of similar conduct and, where similar conduct has previously been the subject of disciplinary action or termination, the employer should administer its policy to preserve uniformity.

Before terminating an employee, the employer should thoroughly document the event or behavior prompting dismissal. Documentation should concentrate on the work performed (or not performed), not on assumptions regarding its cause (e.g., substance abuse). The meeting during which an employee is to be terminated should also be attended by a third party—a member of management—who can attest in writing to the conversation between the supervisor and employee. Third-party attendance aids in preparing a defense if the employee should later file a lawsuit for discrimination or wrongful termination.

While terminated employees are usually entitled to collect unemployment compensation, unemployment benefits may be denied in certain circumstances. A dismissed employee could sue the employer for denied unemployment compensation or for damages based on discriminatory or other unfair practices by the employer. To avoid such a suit, an employer should establish and fairly apply a policy of progressive discipline and carefully record reasons for dismissal.

EMPLOYER LIABILITY

Real estate managers must understand the potential liability involved in the role of employer. Employers may reject applicants or terminate employees who pose a direct threat to the health or safety of others in the workplace. (In real estate management, the workplace includes not only the managed property but also the property of residential and commercial tenants and the latter's employees as well as the management employee's coworkers.)

Apart from the problems that arise directly from an employee's actions, the potential exists for legal action by others. If a preemployment background check would have revealed a prior conviction for a felony (e.g., assault), the employer of an individual who assaults someone on the job could be sued successfully for *negligent hiring*. If an employee who exhibits dangerous behavior on the job (e.g., showing a weapon, making or carrying out threats of harm) is allowed to repeat the behavior and someone is hurt, a lawsuit could be filed based on *negligent retention*. If training and oversight of an employee is inadequate and an incident results in injury to another person (employee, tenant, visitor), the employer could be sued for *negligent supervision*. Criminal background checks and drug testing are among the tools available to help prevent problems caused by employees.

SUMMARY

In real estate management, relations with employees are central to maintaining good relations with tenants and with the property owner. All staff members, whether supervisors or subordinates, are colleagues and should work toward fulfilling the owner's goal for the property. The size of a management firm's staff depends on specific attributes of the properties managed as well as the attributes of other properties in the firm's portfolio. People who work at a property may be employees of the management firm or sometimes of the property owner. Contractors may be hired for specialized work. All workers must perform their duties harmoniously and cooperatively.

Wise selection of staff members is as crucial to successful real estate management as it is to any other business. The key to hiring superior employees is searching for qualified candidates who possess the appropriate skills and are willing to share the same goals as the manager of the property. Continual training and encouragement to pursue additional education fosters individual productivity. Such programs are good investments when companies can afford to implement them.

Employers can retain employees by treating them fairly, respecting them, and regarding them as colleagues. This includes providing fair compensation and benefits. Honest communication and genuine concern should be at the forefront of employer-employee relationships. The rules in these relationships differ very little from any other human relationship involving mutual respect.

Employees may be lost through their own volition or through a layoff. Discipline is problematic, primarily because the employer must ensure that disciplinary actions are fair. If the employer must discipline or terminate an employee, all infractions of the rules and regulations as well as job performance (or nonperformance) must be carefully documented.

7

Maintenance

Maintenance is the key to superior presentation and optimal function; it preserves—and sometimes improves—the condition and, therefore, the value of the property. Regular cleaning and repairs are necessary to keep tenants comfortable. The objective of maintenance, like that of every other aspect of real estate management, is to meet the goals of the owner. A comprehensive maintenance program can provide the following benefits for the owner.

- *Tenant retention.* If the property is immaculate and the building components are in good working condition, tenants will be comfortable in their surroundings. Tenant satisfaction will result in a lower vacancy rate. The owner will have less expense for turnover of rental space because tenants will be inclined to renew their leases.

- *Reduced operating costs.* Maintenance and repair costs may be a large part of a property's operating expenses, but investment in maintenance and repair may reduce other operating costs such as utilities, rubbish removal, and insurance premiums. Rental income may increase because of increased tenancy in a well-maintained property. The real estate manager who investigates reducing maintenance expenses should also consider the indirect savings and improved income that good maintenance programs can produce.

- *Preservation and enhancement of property value.* If the manager establishes a comprehensive maintenance program, the property's

---

Objectives of Maintenance

- Accomplishment of owner's goals
- Tenant satisfaction
- Higher tenant retention
- Lower operating costs
- Optimal function of the property
- Maximized property value
- Safety of employees and occupants

---

value will be preserved and enhanced during the course of regular operations. Deferred maintenance may cause the greatest loss an owner can suffer on a real estate investment. Even if a fire consumes the property or a natural disaster destroys it, the owner can usually regain the financial investment if the property is properly insured. However, there is no insurance against neglected maintenance; cleaning and repair are major concerns the manager of real property must address daily.

Safety is also an issue. If an injury occurs because of neglected maintenance, the economic repercussions could be severe, even with liability insurance in place. Regular maintenance reduces potential hazards and provides a safe environment for everyone on the property—prospective tenants and other visitors, residents, businesses' employees and customers, and the on-site staff.

Maintenance falls into four categories: custodial, corrective, preventive, or deferred. *Custodial maintenance* is the day-to-day cleaning and upkeep that should be part of every property's ongoing program to retain value—and tenants. *Corrective maintenance* involves the ordinary repairs that a building and its equipment require on a day-to-day basis. *Preventive maintenance* is a program of regular inspection and care to avert problems or at least detect and solve them before major repairs are necessary. *Deferred maintenance* is ordinary maintenance of a building that is *not* performed at the time a problem is detected. If left unchecked, deferred maintenance will eventually diminish the use, occupancy, and value of the property.

Regulatory compliance sometimes demands specific maintenance procedures and related activities. For example, some locales require fire drills that include all tenants and property staff evacuating the building twice a year. Inspections and monitoring of some equipment may be necessary to safeguard the environment from potentially hazardous emissions (more likely for industrial than other types of properties). Maintenance for regulatory compliance is not necessarily separate from the maintenance categories described above; most compliance activities fall into the preventive or the corrective maintenance categories. Establishing and enforcing strict standards for custodial and preventive maintenance can significantly reduce corrective and deferred maintenance.

SCHEDULES, INSPECTIONS, AND MAINTENANCE TASKS

In the effort to minimize monthly operating expenses, some real estate managers unwisely have cleaning and maintenance work done only when absolutely necessary or in an emergency. On any property, some deferred maintenance is inevitable, but too much will eventually result in excessively costly repairs. As an example, not heeding the manufacturer's recommendations for maintaining a motor may temporarily delay the expense of a service call or replacement parts. However, excessive wear on the motor from lack of maintenance can lead to temporary loss of service from the motor and perhaps premature replacement—which will eventually cost much more than timely maintenance.

Because of budget constraints, the manager may have to tolerate some deferred maintenance. When this occurs, the real estate manager should list the deferred maintenance in order of priority and incorporate it into the list of routine maintenance procedures. In that way, the manager and staff can gradually reduce the list of deferred projects while they keep pace with ongoing maintenance.

Schedules and Inspections

Planning is the first step in any maintenance operation. Planning starts with a list of every component that requires maintenance, the type of maintenance each requires, how often each procedure is to be done, and how much time a procedure requires. To develop this list, the manager should survey the condition of all functional components of the property. From the list, the manager can develop schedules for inspections and routine service.

Communication with maintenance personnel is vital to ensure that they maintain work schedules and handle emergency work orders promptly. Today, pagers and cell phones are used routinely for such communications. Newer high-tech cell phones include a digital camera and a personal digital assistant (PDA) in addition to voice communications. Using such phones, maintenance personnel can download work orders to their PDAs (using e-mail or a Web browser), and they can photographically document equipment repairs or damage in a unit.

Inspection Reports.   Scheduling of inspections and cleaning is crucial. Some building components (lobbies, corridors) require daily cleaning or maintenance, while other components (fan motors) need only periodic maintenance to function optimally. The roof may only require annual (or semiannual) inspection. The real estate manager can assemble these considerations in a master maintenance chart and use them to establish a regular and efficient pattern of inspection, cleaning, and repair. An *inspection report* (exhibit 7.1) usually lists all of the major components of a property (e.g., grounds, foundations, exterior walls, electrical network), with numerous subentries under each major component. For example, transformers, circuit breakers, fuse boxes, wiring, wall plugs, light switches, and light fixtures might be subentries under electrical system. Space is provided to record the condition of the component, specific work to be done to it, an estimate of the cost of the work, and timing of reinspection.

For a residential property, a laundry room, recreational facilities, or other amenities would be added items for inspection along with appropriate subentries. Managers usually use a separate form for inspection of apartment interiors, including individual rooms as items and appliances and fixtures as subentries. An office building form would include restrooms and other employee (or public) facilities, light wells or atriums, equipment rooms, fire escapes, and office interiors as items. Most managers use separate forms for the building exterior and interior since they do not inspect the exterior as frequently as they inspect the interior common areas. A separate janitorial survey may be used to review the level of cleanliness of entrances, public areas, lobbies, restrooms, and their components. Managers may record inspections of vacancies on a form that also serves as a work order to prepare the space for re-leasing. Inspection of a shopping center includes examination of the surrounding area and access to the property along with parking lots, signage, and vacant and occupied stores. There, too, separate exterior and interior inspection forms are typical.

Maintenance Schedules. Inspection reports are coordinated with a maintenance schedule to assure timely follow-up. The *maintenance schedule* (exhibit 7.2) usually lists specific tasks and their frequencies. It may also provide spaces for assignment of specific personnel and a specific time of the week, month, or year for completion of the task. Preventive maintenance of equipment is usually addressed on a separate schedule that lists each piece of equipment and its location on the property, with columns for each month of the year so the real estate manager or the maintenance supervisor can indicate how often work is to be done.

The organization of inspection reports and maintenance schedules depends on the design of the structure and its surroundings, the individual components that require service, and the availability of personnel qualified to do the work. The maintenance supervisor must integrate all of these factors into a logical and efficient program for maintaining the property. Computer software can expedite the scheduling process while also documenting

Exhibit 7.1
Sample Property Inspection Report

Property _____

Inspected By _____ Date _____

Item	Condition	Repairs Needed	Est. Cost	Next Inspection
Grounds				
Foundations				
Exterior walls				
Roof				
Gutters and downspouts				
Windows and casings				
Lobby				
Common areas				
Elevators				
Stairways				
Boiler or furnace room				
Air-conditioning plant				
Electrical system				
Plumbing				
Gas lines				
Fire safety equipment				
Garbage disposal area				

This example includes most of the *major* categories of items inspected. Mechanical rooms, storage areas, and parking facilities are other items common to all types of properties. In actual use, an in-spection form is customized for the property, including numerous subentries under each of the items listed here. Condition might be noted as good, fair, or poor (definitions should be included to ensure consistent evaluation); or items might be marked as okay or not okay, the latter meaning an item needs attention.

Exhibit 7.2
Sample Maintenance Schedule

Date _____

Property _____

Project	Frequency	Month of Year
Patch parking lot and other concrete	Once per year	
Clean windows	Twice per year	
Inspect and oil exhaust fans	Once per quarter	
Clean gutters and downspouts	Once per year or after heavy rains	
Inspect and test fire safety equipment	As needed, at least monthly	
Recharge fire extinguishers	Once per year	
Inspect common area lighting	Once per week	
Clean or replace HVAC filters	Once per month	
Polish chrome and brass in lobby	As needed	
Wax lobby floors	Three times per year	
Prune hedges	Twice per year	
Touch up exterior paint	Twice per year	
Touch up interior paint	As needed	
Vacuum swimming pool	Twice per week	

Parking lot striping and changeover between heat and air conditioning are examples of other items that such a schedule might include.

specific maintenance activities and helping maintain adequate inventory of parts and supplies.

Establishing effective schedules may take time and experimentation, especially for an older property whose service records are incomplete. However, a new property should have a complete set of owners' manuals and manufacturers' recommendations that can facilitate development of an equipment maintenance program.

The manager should also consider the specific timing of some maintenance activities (groundskeeping and custodial maintenance in particular) so residents or commercial tenants will be aware that the work is being done. More than mere maintenance, such tasks become part of a tenant retention program. Seeing the property maintained gives tenants a sense of added value for their rent dollars—i.e., visible is valuable.

Custodial Maintenance

Custodial maintenance (also called *janitorial maintenance* or *housekeeping*) is the process of keeping the building clean for residents, commercial tenants, prospective tenants, and visitors. This element of maintenance is most noticeable because it relates to people's sensory perceptions, particularly sight and smell. Custodial maintenance is the simplest form of corrective maintenance. It is also the first level of defense in avoiding deferred maintenance by discovering a need for more extensive corrective maintenance. A schedule of the areas and items that must be cleaned on a daily or weekly basis establishes a pattern for inspecting every part of the building. This can also ensure early discovery of damage or wear.

Quantifying the level of traffic that passes through each section of the building will help the manager schedule custodial maintenance. Some areas of the building may require hourly attention; others may require only an occasional spot inspection. Nevertheless, the custodial maintenance schedule should list all rooms and sections of the common areas in the building so they will be inspected regularly and kept clean. This should include equipment rooms and supply closets. Maintenance personnel may question the purpose of cleaning a supply closet that the public does not see, but an orderly supply room saves staff time in finding parts and supplies and helps protect materials stored in it. It also reminds the staff of the importance of cleanliness throughout the building. The following sections describe some of the areas of a property that require frequent custodial (as well as corrective) maintenance.

Walks, Driveways, Parking Areas, and Grounds. The schedule of custodial maintenance duties for the property grounds depends partly on the time of year. In winter, all driveways, parking areas, and sidewalks must be free of ice and snow. Doormats must be regularly inspected and cleaned. In spring or during periods of thaw, the grounds should be cleared of litter that accumulated beneath the snow. In the summer, keeping the lawn mowed and weeded and regularly weeding any flower beds will add greatly to the *curb appeal* of the property. The staff should look for cracks in the concrete or asphalt pavement and patch them if necessary. Weeds growing in these cracks should be removed. Litter should be picked up as it is noticed. Bushes, shrubs, and trees should be watered and pruned regularly, and they should be replaced if they are dead or dying.

Exterior Walls and Components.   The level of traffic around the outside of a property and the exterior finish of the building determines the frequency of custodial maintenance. In addition to cleaning dirt from the outside walls of the building, staff should also regularly clean signs and lights. Touch-up painting and surface finish repairs may be necessary as a part of the regular maintenance of some parts of the property exterior.

Windows and Casings.   Cleaning all of the windows and window casings of a building may not be done routinely, but those on the lobby level require frequent attention. Because these windows are in high traffic areas, they are the first ones seen and they are the ones that become dirty most rapidly. They should be washed daily, if necessary. The interior and exterior of other windows may require cleaning semiannually or annually. The real estate manager usually contracts trained window washers to clean window exteriors on multistory buildings.

Interior Walls.   Interior walls can require frequent painting or cleaning, which is time-consuming and costly. To avoid that, interior walls should have washable paint or wall coverings, and maintenance staff should clean them regularly.

Elevators, Lobbies, and Other Common Areas.   Elevators and lobbies require daily cleaning. Brass or other metallic surfaces need regular polishing, and floors need periodic refinishing. Corridors require the same level of attention, especially in high-traffic areas. Buildings that have information desks in their lobbies have the advantage of personnel in attendance to keep those areas free of litter or report their condition to the appropriate personnel.

Amenities.   A building's amenities usually have unique requirements. People are attracted to amenities such as swimming pools and fitness centers. At the minimum, these areas require daily attention because of health and sanitation considerations. Managers often contract swimming pool maintenance. Swimming pools must be vacuumed frequently, and chlorination or other chemical treatment levels must be monitored. Periodic testing of water samples may be required by law. If the facility supplies towels, staff must collect, launder, and sanitize them. Locker rooms and showers must be cleaned and disinfected frequently.

Preventive Maintenance

Preventive maintenance is the effort to ensure reliable functional performance—and, in some cases, to extend the useful life—of the building and its components. Exterior maintenance requirements vary with the climate.

For comfort, safety, and efficiency, all parts of the building must be regularly inspected and maintained. The number of maintenance personnel and their levels of skill and training will indicate how much of this work outside contractors should do. For reasons of safety, equipment availability, licensing requirements, and special skills involved, contractors should perform some types of preventive maintenance. The following sections discuss components of a property that require regular preventive maintenance.

Walks, Driveways, Parking Areas, and Grounds. Most sidewalks, driveways, and parking lots are finished with asphalt, brick, or concrete. The effects of traffic, vibration, water freezing in winter, and extreme heat in summer cause these materials to crack and crumble. Occasional patching or resurfacing will extend the life of these surfaces, but they will eventually have to be replaced entirely. Parking lots have to be restriped periodically to mark parking stalls and fire lanes. Landscaping that has been neglected may have to be redesigned to be more aesthetically pleasing. Lawns may require reseeding or sod replacement in the spring to restore areas where grass has died.

As an extension of preventive maintenance, grounds should be inspected during (if possible) and immediately after major weather events such as high winds, severe thunderstorms, or heavy and prolonged rains. Shrubs are easily uprooted. Branches can be torn from trees. Signs and property lighting can be damaged in various ways. Such damage requires prompt attention to avoid potential hazards to people and vehicles.

Foundations. Building foundations should be inspected periodically for evidence of water penetration, settlement, cracks, and other signs of deterioration. To prevent further deterioration, staff should correct problems when they are discovered. When problems are severe, the real estate manager should consult professional engineers.

Exterior Walls. Preventive maintenance of exterior walls depends on the construction or finishing material. Because of repeated freezing and thawing, cracks can develop in the mortar of brick walls, and *tuck-pointing*—the periodic replacement of mortar—becomes necessary. Painted walls should be examined for cracked or peeling paint; occasional touch-ups will protect a painted surface, but complete repainting will eventually be necessary. Wood surfaces should be inspected for splintering, decay, and insect damage caused by termites, carpenter ants, etc. It is often possible to replace portions of a wood surface without completely refacing the building. To prevent reinfestation, a professional contractor must exterminate insects before repair work begins. Concrete walls must be checked for cracks or chipping. Glass curtain walls should be examined for stability and to detect cracks or other damage.

Roof.   A roof endures extremes of heat, cold, and moisture. Over the years, an owner may have a building reroofed many times. Severe weather may weaken areas of the roof, necessitating occasional patching. The manager of the property should routinely inspect the surface of the roof for wear. Roof inspections should be at least annual, and a qualified roofing contractor should usually accompany the manager. A *thermal scan* may help identify problems that are not visible to the naked eye (e.g., areas of heat loss due to absent, inadequate, or wet insulation).

Antennas and satellite dishes may be installed on the roof to provide communications and television services. These require little or no ongoing maintenance, but the contractors who installed them should do any work required. Installers must take care not to compromise the integrity of the roof system. The real estate manager should carefully check these areas when inspecting the roof.

Gutters and Downspouts.   Many buildings have exposed gutters and downspouts. These prevent the accumulation of water on the roof and protect the exterior walls from excessive water flow. Gutters usually have to be replaced as often as the roof. They should be inspected frequently, especially after heavy rains, and they must be kept clear of leaves and other accumulating debris.

Windows and Casings.   In addition to cleaning, windows require maintenance of their moving parts and frames. The maintenance staff may have to install separate storm windows in the autumn and remove them in the spring. When windows need replacing, the manager should investigate double-paned windows that serve as their own storm windows. They are energy-efficient in all seasons and require less maintenance. These issues are more generally applicable to residential properties. Newer office buildings usually have windows that do not open, and older buildings are often retrofitted to prevent the opening of windows.

Elevators.   The real estate manager should contract for elevator maintenance. The elevator timing should be recorded, and the manager should work with the contractor to develop the system that is most efficient for handling the volume of traffic in the building. The elevator contractor will provide preventive maintenance such as lubricating parts, inspecting cables, and cleaning the rails.

The real estate manager can devise strategies to protect the building's elevators from improper use. While not specifically preventive maintenance, such strategies can minimize damage and prolong an elevator's life. To discourage use of passenger elevators for freight, and vice versa, the freight elevator should be separate from those for passengers. In buildings that lack a freight elevator, passenger elevators must serve as freight elevators. The risk of damage to passenger elevators used for freight warrants a creative approach. One possibility is to reserve one of the passenger elevators for freight use and make it accessible only to appropriate personnel who have a key. When using that practice, the manager must provide pads for the elevator walls and designate a particular time of the day when the elevators may be used for moving freight. This will avert disruption during periods of peak traffic. Another possibility is to load furniture on the top of the elevator cab rather than inside. The ability to do this depends on the system in place (elevator cab construction, door controls, etc.).

Stairways.   No matter how they are constructed, stairways require close attention because they are frequently the site of accidents involving injuries. Step surfaces show wear over time, and this alone can be a potential hazard because the surface (tread) is no longer smooth or level. The manager should check stairs for any loose or deteriorating steps. All staircases should have a handrail that is easy to grasp. All handrails should be securely fastened to the wall or staircase. The most common challenge is keeping stairways free of debris. Stair edges should be clearly marked if it is difficult to distinguish the surfaces of successive steps, and all stairwells should have adequate lighting for emergencies as well as for normal use.

Heating, Ventilating, and Air-Conditioning (HVAC) Equipment.   Controlling the climate in buildings is an ongoing challenge. In addition to temperature, HVAC equipment regulates humidity, supplies fresh air to the building, and removes stale air. Regulating all of these conditions requires a system of controls and precise monitoring of each room or floor in the building. A malfunction or error in programming this equipment can cause tenants extreme discomfort. Maintenance staff may be trained to clean and replace filters, lubricate portions of the mechanical equipment, or monitor thermostat settings. However, real estate managers usually contract maintenance and repair of HVAC equipment unless the size of a property justifies the skilled labor needed for that work. Local ordinances may require licensing of boiler operators. Heating and air-conditioning systems usually require special maintenance for start-up and shutdown when the seasons change.

Electrical Network and Plumbing.   As demand for electrical service grows, the real estate manager must monitor whether the capacity in the building can meet that demand. In particular, the manager should ask prospective commercial tenants about their electrical requirements to determine whether the building can accommodate them. Computer networks and telephone systems are increasing in complexity. An existing building can often be retrofitted for the electrical and network cabling required for computers and their adjunct equipment. However, that may be a major undertaking that warrants retrofitting the entire building rather than only one tenant's leased space.

The maintenance supervisor should regularly inspect all electrical wiring and all electrically operated pumps and motors. All property staff should know the location of transformers on or near the property, the location of the transformer identification number, and the telephone number of the electric utility company. The main shutoff switch should be identified; employees should know its location in the building and the circumstances that warrant disconnecting the property from its power supply. Licensed personnel should make any changes in the wiring, and they should appropriately document those changes.

Plumbing should be inspected regularly. Work required to clear drains, repair leaks, and otherwise maintain the integrity of the system should be done immediately. Residential properties usually have more plumbing fixtures than any other property type. Consequently, they have the most plumbing problems. To minimize service calls and reduce the amount of toxic drain cleaner released into the environment, residents should learn responsible and proper use of plumbing fixtures. Managers should give commercial tenants information to use to educate their employees about proper disposal of refuse (i.e., what not to put into sinks or toilets). The main water shutoff valve should be identified, employees should know its location in the building and the circumstances that warrant its use.

Gas Lines.   Only trained personnel from the gas company should perform the maintenance of gas lines. The manager should remind maintenance staff to check for gas leaks, to report them to the proper authorities, and to initiate appropriate emergency procedures. If the property is equipped with a primary shutoff valve and the gas company provides instructions on how to use it, the manager should convey that information to the employees.

Cogeneration Equipment.   On properties that produce electricity using a cogeneration plant, the maintenance staff may be responsible for certain routine tasks. However, authorized contractors must perform most preventive and corrective maintenance.

Fire Prevention and Safety Equipment.   To minimize the threat to life and property from fire, the manager should inform everyone in the building about fire safety procedures, make sure that the associated equipment is functioning properly, and verify that all equipment meets local fire codes. All fire exits and fire doors should be marked clearly and kept free of obstructions. Proper operation of fire doors, alarm systems, fire escapes, and interior sprinkler systems should be verified at least once a year. Certificates of inspection may be required, and maintenance may have to be contracted.

Fire Safety—Additional Considerations

Thousands of buildings catch fire every year, and thousands of people lose their lives in those fires. Real estate managers must know how to minimize the risk of fire and, in the event of a fire, how to properly react to minimize injuries and property damage. A fire prevention and safety program may start with a call to the local fire department—many fire departments will conduct fire safety inspections of properties. An inspection of the site by the fire department will identify potential fire hazards and equipment that must be installed or upgraded to comply with safety standards or codes.

Lights in exit signs must be inspected regularly to ensure they are functioning. Installing emergency lighting that automatically turns on in a power failure in corridors and stairwells may be advisable; some jurisdictions require it. Such lights also require regular inspection.

Sprinkler systems are often installed in building common areas and leased premises—some jurisdictions require them in high-rise structures. Fire extinguishers and smoke alarms should be installed in common areas. If local law does not require the installation of fire extinguishers or smoke alarms within discrete leased spaces, the manager may want to encourage tenants to purchase these items themselves. Because the cost of alarms and extinguishers is nominal compared to the cost of lives and property, the manager may even want to encourage the owner to install this equipment in every leased space. Insurance premiums will be lower if alarms, extinguishers, and/or sprinkler systems are present.

The local fire department may also help a real estate manager prepare a fire safety training program for site staff and tenants. Such a program includes prevention advice (e.g., proper storage and use of combustibles) as well as procedures to follow to escape from a fire. The core of any safety program is to establish an *evacuation plan* and to begin evacuation as soon as a fire is discovered or an alarm sounds. Management staff and tenants should know how to call the fire department and how to activate the building alarm system if they discover a fire or encounter smoke.

Advice from the fire department and occasional fire drills help to ensure the appropriateness of an evacuation plan. Many safety tips about exiting a burning building may seem to be common knowledge (e.g., knowing where the nearest exits are located, touching a door with the back of a hand before opening it, staying near the floor for fresh air, closing doors when possible to contain the fire), but they should be reiterated frequently. If the fire department does not offer safety training, it may have brochures available that list safety procedures, or it may direct a manager to the nearest resource for this information.

Most jurisdictions require the installation of smoke alarms; batteries must be checked and replaced in smoke detectors that are not connected to a central system. Some jurisdictions even require supervised fire drills, especially for multistory office buildings. Regardless of requirements, the manager should provide routine drills for all property personnel, residents, and commercial tenants on how to summon the fire department and evacuate the building.

An outside service must recharge and tag *fire extinguishers* as prescribed by the manufacturer. In the United States, fire extinguishers are classified by the extinguishing material they contain. The extinguishers in the building should be placed by class according to the combustibles nearby. *Class A* is ordinary combustibles, such as paper and wood, which can be extinguished with water. *Class B* is flammable liquids such as fuel oil, paint, and paint thinner; these must be extinguished with foam. *Class C* involves electrical equipment and systems that must be deprived of air by using carbon dioxide (CO_2) gas. In other words, a water-based extinguisher should not be used on an electrical fire. Managers commonly install type ABC (dry chemical) extinguishers because they are effective against all types of fires. Fire-suppression systems in computer rooms may contain halogenated compounds (Halon) that are similar in action to CO_2 gas.

Pest Control. An ongoing concern among real estate managers is the control of insect pests and other vermin. Most properties contract for regular extermination service, and many states require pest control operators to be licensed. The frequency of the exterminator's visits depends on the severity of infestation, the season, and the locale. Cockroaches are ubiquitous and particularly difficult to exterminate. Other troublesome insects are termites, carpenter ants, and fire ants. Because these insects burrow into foundations and wooden beams, they may be noticed only after they have done extensive damage.

To eliminate an infestation, fumigation may be necessary. However, if only one leased space is fumigated or sprayed after a tenant has vacated, the pests may not die; they may merely relocate to adjoining spaces. To ensure complete extermination, the exterminator should spray the entire building or a large section of it at one time. Properties whose tenants include restaurants or food stores are especially prone to vermin infestations. However, local health departments require most food stores and restaurants to spray periodically for pests.

The most effective way to control pests is to remove their food sources. Mice, rats, and cockroaches thrive in unsanitary conditions. Managers should stress to residents and commercial tenants the proper frequency and method for disposing of garbage on the premises. If no place is available outside the building to maintain dumpsters, garbage must be stored inside the building. The garbage room (or storage area) should be inspected regularly—cracks in the walls and other types of damage provide conduits for pests to spread throughout the building. To control odors and inhibit bacterial and fungal growth, routine cleaning and disinfection of the garbage room are mandatory. The garbage room should be insulated from heat, especially if the room is near the furnace or boiler. Good illumination and walls painted a light color imply to tenants the desire to keep the room clean and facilitate the detection of insects on the walls. Regardless of where garbage is stored, a program to sort trash for *recycling* may also help control pests by concentrating the organic garbage in fewer containers. (Recycling of paper, glass, metals, and plastics is mandatory in many states.)

In many areas, squirrels, bats, birds, and other wildlife also become pests and can cause serious damage to the outsides of buildings. Campus-style commercial and residential properties are particularly vulnerable. The animals can also present hazards to people (scratches, bites, disease transmission). As the habitats available for animals diminish, encounters with wildlife increase. Real estate managers must be aware that federal and state laws protect most wildlife species and their management. Managers should proactively institute measures to eliminate food sources and discourage habitats that attract animals. They should seek advice from wildlife rehabilitators, other wildlife experts, or animal control on additional ways to keep wildlife away from the property.

OTHER ASPECTS OF MAINTENANCE

Regulations enforced by local, state, and federal governments establish minimum standards for the safety of employees and building occupants and affect many maintenance procedures. Laws governing minimum standards change frequently, so real estate managers must stay abreast of new laws and court interpretations. In addition, properties must comply with current environmental regulations, and such compliance relates to the safety, health, and well-being of tenants through maintenance practices. Operating economies and maintenance procedures conserve energy. Maintenance is also the key to building security and crime prevention.

Safety

The Occupational Safety and Health Administration (OSHA) of the U.S. Department of Labor establishes job safety standards and is authorized to conduct inspections and to cite businesses for violations. The manager should know the OSHA standards that apply to activities on the property and explain them to the employees who work there. Unsafe work practices should be corrected. The manager should provide employees with proper equipment for their duties and be sure they know how to use the equipment correctly. Appropriate and approved protective devices for equipment and personnel (shields on power saws, safety glasses, rubber gloves) must be readily available.

Various chemicals and other materials used on-site (e.g., cleaning products) may include potentially combustible, flammable, or toxic substances. Personnel who work with such chemicals should be aware of the specific hazards and wear protective gloves and other appropriate equipment. Product labels identify the hazards and indicate how to treat persons who are exposed to the materials as well as how to dispose of the products and their containers properly. A *material safety data sheet (MSDS)* accompanies chemicals purchased in bulk in drums. Hazardous materials are also an environmental issue.

The issue of safety of building occupants and visitors goes beyond those items noted in the discussions of specific area inspections. Temporary barriers or fencing should delineate construction and other work areas. The barriers should be clearly identified with signage, and they should be locked to prevent unauthorized persons from entering. Even such tasks as mopping and waxing lobby floors require clear delineation and signage to minimize the potential for slip- or trip-and-fall accidents.

Protecting the Environment

Understanding proper ways to handle wastes and dispose of them ensures safety, compliance with regulations, and preservation of the environment, yet waste disposal is only one aspect of environmental protection. Many materials once considered safe for use in buildings have been found to be harmful to humans. The U.S. Environmental Protection Agency (EPA) and state and local governments have enacted regulations to protect people and the environment. The real estate manager must know whether harmful materials are present on the property and whether they are potentially hazardous in their current state. The presence of hazardous materials can lower the value of a property, even if the materials do not pose a threat. Liability for leaving such materials in place or for removing them has received considerable attention.

Of primary concern to real estate managers are asbestos, radon, and polychlorinated biphenyls (PCBs). Chlorofluorocarbons (CFCs) used in chiller components of many air-conditioning and refrigeration systems are of concern. Lead-based paint found in older buildings is especially hazardous to children who live there. Formaldehyde gas is yet another hazard. Bloodborne pathogens may be an issue when health care professionals or medical laboratories lease office or store spaces.

- *Asbestos* is a fibrous mineral that was used in buildings prior to 1981 for flooring, insulation, and fireproofing. Though not banned entirely, its use is banned in new flooring felt, rollboard, and corrugated, commercial, or specialty paper. Only licensed contractors can assess the condition of asbestos-containing material (ACM) in a property— i.e., whether it is *friable* (easily crumbled). Only they can remove it *(abatement)* or maintain it in place *(containment)*.

- *Radon* is a colorless, odorless, tasteless gas that occurs naturally in the radioactive decay of radium and uranium. It became a problem

Hazardous Materials in Buildings

- Asbestos-containing material (ACM)
- Radon gas
- Polychlorinated biphenyls (PCBs)
- Chlorofluorocarbons (CFCs)
- Lead-based paint
- Formaldehyde gas
- Bloodborne pathogens

Poor indoor air quality (IAQ), mold, and leaking underground storage tanks (LUSTs) are other examples of hazards at managed properties.

with the advent of energy-efficient buildings that allow only minimal transfer of air between the building's interior and the outside. If high levels of radon exist in a building, a qualified contractor can identify the sources and recommend ways to seal them or better ventilate the building.

- *Polychlorinated biphenyls (PCBs)* in electrical transformers are relatively harmless if left undisturbed. However, if a PCB-containing transformer leaks or burns, lethal *dioxin* gas may be released. Local or state law may require removal of PCBs during rehabilitation. An authorized hazardous waste hauler must transport transformers that contain PCBs to a licensed location for disposal. The property owner may be liable for any PCB contamination caused by the transformer even after it has been removed from the property. However, when the utility company owns the transformers (which is often the case), it has the burden of responsibility for correcting transformer-related environmental problems.

- *Chlorofluorocarbons (CFCs),* which contain two types of halogens— namely chlorine (Cl) and fluorine (F)—are being phased out and replaced with similar compounds that do not include chlorine atoms. (Many were banned when the United States signed the Montreal Protocol.) Newer refrigerant chemicals are not always compatible with existing air-conditioning systems, but it is possible to modify the equipment to use them. Information on refrigerant chemicals and equipment modifications and costs is available from the American Society of Heating, Refrigerating, and Air-Conditioning Engineers (ASHRAE).

- *Lead-based paint* in housing built prior to 1980 poses a serious lead-poisoning hazard to resident children. (Its use in the United States was outlawed in 1978.) The hazard may be abated by removing the paint (e.g., dipping removable components in chemical strippers); encapsulating it by covering painted surfaces with other materials (e.g., installing wallboard); and replacing painted window frames, doors, balustrades, and other easily removed components. Only qualified contractors should perform abatement work and disposal of the hazardous waste. (The property owner must disclose the presence of lead-based paint to potential buyers, residents, and commercial tenants.)

- *Formaldehyde gas* is a foaming agent once used in foam insulation and still present in adhesives used in making pressed-wood products. Its presence in a building can be harmful. Manufactured homes are most susceptible to high levels of formaldehyde gas because of the amount of pressed wood and the type of insulation in them. Although formaldehyde gas will dissipate eventually, removing some of the formaldehyde-containing materials or increasing interior ventilation to hasten the dissipation and eliminate harmful effects may be necessary.

While *indoor air quality (IAQ)* problems can arise in any type of building, office buildings are the most susceptible. That is partially because their centralized HVAC systems serve such a large space and partially because they are built new or retrofitted as entirely enclosed systems (the windows cannot be opened), which results in poor air circulation. Contaminants, including *volatile organic compounds (VOCs)* and bacteria, can be distributed throughout the building causing occupants to experience headaches, dizziness, drowsiness, nausea, and other symptoms of *sick building syndrome (SBS)*. *Legionella* bacteria, which can grow in fouled water-cooling towers, are the cause of *Legionnaires' disease* (an often fatal respiratory infection). As yet, there is no federal regulation of IAQ, but ASHRAE established IAQ standards in the early 1990s that have since been formalized as Standard 62-1999 and continue to evolve. The standards specify minimum ventilation rates and IAQ that are acceptable to human occupants.

Mold and mold-like substances can exist in rental homes, condominiums, apartments, and commercial buildings. Water damage, leaks, and other moisture intrusions (e.g., seepage) are the primary sources of mold growth. Mold may adversely affect human health. However, it appears that the effect of mold on humans is short term rather than long term—removing the mold removes the effect. Not all mold that grows in buildings is the toxic mold that has sensationalized this subject. When mold is detected, actions to remediate the problem should be initiated promptly. A qualified contractor should remove the mold and repair the damage area. Straightforward, informative communications with building occupants will help diminish the perception of mold hazards and minimize the risk of liability for the property's owner and manager.

Many older buildings used to maintain their own fuel supply for their boilers, usually in storage tanks on the premises. The threat of contamination of groundwater by *leaking underground storage tanks (LUSTs)* has led to regulations requiring inspection and replacement of tanks that are still in use. Those no longer in use may have to be removed. The presence of extra pipes may indicate a forgotten underground tank. If an abandoned tank is found on the premises, the alternatives for making it completely safe are to remove it or to fill it with cement. The real estate manager should always contact the local authorities regarding the legally correct procedure to use when dealing with environmental issues.

Controlling Energy Consumption

Managing energy usage is an ongoing aspect of maintenance, and energy savings reduces operating costs and increases potential profit for the property. *Energy conservation* is a way to ensure comfort and reduce fuel consumption.

Basic Energy Conservation Programs.   Some energy programs cost very little to implement. A reminder to residents and commercial tenants to report leaky faucets can reduce wasted water and fuel. (If tenants pay for utilities, less waste saves them money.) A policy that cleaning staff is to turn off the lights after cleaning a room can save an enormous amount of electricity. A maintenance program that emphasizes energy management can begin generating savings with the following month's fuel bills. Although new energy-saving equipment can be expensive, some devices have the potential to reduce energy consumption by more than half. As a simple example, low-wattage fluorescent lamps can replace conventional incandescent lamps. The cost of one of these fluorescent lamps is higher than the cost of an incandescent lamp, but its life expectancy is also many times greater. The savings results from much lower energy consumption—the fluorescent lamp produces the same intensity and quality of light as a conventional incandescent lamp but uses about one-fourth the wattage.

New types of incandescent lamps that burn brighter and last longer are marketed from time to time. Mercury vapor lamps are more efficient and have a longer operating life than incandescent lamps; they are often used outdoors to light walkways and parking areas. Sodium vapor lamps offer higher efficiency for the same uses as mercury vapor lamps and are especially useful in areas subject to dense fog. Metal halide lamps have a longer rated life and are typically used in large open spaces (parking garages, mechanical rooms).

Another method of conserving energy and reducing costs is to adjust thermostats throughout the building, especially in office buildings that have central HVAC systems. By setting the temperature a few degrees *lower* during the heating season and, similarly, a few degrees *higher* during the cooling season, the manager can realize substantial energy and cost savings. Many residential buildings also have central HVAC systems, and these can be adjusted similarly. To avoid constant complaints, the temperature maintained should satisfy the residents' or commercial tenants' comfort levels. Local ordinances may dictate thermostat settings during certain hours of the day or night or require certain levels of heating (or cooling), and compliance with these requirements is important.

Other Energy Conservation Tactics. Numerous controls can be installed on existing equipment; replacement with completely new equipment is another possibility. A *retrofit* is the replacement of an old building component with a new, energy-efficient one—installation of a new boiler, for example, especially one carrying the ENERGY STAR® label. Retrofitting can be very expensive, but the installation will eventually pay off, especially if the component was due for replacement anyway. Although the payback may take years, such a retrofitting can become a strong competitive advantage if energy costs soar. (Chapter 4 discusses the calculation of payback.)

A manager should learn about the energy consumption of a property, the billing procedures used by utility companies, and the energy control devices available on the market. Alternatives can be compared and appropriately implemented. To optimize energy conservation, a manager must think creatively about energy costs and usage. Low-flow showerheads greatly reduce consumption of water and fuel. Motion or infrared sensors on parking lot lights may reduce electricity consumption without compromising security. A combination timer-thermostat on a boiler can match high water temperature with peak demand. Routine cleaning and oiling of machinery results in better performance, longer life, and lower energy consumption. Frequent inspections of the property and routine maintenance are essential to prevent energy waste.

The goal of energy management is to strike a balance between the initial cost of an energy-saving device or program and the amount of time before it pays for itself. Reducing expenses in this manner also improves NOI and adds to the property's value.

Maintaining Property Security

Successful maintenance programs contribute to a building's security. Although preventing crime in buildings is very difficult, many crimes do not result from forcible entry. Complacency about security measures provides greater opportunities for crime. Regular inspections and thorough preventive measures are the best defenses against crime at a property.

Some real estate managers and property owners may consider a security staff or surveillance equipment crucial. Before making such an investment, however, they should consider the issue of liability. The presence of a security force or monitoring equipment—or the promotion of these services when marketing the property—may be construed as a "security guarantee." If that guarantee fails, the owner and the manager may be liable. Despite this risk, security personnel are crucial for some types of property, especially office buildings and shopping centers. In residential properties, providing residents with security devices they can use themselves (peepholes in doors, deadbolt locks) may be most appropriate.

Whatever security program is in place, staff should continually monitor to make sure it works exactly as planned. The real estate manager should advise tenants and staff to consider the consequences of their actions. Doors that lock automatically should not be propped open. Most crimes in apartment buildings result from entry and fire doors being propped open. Maintenance staff should replace burned-out light bulbs as soon as they discover them. In scheduling, the manager should give immediate priority to repair of any component that may provide access to the property. In addition, monitoring and adjusting outdoor lighting levels and frequently trimming overgrown shrubbery help eliminate potential hiding places.

In the aftermath of September 11, 2001, security has tightened in general. In office buildings, scanners may check packages as well as building personnel and visitors. Biometric identification (fingerprints, handprints, retinal scans, etc.) will become more common as those devices become more economical to purchase and operate. At the same time, managers of all types of buildings must stay alert to the threat of acts of terrorism. Buildings may be evacuated because of bomb threats, dangerous air pollutants (including biological and chemical agents), nearby hazardous materials spills, and other incidents. Real estate managers should work with local authorities in planning for emergencies and keep abreast of alerts issued by the various governmental authorities. In this context, greater scrutiny of prospective tenants and of current tenants' activities is also warranted.

MANAGING MAINTENANCE WORK

The manager and the owner must choose the most effective method of maintaining the property. They must find qualified personnel to do the work, and they must keep records of the work performed.

Staffing Choices

Real estate managers can find personnel to do maintenance work in three ways: hiring on-site staff, using management firm employees, using contractors. (See also chapter 6.) Managers commonly use a combination of the three approaches.

On-Site Staff.   Hiring on-site staff is a customary practice and an effective way to quickly provide custodial and preventive maintenance. The size of the building usually determines the number of people and the range of specialized skills required.

Management Firm Employees.   The real estate manager or the management company may manage enough properties to sustain a full-time maintenance staff. When providing nonroutine maintenance to a managed property, the manager or management company bills the property owner for labor and parts in addition to the regular management fee. With such an arrangement, disputes may arise between the owner and the manager over the amount of extra charges; if the management company provides maintenance services, negotiating a totally separate fee or billing arrangement may be more appropriate.

Contractors.   For maintenance that requires specialized skills or licensing of those who do the work (e.g., elevator maintenance), the real estate manager may use contractors in addition to or in place of on-site staff. The manager may also contract regular janitorial services, and independent security agencies usually provide on-site security officers on contract.

All contractors should be bonded, and if their particular duties require licensing, the manager should verify that their licenses are current. Janitorial, security, and other contracted personnel who will work on-site for extended periods should undergo preemployment criminal background checks. The manager should require contractors to show proof that they have adequate and appropriate insurance (workers' compensation, liability) and to supply several references, all of which should be checked.

Before choosing a contractor to perform a certain job at a property, the real estate manager should draft precise *specifications* for the work. The specifications should describe the work to be done, the materials to be used, any special equipment or tools required, and any time constraints that may apply. The manager should then invite contractors to *bid* on the job. They will submit *quotations* that state their analysis of the job, the time it will take, and the cost.

After receiving the quotations, the manager can select the contractor who will provide the necessary level of quality for the fairest price. In some instances, stating a firm price is impossible, especially if a job—elevator repair, for instance—could take on a different character after the work begins.

The contractor may submit an *estimate* showing known costs (for parts) and specific rates to be charged for variable components of the job (an hourly rate for labor; mileage charges for travel). Contractors typically use specific written contracts for technical or repetitive maintenance services; they may use purchase orders for work not covered by a contract.

Record Keeping

Whether the maintenance work is done by on-site staff, employees of the management firm, contractors, or a combination of the three, the record-keeping requirements are essentially the same.

Work Order. Each specific maintenance or repair activity should have an individual *work order* (exhibit 7.3) that indicates what is to be done, when it is to be done, and who will do the work. The work order form usually consists of an original and two copies. The original may remain with the manager, the maintenance supervisor, or the person who files the orders. The second and third copies are for the maintenance worker. After the job is done, the worker should fill in the rest of the work order and return it to the manager or the maintenance office.

Maintenance Service Request. The real estate manager may initiate maintenance work because of a property inspection. Commercial tenants and residents usually complete a *maintenance service request* to initiate work to be done in their leased spaces. A staff member may also fill out the form when a request is phoned to the manager's office.

Some properties provide this form on their Web sites, and tenants can complete them online and send them to the management office via e-mail. The service request form identifies the tenant and the leased space, indicates contact information, and describes the work requested. Space is available for the tenant to sign the form and grant permission to enter the leased premises and for the manager to indicate the priority of the task. Some maintenance systems include an e-mail confirmation to the tenant of the work performed and any cost to be charged. The communication requests the tenant's response as to whether the work was satisfactory.

An expanded form might include space for information about parts, scheduling, and actual work done, along with space for the maintenance worker to sign the form when the work is complete, which effectively combines the service request with the work order form.

Work Log. Real estate managers commonly use a *work log* to record maintenance jobs on a cumulative basis. Some keep a master work log for all property staff and contractors, listing what has been scheduled for each of them and the cost of the work (exhibit 7.4). Supervisors may ask staff

Exhibit 7.3
Sample Maintenance Work Order

Work Order Number _____Assigned To _____

Property _____Date _____

Maintenance required _____

_____

_____

Location on property _____

Maintenance performed _____

_____

_____

Materials used _____

_____

_____

Time required _____   Cost of labor $ _____

                                          Cost of materials $ _____

                                          Total $ _____

Maintenance performed by _____

Unable to complete because _____

_____

This is a generic example. For work to be done in an apartment, a work order form would include spaces for the resident's name and home and work phone numbers, the presence of a pet, and whether permission to enter the unit has been received, as well as whether the resident is to be charged for the work and the reason. A commercial property work order would also include tenant contact information. Work done for commercial tenants is usually charged back to the tenant. Space may also be included for the tenant to acknowledge the completion of the work. Some managers combine this form with a *maintenance service request* form.

Exhibit 7.4

Sample Maintenance Work Log

Order Number	Location	Description of Work	Written		Assigned To	Completed	Cost
			Time	Date			

The information displayed in this generic form is usually sufficient for most purposes. The location column may be used to identify the space and the resident or commercial tenant or separate columns can be created for this information. Columns may be added to track other details such as the amount of time to do the work, purchase order numbers, additional work to be done, and when the work was inspected.

members to maintain a separate log record of assigned tasks and time allotments. The worker then checks off the work as it is completed, indicating the actual time required and reasons for any time variances (or if a task is not completed, the reason).

Purchase Order.   Although a staff member who is not directly involved with maintenance may complete a *purchase order* for supplies or equipment, this record has a direct effect on the maintenance staff and maintenance efficiency. A purchase order should show the name of the vendor; the date of the order; the kind, quantity, and price of each item ordered; the delivery date and terms of acceptance; and whether any substitutions are allowed. Purchase orders help the manager monitor inventory levels and ensure an adequate supply of replacement parts. Tracking inventory through purchase orders can prevent purchasing too many or too few supplies and spare parts. Both situations are costly. Overstock represents cash that is not available for other uses, and having too many parts on hand can lead to pilferage by employees or tenants. Inadequate inventory is also expensive, especially in terms of the staff time involved in making a special trip to purchase a part.

Inventory Control System.   To verify inventory levels and track the frequency of restocking, the manager may develop an *inventory control system,* such as a checkout list in the supply storeroom. Each item is recorded as it is removed from inventory, and the remaining inventory count (item total) is reduced. Regular review of the list indicates what needs to be restocked and when. When managing large or many properties, real estate managers increasingly use computerized inventories to perform this function.

SUMMARY

Maintenance involves more than cleaning and repairs. A good maintenance program also anticipates malfunctions and schedules regular examination and care of building components. Appearance is the best marketing tool for any property, so the site must be immaculate at all times. Managers can optimally schedule custodial maintenance by monitoring traffic flow through various parts of the building and by making sure the maintenance staff know how often inspections are required under various conditions. Preventive maintenance lowers repair costs overall. It can help deter crime by ensuring that security devices (door locks, alarms) and strategic lighting (parking lots, stairwells) are operational.

   Maintenance and repair of equipment poses risks and hazards to staff; to minimize these and provide a safe working environment, a property must comply with OSHA regulations. The variety of chemicals used in cleaning and maintenance must be disposed of safely, so staff must know the proper procedures. If hazardous materials are on the premises, the manager must know what to do about them in order to comply with federal, state, and local environmental regulations.

Keeping accurate records is an integral part of maintenance and management. Use of purchase orders and inventory controls can save the owner the costs of excessive or inadequate inventory. Records are also necessary to track specific maintenance work and when or whether it is completed.

8

The Cycle
of Tenancy

The principles of tenant relations are essentially the same regardless of property type. In fact, a *cycle of tenancy* is common to all properties. All current tenants were once prospects; they were attracted to the property because of its marketing. They signed a lease and they regularly pay rent to occupy space in the property. When the lease expires, they may or may not renew it based on their evaluation of the benefit of renewal versus the amount of the rent increase or the expense of relocating. Tenants eventually move out, but satisfied tenants may refer others to the property. In all phases of the cycle of tenancy, the attitude, skill, and dedication of the real estate manager are as important to tenants' satisfaction as the location, appearance, and structural integrity of the property. Tenants will also be less inclined to move out of a property where the management personnel have implemented specific programs designed to retain them.

MARKETING THE PROPERTY

For every product or service, a market of willing consumers exists. One function of *marketing* is to identify prospective customers whose specific needs, wants, and finances a particular product or service will satisfy. The objective of marketing rental space is to attract as many potential tenants as possible from the market of renters. That requires a thorough knowledge of the property for lease and a clear understanding of the market for that type of space. The real estate manager should already know the characteristics of

---

Factors That Determine Market Size

- Property type
- Size of the rental space
- Location
- Rental price

---

the property from the regional, neighborhood, property, and market analyses conducted during development of the management plan (see chapter 4). Those analyses indicated the features and amenities of the property to highlight and the type of prospective tenant they will attract. In the absence of a specific management plan, the real estate manager, marketing director, or leasing agent should perform those analyses before planning a marketing program.

Understanding the Market

Marketing real estate is different from marketing other types of products and services. Real property is immovable. Altering it to meet market demands is difficult and expensive. Specific features of a property may limit the size of its market and the number of its potential tenants. Therefore, the real estate manager (or leasing agent) must thoroughly understand the property's features and its location before he or she can identify the market and concentrate promotion in media appropriate to that market. Money spent to reach extraneous markets—those individuals who have no reason to respond to the marketing effort—is money wasted. Careful study of the limitations on the market before initiating a marketing program will reduce the time and expense required to produce results.

The primary factor that limits the potential market is the *property type*. The leasing agent must market store space to merchants, office space to business people, apartments to individuals who want a place to live. The second limiting factor is the *size of the rental space*. Supermarkets must have 50,000 or more square feet of space—some may need up to 100,000 square feet—while a gift shop usually requires 2,000 square feet or less. Numbers of employees and the amount and size of equipment they use determine the square footage an office needs. The number of people in a household and their income generally define the size and layout of their living quarters. Factors such as these narrow the range of potential tenants for a specific store, office space, or apartment. The third limiting factor is *location*—where the property is situated and how far it is from its market. This, too, relates to the type of property. Shopping centers can seek tenants nationally. Rental housing and office space generally attract prospective tenants from the surrounding neighborhood or region. A time-share condominium in a resort area may attract residents from all parts of the country or the world. Specific features related to location (access to transportation and proximity to local attractions) define the market as well. *Rental price* is the fourth limiting factor. Those in the market must be able to afford the rent and be willing to pay it.

Once the general characteristics of the tenant profile become evident, the real estate manager can examine what will attract the greatest number of prospects to visit the site. The effort at this point is to make the market for the property aware of its existence, its advantages, and its available space. This means choosing the medium and the message that will generate the most responses—the greater the number of responses, the larger the number of prospects—and ensure that the property will lease up quickly.

By its nature, a new property attracts attention. Its location, size, and state of completion invite curiosity. In this regard, a new development benefits from the free publicity it receives simply because it is new. People's natural inquisitiveness can be further encouraged with specific advertising. On the other hand, an older property may not generate much curiosity. However, compared to a new structure, an established property may have fewer vacancies to fill.

New residential properties usually have impressive model units. A model should reflect the manager's understanding of the market and the most probable type of resident. Models help prospects envision the space as their home. While the furnishings of a model space should suit the market, the furnishings themselves should not be the focus of attention—they should subtly enhance the space, not overshadow it. Models, as such, are rarely a factor in leasing office or retail space. However, the on-site leasing office or the management office usually has typical building finishes. An upgraded office may also be available to show above-standard finishes for tenant improvements. Store spaces are uniquely built out for a particular tenant.

Developing a Marketing Program

Knowing the marketable features of the property and the profile of the most likely prospects, the real estate manager can plan a specific promotional message and choose the best medium to convey it. Advertising and promotion cost money, so the first step in developing a marketing program is to quantify how much money is available for it. An advertising program generally requires its own budget. Another early step is to determine whether and to what extent to use an advertising agency. Because of the extra expense involved, managers are most likely to hire advertising agencies to promote very large developments—especially new ones—or a group of properties under one ownership. If an advertising agency is considered, the manager

---

Common Advertising Media

- Classified newspaper ads
- Display advertising
- Signage
- Brochures
- Direct mail
- Broadcast advertising
- Internet (Web page, locator services)

---

and the owner must verify the extent of the services desired, the precise cost of those services, and the length of time the contract will last. Whether an agency is used or not, a comprehensive marketing program includes a variety of media. The sections that follow discuss the advantages and disadvantages of some specific promotional vehicles.

Newspaper Advertising. Newspaper advertising has long been one of the most cost-effective ways to convey a message to the greatest number of people, but the Internet is challenging that dominance (see discussion later in this chapter). One newspaper usually dominates the coverage of a community's business and real estate, and real estate managers should prefer that paper for marketing space for rent.

Newspapers offer several methods for advertising rental space. *Classified advertising* usually appears in a special section of the newspaper and is the most common medium for announcing available rental space. Classified advertisements should be straightforward. They should identify the space, its location, the rent, and a phone number to call. Purposely omitting any of this information is not necessarily an enticement; it can dissuade prospects. Apartments, condominiums, some office space, and some small retail spaces successfully advertise in the classified section.

Display advertisements (exhibit 8.1) are larger and more expensive than classified ads. These advertisements must be attractive and well designed. They are most helpful during initial lease-up of any type of property and are very effective for inviting the public to visit a new or renovated building. When display advertisements are used, their placement on the newspaper page should be as prominent as possible.

Newspapers with large circulations periodically publish special real estate sections that include information on properties, neighborhoods, property owners, real estate brokers, developers, and managers. They often appear in a magazine or tabloid format and appeal to numerous audiences. The manager must weigh the appeal and potential success of advertising in these special sections against the added cost.

Exhibit 8.1
Sample Display Advertisement (Residential)

RIVERVIEW TERRACE APARTMENTS
Distinctive Rural Living
1500 North Main Street

- 1, 2, and 3 bedroom apartments from 800 to 2,500 square feet
- Private balconies
- Charming river views from most apartments
- Hardwood floors, wood-burning fireplaces
- European-style kitchens
- Assigned parking
- Choice location near commuter rail station
- Health club, tennis courts, and indoor swimming pool

Call 555-5555

EQUAL HOUSING
OPPORTUNITY

Other Print Media. Other print media accept display advertisements. Major cities often have one or more *apartment guides* that are distributed free of charge; many also have a commercial guide that lists available office space. Managers of office buildings can advertise in periodicals directed to specific businesses or professions. Shopping center space can be promoted in periodicals directed to general retailing audiences as well as to specific types of retailers. The purpose of these ads is to promote the property to a broad audience rather than to attract prospects to lease a specific apartment or commercial space.

Signs. Every property, whether it has vacancies or not, should display a tasteful sign that identifies the site, shows the name of the managing agent or firm, and tells where or how to obtain rental information. Those who respond to on-site signage are usually strong prospects; they have seen the property and its surroundings and are already sufficiently impressed to inquire.

Using signs to enhance the prestige of a building is productive. However, signs on the site have an understandably limited effectiveness; only people passing the property will notice the signs, and they may already know the information presented. *Billboards* announcing the location, type of space, and projected occupancy date have the advantage of reaching a

Signage

The term *signage* means the signs in and on a property. A building's signage conveys an integrated message and impression about the site. The property name and any logo or other symbol used to represent the property should appear consistently in all signage and other promotional vehicles. It should have the same typeface and logo placement to present a *unified theme*. Three types of signs comprise a property's signage: identification signs, directional signs, and informational signs.

• **Identification signs** include the permanent identification sign (*monument sign, keystone-entry sign*) showing the property's name. Freestanding signs should be designed to be part of the property's landscaping. On high-rise buildings, an engraved plaque may be coordinated with the building exterior. (For commercial properties, the addition of tenant signage to the exterior of the building—a property owner's concession to a tenant—can attract prospects, especially in overbuilt markets.) Signs placed on or above doors to indicate entrances, exits, and unit or suite numbers or special rooms (e.g., leasing office, laundry room) are other examples of identification signs.

• **Directional signs** guide visitors and tenants to their destination in the building. The building directory and signs on walls or in hallways leading to various building facilities are directional signs. Buildings that have numerous entrances may have signs directing visitors to the main entrance. Off-site directional signs lead prospects to the building and to the on-site office. Such signs contain few words and may use arrows to indicate direction.

• **Informational signs** convey messages, and while they must be used from time to time, they should be kept to an absolute minimum. Many informational signs are negative (Keep Off the Grass, Wipe Feet Before Entering). They tend to detract from the building's image, and their effectiveness is open to question. On the other hand, legal requirements mandate the posting of some types of informational signs. Examples are warning signs concerning safety (swimming pool rules, emergency procedures, fire exits). Temporary signs are occasionally necessary to warn tenants about a malfunction, a wet floor, or wet paint; however, staff should immediately remove these signs once the problem is corrected.

Even though signs do not necessarily enhance the appeal of a building, mismatched signs, handwritten signs, and signs that give commands do detract from a building's image.

wider audience. Signage is not adequate alone, however; other forms of advertising must accompany it.

Brochures. A *brochure* is usually the most detailed piece of advertising a property uses. A colorful, appealing brochure that fully describes the property and the rental space should be available as a handout to prospects who visit the property. A brochure may also be suitable for mailing to those who inquire by telephone. Brochures for residential properties should include sample floor plans; those for large shopping centers should include a plot plan, traffic statistics, and consumer demographics. Brochures for office buildings usually include photographs of the building and information about building amenities and nearby facilities, while those for shopping centers may include aerial photographs of the site and the neighborhood.

To minimize costs, before a brochure is designed, the manager should consider how long it will be in use. In particular, a design that provides for updating information on rents can make a brochure effective for several years. Additions or changes should use the same typeface as the brochure itself. Computer design software allows businesses to customize brochures quickly and to change them as needed. Computer-generated brochures also allow smaller, less expensive print runs.

Primary design elements (logo, typeface, graphics) are the most likely elements to be adapted for or used in conjunction with outdoor signs and display advertisements in newspapers and trade magazines. Brochures are often a component of direct mail campaigns, and they are most useful in promoting properties that are very large, brand new, or recently renovated.

Direct Mail. Every individual is a prospect for rental housing and most businesses are prospects for office or retail space, but not all of them will be prospects for a particular apartment, office, or store. If the legitimate prospects for a particular property can be identified, a direct-mail campaign may be profitable; but identifying prospects with any accuracy is problematic. While producing, printing, and mailing a direct-mail advertisement is costly, preparing or purchasing mailing lists is usually even more expensive. Most purchased lists are ineffective for reaching rental space users directly; however, lists of brokers who represent tenants (often called *tenant reps*) are useful for leasing office, retail, and industrial space. Because of the costs involved, direct-mail advertising is *not* a *primary* means of promoting rental real estate; but it can be effective if sent to a targeted market (e.g., all local dry cleaners within a certain radius of an available store space) and followed up with a personal contact.

Press Releases. A manager should be sure to send a press release about a newsworthy item to the business or real estate editors of local newspapers and broadcast media. Information about a new development or a property that has undergone substantial rehabilitation can lead to rental inquiries at virtually no cost. Using the following pattern will increase the chances of a press release attracting an editor's attention.

- The name and phone number of a person to contact should be at the top of the page.

- The release should be short—two pages double-spaced at most; one page is preferable.
- The pertinent information (who, what, when, where, and why) should be contained in the first paragraph.
- The subject should be a legitimate news item, not a veiled advertisement.

Today many businesses distribute press releases as e-mail messages. In fact, many publications prefer to receive releases just that way. Regardless of the method of distribution, the presentation should be clean, attractive, and free of errors.

Press releases do not replace advertisements; they will not lease space directly. However, managers and leasing agents should maximize their publicity and public relations value.

Broadcast Advertising. Real estate managers occasionally use *television* advertising to lease a new residential development or to promote tenant businesses in large shopping centers. Television advertising is extremely expensive because both production and airtime costs are high. In certain markets, cable-access channels run local advertising. The cost of the airtime is usually much lower than on network television, and the advertisement can target a specific market based on the programming of the particular channel.

Production and airtime costs for *radio* advertisements are much lower than they are for television. Radio promotion is primarily useful for residential space, although office and retail space may benefit from advertising on all-news or business stations or programs. Saturday or Sunday afternoon radio commercials may effectively direct drivers to open house showings.

The Internet. Most companies and individuals with home computers have access to the Internet, which is an increasingly popular advertising vehicle. Information about the property, including photographs, site plans, floor plans, and the contents of printed promotional materials can be presented on a *Web site*. Some property Web sites include 360° virtual tours of the rental space they offer.

A Web site can include mapping capabilities to facilitate directing prospects to a property. It can also allow prospects to send messages and receive responses via *e-mail*. (E-mail can "broadcast" messages to tenants of the property as well.) Managers should note, however, that Web page creation is a specialized skill, and keeping the information up-to-date involves ongoing costs.

Many existing Web sites offer opportunities to advertise space for lease—some charge a fee, others do not. Prospects can search these listings by geographic area, rental price, and other criteria. Commercial property listing services are available. Real estate managers and sales agents routinely list available space on the Internet, and they receive inquiries from prospects throughout the United States and around the world. Some Web sites list available apartments, both locally and nationally. They feature search functions that allow the prospect to define a location. In fact, many newspapers place their classified "for rent" ads on the Internet at no additional charge.

Locator Services and Referrals. Advertising generally attracts the largest proportion of prospective residential tenants and is therefore the major part of a marketing program. However, two methods of *prospecting* for tenants are also valuable. Because both of these services require compensation, managers must budget their use appropriately.

In major cities and many large communities, businesses exist whose sole objective is matching prospective tenants with rental spaces. These *locator services* are more common in the apartment market, and they often assist people who are relocating into the area. They provide a centralized listing of available rental space, and they usually offer their services directly to the prospect. However, the owner of the property whose space is rented pays their fee—typically a percentage of the first month's rent.

In the commercial market, leasing agents and real estate brokers provide a similar service to owners and prospective tenants. These representatives seek out prospects if they work for an owner. If they are tenant reps, they search for office, retail, or industrial spaces that meet the prospect's criteria. The broker's fee (*leasing commission*) relates to the negotiated rent. In a soft market, the owner of the leased space pays the fee. In a tight market, the tenant may have to pay the commission. Commercial brokers and leasing agents are often part of a network. (The local Commercial Board of REALTORS® provides a gathering place to exchange information.) Many have multiple-listing services and mechanisms for distributing flyers on available properties to their members. They may refer properties or prospects to other brokers if they are unable to match a commercial tenant to a particular space. In such situations, a reciprocal arrangement may be made regarding commissions if a lease is arranged.

Referrals are excellent sources of prospects for any type of property. Satisfied tenants actively discuss their satisfaction with friends and business associates, and real estate managers can encourage that by offering referral incentives. Managers must carefully evaluate the choice of the incentive to offer and its cost. A rental discount may appear to be the most attractive incentive to offer, but other incentives may be more effective, especially for a residential property. Prospects referred by residents are usually of the same caliber, and because of this, a referral based on a rental discount may be counterproductive. The most desired referrals are from residents who pay their rent on time and meet the other lease requirements, yet they may hesitate to refer their friends if they feel they are being paid for the referral. On the other hand, residents who have difficulty paying their rent are likely to take advantage of a rental discount offer, and prospects they refer may have similar difficulty paying rent. A good incentive offer is usually indirect—e.g., an improvement to the current resident's apartment, such as a new appliance or fixture, if an acceptable referral becomes a resident. The resident should be required to introduce the referral prospect to the manager in person. This will prevent any questions or conflicts over the referral source or awarding of the incentive. Before instituting a referral incentive program, the manager should investigate any legal limitations on tenant referrals or compensation for them. (Restrictions may relate to state real estate licensing requirements, and some states may prohibit monetary incentives.)

Offering Marketing Incentives

The list of incentives and concessions that an owner can offer to new tenants is endless. Incentives to lease residential space tend to center on courtesies or amenities such as free cable television, a lower security deposit, or interior decorating (paint, wallpaper)—even lottery tickets. However, the choice of incentives should not detract from the property's image or reputation.

Real estate managers also commonly offer leasing incentives to prospective tenants for office, retail, or industrial space. Upgraded tenant improvements or reimbursement of part or all of their moving costs are examples. At shopping centers, managers may grant a modified percentage rent or caps on pass-through expenses. Market conditions as well as how desirable a particular space is to a particular tenant (and vice versa) are considerations in offering such incentives.

Concessions. In areas with high vacancy and a poor economy or a large amount of new competitive space, offering a period of free rent as a marketing incentive is common. Such a marketing incentive is called a *concession*. Free rent is a costly concession for an owner to make—the reduction in NOI reduces cash flow and property value. However, if the market is poor and competitors are offering rent-free periods, the owner may have no choice but to offer such a concession.

Offering an incoming tenant a period of free rent technically reduces the amount of income derived from the rental space. However, the impact of this concession on property value and long-term income is not as great as a straightforward reduction of the rent, provided the rental space is priced competitively. When a financial concession seems necessary, the owner and the real estate manager must strive to minimize the negative effects of the concession on NOI. At the same time, the owner and the manager must

---

Exhibit 8.2

Residential Rent Concessions and Effective Rent

Assume the quoted rent for an apartment is $840 per month and the lease term is one year (12 months). The impact of one month free rent on effective rent would be as follows:

Quoted rent	$840/month
Expected effective rent	$10,080/year ($840 × 12 months)
Actual effective rent	$9,240/year ($840 × 11 months)
Average rent collected	$770/month ($9,240 ÷ 12)
Amount of rent loss	8.3% ($840 ÷ $10,080)

Note that if the quoted rent were reduced to $770 per month, the effective rent would also be $9,240 ($770 × 12 months). Either way, the loss of income is more than 8%. However, the impact of the rent reduction is greater going into the future.

Suppose greater operating expenses necessitate a rent increase of 5% in the second year of the lease. The impact of the increase in rent would be as follows:

Rent increase in second year	5%
Increase applied to original	
quoted rent	$882 ($840 × 1.05)
Effective rent for second year	$10,584 ($882 × 12)
Increase applied to reduced rent	$809 ($770 × 1.05 = $808.50 rounded to $809)[1]
Effective rent for second year	$9,708 ($809 × 12)
Second year loss (additional)	8.3% ($882 − $809 = $73 ÷ $882)

Reducing the quoted rent in the first year results in even less increased rent in the second year, an additional 8% loss of potential income. In order to increase the second year's reduced rent to the quoted rent (from $770 to $882 per month), a 14.5% increase would be necessary.

Few residents would be willing to renew their leases under such conditions. That could result in another period of vacancy, and the owner might have to offer another concession to lease the apartment again.

Because lowering quoted rent can cost so much income, prudent management of real property often includes promotion of carefully planned nonmonetary concession packages.

1. The number is rounded because rent is not quoted with cents.

---

realize that if they do not offer a concession, the damage to NOI may be more severe.

Effective Rent. To evaluate the ramifications of a rental concession accurately, real estate managers must understand the concept of effective rent. *Effective rent* is the cumulative rental amount collected over the term of a lease expressed as an average monthly rental (residential) or an annual rate per rentable square foot (office, retail, industrial). If a lease term is 12 months (more common in residential than commercial leasing), the effective rent is the total rent collected during the 12-month period. When one

Exhibit 8.3
Commercial Rent Concessions and Effective Rent

Suppose the base rent for 1,000 square feet of office (rentable area), retail (gross leasable area), or industrial space is $18.00 per square foot per year. On a three-year lease with three months' free rent, the effective rent for the lease term is calculated as follows:

1,000 sq ft × $18.00 = $18,000 annual rent × 3 years = $54,000 total rent due

$18,000 annual rent ÷ 12 = $1,500 monthly rent × 3 months = $4,500 free rent

$54,000 total rent − $4,500 free rent = $49,500 total actual effective rent
÷ 36 months = $1,375 actual effective monthly rental income

$1,500 monthly rent − $1,375 actual effective monthly rent
= $125 (more than 8% lost income)

On a square-foot basis for the three-year term, the base expected rent of $18.00 would be effectively reduced to $16.50 ($1,375 × 12 months ÷ 1,000 sq ft).

If the base rent were reduced to $16.50 per square foot instead of giving three months' free rent, the total effective rent for 36 months would still be the same: $49,500. However, if the lease were renewed for another three years at a 4% increase, the total effective rent for the new lease term would be only $51,480 ($16.50 × 1.04 × 1,000 sq ft × 3 years) as opposed to $56,160 ($18.00 × 1.04 × 1,000 sq ft × 3 years), a difference of $4,680. In order to achieve the equivalent total effective rent of $56,160 for the new lease term, the reduced rent would have to be increased 13.5% ($56,160 − $49,500 = $6,660 ÷ $49,500).

This example presents the basic method for arriving at effective rent for commercial space. However, it does not take into account the *time value of money* (a valuation concept usually applied in calculating effective rent for leases that have a term of more than one year). A calculation of effective rent incorporating the time value of money would produce a rental rate per square foot lower than the stated $16.50.

---

month's free rent is given as a concession, the effective rent is equal to only 11 months' total rent. Averaged over the entire lease term of 12 months, this total is less than the quoted rent for the space per month, even though the full quoted monthly amount is collected in each of the 11 months. However, a period of free rent is preferable to actually reducing the quoted rent because the latter may reduce the effective rent for many years, not just one. Exhibits 8.2 and 8.3 demonstrate this. The impact of lowering quoted rent is magnified when seen in the context of the whole building or property. Above all, it reduces NOI and property value.

Measuring Marketing Effectiveness

The goal of all marketing programs is to lease space by attracting as many legitimate rental prospects as possible. The effectiveness of each marketing effort (or advertisement) is measured in terms of the number of prospects

Measures of Marketing Effectiveness

- Number of prospects attracted
- Cost to reach each prospect
- Conversion ratio—prospects to signed leases
- Duration of vacancy

who come to the property, the cost to reach them, the number of prospects who become residents or commercial tenants, and the length of time the space remains vacant. The amount of advertising needed depends on the occupancy level. If the property is fully leased and no move-outs are expected, no advertising is necessary. However, most large buildings have continual turnover, and continual advertising is essential.

Location of a property has an effect on the advertising required. A prominent location may generate enough walk-in traffic at a residential property to reduce the advertising needed; less prominent properties may require significantly more promotion to achieve sufficient rental traffic. No set rule can determine how much advertising an individual property needs, but thinking of advertising as an investment underscores its monetary value. The return on this investment is finding a qualified tenant to fill a vacancy as quickly as possible.

With that in mind, the real estate manager should calculate advertising expenses in terms of the *cost per prospect.* For example, a manager spends $100 to advertise in the classified section of the newspaper to fill a vacancy in an apartment building. Because very few vacancies exist in the community, ten prospects respond to this ad, and two of them are intent on signing a lease for this $800-a-month apartment. The $100 investment certainly would be a value at a cost of $10 per prospect. The number of strongly interested prospects was two out of ten, making the prospect-to-tenant ratio five to one. This ratio is called the *conversion ratio.* The advertising cost, the selected medium, and the length of time before a new tenant is found must be evaluated in relation to the resulting conversion ratio to determine the effectiveness of a particular marketing campaign.

Managers commonly use a *traffic report* to record what attracted a prospect to visit the subject property. The example shown (exhibit 8.4) is for a residential property; a traffic report for an office building would record similar information with prospects' space needs indicated as ranges of square footages. By evaluating traffic reports, the property manager can determine the effectiveness of different marketing methods. The most effective approach is the one that produces the most prospects at the lowest cost per prospect in the least amount of time.

Another management form used to measure marketing effectiveness is

Exhibit 8.4
Sample Weekly Traffic Report (Residential)

Property _____ Week of _____ Prepared By_____

	Mon	Tue	Wed	Thu	Fri	Sat	Sun	Total
Nature of Inquiry								
Telephone call								
Visitor								
Time of inquiry								
Before noon								
Noon to 5 p.m.								
After 5 p.m.								
Referral Source								
Classified ad								
Display ad								
Billboard								
Drive-by								
Telephone directory								
Word of mouth								
Direct mail								
Television								
Radio								
Internet Web site								
Apartment locator service								
Current resident								
Prior visit								
Apartment Desired								
Studio								
One-bedroom								

(*Continued*)

Exhibit 8.4 (*concluded*)

Two-bedroom								
Three-bedroom								
Other								

Weather conditions _____

Comments _____

_____

_____

a rental inquiry or *prospect card*. The information required in the residential example (exhibit 8.5) is minimal. It might also document the prospects' parking needs and how they learned about the property as well as specific follow-up contacts and the results of the showing. As is evident in exhibit 8.6, a prospect card for a commercial property includes some financial information to qualify the business as a tenant. At a shopping center, specific information about the retailer's current operations—rent and sales per square foot, percentage rent, amount of pass-through charges—is likely to be included along with the number of stores operated and years in business.

Using Sales Techniques

The most that advertising and promotion can do is to generate prospects. Prospects become tenants only after visiting the property. The rental space may sell itself, but regardless of the condition of the available space, there is no guarantee that will happen. The person who shows the rental space must use sales techniques to try to persuade the prospect that a particular rental space is the best value to accommodate the prospect's particular needs.

Many books are available about sales techniques, and everyday life offers countless demonstrations of their effectiveness. Real estate managers and leasing agents must master three fundamentals concerning leasing:

1. Know the features of the property thoroughly.
2. Discover the needs and wants of each prospect.
3. Demonstrate how the features of the property result in benefits that meet the prospect's needs and wants.

Exhibit 8.5
Sample Prospect Card (Residential)

Name of Prospect _____

Address _____

Home Phone _____Other Phone _____

Unit Desired _____ Rent Desired $_____

Date Desired_____ Number of Occupants _____

Unit Shown _____Rent Quoted $ _____

Reason for Move _____

Follow-up Remarks _____

_____

Date Inquiry Received_____Inquiry Taken By_____

All three are critical; the last is most important of all and must go beyond the obvious. For example, if prospects who are considering an apartment mention that they have children, simply saying, "There is an elementary school in the next block," is not sufficient. The prospects probably noticed the school themselves. Instead, leasing personnel should be able to volunteer detailed information about the school. In fact, they should be thoroughly familiar with the neighborhood (shopping, transportation) so they can answer specific questions as well as describe the setting in which the property is located. A leasing agent who shows office space should be able to discuss features and businesses in the vicinity that may be of use to prospective office tenants and their employees. Examples are the proximity of business-to-business services such as attorneys, commercial banks, restaurants, health clubs, and public transportation. Information about the trade area population, traffic counts, and the competition (or lack of it) should be available for retail prospects.

Approving a Prospect for Tenancy

In the leasing effort, diligence is necessary to ensure that the prospect can and will pay the rent, care for the property, and be a cooperative tenant. Most of this *qualification* process involves financial history, but it should include other pertinent credentials as well. For residential or small commercial properties, the prospect usually supplies the information on a *rental*

Exhibit 8.6
Sample Prospect Card (Commercial)

Agent _____ Date _____

Name of Contact _____

Company Name _____

Address _____ Phone _____

Type of Business _____

Space Requirements _____ sq ft; No. of Employees _____

Date Needed _____ Rental Range $ _____ per sq ft

Location (suite or store no.) _____

Amenities Required _____ Parking _____

Other _____

Moving from? _____ Why? _____

_____

Expansion _____ Future Needs _____

Current: _____ sq ft, $ _____ per sq ft, Month or Year? _____

Banking Institutions _____

Credit Report _____ Net Worth $ _____

Indication of Interest _____ Negotiations Started _____

Date of Contact	Person Contacted	Space Shown	Rate Quoted	Comments

application form. A credit card bureau can verify information about current loans, activity on credit cards, payment history, and delinquent debts. Appropriate consumer reporting agencies, such as tenant-screening and reference-checking services, can provide other types of information, such as an applicant's rental history. Managers may ask residential prospects to pay a fee for such a credit check, and they customarily leave a *refundable* deposit to reserve the space until the credit check is complete. If the prospect is approved, the initial deposit should be applied toward the security deposit rather than the rent, and if any amount is due, the manager or leasing agent should collect the remainder of the security deposit when the lease is signed. (Under the *Fair Credit Reporting Act,* prospects who are denied a lease based on a credit report must be notified in writing of the adverse action.) A residential rental application should request the prospect's current and previous addresses so the manager can contact both property owners. The information they can provide about the prospect as their resident is not available anywhere else. To establish creditworthiness for commercial tenant prospects, the real estate manager uses the financial statements, federal tax returns, etc., for the entity legally responsible for paying the rent. (Qualification of tenants is discussed in the following chapters: chapter 9, residential; chapter 10, office; chapter 11, other commercial tenants.)

Real estate owners and managers are not responsible for implementing the Customer Identification Program of the U.S.A. PATRIOT Act. However, they should verify the applicant's identity and citizenship or immigration status because of the risk associated with renting to a terrorist and the increase in identity theft. Real estate managers routinely require photo identification in the form of a driving license, federal (green card) or state-issued identification, or a foreign passport. The tenant's file should include a copy of the identification record.

Another critical piece of information that the rental application should require is the prospect's Social Security number (SSN) or *individual tax identification number (ITIN).* Issued by the Internal Revenue Service, ITINs are available to noncitizens who need to report income for tax purposes but are not eligible for Social Security numbers. The Gramm-Leach Bliley Act, which became effective in July 2001, requires property owners and managers to safeguard personal and financial information collected from prospective tenants and to dispose of it properly to protect against misuse and identity theft.

THE LEASE DOCUMENT

The culmination of the marketing activity is a written agreement between the owner and the resident or commercial tenant. By definition, a *lease* is a contract between a property owner *(lessor)* and a tenant *(lessee)* for the use or possession of real property for a specified time in exchange for fixed payments (rent). The real estate manager may sign the lease as the agent of the owner. The contract should be in writing, and it is legally binding on both parties.

Although any agreement, even an oral one, is legal and enforceable within the bounds of applicable law, provided the intent is clear, good management practice requires a written lease. A written lease offers greater protection to both parties, and it assures the property owner that the tenant will occupy the space for a certain period and that he or she can anticipate a prescribed income for that period. In theory, no financial loss should occur because of a sudden vacancy. The tenant has possession of the space for the duration of the lease at a set rental rate. The lease may also outline procedures for rent increases. (That is more common in commercial leases that have multiyear terms.) The lease should also clearly delineate the property owner's and tenant's responsibilities.

The lease should reduce or eliminate misunderstandings between the owner and the tenant, so both of them must understand its provisions. The real estate manager or the leasing agent should ask new tenants whether they have read and understood the lease. Any unclear provisions should be explained at that time.

The manager should use a lease form that is reasonable, standardized, and suitable for all tenants. As a matter of goodwill, the lease form should not contain clauses to which informed people will object or that uninformed people will ignore. When properly prepared and presented with equal emphasis on the tenant's point of view, the lease has excellent marketing value.

Fundamental Elements of Leases

Numerous leases are suited to different types of rental space, but all leases should describe the *demised premises* (the leased space that is conveyed from the owner to the tenant) and state the duration of the agreement, the amount of rent, and when and how payment is to be made. The following are the principal contents of a lease.

- *The parties.* The full legal names of the property owner and tenant, both of whom must sign the lease to validate it.

- *Description of the leased premises.* The apartment number and address of the building for residential units; the amount of space (square feet), location in the building (suite or store number), and street address for offices, stores, and other commercial space. Often a legal description or a floor plan augments the description.

- *Lease term.* The duration of the lease (including the starting and ending dates) and any specific provisions relating to renewal or can-

---

Components of a Lease

- Parties to the lease (property owner, tenant)
- Description of the leased premises
- Term of the lease (including commencement and termination dates)
- Rent and additional payments (if any)
- Use of the premises
- Tenant's obligations and rights
- Owner's rights and obligations

In commercial leases, compensation to the property owner (rent) often includes pass-through charges. For retail tenants, the property owner's compensation often includes percentage rent. Separate provisions detail such charges.

---

cellation. If commercial leases involve construction (or free rent), they may show separate dates for occupancy and for the first rent payment.

- *Rent.* The amount of rent for each period and the date it is due. Rent is usually monthly and is due on the first of the month. The lease may state the aggregate rent for the entire lease term (most commonly in commercial leases) to indicate the full financial obligation. Commercial leases often include provisions for rent increases, especially when their duration exceeds one year. Nonpayment of rent is cause for termination of the lease.

- *Use of the premises.* Inherent in the lease agreement is a specific use of the space (living quarters, a business office, an apparel store), and any other use may be cause for termination of the lease.

- *Other provisions.* Leases usually include lengthy clauses that detail the rights and obligations of the parties with respect to their relationship to each other (as property owner and tenant) and to the property. Of particular concern are the responsibilities to pay specific utilities (residential) or increases in operating costs (commercial) and to maintain the property. The lease also states the amount and condition for return of any required security deposit.

Types of Leases

The type of lease depends on the kind of property. There are three basic types of leases. The first is a *gross lease,* under which the tenant pays a fixed rent and the owner pays all of the operating expenses of the property, including property taxes and insurance. The common residential lease is a form of gross lease. Residents are usually responsible for utilities *inside* their apartments.

The second type of lease is a *net lease,* under which the tenant not only pays rent but also assumes responsibility for certain expenses connected with the property as a whole. Net leases are used primarily for space in large office buildings, shopping centers, and industrial properties that rent for longer terms. Net leases generally prorate itemized pass-through expenses based on the amount of space the tenant occupies as a percentage of the total leasable space in the building. (See chapters 10 and 11 for further discussion of net leases.)

A third type of lease, the *percentage lease,* is sometimes used for retail properties. Under a percentage lease, the rent is a percentage of the tenant's gross sales made on the premises. The lease usually states a fixed minimum rent, and the tenant pays a percentage of its gross sales in excess of that amount, depending on the volume of business.

COLLECTION POLICIES

Effective real estate management requires collecting rent and other amounts due from tenants. Traditionally, renters have paid in cash or by check or money order. Recently, the convenience of paying with credit or debit cards or direct electronic funds transfer (using online or telephone authorizations) is overtaking these methods as electronic payment systems become more readily available. For the real estate management firm, such payment methods offer the benefit of quick verification of money transfer and predictable cash flow.

Rental Collection

As with all other aspects of tenant relations, tact, diplomacy, and goodwill are essential to the collections process, but the manager must also be firm in requiring payment of rent on the date it is due. The real estate manager pays operating costs, taxes, and other property expenses out of the rental income, and expenses accumulate daily. Timely collection of rents is imperative for timely payment of the property's bills. In addition, some portion of the manager's compensation is usually a percentage of the total rent collected, and any decline in that amount reduces the manager's income. These two concerns—operating expenses and personal compensation—are the manager's incentives to collect the full amount of rent on time.

Rent Due Date. The advance payment of rent is an accepted practice. (Leases with federal agencies are exceptions. The federal government always pays one month in arrears.) Monthly rents are usually due on the first day of each month, although some are due on the lease date. (For example, if the lease is signed on the 19th of the month, the rent is likewise due on the 19th unless the lease provides otherwise.) To streamline accounting, rent collections, and payment of the property's expenses, all leases should have rent due on the same date. To accomplish this effectively, the manager should prorate the first month's rent for tenants who do not take possession on the first of a month.

Most tenants pay their rent on the date it is due, but inevitably, some will be late. Three significant reasons for not tolerating any delay in rent payments follow.

1. Rent is one of most tenants' largest expenses, and each day's delay increases the chances that the tenant will not pay the whole amount for that month.

2. Acceptance of a partial payment increases the tenant's obligation in the following month, and the tenant's financial situation may not improve.

3. Most leases require payment in full on the first, and habitually accepting late payments may compromise the property owner's right to require timely payment and to evict a tenant for nonpayment.

Late Fee. Some managers and owners state that they expect payment in full by the first of the month, and they impose *late fees* as a reinforcement of their policy. Late fees may be a residual source of income for management, but the delay in receiving the rent and accounting for the fees tend to cancel any expected benefit. A small late fee actually encourages late payment because such a policy has an inherent grace period associated with it. For example, if management imposes an extra charge for payments received on the sixth of the month or later, the tenant has no compelling reason to pay the rent until the fifth. If late fees are used, they should be large enough to encourage prompt payment. Some municipalities limit the maximum late fee that a property owner can charge on residential rent, and this must be a consideration as well.

Back rent is a debt, and collection of back rent is subject to the requirements of the Fair Debt Collection Practices Act. Statutes always control delinquency, collection, and eviction rights and procedures. The real estate manager must be familiar with and understand the laws and the practices that govern these matters. Local law may be more favorable to residents and commercial tenants than to property owners, and the laws in nearby municipalities may differ from each other.

Delinquency. The manager should encourage payment on the first day of each month. That policy justifies distributing notices of delinquency very early in the month, followed by a personal contact soon thereafter if payment is not received.

Collection System. All residents and commercial tenants should have a clear understanding of the rental collection policy before they move in, including the actions the real estate manager will take in case of delinquency. However, the manager must be careful not to compromise any of the owner's legal rights by presenting a policy that is more lenient than the law requires. The manager can explain the policy in a firm manner that does not jeopardize the extension of goodwill toward the tenant.

Some property owners fear that aggressive pursuit of rent will result in vacancies. They hesitate even more when the market is declining and vacancy in general is high. During these periods, managers sometimes tolerate substantial rent delinquencies rather than take action to collect the rent or evict the delinquent tenant. However, a vacant unit is less costly than one that is occupied by a delinquent tenant—when a space is vacant, it is less likely to incur damage, and utility costs will be lower. More important, the vacancy allows the manager to find a new tenant who will pay rent.

Even though the great majority of residents and commercial tenants pay their rent when it is due, the few who do not will be responsible for the majority of the time the manager must devote to collections. The effectiveness of a collection procedure depends on the diligence of the people in control of it.

A series of forms is the basis of a good collection system. A notice should be delivered to the resident or commercial tenant on the first day the rent is delinquent. This notice should be a strongly worded but friendly reminder. The check may be delayed in the mail, so the reminder notice should simply state that the rent has not been received and ask the tenant to contact the office about the matter. Personal contact by the manager is also appropriate at this point.

Eviction. If the resident or commercial tenant does not respond to the reminder notice and the rent is still delinquent, the next step is to send or serve an eviction notice or such other notice as state or local law may require to initiate eviction.

Eviction is ejection of a tenant from the leased premises by the property owner. It is a drastic measure. It can result in the forcible removal of the tenant's possessions from the premises if the tenant refuses to move out. State laws governing eviction vary widely, but most provide for the property owners or their attorneys to serve eviction notices or notices to cure a lease violation within a specified period. Municipalities frequently have laws concerning evictions and tenants' rights as well.

Eviction Notice. This notice should be a demand that the tenant pay the rent within a specified period or vacate the premises within that same pe-

Bankruptcy

Residents' and commercial tenants' ability to pay rent in full and on time may be compromised in a down economy or when an individual or a company experiences financial difficulties. Sometimes a situation deteriorates to the point that an individual or a company declares bankruptcy. In a commercial property, a tenant's bankruptcy can have a greater impact because of the longer lease terms. In retail properties, the shopping center's tenant mix and the amount of percentage rent payable under the lease are additional considerations.

Leases commonly include a provision that protects the owner from a resident's or commercial tenant's bankruptcy and debt reorganization. The 2005 Federal Bankruptcy Act changed many provisions of the previous bankruptcy laws. To protect the property owner and ensure compliance with applicable laws, the owner or manager should have an attorney who is familiar with the new bankruptcy law draft a bankruptcy lease provision.

riod. State and/or local laws prescribe the time allowed, the form, and the content of the notice. If the law permits a late fee, the notice should state that amount.

By law, such a notice may automatically terminate the lease, so the manager must understand its effect. In some states, an owner may accept a partial payment of the amount due without compromising the notice or the owner's right to bring suit for the whole amount of the delinquency. Managers should be aware, however, that in some jurisdictions accepting a partial rent payment may preclude collection of the total amount that is in arrears. Because an error can lead to the owner's or the manager's liability to a tenant, they must consult an attorney to determine the requirements of state and local law.

Eviction Proceedings. If a tenant refuses to pay all the delinquent rent specified in the notice or violates the lease in some other way and fails to cease or cure the violation within an allotted period, the manager can initiate eviction proceedings. (The management agreement should expressly grant the manager discretion to evict tenants or specify a procedure for obtaining the owner's approval. The manager should not begin an eviction without the owner's approval.)

In the case of *nonpayment,* if the tenant has not responded to the demand for payment within the time allowed, the manager must file a complaint with the court. The complaint prompts the court to issue a summons to appear in court, and that document is served on the tenant with the complaint. A third party, such as a sheriff or private process server, delivers the summons. If the summons and complaint cannot be delivered personally to an occupant, state or local laws will specify alternate procedures, which *must be followed exactly.* Sometimes a notice may be affixed face-up on the front door of the premises or in another conspicuous place. Some jurisdictions allow for substituted service upon another occupant of the premises, even a minor.

The complete form usually includes an affidavit of service (a sworn statement that the notice has been properly served), which the process server completes. This affidavit is then presented in court. The form must be completed and delivered *exactly* as stipulated by the legal procedures specified in it and by state and local law or court rule, or it may be ruled invalid.

The real estate manager should review the property's internal policy for serving the eviction notice to ensure that the notice is served impartially. Any procedural inconsistency may permit the tenant to avoid the eviction (necessitating a complete restart of the process) or leave the tenant with a claim for a countersuit. The tenant should not be harassed, intimidated, or denied access to or use of the rental unit or specific services; such actions can also be cause for a countersuit.

In court, the judge may give the tenant an opportunity to pay the rent. State or local law determines whether the property owner has a legal obligation to accept the rent. However, if the tenant offers to pay, the judge may direct the owner to accept payment. If the tenant cannot pay, the judge will usually render a decision or award judgment in favor of the owner—for possession, for rent due, and (possibly) for court costs. As part of the judgment, the tenant will be given a date by which to vacate the premises. If the tenant does not yield the space by that date, state and local law dictate further procedures.

Eviction Types.   Eviction is the result of a resident's or commercial tenant's failure to perform under the lease *(for cause)*. The two types of causes are monetary (nonpayment of rent) and nonmonetary (breach of a lease covenant). Examples of the latter are keeping a pet when the lease stipulates that no pets are allowed (residential) and light manufacturing in space leased for use as offices (commercial). In addition, the property owner may terminate a tenancy without stating a cause if the tenant has a month-to-month lease (this is a *no-cause action,* not an eviction). The real estate manager must understand the differences between the two types of evictions and the owner's right to terminate a month-to-month lease because they involve different procedures.

Eviction can be expensive, although the real estate manager may be able to negotiate a reasonable fee with an attorney who specializes in evictions. Even in the best circumstances, eviction may require months to complete. Winning an eviction for cause (other than nonpayment of rent) in court is particularly difficult unless a felony is involved.

The best way for a real estate manager to minimize the need for eviction is to be diligent in selecting tenants, perform credit checks, and verify credentials for all prospects before they sign leases. Although the staff of a property must be diligent and prompt in taking action when rent is late or if tenants fail to respect any section of the lease, the most effective means of maintaining harmony on the property is to give tenants the respect they deserve. If the property owner, the manager, and the staff treat residents and commercial tenants properly and professionally, give them prompt service, and respect their privacy, the great majority will faithfully observe the requirements of the lease.

Security Deposits

In addition to rent payments, most residential and commercial leases require a *security deposit* that the resident or commercial tenant pays in advance and the property owner holds as a guarantee to ensure the tenant's performance under the lease. The amount of the security deposit is often equivalent to one month's rent, although it can be any amount. Managers should not permit tenants to apply the security deposit to the last month's rent; if damage occurs to the premises, the deposit will not cover both repair expenses and the rent. The deposit must be large enough to be an incentive to the tenant to take care of the premises, but that does not always necessitate the equivalent of one month's rent. On the other hand, a leased residence that includes furnishings has greater potential for damage and warrants a larger security deposit.

If the tenant fulfills all the obligations of the lease, the real estate manager must return the security deposit within a reasonable amount of time after the tenant moves. State statute and/or local ordinance often dictate that period. However, the manager should hold the deposit until damage charges can be itemized and deducted. The manager should do this quickly so the space can be made market-ready right away. If feasible, the real estate manager should inspect the unit in the tenant's presence on the last day of the lease to explain the need for damage or cleaning charges. (Chapter 5 discusses financial management of security deposits.)

RETAINING TENANTS

The most important element in keeping tenants satisfied with their choice of rental space is to let them know that their business is valued. Thinking of and treating tenants as customers, rather than simply rent-payers, fosters the notion that they are valued. Rent is usually a major expense for tenants, and for that, they expect the components of the building to operate properly and efficiently and the property as a whole to be pleasant, comfortable, and secure.

Building a business relationship with residents or commercial tenants requires months or even years, especially if the manager is new to the site and some of the tenants have been there for several years. Any dissatisfaction with the previous manager or management firm must be dispelled. Tenant dissatisfaction can be very damaging in terms of current occupancy and the property's reputation into the future. The real estate manager can rectify legitimate concerns such as deficiencies in service, however, regaining the respect of the tenants may be extremely difficult if service was substandard for a long time.

Welcoming New Tenants

A real estate manager's efforts to retain tenants begin before they move in. Between the time that one residential tenant vacates a unit and another moves in, the property staff should inspect the premises to make sure all components are operating and are properly installed. Thorough inspection and repair at this time will avert dissatisfaction on the part of the incoming resident. If a repair cannot be completed until after move-in, the manager should tell the new resident approximately when the task will be finished. Commercial property owners may lease vacant space "as is," or they may completely gut the space to allow for new tenant improvement construction.

Incoming residents and commercial tenants should receive a handbook that outlines the rules and regulations of tenancy as well as a list of important names and phone numbers. The handbook should define emergencies and nonemergencies. Management and staff of residential properties in particular may receive calls at any time of day or night unless guidelines are provided. Although a resident should never be dissuaded from calling about a problem, he or she should be able to distinguish a repair that can wait from one that is a true emergency.

Handling Requests

Residents and commercial tenants at times request improved services or products. The real estate manager and the staff must deal with all requests respectfully, conscientiously, and promptly. They should not consider requests as complaints. Although some tenants may think the motto, "The customer is always right," grants them the privilege to make outrageous requests or demands, most understand the limitations involved in operating a property. All requests should receive a response as quickly as possible. However, requests that are particularly complex may require research, and the manager should advise the tenant of that fact and when an answer may be expected. Not all requests can be granted, and delaying a negative response (saying someone else must make the decision or that the request is still under consideration) may be tempting. Saying "no" is never easy, but delivering bad news as quickly as good news will gain the confidence of most tenants. Tenants are typically more concerned about receiving an honest response than about having a problem corrected immediately. They would much prefer a forthright estimate of when a problem will be corrected to a promise that will not be kept.

Building Goodwill

Every communication with tenants is an opportunity to build goodwill. Special events sponsored by the property's management (e.g., a picnic or outing for a "tenant appreciation day") can build morale. Residential and commercial properties can use newsletters effectively to update tenants about events on or near the site or to provide other information that pertains to all building occupants.

Yet another retention strategy is to perform housekeeping tasks as tenants are entering or leaving the building so they can see *what the management does for them*. Seeing the work in progress, as well as the results, tends to make that work more valuable to the tenant. *Visibility adds value.*

Real estate managers can also employ customer service strategies to retain tenants. They can use written questionnaires, send e-mails, or place telephone calls (and make written notes) to find out whether service requests have been handled promptly and satisfactorily—and ask if any additional service is needed. Managers can use exit surveys to find out why tenants move out and ask them what improvements to their leased premises, the building itself, or the property's amenities might have encouraged them to stay. Asking about the rent structure and the value they received is also a good idea.

LEASE RENEWAL TECHNIQUES

Lease renewals are very important in the overall economics of property performance. Renewing the lease of an existing tenant is usually more profitable than finding a new tenant for the space for several reasons.

- Renewal eliminates the rent loss that occurs when a new tenant does not move in as soon as the current tenant moves out.

- The expense of finding a new tenant (marketing the space) is saved.

- The cost of improvements related to a renewal is usually less than the cost of preparing the space for a new tenant.

- The current tenant is a known quantity (payment history, level of respect for the property and the other tenants), and evaluating prospects entails the investment of time and money.

Only tenants who are satisfied with the property and the service they receive will renew their leases. In this regard, every contact with the tenant is an indirect renewal effort. Some reasons for not renewing a lease are beyond a manager's control; but if the tenant is under no pressure to move, renewal of a lease is a reasonable expectation. However, market conditions usually change during the lease term, rents may go up or down, and vacancy may increase or decrease. Lease expiration usually requires negotiating new lease terms unless the lease that is expiring contains an *option to renew* that already has specified terms and conditions of renewal. The starting point of negotiations may be whether the parties are willing to renew the lease, and the conclusion may be whether the proposed terms are acceptable. The following are principal bargaining points:

- The amount of any rent increase
- The length of the new lease term
- The extent of repairs, service, and rehabilitation that are conditions of renewal

Both parties usually expect the rent to increase, but the exact amount may be subject to negotiation, depending on market conditions. Renewal terms are more likely to be negotiated for commercial leases, and the negotiations may be as comprehensive as for a new lease.

To facilitate lease renewals, the real estate manager must perform two basic administrative tasks. First, the manager should use the property's rent roll to generate a list of all tenants' lease expiration dates. He or she should update the list monthly to show renewal progress. Second, the manager should prepare and mail a letter to tenants whose leases are about to expire. The timing of renewal negotiations should be adequate for tenants to make their decisions and for the manager to find replacements for those who decide to move. For residential tenants, managers usually mail renewal notices 60 to 90 days in advance of lease expiration; for commercial tenants with long-term leases, renewal negotiations may begin a year or more in advance.

SUMMARY

Throughout the cycle of tenancy, a real estate manager's dedication to goodwill is essential for the property to thrive. The manager must examine the property and its potential tenants to estimate the size and nature of the market and to plan a marketing strategy. By persuasively matching the qualities of the property with the prospect's expressed needs and wants, the manager (or leasing agent) attempts to convert the prospect into a tenant. If the prospective tenant's credentials are acceptable, a written lease is executed to protect both parties to the agreement.

One of the most important aspects of tenant relations is the collection of deposits and rent. In enforcing collection policies, the manager must treat all residents and commercial tenants fairly. To meet the expectations of the owner, the manager must firmly uphold the policy on when rent is due. If the tenant is unable or unwilling to pay, or if some other serious infraction of the lease occurs, the manager must start eviction proceedings.

Real estate managers play an essential role in the retention of tenants. Tenants' requests for repairs and services should be handled conscientiously and impartially to provide the tenants with the best possible service. Throughout each phase of the cycle of tenancy, how the manager and the staff treat the tenants has a strong bearing on lease renewals. The manager should regard lease renewal as an expression of goodwill toward the tenant and a part of the sound economic operation of the property.

9

Managing
Residential Property

Residential property offers some of the greatest opportunities in real estate management because of the diversity and number of properties involved. In the public's perception, rental apartments are most commonly associated with professional management, and apartments come in a wide variety of sizes and configurations. One primary difference that managers face in managing rental housing is whether it is a conventional site (a market-based operation) or government-assisted (residents or owners may receive some form of financial assistance that affects policies or procedures). Management of all types of rental housing requires that the manager select qualified residents and enforce lease terms. In addition to rental apartments, professional real estate managers also provide services to common interest realty associations (condominiums, cooperatives, and planned unit developments), rented single-family homes, manufactured housing communities (mobile home parks), and specially designed housing for the elderly. This diversity creates numerous challenges and opportunities for real estate managers who specialize in residential management.

RENTAL HOUSING

Rental housing ranges from apartments of various sizes in high-rise buildings to single-family homes. Unlike commercial property, rental housing is in use 24 hours a day and must meet all of the housing needs of the residents' daily lives. This continuous occupancy tends to increase the demand for

---

Professionally Managed Housing

- Apartment buildings
- Government-assisted housing
- Common interest realty associations (CIRAs)
  — Condominiums
  — Cooperatives
  — Planned unit developments (PUDs)
- Single-family homes
- Manufactured housing (mobile home parks)
- Housing for the elderly

---

maintenance and repair. When people rent housing, they expect that management will provide specific services such as yard work, window cleaning, and snow removal. If service lapses for any reason, the manager of the property may become the personification of the problem in the resident's mind. This is unavoidable at times, and it is not necessarily a reflection on the ability of the real estate manager or the quality of service. Because residents consider where they live their home, they have an emotional as well as a monetary investment in their dwelling. Therefore, managers of residential property must have superior people skills in addition to proficiency in the administrative functions of the profession. Because the rental income of the property is usually the basis for managers' compensation, their efforts focus on maintaining the highest levels of occupancy. Satisfied residents are likely to want to renew their leases.

Management of residential property requires specific applications of the principles of real estate management already outlined in this book. The personal nature of the use of the leased space places special demands on the property's staff. The following sections discuss characteristics of rental housing that make its management unique.

Apartments

Technological advances have changed the concept, design, size, and features of apartment buildings. At one time, a prospective resident could tour numerous apartments of about the same size and never see the same floor plan twice. Newer apartments usually have more standardized floor plans; variety appears in the types of amenities built into the individual units and the building or the property as a whole. Although new buildings are generally more popular with renters, a fair portion of the rental population seeks "vintage" property, especially in urban areas. Location, size, age, and amenities make every apartment building unique. The special challenge of

managing apartments is to recognize and accentuate the positive characteristics of the individual property. This creates a more pleasant residence and
helps enhance the property's value.

Apartment Types.   *High-rise apartment buildings* are popular in major
cities where land is at a premium and intensive use of the land is a necessity. The minimum number of stories that constitute a high-rise apartment
building varies by region, but most buildings that are 10 stories and taller
are classified as such. The largest high-rise apartment buildings can contain
hundreds of apartments and house thousands of residents. These buildings
may have a variety of recreational amenities such as fitness centers, tennis
courts, swimming pools, saunas, and hot tubs. The availability of parking
on decks or in underground garages connected to the building may be another amenity, although the number of parking spaces allotted per resident
or apartment may be limited and a separate monthly rent may be charged.
A high-rise apartment building may warrant a continuously staffed "front
desk," or it may have all-night attendants on duty when the on-site office is
closed. Large high-rise apartment buildings may also include retail space on
the ground floor for convenience stores or newsstands.

A type of multiple-unit development that exists in both cities and suburbs is the *mid-rise apartment building*. These buildings have between
four and nine stories, and they may include recreational facilities. A central
lobby and mailroom are standard. Mid-rise apartment buildings in urban
areas usually do not provide parking, but their counterparts in small cities
and suburban areas usually have parking available. Most buildings that are
four or more stories have elevators, although older four-story apartment
buildings may have stairs only. Such a building is often referred to as a
walk-up.

Garden apartments are often located in suburban areas where land is
comparatively less expensive. Garden apartment communities may occupy
several acres and consist of numerous *low-rise buildings* of one to three
stories. Each building may have as few as four apartments. A separate building may house laundry facilities, the management office, or recreational
amenities. Such amenities are often comparable to those in high-rise apartment buildings. Part of the attraction of suburban garden apartments is their
appealing landscapes.

Traditional smaller properties with 2 to 12 units are also popular. Most
of these buildings do not have elevator service and consequently are rarely
more than three stories. Many of them have been rehabilitated, particularly
in urban areas. Even though these small properties do not provide the
recreational amenities found in other types of apartment buildings, they
generally offer greater privacy along with the conveniences most apartment
dwellers expect in return for rent.

Apartment Management.   The architectural design and the size of multiple-unit apartment developments directly affect the complexity of managing them. For instance, high-rise apartment buildings include sophisticated
elevators, centralized HVAC equipment, and other systems that require
specialized maintenance. Large garden complexes offer a different set of
management challenges because they have more spacious lawns and separate systems and equipment in each of several buildings. Small apartment
buildings usually provide few extra services and facilities and consequently
are less management-intensive. However, those structures are usually older,
and their general maintenance may be time-consuming. Older structures
usually require a greater amount of work per apartment as well.

In addition to the physical upkeep that apartment buildings require,
the number of properties in a manager's portfolio influences administrative
time. The preparation of an operations report on 300 apartments may be a
relatively light exercise if all the units are in one building owned by a sole
proprietor. On the other hand, 300 apartments in thirty individually owned
10-unit buildings will require more involved reporting.

Government-Assisted Housing

Government-assisted housing is defined as any residential rental property
in which the property owner receives part of the rent payment from a governmental body. *Public housing,* on the other hand, is generally owned and
managed through a local or state governmental agency. As a rule, governmental housing subsidies are either resident based or property based.

Private investors usually own rental property in which a subsidy is
provided. The common forms of real estate ownership (partnerships, corporations, REITs) also apply to subsidized housing, and the owners' desire
for a fair return on their investment is the same as in conventional housing.
However, a portion of the return on investment in subsidized housing may
result from additional tax advantages granted for development, for leasing
part of the property to residents eligible for housing subsidies, or for leasing
to the local housing authority. Lower debt service payments due to special
loan arrangements can also increase the return so that the investment is
competitive with conventional housing. Another common arrangement is
for the developers and investors to build the complex and sell it to the
housing authority or to a nonprofit (religious or charitable) organization that
specializes in subsidized housing.

The Housing and Community Development Act of 1974 authorized the
Housing Assistance Payments Program commonly referred to as the *Section
8 Housing Choice Voucher Program.* The program provides rental assistance
nationwide to low-income families and elderly and disabled individuals.
Public housing agencies (PHAs), which receive funds from the U.S. Depart-

ment of Housing and Urban Development (HUD), locally administer housing choice vouchers.

Resident-Based Rental Assistance.   The individual or family who receives a housing voucher is responsible for finding a suitable housing unit. The PHA pays the subsidy directly to the property owner on behalf of the participating renter. The renter then pays the difference between the amount subsidized by the program and the actual rent charged by the owner (usually limited to 30 percent of the renter's adjusted monthly income). The voucher program also has provisions that outline resident and owner responsibilities. In addition to the traditional resident screening by property owners, HUD permits PHAs to screen applicants for assistance.

A PHA may choose to use up to 20 percent of its voucher funding to implement a project-based voucher program to provide rental assistance for eligible families who live in specific housing developments or units. After one year of assistance, a family may move from a project-based voucher unit and switch to the PHA's tenant-based voucher program when the next voucher is available. A PHA may commit to pay project-based assistance for a term of up to 10 years, subject to availability of funding from HUD.

Project-Based Rental Assistance.   Section 8 *Project-Based Rental Assistance* is also available directly from HUD. Under this program, HUD makes up the difference between the rent a low- or very low-income household can afford and the approved rent for an adequate housing unit in a multifamily project. Eligible renters pay rent based on their income. HUD originally provided such project-based assistance in connection with new construction or substantial rehabilitation of existing structures. However, the government repealed those programs in 1983. While funding is no longer available for new commitments, units previously approved under long-term contracts (20 to 40 years) may continue to receive subsidies.

In addition to these Section 8 programs, many other federal housing programs exist. In most cases, they are available to a particular segment of the population. For example, the *Section 202* and *Section 811* programs cover supportive housing for the elderly and the disabled, respectively. The U.S. Department of Agriculture, Rural Development, administers other housing programs, including rental assistance.

Federal housing programs are often subject to the availability of funds, and the government may modify requirements for participation (by property owners and low-income residents) from time to time. Sometimes a program is discontinued, as noted above, but aspects of it do not change immediately because of the long-term commitments involved.

Subsidized Housing Management.   The need for effective management of subsidized and public housing creates a demand for real estate managers who are skilled in balancing the interests of all the parties involved—owners, governmental agencies, residents who receive subsidies, residents who do not, citizens' action groups, and resident (tenant) associations. In addition to understanding the principles of real estate management, managers of subsidized housing must thoroughly understand all applicable regulations. (For example, residents of subsidized housing must be recertified periodically to continue to receive housing benefits.) These managers must also understand the role and structure of the governmental agencies involved, and they must work within budgets that are limited because of lower rental income. Under most federal, state, and local housing programs, the real estate manager must submit an extensive series of forms and reports. Completing these reports is often time-consuming. If the manager completes the reports improperly, he or she may have to correct the reports before the governmental agency will send compensation.

Real estate managers who work with public or government-assisted housing often think of themselves as a special breed. Their specialization extends beyond the ability to work with governmental agencies. Interactions with residents are often more demanding than in other professionally managed housing because the objective of assuring resident comfort has additional social, political, and fiscal dimensions. In subsidized housing, the manager must establish lines of communication to overcome a multitude of barriers—ethnic, economic, social, and linguistic. In addition to maintaining peaceful coexistence at the property, the improved relations that result from the manager's efforts help the community and society.

Selecting Qualified Residents

One of a residential manager's most important responsibilities is qualifying prospects for residency. Before agreeing to establish a lease, the manager must obtain certain information about a prospect.

- Does the prospect have sufficient resources to pay the rent and his or her existing financial obligations?
- Will the prospect pay the rent on time?
- Will the prospect respect the privacy and property of others?
- Will the prospect maintain the rental space?

The prospective resident usually provides the answers to these questions on a *rental application form* (exhibit 9.1 outlines information guidelines). With the exception of the financial data, verifying some of this information may be difficult. The amount of information that is actually validated may be left to the discretion of the manager. In particular, inquiries pertaining to prospective residents' behavior must be made cautiously and without any bias; a decision that can be perceived as discriminatory can lead to liability.

Exhibit 9.1

Information Commonly Requested on an Apartment Rental Application Form

Property/Lease Information
- The space to be rented (street address and apartment number)
- Rental rate (dollars per month)
- Duration of the lease term (if applicant approved)
- Amount of security deposit

Applicant Personal Information
- Name and Social Security number—or federal individual tax identification number (ITIN)—of principal applicant (and all adults who will sign the lease)
- Name(s) of all other occupants, including minor children
- Description(s) of any pets (if allowed)

Applicant Residency Information
- *Current* address and phone number
- Name and phone number of current property owner; address (if different from applicant's)
- Duration of current tenancy
- Reason for leaving
- The same information for *prior* residence

Applicant Employment Information
- *Current* place of employment (company name, address, and phone number), job title, years with the company, immediate supervisor(s), and salary
- Same information for *prior* employer

Applicant Financial Status
- Institution names and account numbers for bank savings and checking accounts, credit cards or charge accounts, automobile and other outstanding loans

Other Information
- Identification of any requisite deposits or fees to be paid at the time the application is completed (e.g., for processing the credit check) and their refundability
- A statement of authenticity of all information provided and authorization to verify it (including credit and criminal background checks)
- Applicant signature
- Spaces for initials of staff who process the application and the date

A standardized rental application form ensures the uniformity of information requested from each applicant, avoids the possibility of discrimination, and facilitates verification of the data for a rental decision.

Of utmost importance in the selection of residents is an understanding of local, state, and federal fair housing laws.

Fair Housing Ground Rules. The federal *Fair Housing Act of 1968* (Title VIII, Civil Rights Act of 1968) prohibits housing discrimination on the basis of race, color, religion, and national origin; a 1974 amendment added sex as a *protected class*. *The Fair Housing Amendments Act of 1988* further prohibits discrimination based on *familial status* (children) or mental or physical *handicap*. It is unlawful to refuse or to fail to show an apartment, to supply rental information (e.g., rates), or to rent an apartment because of an applicant's protected status. It is also unlawful to impose different terms or conditions (e.g., security deposit amounts) or extend different privileges in regard to the rental of an apartment or to discriminate in selecting or qualifying applicants or in providing services based on a resident's protected class (except for the provision of reasonable accommodations for individuals with disabilities).

Interpretation of fair housing laws has been very strict, partly because very few people overtly say to a prospective renter, "I will not rent this apartment to you because. . . ." Even an unwitting breach of the law can result in a discrimination lawsuit, an event that can end a career and result in a substantial monetary fine. One of the most common discriminatory practices involves a prospect who inquires about available property and is dissuaded from living at a particular site or encouraged to look elsewhere. This is called *steering*. An applicant from whom some vacancies are hidden is also a victim of steering.

The number of people allowed to reside in an apartment is yet another area in which prospects may claim discriminatory practices. Occupancy standards vary by state and local jurisdiction. Apartment managers should check their state landlord-tenant law and local ordinances before establishing specific occupancy standards or guidelines. Consultation with an attorney is advisable to ensure that any guidelines followed are in compliance with existing laws.

The intent of fair housing laws is to give every prospective resident an *equal opportunity* to live where he or she desires. To uphold the spirit of this law, management must maintain consistency in all phases of relationships with prospects and residents. To maintain such consistency, all employees who interview prospects at the property or at the management firm should receive thorough training in this subject, and all policies should be clearly stated in writing. For example, if income level compared to rent is an important selection criterion, the formula to calculate the ratio should be standardized, documented, and applied to all applicants consistently. Fair housing law also applies to marketing materials. Advertisements must not include words or images that would indicate or imply any limitations or preferences in the rental of apartments (or sale or other transactions related to housing). Some state and local jurisdictions may publish lists of words that rental advertisements may *not* use.

Fair housing laws are subject to change, particularly as states and local jurisdictions enact their own rules and courts adjudicate discrimination lawsuits. Local requirements are often more stringent—they may include additional protected classes (e.g., sexual orientation)—and the most stringent law that is in place locally is the one that applies. Consultation with an attorney and reading on the subject of fair housing are two ways to remain informed on these important laws.

Rent-Paying Ability. A prospect's past payment record, sources and amount of income, and level of indebtedness are the main considerations in determining rent-paying ability. The amount of rent as a percentage of the individual's income is not by itself a definitive indicator of an individual's ability to pay rent. The size of a household and the number of its members who are employed affect the amount of money available for rent.

Most occupants of rental housing in the United States pay their rent from current income. Use of reserves or proceeds from financial investments is not common. The resident who loses a job may soon be unable to pay the rent because he or she does not have enough cash in reserve to meet living costs for an extended period. Housing may be essential, but in times of financial difficulty, other essentials such as food, clothing, and transportation may take precedence over rent payment.

Income Sources. Examining prospective residents' sources of income to verify their ability to pay rent is fair and necessary. Factors to consider are the length of time that a worker has been in a position with a company, the amount of income and frequency with which it is paid, and the nature of the employer's business. Individually, these factors may not qualify or disqualify a prospect, but taken together they can be a good indicator of personal financial strength.

- *Duration of employment.* The longer someone has been in a position, the more likely it is that employer and employee are mutually satisfied with each other's performance, which increases the probability of the prospect's job security.

- *Amount of income.* Although a real estate manager can use the amount of rent as a percentage of income to estimate the prospect's ability to pay the rent, that is not the only deciding factor. In addition to wages or salary, the manager should ask the prospect about other financial resources.

- *Frequency of payment.* Because renters usually pay rent from current income, knowing how often the prospect is paid can be helpful in predicting the timeliness of rent payments.

- *Nature of the business.* People once thought that some jobs were more secure than others and that workers paid by the hour were at greater risk of being laid off than salaried workers. The changing economic climate from decade to decade indicates that there are no guarantees. Anyone can be laid off at any time. Because the prospect probably works in or near the community, the manager can easily learn about the company, its outlook, and its reputation as an employer.

Review of these factors may cast a favorable light on a prospect, but none of them indicates whether he or she manages money wisely. A large family with limited means may be very frugal while someone with a large income and a secure position may not. Just as verification of sufficient income is important, so is checking the applicant's payment record for loans and revolving credit programs. Regular and timely payments signify responsibility and ability to manage money.

Credit Reports. Apartment managers generally hire credit bureaus and/or consumer reporting agencies to conduct the financial investigation of an applicant. The resulting credit report includes information on bank accounts, credit card debt, outstanding loans and judgments, and bankruptcy filings that can help the manager determine how much of a prospect's income is already committed. Credit bureaus give individual consumers a credit score based on their credit activity. Many real estate management firms require that prospects meet a minimum credit score in order to qualify for a lease at properties they manage. Businesses are willing to provide a reputable credit bureau with accurate information because they may rely on the credit bureau for information themselves or they may foresee a use for the service. A credit bureau's reputation for maintaining confidentiality is also well-known in most circumstances, and reputable organizations know precisely what to ask without inadvertently requesting information that cannot be shared. (Using a third party to check credit tends to shift responsibility away from the property at lease initiation.)

However the manager acquires the information, the *Fair Credit Reporting Act (FCRA)* requires that the prospect be advised that his or her credit is being checked. A standard rental application form usually includes a statement that the prospect—by signing the form—authorizes the property owner to verify the information provided. (The FCRA also requires written authorization to investigate any other aspect of the applicant's background—e.g., occupancy history, employment, criminal record.)

The FCRA further requires that an applicant who is rejected based on a negative credit report must receive written notification of the adverse action. The letter must include the names, addresses, and telephone numbers of all consumer credit reporting agencies that provided information. The letter must also state that the agencies only provided information and were not involved in the rental decision, and it must advise the applicant of his or her rights to obtain additional information from the credit reporting agency, dispute its accuracy, and provide a consumer statement describing his or her position.

Some Laws That Affect Residential Rentals

In addition to fair housing and consumer credit laws, a number of other laws affect residential rentals—some directly, others indirectly. Managers of apartment properties must keep up-to-date with these and other laws that affect their responsibilities concerning apartment rentals. (See also the discussions of environmental regulations in chapter 7 and bankruptcy in chapter 8.)

- **Americans with Disabilities Act (ADA)** Under the ADA, public accommodations must be accessible to disabled individuals. Management may need to modify the rental office and other common areas of an apartment property (e.g., parking, lobbies) to comply with this requirement.

- **Residential Lead-Based Paint Hazard Reduction Act** This act requires owners and managers of apartment buildings constructed before 1978 to give renters (1) a disclosure form detailing the presence of lead-based paint; (2) a government pamphlet on lead paint hazards; and (3) a copy of any existing reports that describe lead paint hazards at the property.

- **Megan's Law** In 1996, the federal government passed House Resolution 2137 (called Megan's Law), which requires disclosure to the public of the presence of convicted sex offenders (names and addresses). This information is available from a variety of sources including local police departments and the Internet. As interpreted up to 2005, the federal law does not address the responsibility of a property owner to a tenant regarding disclosure. A number of individual states have passed similar laws that require disclosure of the presence of a convicted sex offender on the property as a "material fact" of a real estate transaction. While the states' laws up to 2005 related to property sales, they could extend the disclosure requirement to rental properties. If that were to happen, the owner or manager of the property might be held liable in the event of a criminal incident.

- **The USA PATRIOT Act and Executive Order 13224** Executive Order 13224 of the PATRIOT Act prohibits any business, including real estate professionals, from entering into business relationships (e.g., leases) with entities identified on the Specially Designated Nationals and Blocked Persons List (SDN). The order also prohibits those on the SDN list from benefiting from properties they already own by receiving rents or other payments. The order applies to both residential *and* commercial properties. Managers should screen prospective tenants against the SDN list. This can be part of a personal credit check. Real estate managers should check the list periodically to ensure that they are not leasing to a restricted entity. If they find an apparent match, they should verify the match with the U.S. Treasury Department.

- **Terrorism Risk Insurance Act (TRIA)** This act requires insurers to offer terrorism insurance to commercial industry and provides a federal backstop to support the insurance industry in the event of catastrophic terrorist attacks. Congress signed TRIA into law in 2002. The act was scheduled to expire at the end of 2005, but legislation was introduced to extend the act for two years.

Respect for Property and Neighbors. While financial investigation of all applicants is important, verification that applicants will be good neighbors and treat the property with care is equally important. However, that is more difficult to verify. The information is usually beyond the scope of a credit bureau's investigation, although other local firms may perform such background checks. Such firms may also scan public records for evidence of evictions and checks returned because of insufficient funds. (Care must be taken not to invade a prospect's privacy.)

The definitive sources for verification of an applicant's respect for property and neighbors are his or her previous landlords. A phone call or visit to the prospect's present landlord is often the best way to learn about the prospect's rental payment record, respect for neighbors, and treatment of the premises. However, the manager should interpret a current landlord's comments carefully. A property owner may commend the prospect even if he or she has not been an ideal resident; knowing a problem resident has a place to move is one way to ensure the problem will soon be gone. (Within a small network of real estate managers and property owners, such a tactic would result in few referrals and hinder professional cooperation.) If a landlord's responses seem dubious, checking with an earlier landlord may remove any doubts. A former landlord may be more candid because the prospect is no longer a resident.

Length of residency is additional evidence of reliability. A succession of moves may imply instability, while long-term occupancy tends to indicate that the prospect is dependable. However, in an active market with substantial new construction, a succession of moves may only indicate a prospect's search for the best rental deal.

As a matter of safety for residents and site employees, including a criminal background check on rental applicants may be prudent. Whatever checks are used, they must be done for *all* applicants.

Permanence Potential. Although predicting how long a prospect may be a resident is difficult, prospects whose records indicate prior long-term occupancies will probably reside in a new rental space for a long period as well. Most stable households dislike moving, yet turnover in residential properties is common. Frequent turnover reduces income and increases the costs of repair, cleaning, and leasing. Therefore, long-term residents are desirable.

The Residential Lease

A *lease* is a contractual agreement between a property owner and a residential tenant to provide the resident with a private dwelling and the owner with regular payments in the form of rent. A lease is important because it

---

Principal Clauses of a Residential Lease

- Names of parties (property owner and residential tenant)
- Description of leased premises
- Amount of security deposit
- Amount of rent and due date
- Late fees and other charges
- Term of lease (including start and end dates)
- Right of reentry
- Subleasing
- Rules and regulations
- Insurance requirements
- Services, utilities, etc., provided by the property owner (if any)

---

protects the resident's interests as much as it protects the property owner's interests. In an attempt to dispel negative connotations of the word *lease,* management firms sometimes call a residential lease an *occupancy agreement.* However, an occupancy agreement is legally just as binding; in fact, it is a lease. Some states require residential leases to be written in "plain language"; the state may require preapproval of the lease, and violators may face stiff penalties.

The lease for any rental property is based on the intended use of the space and any special provisions for that usage. Residential leases by nature are not complicated, but they must include certain provisions and clauses that are discussed in the following sections.

Lease Clauses and Provisions. Printed lease forms include specific clauses that define the leased space, govern the payment of rent and handling of security deposits, and state the responsibilities of and the relationship between the property owner and the resident. These forms usually include various protections for both parties. The items discussed here are especially important.

Parties to the Lease. In addition to the owner or the owner's agent, the lease should identify all adults who will occupy the apartment, and they should sign it. The lease should state that all of the signers are responsible for paying the rent and otherwise fulfilling the lease agreement (i.e., *joint and several liability*). This is especially important when unrelated adults share an apartment. In some situations (e.g., college student housing), having unrelated individuals sign separate leases may be appropriate. While having multiple leases for one rental unit may seem cumbersome, it facilitates changes in occupancy. Having an individual lease for each roommate makes evicting one resident who is irresponsible or behind in paying rent easier. That arrangement also prevents friends of the residents from becoming long-term guests.

Lease Term.   While no standard *lease term* for residential property exists, one year is the usual period; six-month and month-to-month terms are also common. The length of the term is often based on what is popular in a given market. In most markets, a written lease that lasts at least one year covers residential units that command high rents.

Establishing the term of the lease has advantages and disadvantages. When a lease is signed, the rent is probably the highest the market will bear at the time for the space leased. If market demand rises during the lease term, the owner has essentially undersold the space. If the market declines, the resident has agreed to a rent that may exceed the rate for comparable space.

Although a residential lease term of more than one year is uncommon, the manager should always remember that the length of the lease term can be used to advantage. Chapter 8 discussed the incentive of a free period of rent and the adjustment of the lease term to compensate for that period. Other circumstances may also justify a modified lease term. For example, a prospect who needs to find a place to live during the winter and an owner who wishes to fill a vacancy during that period are both limited in their options because little turnover occurs in winter, especially in northern regions. If a qualified prospect is found, a 16- or 17-month lease may benefit both the owner and the resident even though the period is unusual. The longer lease term would preclude the unit becoming vacant the following winter, and it would protect the resident from having to move again in the cold.

Condition of Premises.   A *statement of condition* is usually a reflection of what a manager notes during an inspection of an apartment just prior to a resident's moving into it. Incidental damage may be noted so a new resident will not be charged for it on move-out.

Some residential leases spell out residents' responsibilities for maintenance within their leased premises—e.g., cleaning carpeting once a year, keeping appliances clean and in working order, not keeping hazardous substances other than appropriate cleaning aids, etc. While a resident's handbook often previously spelled out these requirements, managers increasingly incorporate them into the lease itself, either in the condition of premises provision or in a separate maintenance provision.

The statement of condition may include information about what charges for damage the management will assess at move-out and what it will consider normal wear and tear. This can be a delicate subject because the manager and the resident may have different interpretations of the word *damage.* Finally, the statement of condition may establish the overall state to which the resident is expected to restore the apartment at the time of move-out.

Pets.   Real estate managers and property owners often prohibit pets because animals can be a nuisance and can damage property. However, such a policy can also limit the potential market for an apartment. Fair housing laws also apply. A person with a disability that requires an "assistive (or service) animal" may not be denied housing because of a "no pets" policy.

A *pet clause* is necessary regardless of whether pets are allowed. Instead of outright prohibition, the lease can establish thorough guidelines that specify what is allowed and what is not. Alternatively, pet policies may be stated in a separate *pet agreement* that the pet-owning resident signs, or they may be listed in the resident's handbook (discussed later in this chapter). The provisions in a pet agreement may only reiterate local ordinances, but if they are a stipulation of the lease or of house rules, they are easier to enforce.

Guidelines often set limitations on the type, size, and number of pets allowed; list requirements for damage deposits, use of leashes, and cleanup of animal wastes; and reiterate legalities related to licensing and vaccinations (see exhibit 9.2).

Although a pet policy may appear harsh when itemized and listed in an agreement, the manager can remind the resident that these measures are similar to advice given by pet associations and humane societies. In addition to protecting the owner's property, these policies safeguard the pet and protect all residents of the property from the nuisance and danger that animals can sometimes pose.

Right of Reentry.   The resident is entitled to *quiet enjoyment* of the leased premises, free from disturbances by others and by the management. However, the property owner is granted the right to enter an occupied apartment to make repairs, provide agreed-upon services, and show the apartment to prospective tenants and others, subject to certain limitations. The lease should specifically state those limitations. For ordinary repairs, the manager should obtain written permission to enter the premises (notification requirements may be prescribed by law). In emergencies, the property owner may enter regardless of whether anyone is available to grant admittance.

Subleasing.   A prospect may request inclusion of a *transfer clause* that allows the resident to break the lease without penalty in case of a job transfer. If that is the case, the manager should request documentation from the resident's employer to that effect. On the other hand, a prospect who is renting while also looking for a house to buy may ask for a *home purchase*

Exhibit 9.2
Guidelines for Developing a Pet Policy

Type of Pet Arguments can be made for allowing some types of animals and excluding others. Consider these elements in deciding which animals to permit. Other residents may consider barking dogs a nuisance. Cats have a tendency to roam when let out and to scratch woodwork indoors. Exotic or wild animals, if not illegal, may be too large for the premises or inappropriate as pets. Pets also produce odors that linger.

Size of Pet State specific weight and height requirements to exclude extremely large dogs or exotic animals.

Number of Pets Specify a maximum number of pets to preclude residents from having too many animals.

Pet Deposit Require an extra deposit for each pet. The deposit should be sufficient to cover any damage to the leased space or the property as a whole and to deter the resident from allowing the pet to cause damage. (Like a security deposit, the pet deposit should be refundable if no damage occurs.)

Pet Registration Require the pet owner to register each pet with the manager of the property. This links a specific pet to the deposit and verifies the number of pets on the premises. An instant photo of the pet for the resident's file is an added measure of verification

Leash Requirement State that all dogs must be kept on a leash when outside the pet owner's apartment; the same policy should apply to other animals as appropriate. Pets may break loose from their leashes occasionally; the intent of such a statement is not to penalize a resident for this rare occurrence but to encourage residents to take extra care with their animals and not allow them to roam. This is also a safety measure for the pet.

Cleanup Require pet owners to clean up after their animals. Animal wastes are a danger to health and sanitation. Many communities have passed such ordinances, and this should be a policy of managed residential property as well.

Vaccinations and Licenses Require proof that all animals have appropriate vaccinations and licensing as required by law. Neutering or spaying may also be required.

Insurance Require pet-owning residents to carry renter's insurance that includes liability coverage. (Renter's insurance may be specific regarding pets—dog bites may be covered but not other animal-related injuries, and property damage by a pet may be excluded.)

Prohibited Areas Indicate where animals are prohibited on the property (e.g., the sandbox in a children's play area, the swimming pool and surrounding area).

Animal-Friendly Areas Clearly identify animal-friendly areas of the property (e.g., a designated dog-walking area) with signage. Spell out rules and regulations regarding their use in the pet policy, the pet agreement, or other relevant documentation.

---

clause that similarly allows the resident to break the lease in the event a purchase transaction is closed before the lease term ends.

Instead of either of those specific clauses, the lease may contain a *sublet clause* that states that, in order for the resident to vacate the premises before the end of the term—whether because of a transfer or other extenuating circumstances—he or she must find a suitable resident to sublet the space for the remainder of the lease obligation. The manager must approve that person, and the resident or the subtenant must pay for the credit check. In the event of a job transfer, the employer may use its resources to help find a subtenant or, it may pay, on the employee's behalf, a negotiated penalty for breaking the lease without finding a subtenant.

Utilities.   Occupants of rental apartments are usually responsible for payment of utilities, such as gas and electricity, for which the utility provider bills them directly. The lease should state specifically what utilities are the resident's responsibility. This is especially important if residents pay for their own heat, water, and sewer. If some utilities are charged to the property, a system for prorating such expenses (based on apartment square footage) and billing each resident may be implemented. Some residential properties include utilities in the rent. This is a common practice in older buildings in which the apartments are not individually metered.

Rules and Regulations.   To assure residents' safety, protect their rights, and protect the physical integrity of the property, the manager may distribute a set of rules and regulations to new residents. (Items not covered specifically as lease provisions should be listed in an addendum or rider and incorporated into the lease by reference.) Rules and regulations may also be part of a *resident's handbook*. In addition to recapitulating information from the lease (such as when rent is due and the owner's right of reentry), a handbook is an appropriate format in which to state policies regarding trash disposal, laundry room and common area amenity use, and permissible or prohibited furnishings (e.g., water beds). To encourage all residents to abide by these rules, a form for the residents to sign and return that states that they have read and understand the rules may accompany the handbook. In addition, a clause in the lease stating that the resident understands and will abide by the house rules is often appropriate. To make the house rules more palatable, they may be called "policies" rather than rules and regulations—positive statements are more readily accepted than a list of what is not allowed. Exhibit 9.3 lists some items that a resident's handbook may include.

Compliance with Landlord-Tenant Laws.   Most if not all local jurisdictions have laws that affect the rights of residents; these are known collectively as *landlord-tenant laws*. They state the rights and obligations of property owners and residents and detail what either party can do if the other does not comply with the lease or the law. Landlord-tenant laws usually govern issues that the lease, its clauses, or the policies (or rules) for the property address. In particular, they define *habitability* and regulate the handling of security deposits. They may also set the maximum late fee,

Exhibit 9.3
Resident's Handbook—Typical Information

* Rent due date and treatment of delinquencies (what constitutes late payment, fees assessed for late payments and NSF checks)
* Purpose of the security deposit and conditions for its return
* Limitations on occupancy by visitors and persons other than those named in the lease
* Limitations on parking by residents and visitors
* Pet agreement conditions
* Limitations on particular furnishings, wall hangings, etc.
* Use of laundry room, pool, and any other amenities of the property
* Fundamental maintenance and upkeep the resident is expected to perform (e.g., provide and replace own light bulbs within residence; replace batteries in smoke detectors when necessary)
* Numbers to call for emergency repairs and other services
* Utilities that are the resident's responsibility
* Insurance the resident is expected to carry
* Evacuation procedures and exit routes from the specific apartment
* Requirements for notice of renewal, nonrenewal, or termination of the lease
* Procedures for management inspections of the premises before move-in and after move-out and the effect of the latter on security deposit refunds (amounts charged for cleanup and repairs to restore the apartment to move-in condition)
* Need for and right of the property owner to enter the premises and conditions that would require the owner to enter the premises without notifying the resident first
* Rules governing subletting
* Grounds for eviction
* Other limitations or proscriptions on the resident's actions

The handbook may also include information regarding proper care of built-in appliances such as ovens, refrigerators, air conditioners, furnaces, or thermostats. Such instructions (e.g., do not use a sharp object to defrost the freezer compartment of the refrigerator; always run cold water when using the garbage disposal) can avert damage or minimize wear on the appliances. Other suggestions, particularly those pertaining to energy conservation (e.g., replace air-conditioner filters regularly, keep windows and doors closed in the winter or when operating the air conditioner in the summer), will reduce the resident's utility bills or the owner's expenses for master-metered fuel.

A resident's handbook may be expanded to be more useful to and welcoming of new residents. Information about the neighborhood such as schools, shopping, public transportation stops, and places of worship will help orient newcomers. Other appropriate additions might be sources for personal services (barber and beauty shops, dry cleaners), nearby restaurants and entertainment (cinemas, amusement parks), and local social service agencies.

---

state provisions and requirements for subleasing, and specify procedures for eviction.

Certain locales have *rent control laws* that set a ceiling on the amount of rent that an owner can charge or the maximum allowable increase on renewal or both. Rent control is a concept that some metropolitan areas see as a way to maintain affordable housing, but it benefits neither owners nor residents over the long term. If rent is held below what the market will bear, the income of the property may not be adequate to maintain it properly. The result will be a greater concentration of poorly maintained residential space. Properties that are not maintained lose value. Depressed property values reduce municipal income because of the lower real estate taxes they yield. Because it reduces or precludes the potential for financial success, rent control also discourages new construction. (Chapter 2 also discusses rent control laws.)

Encouraging Renewals.   Reputable residents are the most valuable assets of any income-producing residential property. The real estate manager should contact a resident whose lease is nearing expiration two to three months before the expiration date. (The specific period of notice may be set by statute.) Some managers send out a new lease. Others send only a renewal notice stating any change in the rent and noting any specific changes in terms and conditions of the prior lease. Personal contact regarding renewal is a good management tactic. Hand delivery of a renewal lease or a follow-up visit is a way of showing residents that their tenancy is valued.

Even though residents generally anticipate a rent increase, they may protest it. Because of the potential for reaction, managers often focus on lease renewal as the time to improve the unit. Upgrading is a sound business practice and can be an incentive for the resident to renew. The upgrade may be a new appliance, painting one or more rooms, or some other work. (Some improvements may be necessary in the unit regardless of the resident's decision.) Improving a unit as part of a lease renewal has at least three benefits.

1. *Good resident relations.* Even if the improvement is not necessary for the resident to commit to a new lease, the extension of goodwill strengthens the relationship with a good resident. If the improvement alone wins the renewal, it is most likely a cost-effective means of keeping the unit leased. The cost is usually equivalent to or less than one month's rent. If the improvement averts a rent loss because of temporary vacancy, it also averts the expense of advertising and marketing. The improvement may be necessary anyway to keep the unit competitive in the market if the resident does not renew the lease.

2. *Increased property value.* A comprehensive program of individual unit improvements increases the value of the property as a whole, which may lead to higher income both in the short term and in the long term. The investment may increase the resale value of the property by much more than the actual cost of the improvements.

3. *Tax benefits.* Apartment upgrades can be tax deductible in one of two ways. An improvement that will increase the value of the prop-

erty and will endure for more than one year may be depreciable over several years. On the other hand, the cost of repairs done to preserve the integrity of the property may be deductible as an operating expense for the year in which it is paid.

COMMON INTEREST REALTY ASSOCIATIONS

Properties in which individuals own dwellings, along with a shared interest in so-called common areas, are called *common interest realty associations* (*CIRAs*). Examples are condominiums, cooperatives, and planned unit developments (PUDs). Managing CIRAs is quite different from managing residential rentals because of the ownership structures involved.

Condominiums

A *condominium* is a multiple-unit residence in which the units are individually owned. "Condominium" literally means "joint dominion"—the domains (homes) are arranged together in a single property. An individual who owns a unit in a condominium development actually owns the space bounded by the floor, walls, and ceiling of a particular unit (or townhouse).

Common Area.   The rest of the property (hallways, lobbies, grounds, and any other part of the property that is not individually owned) is called the *common area*. The individual owners technically own a percentage of the common area, and this percentage is usually based on the square footage of their living areas compared to all of the living area in the building. It may also be based on the desirability of the individual unit—irrespective of square footage, some units will have higher values because of various amenities and therefore represent a greater percentage of the entire property value. However, common area ownership is *undivided,* so no owner can claim a particular section of common area as his or her own.

Condominium Association.   State law requires that condominium unit owners form a not-for-profit corporation comprised of all the individual owners; this *condominium or home-owners' association* discusses and acts on common concerns of the property owners. All owners are association members. The association elects a board of directors from among the membership. From the board of directors, the association members elect individuals to serve as officers. (A large association may have a president, vice president, secretary, and treasurer; a smaller association may combine responsibilities.) The remaining board members who are not officers are at-large members. The condominium board is responsible for managing the property, and it normally hires or contracts for professional management.
    Ownership of a condominium does not mean that the owner must

live in the unit. An owner may move out but not want to sell the unit. As an investment, the owner may lease the unit to someone else whose rent payments ensure that the mortgage and monthly assessments are covered. Some people invest in condominium units solely to lease them to others. Because renters have no vested interest in the condominium, they cannot participate in the association, so having a large proportion of a condominium's units occupied by renters can pose problems. In particular, lenders may be reluctant to finance a condominium purchase if more than a certain percentage of the units are not owner-occupied. (Whether and how many units in a condominium may be rented to others is an issue that the condominium association must address.)

Governing Documents.   In addition to hiring and communicating with the manager, the condominium association upholds and fulfills the tenets of the *governing documents,* which usually include the following.

- *Declaration.* The declaration commits the land to condominium use, provides for the association's creation, defines the method to determine each owner's share of expenses, and outlines the relationship between the individual owners and the association. The declaration is effectively the constitution of the association.

- *Bylaws.* While the declaration establishes the broad administrative framework for the association, the bylaws provide specific procedures for handling routine matters. They detail procedures for accounting, maintenance of common areas and individual units (the unit owner is responsible for repair and maintenance within his or her unit), election of officers (and their duties), votes by the association members, collection of assessments, and other administrative business.

- *Unit deed.* The individual unit deed is the document that legally transfers to the purchaser the title of a condominium unit and its undivided portion of the common areas.

Other documents relate to the establishment and operation of a condominium. The *articles of incorporation* state that the condominium association is a corporation under the laws of the state. House *rules and regulations* are the guidelines for day-to-day behavior on the premises and for settling disputes that may arise. Although many rules are common among condominium properties, each association is likely to establish some rules that are unique. The rules may cover anything from pets to noise to parking.

Assessments.   The bylaws or a separate document usually specify the percentage of the property owned by each unit owner by taking into account the amount of living area—and possibly the desirability—of each unit. These percentages are the multipliers used to calculate the monthly *assessment* paid by each owner. The assessment is used to pay the operating expenses for the whole property—common-area services, maintenance, management. For example, if the board determines that operating expenses for the whole property are $6,000 a month and the bylaws state that the owner of unit 6B owns five percent of the property, the owner of 6B will pay the association at least $300 every month.

The regular assessment collections must also factor in reserves. *Reserve funds* may be used to pay for anticipated and unanticipated capital expenditures. If a capital expenditure is required and reserve funds are not sufficient to pay it, or if the association chooses not to deplete reserves to pay the expense, a *special assessment* will be necessary to defray the cost. For example, if the property needs a new roof and $30,000 of that cost will not be paid from the reserves, the owner of unit 6B (who owns five percent of the property) will be required to pay a special assessment of $1,500.

Timeshares.   The *timeshare* is a specialized form of condominium found mostly in resort areas. As the name implies, the owner has the right to occupy the unit for a specific period. There are several ways to set up a timeshare condominium. In order for the owner to have an actual share of property and its accompanying tax advantages, he or she may cooperatively own a percentage of a condominium unit. In other words, a person who owns one month's possession of one unit every year may own 30/365 of a unit. On that basis, a 100-unit building could have 1,200 or more owners.

Cooperatives

Cooperative ownership differs from condominium ownership in that the *cooperative* incorporates itself to purchase or build a multiple-unit dwelling and issues shares in the corporation to represent the proportion of ownership of the entire property. A single mortgage covers the entire cooperative property, and shareholders receive a *proprietary lease* that entitles them to occupy one unit. While this traditional ownership structure is common, unit owners can also "pledge" their shares in the cooperative corporation as collateral for a loan. The proprietary lease is assigned to the lender (the transaction is recorded in the land records), and the lender obtains a *recognition agreement* from the cooperative corporation. Under the agreement, if the borrower (unit "owner") defaults on his or her obligation to the cooperative corporation, the corporation will give the lender an opportunity to cure the default before the cooperative forecloses on the unit.

Managing a cooperative differs from managing a condominium in several ways. Residents tend to be long-term—the resident profile is highly stable and homogeneous. Decisions for the cooperative are made by a board, which is comprised of shareholders in the corporation. However, cooperative boards can be more active than condominium boards, and sometimes they enforce greater restrictions on the property. The board must interview and approve new residents. It may have the right to approve or deny improvements to units. The board may stipulate that all sales of shares must be on an all-cash basis, and it may state that only shareholders may reside in units (i.e., they cannot be bought as investments and leased to others).

Planned Unit Developments

The residential *planned unit development* (*PUD*) combines the concept of the conventional neighborhood subdivision with characteristics that are similar to condominium ownership. Most residents purchase their dwelling, the property it is on, and an undivided share of the common area within the PUD (roads, parks, recreational amenities). The residents pay a monthly assessment to maintain the common areas. The assessment may also pay for lawn care, snow removal, and other services for individual units.

A developer normally designs a PUD as a single entity before ground is broken, much as the plans of a building are completely drawn prior to construction. Unlike a single building, however, the PUD may be constructed in stages over several years. A characteristic of PUDs is that the developer pays as much attention to the location of open space as to the placement of buildings. Although open spaces are emphasized, land is used more intensively than in conventional subdivisions because townhouses and multiple-unit dwellings are more common than single-family homes. This concentration of land use particularly benefits three groups.

1. *The developers.* The profit margin on land resale is higher, both because a PUD has more living units per acre and because careful planning of the development as a whole makes it aesthetically attractive.

2. *The community.* More real estate taxes can be collected per acre.

3. *The residents.* Assessments for common area services are minimized because of the large number of residents per acre and because the intensive use of the land reduces the amount of common area to maintain.

A PUD is a departure from conventional residential zoning; therefore, the term *planned unit development* also refers to a special zoning apparatus that permits the undertaking. Because it is a unique zoning form, public officials can be heavily involved in the site plan review and may play a key role in determining the nature and shape of the PUD.

In addition to dwelling types that may range from detached houses to rental apartments, a very large PUD may include retail and service facilities if such facilities are not immediately accessible from its location. In most cases, a home-owners' association comparable to that of a condominium governs the PUD. However, the developer may be more prominent in the home-owners' association of a PUD, especially if the property has rental units. Because only property owners can be association members in PUDs that have both privately owned and rental residences, renters do not have a voice in the association.

Collection of assessments for common area maintenance is a major responsibility of the manager of a PUD. The association may rely on the manager to create the assessment structure, which may provide for a variety of separate collections, including standard assessments, special assessments, rental security deposits, and rents. Maintenance services provided may encompass landscaping as well as general upkeep and repair of apartments, building exteriors, roads, and amenities.

The Role of Management

Perhaps the most important attraction to owning and occupying a portion of a multiple-unit building or property is that it combines the advantages of apartment living with the advantages of home ownership. The owner of a condominium unit reaps all of the tax advantages of home ownership, and his or her equity in the property grows as the mortgage on the unit is paid down. As with maintenance of a single-family home, the owner can make repairs and improvements to his or her individual unit.

While the home-owners' association governing a small number of units may manage the property on its own, larger properties require full-time supervision, which is usually why a real estate manager is hired (or retained as a consultant). Unlike rental property, condominiums and cooperatives have no effective gross income (PUDs may have some rental income as noted earlier); their monthly assessment collections are based on anticipated expenses, including management fees and funds for reserves. Because of this, compensation for management is usually a fixed monthly amount, which is prorated into the owners' monthly assessments. However, the manager may negotiate separate fees for specific additional services or for attending after-hours board meetings.

Owner Relations.   Because each encounter between a staff member and a resident is an encounter with one of the property owners, all management employees must understand their relationship to the owners. Their efforts to extend goodwill should not compromise the agreement between management and the board of directors. Because the residents actually own the property, they may think the staff is at their service for any maintenance or repairs in their individual units. However, owner-residents usually have to pay separately for such services. (Depending on the management agreement, the residents may have to call an independent service of their choosing or pay the association to have the work done by staff.) To be fair to the other unit owners, the individual owner must reimburse the association for an employee's work on an individual unit. As a convenience, some properties may provide service in individual units at no extra charge to residents. However, the association members must agree that such a benefit is worth higher assessments for everyone.

Working with a Board of Directors.   The association usually elects a board and new officers each year, or it may have an annual election with staggered multiple-year terms to ensure consistency of board decisions. The meetings are usually after-hours in one of the resident's units or in an office or common room on the premises. Because the board meeting is also a gathering of neighbors, the agenda may yield to tangential discussions. Complications can also arise when disputes occur among the owners, the board of directors, and the manager of the property.

The proximity of the board members, by virtue of living in the same building or property, may also encourage frequent meetings. The manager is usually required to attend *some* meetings. However, the amount of time the manager must spend at these meetings can often be minimized if the management agreement includes an hourly fee for attending meetings.

The board makes management decisions, but the manager may be the one who carries out those decisions. This may require the manager to mediate differences of opinion among the board members. With regard to issues of real estate management, the manager is probably better qualified to decide which course of action to take. However, management decisions may provoke dissent because some board members may consider the manager's viewpoint biased. These differences of opinion can be extremely frustrating for a manager and can impede successful management. To prevent conflicting demands on the manager, the board should name one individual—usually the president—to be responsible for communication with the manager.

Maintenance.   As owners of the property, the residents will be especially attentive to maintenance of the building and grounds. While a rental property must be sold as a whole, the units in a condominium or PUD or the shares of a cooperative may be bought and sold independently. Rental property can tolerate some deferred maintenance for a limited time without losing value. However, once the owner decides to sell a rental property, he or she must correct its deferred maintenance to assure the highest sale price possible. In contrast, any deferred maintenance of a resident-owned property, whether in a particular unit or in a common area, lowers the individual unit or share value. The manager may have to remind the board or the president of that fact occasionally, especially when a repair is extremely

costly. Because resident-owned properties are investments and resale potential is paramount to the resident-owners, management must be aware of
a heightened demand for custodial maintenance. The manager should work
diligently with the association to ensure that funds for maintenance of the
property are budgeted adequately and that sufficient funds are in reserve.

Fiscal Affairs. The assessments paid by unit owners are primarily to
cover the operating costs of the property that they own in common (e.g.,
insurance, utilities). These costs must be kept under control to minimize the
residents' individual assessments. However, assessments should not be so
low that a provision for reserves is lacking. Low monthly assessments usually result in requirements for special assessments every time the property
needs a major repair. If only one or even a few residents do not have the
money available to pay a special assessment when it is levied, the necessary work may be jeopardized. For this reason alone, accruing an adequate
reserve fund through the regular assessment is important. The manager
should encourage the board to develop ample reserves because it is in the
owners' best interests to preserve the value of the property as a whole, and,
if possible, to enhance it. Prospective buyers recognize the value of a large
reserve and will be more inclined to pay a higher price for a condominium
or PUD unit or shares of a cooperative because of it.

As a general rule, a home-owners' association can apply for tax-exempt
status under the Internal Revenue Code if (1) a prescribed percentage of its
gross income comes from unit owner assessments; (2) a prescribed percentage of its expenses are for managing, maintaining, and caring for common
areas; (3) substantially all of the units are used as residences; and (4) no
part of the net income benefits any individual member of the association.
Some sources of income—interest earned by reserve funds, fees received
for special use of amenities, and the like—are not exempt under any circumstances. Tax exemption protects the principal of the reserve fund. If
the association does not have exempt status, the IRS could construe that
the reserves collected as part of the assessment are the association's profit,
and it could tax them accordingly. A real estate manager should periodically
consult a tax specialist for updates on rules governing tax exemption of a
home-owners' association. It is also good practice to keep up with changes
in state laws regarding different types of common interest realty associations.

OTHER RESIDENTIAL PROPERTY

Variations on traditional rental and ownership arrangements abound. These
include single-family homes, manufactured housing (mobile home parks),
and specialized housing for the elderly. Few real estate managers work
exclusively with these types of properties, but these properties represent a

large part of the housing market. In some localities, one of them may be the dominant type of housing.

Single-Family Homes

References to "the American dream" frequently conjure notions of owning a house surrounded by a yard. However, many houses are not owned by their inhabitants but are in fact leased. A *single-family home* is defined as having its own entry. Therefore townhouses, which by definition share a common wall but have private entrances, are also classified as single-family homes.

An extension of the American dream is the investment in a second or third house to rent to others. A house requires a smaller financial commitment than a multiple-unit dwelling; the percentage required as a down payment is often lower, and the owner can usually resell a house more quickly and easily than a larger property. Some first-time real estate investors start in this manner. Those who buy a house to live in when they retire and retain their original house as a source of rental income make up another group of investors. Because these investors may live far away from their rental properties, they often seek professional management services.

Houses as rental units are generally more time-consuming to manage, primarily because they are rarely next door to each other. If an owner demands a level of maintenance that exceeds what can be required of the resident, the general upkeep of the premises can be as time-consuming as it is for a larger property. Marketing and leasing take more time because the manager has to travel to the individual units. In all likelihood, each rental house in a management company's portfolio will be individually owned, and the manager will have to report to numerous owners, many of whom do not live nearby. Despite these seeming disadvantages, some managers have marketed their skills exclusively to the single-family home rental market with great success. Managing rental houses can be very rewarding financially. Because of the value placed on greater privacy, more-accessible parking, and a private yard, a house usually commands more rent than an equivalent-sized apartment.

Manufactured Housing Communities

Manufactured housing is usually built at a factory and, depending on its width, is transported to the installation site in halves or as a whole. At the site, final assembly and connection of the home to gas, electrical, water, and sewer facilities takes place.

Zoning laws commonly prohibit manufactured housing in neighborhoods of conventionally built houses. Manufactured housing is found in areas zoned for *mobile home parks*. Residents of these communities generally own their homes, but they rarely own the land beneath them. They lease

---

Housing Alternatives for Senior Citizens

Aging in Place Persons of retirement age may prefer to remain in their present residences, whether they own or rent.

Congregate Housing For those who want to remain independent but require some assistance with daily tasks, these arrangements include meals, transportation, and some housekeeping services.

Assisted Living Facilities This housing is intended for seniors who need assistance with most (or all) daily living tasks—because of age or frailty but not because of illness. Health care facilities may be nearby.

Senior citizens who are truly ill or require 24-hour supervision need the care of a *nursing home*. Most of these housing alternatives are privately operated. Several federal programs also provide *affordable housing* for the elderly.

---

the land and may have to pay an access charge for the utility connections. The ground rent usually provides for maintenance of community roads and amenities; residents are responsible for maintaining their homes and private yards. The utility company may bill utilities directly to residents of the manufactured housing community. At other times, the community may serve as a distributor and bill residents for the utilities they use. Manufactured housing "condominiums"—an arrangement in which the owner purchases the lot in addition to the manufactured housing unit and pays an assessment for community services and amenities—are popular in resort areas.

The form of management for a manufactured housing community depends on what is managed. Community owners may contract real estate managers to lease lots, collect rents, manage park staff, and supervise the placement of homes on lots in the park. Depending on the type of residents (e.g., families, retirement community), the manager may be responsible for maintaining a clubhouse or other recreational facilities, supervising an activities director, and overseeing any other special services that the community offers.

Housing for the Elderly

As people reach and surpass retirement age, their lifestyles change dramatically, which often changes the type of housing they seek. Some retirees have more time for recreational activities and may be more affluent than other age groups. As they age, people require more medical care and have a higher mortality rate. All of these considerations influence the type of housing the elderly seek. Housing options range from aging in place to full-scale assisted living. Of course, many alternate housing choices are available between the two extremes. When residents age in place in conventional rental housing, managers can sometimes be confronted with a changing occupant profile—they may have to spend more time with the residents, alter building services or building components, and be more aware of the public services available to their residents.

Real estate managers also become involved with developments specifically built for senior citizens. These developments often provide arrangements for independent or assisted living. When the level of service increases in these sites, managers find that they must broaden their skills to include knowledge of recreational amenities, food service, transportation options, and social, psychological, and medical services. In general, management of this type of housing involves providing a greater diversity of services and greater interaction with residents and their off-site families—while also managing the property.

MAINTENANCE ISSUES

Maintenance of residential properties is usually more intensive than that of other types of property because of the amount of wear and tear on them. When maintenance is required within a unit, the staff must inform the resident prior to entering the premises. If they do not, a court of law may interpret the entry as trespassing. Some local or state ordinances require that written notice be given a certain number of hours in advance of entering a unit. However, if a malfunction in a leased unit threatens property or safety, entry is permissible without advance notice to the resident. (This is stated in the lease as the property owner's right of reentry.)

Unit Preparation

After one resident moves out and before another moves in, management has an opportunity to do extensive maintenance and repairs in a vacant apartment. This work may be done principally for marketing purposes. To minimize vacancy periods and maximize rental income, all units must be attractive and all components in them must be operational. Even though a vacancy that lasts a month or more reduces income, it affords significant time to paint and repair the unit. In other circumstances, the period between one resident's vacating an apartment and another's taking possession of it may be less than a day. However, such a limited time should not reduce the thoroughness of the maintenance.

To avoid service calls and assure the resident's comfort, an in-coming resident should receive the unit in superior condition. The staff should inspect a vacant apartment every day, not only as a check on its condition for marketing and showing to prospects, but to ensure that an uninhabited unit remains free of damage. A *unit make-ready report* (exhibit 9.4) can be a useful guide for the staff as they inspect and repair a vacant apartment. After repairs are complete, an inspection using the completed make-ready

Exhibit 9.4
Residential Unit Make-Ready Report

Property _____Date _____

Unit _____

Date vacated _____ Date to be occupied (if known) _____

Initial inspection by _____ Date_____

Checklist Before Move-In	Special Instructions
Check that all plumbing in unit (toilets, faucets, etc.) works properly. Make sure no leaks or drainage problems are present.	_____ _____ _____ _____
Check all appliances (run dishwasher once on each cycle; check for proper operation of refrigerator, disposal, range). Make sure all appliances and kitchen cabinets are clean.	_____ _____ _____ _____ _____
Inspect all windows and screens (no breaks in either). Verify that all sliding components work correctly and easily. Clean out tracks of all windows and sliding glass doors. Clean inside of all windowpanes.	_____ _____ _____ _____ _____ _____
Check painted surfaces for chipping, peeling, discoloration, and stains. Determine whether repainting is necessary.	_____ _____ _____ _____
Check all walls for holes, seams, cuts, cracks, and nail pops.	_____ _____
Check Venetian blinds for proper operation and clean them.	_____ _____
Check flooring (all floors cleaned and waxed, parquet block floors or wood strip and asphalt tile included; vacuum carpet).	_____ _____ _____ _____
Clean bathroom(s) (tub, toilet, basins, vanities, mirrors, medicine cabinets, wall and floor tile).	_____ _____ _____

(Continued)

Exhibit 9.4 (*concluded*)

Verify that all towel bars, toilet paper holders, and soap dishes are secure and clean.

Check tile in bathroom(s) for cracks or
other flaws.

Make sure that all baseboards, cabinets,
shelves, electrical outlet plates, and smoke
detectors are properly installed and secure.

Verify that thresholds and metal strips are
installed properly where needed.

Check that all doors close properly and that
there is no rubbing or warping. Check that
all locks and keys work properly.

Check that all vents and registers are properly installed.

Check heating and air-conditioning units to
verify that they are working properly. Clean
or replace air-conditioning filter.

Make sure that all lighting fixtures work
properly and have new bulbs.

Other _____

_____

_____

Other _____

_____

_____

Other _____

_____

Final inspection by _____ Date _____

Approved by _____ Date _____

report for reference verifies that the unit is ready to be shown or to be inhabited by a new resident. The manager, accompanied by the resident, should inspect the unit both at move-in and at move-out. Use of a combination *move-in/move-out inspection form* with spaces for signatures of both the manager and the resident is helpful. This documents the unit condition and its acceptance by the resident at move-in and helps minimize disputes regarding condition at move-out if the manager must retain part or all of the security deposit to cover the cost of repairs.

Residential Amenities

Some facilities are unique to residential property and require special care and monitoring. The laundry room is a particular source of concern. Because an on-site laundry room is an amenity, it should be as clean and inviting as the rest of the property. If it is tastefully appointed, it will also be easier to keep clean. Maintenance of the washers and dryers is often contracted to a company that specializes in this service, and the cost is paid out of the revenues from the machines. Maintenance of the room itself is a management responsibility. The staff should inspect the laundry room regularly. Air ducts and drains may clog with lint; trash may accumulate in the area, and wet or soapy floors can cause a fall.

A storage area may be provided for residents' use (or rented separately to residents). Storage spaces that are not attached to the units are usually located in a common area, often in the basement. Typical storage spaces are enclosed by wooden or wire floor-to-ceiling partitions that the resident can secure with a padlock. Storage spaces should be protected from seepage and flooding, mildew, and vermin.

Many large developments offer indoor or outdoor swimming pools for residents and visitors. Although these can be a great attraction, pools also pose a serious danger. To minimize the risk, the manager should post and enforce rules for pool use (including hours of access). The staff must monitor the chlorination (or other chemical treatment) level and regularly vacuum the pool. For reasons of safety and security, staff must periodically check fixtures such as fences, gates, and ladders.

While the foregoing maintenance considerations are specific to rental properties, condominiums or cooperatives—especially older properties converted from rental use—may have similar facilities and similar requirements for maintenance. Manufactured housing communities and PUDs will have road repairs in addition to maintenance of amenities, and all properties that provide parking must maintain the parking lots or garages.

INSURANCE ISSUES

To avoid a financial loss from damage to the property, the wisest choice an owner and a manager can make is to consult a capable and knowledge-

---

Curb Appeal of Residential Property

Curb appeal greatly affects the value of every property, but it is particularly important to residential sites. *Curb appeal* is defined as the overall condition and attractiveness of a property as viewed from the outside—from the street or curb. Favorable curb appeal depends on many factors that make the property as a whole inviting to residents and visitors. The effort to make the property appealing on the outside must complement the effort to make it appealing on the inside.

To maintain or improve a property's curb appeal, the manager should examine the building exterior and grounds through the eyes of a prospective resident. A prospect who visits the site most likely has not seen it before and naturally forms an impression about the building and its grounds. Most residents take pride in their dwellings. Where people live makes a statement to society about them and their character. Therefore, a prospect's initial impression of a site will weigh heavily in the decision as to whether to rent an apartment in the building.

After a prospect who is impressed by the curb appeal of a property leaves the site, he or she may not easily remember precisely what features created the favorable impression. Curb appeal is an overall impression of the state of all exterior property components. People will not necessarily notice subtleties such as sidewalks without cracks, clean glass and light fixtures, chip-free paint in entrance areas, coordinated signage, or tidy garbage Dumpsters. However, they will notice—and remember—any individual component that leaves the slightest negative impression (litter on the front lawn, overloaded garbage Dumpsters, damaged or out-of-date signage, or peeling paint).

Besides high standards for maintenance, prospects will also remember obvious enhancements of curb appeal such as flower beds, understated seasonal decorations, or a fountain in the courtyard. The real estate manager must be careful to avoid excessive additions, but a few well-placed enhancements of this nature can be very appealing. Once such an enhancement is on the grounds, maintaining it is vital. A watered, pruned, and weed-free flower bed can improve curb appeal considerably, but an unkempt or dying one will detract from it. In fact, an untended flower bed may make curb appeal less than it would have been without a flower bed.

---

able insurance expert. Unique aspects of a property will require inclusion of certain provisions in its insurance coverage. For example, a residential property in an area that is not prone to earthquakes most likely will not require earthquake insurance; however, insurance for property along the California coast must include this type of coverage. Likewise, a condominium association would not require insurance to protect against the loss of rent in the event of damage to its building, but the insurance of a rental property should include rent loss coverage. In fact, the mortgage holder may require such protection. If the building sustains a physical loss, insurance covering the building will pay to restore the premises. During restoration, however, the property may be partially or completely uninhabitable, resulting in little

or no income. Rent loss coverage provides some income to the owner during restoration and thereby reduces the prospect of foreclosure.

Types of Insurance

There are two principal types of insurance. *Actual cash value (ACV)* insurance is the least expensive and leaves the owner the most vulnerable.
It pays a claim based on depreciation (from use) of the original value of
the item, and the amount may be substantially below the cost of replacement—e.g., a desk that cost $1,000 might be valued at only $700 under
ACV coverage. The alternative, *replacement cost coverage,* pays the cost of
the new or equivalent replacement item: A claim for a desk that cost $1,000
when purchased three years ago and that is priced at $1,700 today would
be reimbursed at the current cost. Naturally, the premiums for this type of
coverage are higher.

An option for lowering the premium cost is to carry a *deductible,* which
is a certain amount the owner agrees to pay before insurance pays for any
of the claim. This practice benefits both the insurance company and the
property owner. The owner pays a lower premium, and the insurer does
not have to investigate or pay small claims. A deductible may be $500,
$5,000, or $5 million, depending on the circumstances, the policy, and the
negotiated terms. The deductible may apply per occurrence, per building,
or per year.

Most insurance policies for damage to a property have *fire insurance*
as their basis. Fire insurance is especially important for residential property because of the numerous opportunities for fire to start in a private
residence. Smoking, stoves, outdoor grills, and carelessness are just some
of the causes. Fire protection itself is not enough, nor will fire insurance
necessarily pay for fire damage under every circumstance. For example, it
may pay for direct loss from a fire but not for related smoke and water damage. Greater protection is provided by adding *extended coverage* insurance,
which usually encompasses damage from specific perils. Coverage is still
limited, however, and broader coverage may be desirable.

A *special form policy* is more comprehensive; it includes most of the
coverages that are commonly obtained as separate policies. A special form
policy pays for anything that is *not* named as an exclusion, and anything
can be excluded. Special needs can be accommodated by paying additional
premiums for specific add-ons.

Insurance for acts of terrorism may be included in a policy or offered
as an endorsement for an additional premium. For most residential properties, with the exception of those in potentially vulnerable locations—urban
centers, near military installations—insuring against acts of terrorism may
be a questionable expenditure. Advice of the owner's insurance agent can
be helpful in this regard. (See also chapter 11.)

Choice of Insurance Packages

To maximize coverage, each residential property usually requires a unique insurance plan. The level of coverage and type of policy vary with the insurance carrier. Insurance for one property may come from several different insurance companies, and numerous *endorsements* or *riders* may ensure protection against particular circumstances that the basic policy does not cover. Possibilities for endorsements are unlimited. If the property has a rare sculpture on its grounds, an endorsement may be added to the basic policy to insure against theft of or damage to that particular piece of art. To obtain the best possible coverage for the lowest premium, the manager should carefully calculate the costs and benefits of each type of additional coverage (endorsement). (An owner of several properties may be able to group them together under a single *blanket policy* at a reduced overall premium. In this way, one or two higher risk properties might be included in the package at a lower rate than they might otherwise receive.)

Administration of such complex insurance coverage is likewise complicated. The property owner usually gives the real estate manager the responsibility to hold the policies, file claims, and ensure that premiums have been paid, although some owners elect to do this work themselves. The property owner is named as the primary insured party in all such policies. However, as the owner's agent, the manager acts in the owner's stead with regard to the property. For that reason, the owner should agree to list the manager as an additional named insured party on all policies related to the property. That protects the manager in his or her operation of the property and expedites the handling of claims for which the manager must contact the insurance company directly.

Physical damage to the structure is only one type of risk that owners and managers of real property must guard against. *Liability* is another. In particular, if an individual is injured or dies on the premises, the manager or owner may be deemed liable. Liability is determined in a court of law, usually in response to a lawsuit. The expense of court time and the prospect of a judge or jury awarding damages to a plaintiff make liability insurance essential. *Liability insurance* protects the owner from financial ruin; it pays the expense of defense against the claim and, if the owner is ruled liable, it pays the settlement. The premium for liability coverage is usually a flat rate per $100,000 of coverage. Additional coverage may be obtained by carrying *umbrella liability insurance,* which is a separate policy that will pay claims that exceed the basic liability coverage. Because the owner is not the only possible defendant in a liability suit, the real estate manager should always insist that he or she be identified as an additional named insured party in the owner's liability insurance. That protects the manager in case of a lawsuit involving the management of the property.

Regardless of the amount of insurance or the types of coverage a property owner carries, the owner's insurance only protects the property, the owner, and the manager. The residents' personal possessions are not covered. For this reason, real estate managers should encourage all residents to carry renters' or homeowners' insurance, depending on the nature of their residency.

SUMMARY

Managing residential property is particularly challenging and rewarding. Rental properties are most commonly thought of as professionally managed. Apartment buildings range in size from a handful of units to high-rise buildings with thousands of units. Although the principles of management are the same regardless of property size, each property has the potential to create unique situations that require specialized management skills. Government-assisted properties require additional administrative paperwork and compliance with legalities.

In rental properties, someone other than the resident is usually the owner. When the residents are the owners, as in common interest realty associations (CIRAs), the home-owners' association employs the manager. Assessments on the owners pay the cost of operating the property, and the manager receives a flat fee rather than a percentage of rental income.

Single-family homes usually require resident participation in their maintenance. Management of units that are not adjacent to each other may be more time-consuming. In manufactured housing communities, the land is usually leased to residents who own their homes, and the residents may pay the community for their utility services. Housing for elderly people is specially designed to accommodate their diminishing independence; rental arrangements may include meals and other services.

Maintenance of residential properties is highly demanding because of the round-the-clock nature of occupancy. The range and complexity of the facilities and the living space influence maintenance requirements.

Insurance of residential property is complex and often necessitates the creation of unique insurance packages. The property owner should carry liability and rent loss coverage in addition to property damage protection, and the manager should be listed as an additional named insured party on all policies for the property.

10

Managing
Office Buildings

The term *commercial property,* in its broadest definition, refers to all real estate development that is not exclusively residential. While managing commercial property is similar in many ways managing residential property, a number of important differences also exist. Two of the most striking distinctions are length of the lease term and complexity of rent payments. (Chapter 8 outlines those differences.) Therefore, the real estate manager's involvement with commercial tenants over the period of their tenancy is much greater than it is with residential tenants.

Office buildings are a unique type of commercial property that has special management requirements. Property analysis for office buildings is done according to class of structure. Tenant selection, rent determination, and lease negotiations also require special consideration. Due to their differences from other commercial property, this chapter details the management of office buildings. Chapter 11 discusses the management of other types of commercial property, marketing commercial space, and insuring commercial properties.

PROPERTY ANALYSIS

The concentration of high-rise buildings within a community has come to be known as the *central business district (CBD)*. In the last half of the twentieth century, people in the largest cities witnessed the development of multiple business districts within cities and in the suburbs surrounding them. The high price of land and increasing congestion of the CBD fueled that development.

While skyscrapers may dominate a city's skyline, the more numerous smaller buildings also require full-time management. High-rise buildings represent only a fraction of the office buildings that require professional management.

When a building owner and a real estate manager or management firm sign a management agreement, they must examine the property objectively to discern its marketable qualities. The manager must learn how the tenants, prospects, and others in the market perceive it in terms of desirability. The manager must not delude himself or herself into believing a property has a greater or lesser strength in the market than it actually has. For this reason, the real estate manager must study the integrity of the property, and the first procedure in this assessment is to examine the building for the purpose of classifying it.

Class of Structure

Although no definitive standard defines what constitutes a specific class of office building, the people and publications in the real estate profession commonly refer to three classes of office buildings: Class A, Class B, and Class C. Age and obsolescence are the two prevailing issues in building classification. An older building has the potential to be notable and appealing, but only if it can accommodate current business needs. If a building cannot be retrofitted for advanced office systems (e.g., wireless technology) or if the space cannot be configured for efficient use by current standards, the class (and therefore the economic potential) of the building is likely to decline.

Class A.   These buildings attract the most prestigious tenants and command the highest rents in their areas. They have outstanding locations and accessibility. They are usually new structures with the latest high-quality amenities and finishes and state-of-the-art systems. Exceptionally well-renovated older buildings in the best locations are often categorized as Class A as well. Class A buildings generally have a complete service staff, including full-time maintenance and security personnel.

Class B.   These buildings attract a wide variety of tenants. The rents are average for the area. The amenities and finishes are fair to good and the systems are adequate. The rents may be lower for many reasons: The building may be older; the location may be less desirable; the building may offer fewer amenities.

Class C.   These buildings attract tenants who need functional space. Rents are below average for the area. Once Class A or Class B, these buildings

---

Twelve Criteria for Classifying Office Buildings

1. Location
2. Accessibility
3. Prestige
4. Appearance
5. Lobby
6. Elevators
7. Corridors
8. Office interiors/efficiency of usable space
9. Tenant services
10. Mechanical systems/communications technology
11. Management
12. Tenant mix

---

are older and reasonably well maintained. Their amenities, finishes, and systems may be below current standards—they may exhibit some degree of functional obsolescence. They may be located on the perimeter of the CBD, and their rents may appeal to those tenants who are most sensitive to price.

The classification of a building is an estimate at best. Visualizing the differences between Class A and Class C buildings is easy, but the distinctions between Class A and Class B buildings can be subtle. Regardless, the building classification can be useful to convey the desirability of the building in general terms.

Criteria for Classification

Not surprisingly, the criteria that influence building classification are those evaluated by prospective tenants as they select office space to lease; current tenants also review these criteria when they consider renewing their leases. The real estate profession uses twelve fundamental criteria for classifying office buildings—location, accessibility, prestige, appearance, lobby, elevators, corridors, office interiors, tenant services, mechanical systems, management, and tenant mix. Most of these factors are interdependent, but examining them separately illustrates their relationship and importance.

Location.   The desirability of an office building is largely measured by its proximity to other business facilities; this desirability can change over time as one section of a city becomes more popular than other sections. Evidence of this is recorded in the history of most large cities. As the CBD develops, most of the buildings on the two main streets are Class A. With each block that is farther away from the main intersection, the property values and prestige diminish, although the buildings may still be Class B. As the area of the CBD expands, some locations on the perimeter may become less desirable because the expansion of the CBD is in the opposite direction (an example of *economic obsolescence*). What was once a Class B building may now be Class C because of location alone.

The effects can reverse as well. As growth of the CBD continues, areas adjacent to it may become popular again because they offer relatively inexpensive land and opportunity for expansion. If so, occupancy rates will increase once the buildings in the area have been rehabilitated or the land has been redeveloped. This will lead to an increase in income and a better property classification.

Buildings developed outside the CBD may also be Class A. Companies that leave the city because land prices and rents are lower in the suburbs generate demand for offices in the outlying regions, resulting in the development of discrete business centers (often called *office parks*) near airports, major highways, and other suburban attractions. Population growth in the outlying suburbs also provides a large pool of workers from the local area.

The attractiveness and cleanliness of neighboring sites influence the desirability of a location. An office building that is well constructed and maintained may rate a Class A designation only if its surroundings are attractive and clean.

Besides the attraction of the CBD or a similar suburban location, the presence of a major corporation can influence suppliers and other associated businesses to locate nearby or in the same building. A major bank may attract investment counselors, brokers, and accounting firms to the site. Likewise, a bank that works closely with large businesses may consider proximity to its major customers when choosing a site.

The desirability of a location because of prestige or convenient access can overshadow most other factors. A strategic location near transportation, within walking distance of major business and financial centers, or adjacent to government services can make a 100-year-old building in sound condition as desirable to a prospective office tenant as the newest construction.

Accessibility. Multistory buildings may house thousands of workers. Because they must have an efficient and rapid way to arrive at and leave the office, access to transportation affects building classification. Office buildings that are served by several transportation alternatives (buses, commuter trains, elevated and subway rapid transit lines, highways) generally have greater value because employers benefit from the availability of a large labor pool.

The availability of parking is also a consideration of accessibility. In general, buildings in CBDs cannot offer as much parking as those in outlying regions; however, buildings centrally located in large cities usually do not require as much parking as those in suburban locations because of the availability of public transportation.

Prestige.   Image and reputation are important factors in business, and location can enhance prestige. A young, ambitious lawyer may want an office in the same building as the city's leading law firms or at least in the same area. The directors of a financial institution will want it to be in the most desirable building in the financial district or as close as possible to such a center. Therefore, the building with a prestigious address and reputation ranks high on the scale of desirability.

Although much of the prestige may stem from location alone, the building's ownership, reputation, management standards, and tenant services can enhance its status. Building size contributes significantly to prestige. A building that is prominent in the city's skyline may command higher rent. A large building may include extensive amenities that further enhance the site's prestige.

Appearance.   A building's architectural design and its exterior appeal are two physical attributes that affect its desirability. Multistoried office buildings are often uniformly cubical or rectangular masses of glass, steel, and stone that lack distinguishing external features, but architectural creativity is giving newer buildings distinctive visual appeal. Attractive older buildings may be retrofitted so they can support today's high-technology uses.

Exterior maintenance contributes to the building's overall impression and attraction. Fresh exterior flower displays, polished entrance doors and signage, and sparkling windows add visual appeal and welcome tenants, prospective tenants, and other visitors.

Lobby.   The appearance, floor plan, and lighting of a building's lobby establish its character. The entrance to any building is part of the setting in which each tenant's business is conducted. A lobby that appears outdated, worn, or neglected will detract from an otherwise attractive building. The real estate manager should pay attention to the primary services that tenants, employees, and visitors expect from a lobby. An updated, well-maintained building directory and unobstructed access to elevators or stairs are essential.

Elevators.   Vertical transportation is vital to multistory office buildings, and each additional story increases the demand for efficient and rapid service. Several factors influence the perception of elevator quality. Location is one of the most important. The desirability of space in the building will be lessened if tenants, employees, and visitors must walk a long distance from the main entrance to the elevators and then walk an equally long distance to their destinations after they arrive on the appropriate floor. Such inconvenience and apparently inefficient use of space create negative impressions of the building.

The appearance of elevator entrances and cab interiors can also affect the perception of the office building as a whole. Passengers expect adequate lighting, proper ventilation, understandable controls, and well-maintained floor coverings in an elevator. To create the illusion of a larger space, a mirror or other reflective surface on the back wall of the cab is sometimes helpful. Any lessening of aesthetic and maintenance standards in the elevator can raise doubts about the quality of the building's tenancy and may even provoke questions about safety in the minds of the elevator passengers.

The most important standards of elevator service are safety and speed, but for passengers, speed includes more than travel time in feet per minute. They judge the amount of time their elevator trip takes from the moment they press the call button to the moment they arrive at their destination. The time spent waiting for the elevator to arrive and the number of stops it makes en route usually influence the perception of quality more than the actual rate of movement does.

Controlling the timing of elevator movement to increase efficiency may be possible. If the building is exceptionally tall, the number of elevators serving a particular floor can be limited. In a 40-story building, for example, one bank of elevators may serve only the second through the twentieth floors, while the other bank serves the twentieth through the fortieth floors. If all the elevators serve one or a few floors in the midsection of the building, passengers will not have to descend to the lobby to go from one half of the building to the other.

Corridors.   Corridors in an office building should be subtle in their decoration and appointments. As much as possible, they should appear to be extensions of the tenants' offices. The corridors should be well lighted and decorated in neutral colors. Any artwork or wall coverings hung in the corridors should reflect the visual appeal of the rest of the building. Staff must diligently maintain corridors in immaculate condition. Signage should be clear, discrete, up-to-date, and uniform in appearance throughout the building.

Office Interiors.   Office suites are usually reconfigured to accommodate new tenants' needs and aesthetic choices. Desirability depends less on existing interior design than on alternative floor plans and the efficiency of the usable space. (The concept of usable space is discussed later in this chapter.) Numerous factors can limit possibilities for changes.

The size and number of windows in a given space and their relative locations often determine the size of the offices. In newer buildings that have expansive windows, the spacing of the *mullions* (vertical bars that separate the panes of glass) usually determines the placement of the walls.

Other factors that limit changes are the existing lighting, the depth of the space from the corridor to the outside wall, the width of the space between supporting columns, and even the view. Older buildings have more load-bearing columns that limit the efficiency of use and the flexibility of the space. Newer office buildings usually have wider column spacing, which permits numerous alternative configurations and efficient use of space.

In addition to layout, the perception of interior quality depends on decoration, wall finish, light fixtures, illumination, and ceiling height. Prospective tenants will judge all of these on their conformity or lack of conformity to the "ideal" office interior, which is generally represented by that available in the most prestigious building in the market. As with any other property, rental value of office space is ultimately based on what else is available in the market.

Tenant Services.   Prospective tenants judge an office building by the quality and variety of the services that the rent includes or that are available. Most important among these are custodial or janitorial services, security, prompt response to service requests by on-site maintenance personnel, after-hours access to the building, availability of after-hours HVAC, and HVAC maintenance.

Some office buildings provide special amenities for tenant use (conference rooms with extensive audiovisual equipment, exercise facilities). The presence of retailers (stock brokerage firms, restaurants, banks, drugstores, newsstands) in the building that serve the needs of workers may also be an asset. In some parts of the United States, office buildings may include concierges and even day-care services, although the latter may be a building tenant. The selective tenant who is shopping for office space or simply considering a move notes these amenities and their direct or indirect costs. The availability of amenities often influences the prospect's decision.

Mechanical Systems.   Advances in office technology place increasing demands on the electrical wiring and HVAC systems in an office building. Often the mechanical systems of a building are a crucial consideration in a prospective tenant's search for space to lease. Tenants increasingly request more power and bandwidth to support the growing use of videoconferencing and other bandwidth-intensive applications. To keep pace with this demand, buildings continue to acquire smarter information systems that require more room for ducting and wiring. New buildings usually have state-of-the-art systems that can keep pace with user demands. They incorporate computer controls into the electrical and HVAC networks to monitor and regulate energy usage, and they include advanced wireless telecommunications systems.

Owners and managers may consider buildings that do not meet the infrastructure demands of new technology for retrofitting. However, many buildings—even relatively new ones—cannot easily be retrofitted to accommodate the many technological advances. In some cases, the costs of retrofitting may be prohibitive. In others, the design of the building may preclude an efficient or cost-effective retrofit. Some buildings cannot be retrofitted at all. This functional obsolescence is one reason Class A buildings can become Class B or Class C despite good locations and high management standards.

Management.   The quality of a building's management adds to the value of its space. Business people are very aware of the influence management has on the appeal of a property and the efficiency of its services.

Of special importance is the level of maintenance. This is often a building service, and it is a direct indicator of management's professional dedication. A well-maintained building with bright wood, polished floors, clean washrooms, dust-free cornices, and general tidiness is more attractive to current and prospective tenants. A prospect that discovers anything less will select a property that is better maintained. Upkeep of mechanical systems and the extent of building security are also indicators of management quality.

The effectiveness of management influences demand for space in the building and contributes to the reputations of the firms whose offices are in it.

Tenant Mix.   Image and reputation are crucial elements in business, and fellow tenants in an office building can enhance (or detract from) these qualities in each other. For this reason, both the prospective tenant and the manager of the property closely examine the *tenant mix* in an office building. A prospect guards against locating in a building whose other tenants will not contribute to its reputation. Prospects sometimes also prefer not to locate near direct competitors.

A building's principal tenant usually governs its tenant mix. For example, if the major tenant is a bank, other financial enterprises (investment and mortgage bankers, brokerage firms, accounting services) may seek space in the building because of that tenant's reputation in its industry and in the community. Sometimes the name of a major tenant may be applied to the building, and that may further encourage a particular type of tenant to lease space there.

Tenant mix is more vital to retail properties (discussed in chapter 11), but managers of office buildings must be wary of prospects whose businesses may detract from the property's image and reputation. Such a tenant may have a negative effect on the businesses of other tenants, which can result in a decline in the property's reputation and its income.

Office Tenant Selection Criteria

- Type of business
- Company reputation
- Financial stability
- Long-term profitability
- Space requirements
- Specific services needed

TENANT SELECTION

Just as an office tenant anticipates being in a building for several years, the real estate manager and the property owner seek tenants who can and will commit to a long-term relationship. The major criteria to consider are the prospect's type of business and reputation, its financial stability and long-term profitability, its space requirements, and its need for specific services. Because these types of information are published or readily available, checking the credit of commercial prospects is often easier than checking that of residential prospects. However, the information is more complex and the consequences of inadequate research can be more damaging.

Business Reputation and Financial Status

The value of an office building is based partly on the business reputations of its tenants. The prospect's business should be compatible with the mix of tenants already in the building, and its reputation should enhance or at least reinforce the reputation of the building as a whole.

The real estate manager should investigate the financial stability of the business. The manager must ensure that the tenant can perform under the terms of the lease and can pay the rent on time. A prospective tenant should fill out an application that lists (among other things): the type of business, the length of time the tenant has been at its current address, its previous address, the principals of the business, the state in which the business is incorporated (if a corporation), the location of the home office (if a branch office), the type of space the business is seeking, the names of its bankers, and credit references (usually vendors). Financial statements, a Dun & Bradstreet rating, the local chamber of commerce or business organization, and the prospect's bankers and suppliers are sources of credit and financial information. The real estate manager should scrutinize every potential tenant, regardless of its size or renown. Large multinational firms are as subject to takeover and bankruptcy as are small ones.

In the aftermath of September 11, 2001, the manager must check the names of all corporate officers, business partners, and sole proprietors who apply for a lease against the *Specially Designated Nationals and Blocked Persons list (SDN)*. Managers should seek legal advice for the appropriate procedures for making these checks. (See chapter 1 for a discussion of the SDN.)

Space Requirements

One of the most complex issues of tenant selection is determining whether the building has adequate space for a specific prospect. Efficient use of space is crucial, and some prospects may not qualify as tenants simply because the available space cannot be designed to comply with their requirements. Three factors must be considered in determining whether the available space is suited to a particular prospect.

1. *Configuration of the available space.* No guarantee exists that a prospect currently occupying 10,000 square feet of space can operate efficiently in the same amount of space in a different building. Exterior walls, columns, elevator shafts, and stairwells cannot be moved or altered to suit the requirements of individual tenants. Those structural elements usually determine the size and configuration of the building's *floor plate*—rentable floor size—and thus determine whether a specific space can be configured to meet a prospect's needs

2. *The nature of the prospect's business.* Some organizations require many executive offices, which usually are along exterior walls of the building because the lighting and view are signs of personal prestige. An organization that has a particularly large clerical staff usually has less demand for perimeter space.

3. *A prospect's plans for future expansion.* If a company expects to grow significantly, the real estate manager must consider whether and how the building can accommodate that growth, especially if the prospect will need contiguous space. While some variances occur among different office uses, in general an allowance of around 150 square feet of floor space per worker will provide a large enough area to accommodate clerical staff, along with the necessary space for cabinets, required equipment that is not part of the employee's work area, and aisles between the desks. (Individual workstations with movable partitions may enclose only 50 to 60 square feet of floor area.) However, if the design is to include a large number of private offices, the manager should consider square footage of individual offices along with separate allowances for conference rooms.

Space needs and office configurations change as technology fosters teamwork in-house, and companies allow or encourage employees to work at home. Cellular telephones, laptop computers, and wireless technology allow staff to do most office jobs almost anywhere. Employers and employees who take advantage of these and newer technologies often need less work space overall. With fewer staff members working in the office, space may be allocated for shared use by workers who come in periodically *(hoteling)* or for groups to work together on projects. Those who work in the field or at home use temporary work space where they can plug into the network and use the phone and other office equipment. They may also use their inside time to attend meetings, give reports, or interact with other staff members. Employees may be able to work at home using a computer linked to their employers' locations via a telephone network *(telecommuting)*. These and other technology-supported strategies have affected how people work in offices, how much space is allocated for individual employees and work functions (sometimes less, sometimes more), and how people and equipment work together to get the job done. Real estate managers need to be aware of changing technology and its impact so they can meet the space needs of current and future office users. (Chapter 2 describes other technological changes.)

Service Requirements

The real estate manager should know the special services that a prospective tenant needs to be able to conduct its business, and he or she should thoroughly consider those requirements in the qualification process. In most cases, the requirements of a prospect that prompt the manager to conduct extra research are (1) a higher level of security than is currently provided; (2) an extraordinary need for electrical power or HVAC; (3) business hours that differ radically from those currently established for the building; or (4) any other service that differs significantly from standard operations. If such factors are not given proper consideration, the building may operate at a loss because of a particular prospect's tenancy.

Before rejecting a prospect outright, however, the real estate manager and the property owner should consider accommodating the prospect. They should analyze the actual costs and the cost-benefit ratio over the long term. Who will pay for the proposed accommodation is one of the lease terms to be negotiated. For example, a prospect may require extensive wireless access capabilities and may be seeking an office building that has a state-of-the-art wireless system. Meeting these requirements may necessitate a large investment, and retrofitting a building for wireless technology cannot always be done successfully. However, evaluation of an accommodation is warranted for the following reasons: (1) The first installation of this kind will make a future installation less difficult or perhaps unnecessary; it can also make securing tenants with similar needs easier. (2) The prospect most likely understands the amount of work and the expense involved in installing the equipment and is therefore more likely to seek a long-term lease in order to avoid repetition of this investment.

OFFICE RENT

New office space is commonly leased as *shell space*—enclosed by outside walls and a roof, with a concrete slab floor and utilities brought in. The plumbing and electrical installations are unfinished, and the space has no partitioning walls, ceiling tiles, wall coverings, or flooring. Office users generally have unique requirements for the space they lease, and it is easier to design and *build out* an unfinished space. (Construction of *tenant improvements* may be done according to the incoming tenant's specifications.) Even a previously rented space may be gutted and rebuilt for succeeding tenants.

Rent is usually charged on a square-foot basis. It may include repayment of some or all of the monies advanced to finance tenant improvements to the leased space. Some property operating expenses (e.g., real estate taxes, insurance, common area utilities and maintenance) may be included in the rent or charged separately on a pro rata basis. Tenants' electricity may be metered individually, and the utility company may bill the tenant directly.

Measuring Rentable and Usable Space

Accurate measurement of the space is crucial to maximize rental income and the market value of the property. Three concepts are central to the measurement of office space. The *gross area* of a building is its entire floor area measured to the outside finished surface of its permanent walls. The *rentable area* of a building is its gross area *less* vertical penetrations through the floor (air shafts, elevators, stairways). The *office usable area* is the rentable area *less* certain common areas that all tenants share (corridors, storage facilities, washrooms). Office usable area is the actual space occupied by tenants.

In order to establish profitable rental rates, the manager must know how much space in the building generates revenue (rentable area) and how much of that space can actually be occupied (usable area). Accurate measurement of the rentable area is extremely important. In a building that has 100,000 square feet of rentable area, a one-percent error would amount to 1,000 square feet. If the average rent were $30 per square foot per year, that one-percent error would result in a loss of $30,000 in rental income each year. The resale value of the property would likewise be reduced—at a capitalization rate of 10 percent, the $30,000 shortfall would lower the property value by $300,000.

Usable Space.   The *usable area of a tenant's leased office space* is the area bounded by its *demising walls* (the partitions that separate one tenant's space from another), the interior of the corridor wall, and the interior of the exterior wall. The usable area is available for the tenant's exclusive use. This area may occupy a portion of a floor, an entire floor of a building, or a series of floors. Although the usable area is the amount of space that is in the tenant's sole possession, rent is usually quoted on the rentable area.

Rentable Space.   *The rentable area of a tenant's leased office space* usually includes certain common areas in addition to its usable area. In a multistory office building, the tenants on each floor pay rent for the common areas on their respective floors. Each tenant's *pro rata share* of the common area of the floor is the percentage represented by the ratio of the tenant's usable area to the usable area of the entire floor (the sum of all defined usable areas on that floor). In addition, all tenants in an office building pay rent for their proportionate share of *building common areas*—the ground-floor lobby and any other areas (conference rooms, mailrooms, building core and service areas) that mutually benefit all tenants.

Standardized Measurement.   To avoid discrepancies, real estate managers employ a standardized method of measurement. The most commonly used method is the one adopted by the *Building Owners and Managers Association (BOMA) International,* a trade association that serves the commercial real estate building industry. (Copies of the current *Standard Method for Measuring Floor Area in Office Buildings,* ANSI/BOMA Z65.1-1996—which includes definitions, illustrations, and calculations—can be obtained from BOMA.)

The BOMA *Standard Method* computes a tenant's rentable area by multiplying the tenant's usable area by an *R/U ratio,* which is the rentable area of a floor divided by the usable area of that same floor. A pro rata share of the building's common areas is then added to the basic rentable area to arrive at the tenant's total rentable square feet. The larger the R/U ratio, the greater the rent paid for the common areas. Prospects are usually more inclined to choose rental space that has the lowest R/U ratio. Older buildings usually have high R/U ratios. This is another characteristic used to classify buildings. (Classes A, B, and C are described earlier in this chapter.)

In some markets, an *add-on factor* (or *load factor*) may be used to account for the proration of the common areas among individual tenants. This may or may not be equal to the ratio between the rentable and usable areas. Some markets may establish a standard or accepted add-on factor. In other words, the R/U ratios of buildings in the CBD may range from 10 to 13 percent, but a standard add-on of 11 or 12 percent might be applied to all usable area rents in the market. This can effectively eliminate one point of negotiation on a market-wide basis. (Exhibit 10.1 is an example of an add-on factor based on the R/U ratio.)

Exhibit 10.1
Use of an Add-On Factor

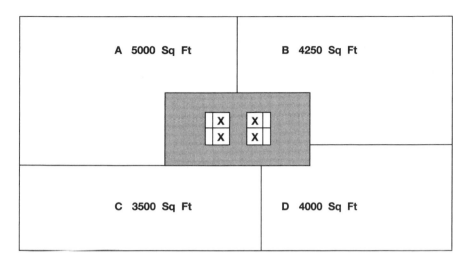

Rentable Area	18,760 Sq Ft
Common Area	2,010 Sq Ft
Usable Area (Total)	16,750 Sq Ft

$$\frac{\text{Rentable Area (18,760 Sq Ft)}}{\text{Usable Area (16,750 Sq Ft)}} = \text{R/U Ratio} = 1.12 \text{ (add-on factor)}$$

	Usable Area	×	1.12	=	Rentable Area
Tenant A:	5,000	×	1.12	=	5,600 Sq Ft
Tenant B:	4,250	×	1.12	=	4,760 Sq Ft
Tenant C:	3,500	×	1.12	=	3,920 Sq Ft
Tenant D:	4,000	×	1.12	=	4,480 Sq Ft
Total:	16,750	×	1.12	=	18,760 Sq Ft

In this sample calculation, the add-on factor is the R/U ratio. In some markets, an add-on factor that is *not* equivalent to the R/U ratio may be used.

Establishing Rates

The rental rate for a building depends on local practice and market conditions. Rent for office space is commonly quoted per square foot, either per month or per year. To determine the rent, the real estate manager must first establish the lowest acceptable dollar amount per square foot that will offset debt service, operating expenses, and vacancy loss—and yield the owner's desired return on the investment. (Chapter 5 discusses market analysis for setting rents.)

If the calculated rental rate is greater than the market will bear, the

Building Standards

The building owner and manager should develop a uniform specification for finish work throughout the building. This *building standard* defines the quantity and quality of construction and finish elements that an owner provides for tenants. It may include materials for partition walls (these may be differentiated for demising walls, corridors, and regular interior walls) as well as the various other components of a build-out—carpeting or hard surface flooring, baseboards, draperies or window blinds, ceilings, light fixtures, paint or wall coverings, and doors, door hardware, and keying systems. The building standard should also address electrical wiring, switches, electrical and telephone outlets, and supply and return air vents for HVAC. The standard should specify compliance with applicable codes.

The owner and manager should establish a dollar amount for an improvement allowance provided to a tenant. The *tenant improvement allowance* is a negotiable item. It may be based on the use of building standard materials, and the tenant may be responsible for any cost overruns. If materials other than the building standard are used, the tenant may be responsible for the difference in (extra) cost.

The building owner and manager should periodically review and update building standards. Market quality standards evolve as new materials become available, and new technology drives other changes. Building codes and other relevant regulations also change from time to time. All these factors can affect building standards. Just one example is the accessibility requirements of the Americans with Disabilities Act (ADA)—they affect both building rehabilitation and new construction and should be a consideration in planning tenant improvements as well.

manager will have to examine alternatives for reducing expenses in order to lower the rent to be competitive. (Otherwise, the owner may have to accept a lower return on the investment.) In ideal circumstances, market conditions will allow rents to be higher than the calculated rate. The marketplace will also dictate whether and which operating expenses the owner can include in the rent or charge directly to tenants on a pro rata basis.

As with any other property, the rent that an office building can earn depends on its condition and its location. The location of a particular office within the building itself, especially in a high-rise building, is also a consideration. In most markets, higher floors and better views command higher rental rates. In terms of height, the manager must examine both extremes of the building. The anticipation of high income from upper floors must often be tempered with lower expectations for office space closer to the ground. Although a high-rise office building will most likely generate a considerable amount of income from its upper floors, that amount may not be sufficient to yield a high income for the building overall.

For instance, a manager may calculate a desired overall average rental rate of $30.00 per square foot per year for a 50-story, Class A office building.

A spectacular view in this structure creates high demand for space on the upper floors, most of which can easily be leased at rates between $40.00 and $45.00 per square foot per year. However, the lower floors cannot expect to command such a high rent, and the manager may have to lease space on those floors for rates that are at or below $30.00 per square foot per year. Ideally, the income the upper floors produce should offset the lower rates.

In CBDs, leasing ground floor space to retailers may be possible, and that can yield additional rent. Retailers may pay higher rates for the space. Sometimes the rents for ground floor retail space are as high as or higher than the rents for the top floors.

Space Planning

Businesses seeking office space are concerned about the comfort of their employees and the efficient use of the space they lease. The tenant who pays for unused space is essentially wasting money, but crowding too many employees into an office may waste the same amount of money through inefficiency. A manager can often help a tenant determine an optimum square footage through a process called space planning.

Space planning is the translation of the prospect's square footage requirements, organizational structure, aesthetic preferences, equipment needs, and financial limitations into the design of a specific floor plan that indicates how office equipment, rooms, and hallways will be placed in the rental space to optimize work flow. Usually a space planner, designer, or architect prepares preliminary drawings. Computer-aided design (CAD) equipment makes exploration of different space arrangements quick and economical. Once lease negotiations are completed, detailed plans are prepared.

Tenant Improvements

Payment of the cost of constructing *(building out)* the tenant's space is often a significant point of negotiation between the leasing agent (or the real estate manager) and the prospective tenant. Usually a *tenant improvement allowance* covers standard items that will be installed at no cost to the tenant (e.g., one telephone jack for every 125 square feet leased, one door for every 300 square feet, etc.). If such a quantitative approach is *not* used, the allowance may be stated as an amount of money the owner will provide per square foot of leased space.

Whether the owner or the tenant pays for construction costs that exceed the standard tenant improvement allowance depends on market conditions and the occupancy level in the building. One of four options is possible: (1) the owner pays; (2) the tenant pays; (3) both owner and tenant pay a portion; or (4) the owner lends the incoming tenant the funds for the construction, and the loan is amortized over the life of the lease and paid back with interest as part of the rent. While a loan paid back via rent is common, the tenant may also seek financing from other sources or pay for the construction outright.

Tenant improvements are more frequently used as an incentive in a renter's market than in an owner's market. Because a commercial lease is usually a long-term contract, sacrifices early in the term may have lasting rewards for both tenant and owner. However, incentives that are too liberal may attract prospective tenants who are less than ideal candidates for the space, and that can burden the property with excessive expense for many years.

No matter how they arrange payment, the property owner and the real estate manager retain final authority on all construction in the office building. The owner of a multi-tenant office building (or the manager on the owner's behalf) usually contracts the construction firm to complete the build-out. This is actually to the tenant's benefit; owner supervision of construction ensures that the integrity of the property's image will be maintained. It tends to ensure high-quality workmanship at lowest cost and realistic timing of the work so that move-in is on schedule.

In the case of offices in *flex space*—single-story structures designed to facilitate different configurations to accommodate both large and small space users as well as some nonoffice uses such as lab assembly or light manufacturing—the building owner (or the manager on the owner's behalf) may allow the tenant to contract for the construction. In such cases, the tenant must meet strict conditions such as owner preapproval of plans, use of approved licensed, bonded contractors and subcontractors, and requirements for specific insurance coverages.

LEASES AND LEASE NEGOTIATION

A written lease, which is a legal contract between the two parties, defines the rights and obligations of the office tenant and the building owner. Because of the complexity of the arrangement and a term that normally lasts more than one year, lengthy negotiations usually precede a lease signing. The building manager often participates in the negotiations. (The leasing agent may work out the details, but the manager will administer the finalized lease agreement.) Even though the manager represents the owner, he or she may be instrumental in clarifying the tenant's perspective or suggesting possible compromises.

The starting point of negotiations is usually a proposal, followed by the presentation of the building owner's standard lease form, which contains clauses that apply to all of the leasable space in the property. However, negotiation of each individual lease generates a unique document that reflects the relationship between the owner and a particular tenant. Many clauses require only minimal discussion. The concerns of the prospective tenant and the property owner usually center on a few specific points. Tenant improvements and any allowances for them are usually negotiated at length. Other clauses that often prompt negotiation relate to rent increases (escalations), pass-through charges, services, and tenant options. Insurance requirements and indemnification clauses may also be negotiated. (Chapter 11 discusses insuring commercial properties.)

Standard Clauses

In developing a standard lease form, one of the owner's objectives is to minimize expenses associated with the rent received. The incoming tenant, on the other hand, wants to maximize the rights and services it receives for that rent. To accommodate these differing desires, a number of specific clauses are common to leases for office space. Two commonly used types of clauses involve rent escalations and pass-through expenses.

Escalation Clauses.   Because a commercial lease is often in effect for several years, it commonly includes an *escalation clause* to provide for a regular increase in rent. Property owners and real estate managers write escalation clauses into a lease to recover increases in real estate taxes, property insurance, and other operating expenses over the term of the lease. Common escalation clauses follow.

Operating Expense.   A lease may contain an *operating expense escalation clause,* under which any increases in operating costs are passed on to tenants on a pro rata basis. For example, if operating expenses for a 150,000-square-foot building were $540,000 one year and $600,000 the next, the owner would pass the $60,000 (40¢/sq ft) increase through to the tenants. The pro rata share of a tenant who occupies a 12,000-square-foot office would be 8% or $4,800 per year above the prior year's expenses.

Base Year.   Sometimes a lease provides for rent adjustments by referring to a *base year* (occasionally the current calendar year but more often the first full calendar year after move-in). The tenant then pays for increases over the amount of operating expenses in the base year. For example, a tenant who moved into offices in September 2005 under a five-year lease would be responsible for increases from the base year of 2006. Escalation of the base rent would take effect in 2007, 2008, and 2009, with a partial escalation for 2010 when the lease term expires. The base year may change when the tenant renews the lease. This may be stated as a specific rate plus accrued escalations. The property owner and real estate manager must take care in establishing the base year for escalations because it will affect the property's cash flow for the full term of the lease.

Lease "Netness"

Net Lease Type	Also Known As	Tenant Usually Pays
Single-Net	Net	Taxes
Double-Net	Net-Net	Taxes & Insurance
Triple-Net	Net-Net-Net	Taxes, Insurance, & Maintenance (TIM)

NOTE: The specific expenses covered under each net lease type may vary from region to region.

Expense Stop.   Another strategy is to include an *expense stop* provision in the lease. This sets a limit on the owner's expense escalations. For example, if the stop is set at $8.25 per square foot per year, the tenant must share in the increased expenses over that amount on a pro rata basis. Often the stop is based on the amount of expenses for the previous full calendar year, and it may be stated as a total amount per year rather than on a per square-foot basis.

In most situations, operating expenses are estimated for the coming year and billed to tenants pro rata on a monthly basis in advance. At year's end, when the actual costs are known, the adjusted amounts are billed (or credited) to the tenants, a process called *reconciliation*.

Inflation Offset.   An escalation clause can also serve to offset the loss in value of the rent dollar over time due to inflation. The owner and the tenant can agree to determine the increase in several ways. (1) In the initial negotiations, the parties can agree to a fixed annual increase for the duration of the lease. (2) They can declare that, at a fixed future date, rent will increase to the then-current market rate, to which both parties will agree at the time and which will never be less than the original rate. (3) They can agree to refer to a standard index such as the *Consumer Price Index (CPI)* to determine the amount of the increase.

In many areas of the United States, the CPI is rarely used as a basis for escalations in new leases because the values can fluctuate widely. However, management firms in the northwestern part of the country still use the CPI—usually with a 5 percent cap and a 3 percent floor. Older, long-term leases may still reference the CPI. (Chapter 2 discusses the CPI.)

Fixed Annual Increase.   The tenant and the manager may prefer to agree on a fixed annual increase for the duration of the lease or on specific rates for set intervals. Annual escalations might be stated specifically ($10 per square foot in year one increasing to $11 in year two and $12 in year three) or as a percentage (8 percent per year). A lease for a very long term might be negotiated to state specific increases only every three or five years.

Pass-Through Charges.   In a commercial lease, not all operating expenses of the property are necessarily collected in the rent. Under a *gross lease,* the owner pays all the expenses of the property and must recover those costs through the rent, but that arrangement is uncommon in large office buildings. Usually the owner bills some expenses to the tenant on a prorated basis in the form of a *pass-through charge.* The pass-through charges are in addition to the base rent charged for the leased space. When the tenant pays any operating expenses directly, the lease is called a *net lease.*

Three types of net leases are common; they are called *net* (or *single-net*), *net-net* (or *double-net*), and *net-net-net* (or *triple-net*). In any locality, with a single-net lease for office space, the tenant pays the smallest number of direct expenses; with a triple-net lease, the tenant pays the greatest number of direct expenses. The expenses covered under each type of net lease may vary by region.

In general, the higher the level of net lease a region uses, the lower the base rent. In other words, a gross lease for office space will state a comparatively high rent because the owner will pay all operating expenses from that rent. The *all-inclusive* rent for that space is its *base rent.* A single-net lease on that same space will state a lower base rent because the tenant will pay part of a certain operating expense or expenses. In the case of a double-net lease, the base rent for the space will be even lower because the tenant will pay more operating expenses. Under a triple-net lease, the base rent on the space will be lowest of all because the tenant directly pays most, if not all, of the expenses. (The three types of net leases are also used for industrial and retail space, and standard definitions are available for those uses, as described in chapter 11.)

The lease states the specific pass-through expenses the tenant will pay and the method of computing the tenant's pro rata share. The most common pass-through expenses are utilities and common area maintenance (CAM) in addition to real estate taxes and property insurance. Owners may pass through capital improvements in the common areas as well, particularly if the improvement reduces an operating expense (e.g., a more-efficient HVAC system may lower utility costs). However, the lease must clearly state that capital improvements will be passed through.

Concessions

A *concession* is an economic incentive an owner gives to a prospective tenant to encourage the leasing of a space or to an existing tenant to encourage the renewal of a lease. It usually provides a monetary incentive but may not reduce the quoted rent. (See the discussion of effective rent in chapter 8 and, in particular, exhibit 8.3.)

Concessions may be in the form of free rent or reduced rent for a specified period, financial assistance with moving from the former location, payment of penalties for breaking a former lease, or payment for above-standard tenant improvements. A concession may be an advance of funds that allows the tenant to invest in certain improvements or incur other costs initially and pay the money back to the owner over the term of the lease. This permits the quoted dollar rent per square foot to stay as high as the market will bear.

Tenant Options

Prospective tenants or current tenants negotiating a lease renewal may seek other *rights*. In a lease, an *option* is the right to obtain a specific condition within a specified time. An option is often written into a lease as an addendum. Except for situations in which a cash payment to the owner is involved, options favor the tenant, and ownership is understandably reluctant to grant them. However, the property owner may need to grant options so a property can be competitive and reflect market conditions.

Option to Expand.   A tenant that anticipates growth may bargain for an *option to expand* that requires the owner to offer specific additional space at a stated time in the future, often at the end of the lease term. Except in very soft market conditions, owners rarely grant such options because they can mean the expansion space will be vacant for some time before the option is exercised.

Right of First Refusal.   As an alternative to an option to expand, the owner may offer a *right of first refusal,* which gives the tenant first choice to lease contiguous space or other space in the building when it becomes available. The lease clause specifies the area.

Right of First Offer.   Another possibility is for the property owner to grant a *right of first offer,* which gives the tenant the right to be the first to make an offer when and if a specific space becomes available. If the subject space is leased to an existing tenant at the time the owner grants the first offer right to the tenant who requests it, the availability date can occur at several times:

1. When the existing tenant does not exercise any renewal options it may have for the space

2. When the landlord first actively markets the space for lease to third parties if the existing tenant does *not* have a renewal right (this often

occurs within 12 months prior to the scheduled expiration date of the existing tenant's lease)

3. When the landlord first receives an unsolicited preliminary offer or request for a proposal from a prospective third-party tenant to lease the space

An owner may also give a right of first offer on unleased new space. This may occur when a building is under renovation or construction and the delivery date is uncertain or marketing has not begun. The tenant that holds the right of first offer usually has a short time after receipt of the owner's availability notice to exercise that right.

Option to Renew.   Sometimes a tenant may seek an *option to renew* on the same terms and conditions as the original lease. However, owners are disinclined to grant such renewal options for several reasons. First, a multiple-year lease usually does not account for all possible market changes during its term—even with escalations still in effect, the actual rent may remain below the market rate. In addition, a renewal option does not guarantee that the tenant will remain. When granted, such options usually refer to a rent adjustment (to an increase to be agreed upon or to market rates current at the time of renewal).

Option to Cancel.   Under some circumstances, a tenant may seek an *option to cancel*. This grants the tenant the right to cancel the lease before its expiration and, if granted, usually requires a financial penalty.

Other Lease Issues

Deregulation of the telecommunications industry expanded the role of the office building manager. Commercial building owners are increasingly responsible for installation, operation, and maintenance of telecommunication risers and cabling in their buildings. The lease document should address the risks that accompany this responsibility. Among the lease issues affected are tenants' insurance, operating expense pass-throughs, escalations, and system failures.

Deregulation of electric and gas utilities means volume users can purchase directly from low-cost sources; however, the electricity and gas will continue to be delivered via the existing local distribution systems. Owners of buildings whose tenants use large amounts of electricity may purchase power to sell to their tenants. Commercial tenants may choose to purchase their own power directly. Leases may need to accommodate these changes in their utilities provisions. In addition, pass-through common area charges may be affected.

Some tenants' leases may need to address regulatory compliance. Disposal of hazardous waste materials is an issue when health professionals lease space in office buildings. Additionally, a separate clause may specify the property owner's and tenant's allocated responsibilities for compliance with the Americans with Disabilities Act (ADA), including provisions for indemnification of either party from liability for costs arising out of the other party's noncompliance.

OFFICE CONDOMINIUMS

Office condominiums are a recent development. They offer ownership of the office space as an alternative to leasing. They appeal to medical and dental practitioners, real estate firms, financial planners, entrepreneurs, and small companies that need 1,000 to 10,000 square feet of space. They are available in Scottsdale, Arizona, the Washington D.C. area, Denver, Nashville, and various locations in Florida, among others.

Not only do owners acquire equity in the property but they are also better able to project and control their costs of occupancy. However, office condominiums do not offer much flexibility to expand or contract as business needs change. Like residential condominiums, office condominiums offer new challenges for professional real estate managers.

SUMMARY

Commercial space is rentable space that is not intended exclusively for residential use. Long lease terms, complex rents, and tenants' desires to maximize the ability of their businesses to prosper in the spaces they rent make lease negotiations crucial to the successful management of commercial property.

Office buildings are a unique kind of commercial property. They are often in the central business districts of cities and suburbs. Whether a building is 100 years old and small or the newest 100-story skyscraper, the value of its rental space to tenants depends on its location, structural components, proximity to transportation, prestige, tenant services, management standards, and tenant mix.

Office rents are based on the square footage of the leased space. They may cover a proportionate part of the operating expenses for the common area (a gross lease). Frequently however, the property owner passes many of the property's operating expenses through to the office tenant on a prorated basis in addition to rent (a net lease).

Office leases often contain escalation clauses that describe the type of rent increases that may occur over the term of the lease and the terms of those increases. Other lease clauses specify the types of expenses (if any) the owner will pass through to the tenant.

Owners may offer potential tenants and current tenants monetary incentives called concessions to encourage them to lease or re-lease space in an office building. In negotiating a lease, tenants may request additional rights in the form of various options.

Condominium offices have recently become popular among professionals, entrepreneurs, and small companies. They combine the advantages of ownership with the opportunity to better control office costs, and they represent new opportunities for professional real estate managers.

11

Managing Shopping Centers and Other Commercial Properties

All real estate development that is not entirely residential is *commercial property*. Office buildings, shopping centers, research and development parks, warehouses, and buildings designed for medical and other professional services are the types of commercial properties professional real estate managers most often manage.

Leased retail space ranges from ground floor space in office or apartment buildings to a variety of shopping centers, including modern shopping malls that enclose a million or more square feet of space and attract shoppers from several states. (Chapter 9 describes retail space in apartment buildings; chapter 10 discusses retail space in office buildings.) This chapter focuses on the management of shopping centers and other commercial properties.

As previously mentioned, some important ways management of commercial property differs from management of residential property are the longer lease term, the greater complexity of rent payments, and the real estate manager's increased involvement with the tenants. This chapter presents two additional important considerations of commercial property management: marketing and insurance.

SHOPPING CENTERS

A shopping center differs from a retail district in a city center or a residential area in that it is usually a single project in a suburban area and it typically has on-site parking. However, shopping centers are not exclusively located in the suburbs; major cities also foster their development downtown, both as new buildings and as adaptive uses of old ones. A shopping center has a unified image, and the property is planned, developed, owned, and managed on the basis of its location, size, and types of shops as they relate to the *trade area* the center serves (i.e., the area from which customers are drawn).

Property Analysis

Unlike property analysis for office buildings, shopping center property analysis does not involve an analysis by class structure. Instead, shopping centers are categorized according to the nature and variety of merchandise they offer and the size of their trade areas. Other considerations a real estate manager takes into account when analyzing the desirability of a shopping center are its aesthetic appeal, location, accessibility by automobile and public transportation, and availability of parking.

The definitive measure of retail space is its square footage, which is expressed as *gross leasable area* (*GLA*) in reference to both the shopping center as a whole and the individual store interiors. In an enclosed shopping mall, the *gross floor area* includes the mall's GLA plus the *common areas*—courtyards, escalators, sidewalks, parking areas, etc., that are not used exclusively by individual tenants.

Most shopping centers have at least one *anchor tenant*. Retailers such as department stores or supermarkets that have large space requirements are common anchor tenants. *Ancillary tenants* occupy the smaller store spaces in a shopping center and may, because of their specialization (jewelry or stationery, for example), attract additional customers to the center.

Shopping Center Classification.   The nature and variety of merchandise a shopping center offers and the size of its trade area determine its classification. However, shopping center categories frequently shift in terms of size and parameters, and new types appear. The categories that follow are among the most common.

Convenience Shopping Center.   A *convenience shopping center* usually has a convenience market anchor and a few small shops (2 to 10 stores). A combination gas station and food store is also common. Most stores of this nature are open all day and all night. When additional store spaces are available, other tenants may be card- or coin-operated laundries, barbershops, dry cleaners, or liquor stores. Convenience centers are often designed in a line, so they are sometimes called *strip centers*. That term can refer to other types of centers as well. This type of center has 5,000 to 30,000 square feet of GLA. The typical trade area comprises the immediate neighborhood of the site, and the traffic on the street. A convenience center can succeed in an area with a population of 1,000 to 2,500 if it is well located.

Neighborhood Shopping Center.   The most common anchor tenant in a *neighborhood shopping center* is a supermarket, a super drugstore, or a combination of the two. This type of center usually has 15 to 25 small shops. Ancillary tenants include dry cleaners, bank branches, beauty salons, and card and gift shops. The GLA of a typical neighborhood center is between 30,000 and 150,000 square feet. A neighborhood center usually thrives in an area with a population of 5,000 to 40,000.

Community Shopping Center.   Junior or discount department stores usually anchor *community shopping centers.* Alternatively, the anchor may be a supermarket or a large hardware store. The 25 to 40 ancillary tenants frequently include men's and women's apparel stores, bookstores, card shops, family shoe stores, and fast food operations. Community shopping centers range in size from 150,000 to 400,000 square feet of GLA. They usually require a population of 100,000 to 150,000 to sustain them.

Regional Mall.   These large shopping centers have one or more full-line department stores as anchor tenants. The presence of a department store tends to attract such ancillary tenants as men's and women's apparel stores, optical shops, electronic equipment stores, and jewelers. Often several stores of one type (for instance, three to five shoe stores) locate in such a center. Many *regional malls* include small fast food outlets arranged in a *food court.* Some also have cinemas. Regional malls contain 400,000 to one million square feet of GLA. Their trade area has a radius of 7 to 10 miles, and they usually serve a population of 150,000 to 300,000.

Super Regional Mall.   These large shopping centers include four or more full-line department stores and 100 to 150 small shops. Ancillary tenants in a *super regional mall* are usually the same types as in regional malls, only there are more of them. Super regional malls, as well as some regional malls (and large community shopping centers), may include separate buildings on sites called *outlots* or *pads.* Banks, restaurants, automotive service centers, and movie theaters are common tenants for these spaces. A super regional mall has one million to three million square feet of GLA. Its trade area has a radius of 10 to 20 miles, and it serves a population of 300,000 or more.

Specialty Shopping Center.   A dominant theme or image characterizes a *specialty shopping center.* Those in downtown areas are often the result of adaptive use of a historic building. They do not always have an anchor tenant, and many rely on tourists for most of their sales. Their uniqueness is their main attraction. They usually vary in size from 25,000 to 70,000 square feet, although some of these centers can be as large as 375,000 square feet of GLA. The specific use defines the trade area, and it may extend beyond the radiuses usually associated with centers of this size. Specialty shopping centers require an area population in excess of 150,000 to survive.

Outlet Center.   At least 50 percent of an *outlet center* consists of factory outlet stores that offer name-brand goods at lower prices by eliminating the intermediary wholesale distributor. They may include off-price and discount merchants. At an *off-price center,* retailers offer name-brand merchandise at well-below-normal retail prices. These centers can give such large discounts because the merchandise consists of factory overruns, seconds and dated items, overstocks from other stores, and consignment purchases from manufacturers. Outlet centers may attract customers from a radius of 20 miles to as far away as several hundred miles in rural areas. They traditionally require a minimum population of 200,000.

Power Shopping Center.   A type of super community shopping center, the name *power shopping center* comes from each anchor tenant's ability to attract customers from a wide area. Several large, strong, high-volume, heavy-advertising retailers occupy most of the space. Home furnishings, office supplies, sporting goods, home improvements, toys, and consumer electronics (computers, major appliances) stores are common anchor tenants in these centers. Power centers have GLAs ranging from 200,000 to 600,000 square feet and at least four category-specific off-price anchors, each occupying 20,000 or more square feet of GLA. The trade area may extend up to 30 miles, depending on local competition; they need a minimum population of 150,000.

Lifestyle Shopping Center.   Anchor tenants such as Ann Taylor, Barnes and Noble, and Pottery Barn are typical in *lifestyle shopping centers.* They have few small shops because they lack the traditional anchor tenants. The trade area may vary greatly from one center to another, depending on the local competition. Lifestyle shopping centers generally have 250,000 to 500,000 square feet of GLA.

Entertainment Shopping Center.   Sometimes difficult to distinguish from lifestyle shopping centers, *entertainment shopping centers* typically consist of entertainment, dining, and other retail stores. Most entertainment centers have a GLA in the range of 150,000 square feet up to 300,000 square feet, but some are well above those figures. The trade area may vary, depending on the location of any other similar center or competition.

Megamall.   These giants can be three to four times larger than a regional center, and some contain five million or more square feet of GLA. *Mega-*

malls, such as the Mall of America, are often connected to or contain hotels, amusement parks, or nightclubs in addition to numerous anchor tenants and hundreds of ancillary tenants.

Trade Area Analysis.   The *trade area* of a shopping center is the geographic area from which it draws most of its customers. The size of the trade area depends on the type of shopping center, the location of competition, and other factors.

The trade area analysis includes a *demographic profile,* which details the social and economic statistics of the population, such as size, density, growth and decline, and its vital statistics, such as age, household size, education, and income. The demographic profile shows the number of people who are likely customers and their purchasing power. The analysis also includes a *psychographic profile,* which goes beyond the numbers to examine the interests and shopping habits of the people who live in the shopping center's trade area.

The trade area analysis indicates the potential for a shopping center to succeed in a particular location. A new shopping center does not create new buying power; it must attract customers away from other shopping centers, so evaluation of the competition in the trade area is important.

Most trade areas are subdivided into three zones—primary, secondary, and tertiary. The *primary trade area* is the immediate area around the site and accounts for 60 to 75 percent of the shopping center's sales. The *secondary trade area* usually extends 3 to 7 miles from the site (for a regional shopping center) and accounts for 10 to 20 percent of sales. The *tertiary trade area* may extend 15 to 50 miles from a major shopping center and account for 5 to 15 percent of sales. Every shopping center, whatever its size, has a trade area and trade zones, the sizes of which vary with the type of center and its location. People will usually travel only one to two miles to shop for groceries, but they will travel three to five miles for apparel and household items and eight to ten miles to comparison shop for appliances and other major purchases.

Aesthetic Appeal, Location, and Accessibility.   The aesthetic appeal of the center plays a strong role in attracting customers, particularly for regional and super regional centers. People who shop at convenience and neighborhood centers live nearby, and proximity is their primary reason for shopping there. Small centers are not dependent on attracting people from a considerable distance, so aesthetic factors are not as critical. Larger centers must blend function and design to create a safe and attractive place for people to spend a lot of time. Important decorative features are lighting, seating, colors, landscaping, and flooring.

Within the trade area, the value of one location over another may depend on the customers' means of transportation. Because most people who shop at large suburban centers travel by car, the center must be easily accessible and provide parking for large numbers of automobiles. Simply being adjacent to a major thoroughfare is not a guarantee of accessibility, especially if traffic patterns make entering or exiting the property difficult or dangerous. Distinctive and appropriate signage to identify the center, clearly marked entrances and exits, and internal traffic controls (i.e., stop signs) also contribute to accessibility.

Parking. Parking must be convenient. Therefore, the plans for a parking lot or garage must receive a great deal of forethought. Parking for downtown shopping centers is usually provided in multistory garages incorporated into or adjacent to the retail building, and shoppers may receive a discount on parking if they make a purchase.

Parking for suburban shopping centers is usually built on the land around the shopping center. The amount of land that is necessary for parking can be gauged in two ways. (1) Local zoning ordinances may specify a relationship between the size of the parking area in square feet and the size of the retail building *(parking area ratio)*, or (2) the number of parking spaces may be based on the gross leasable area (GLA) of the shopping center *(parking index)*. The Urban Land Institute (ULI) recommends 4.0 parking spaces for each 1,000 square feet of GLA for centers that have less than 400,000 square feet of GLA. A center that has 400,000 to 599,999 square feet of GLA should have between 4.0 to 4.5 spaces per 1,000 square feet of GLA. One that has 600,000 or more square feet of GLA should provide 4.5 spaces for every 1,000 square feet of GLA.

Parking ratios and indices are merely guidelines; many other factors must be considered in developing a viable parking plan. Different parking angles and varied widths of driving lanes between parking bays affect the numbers of stalls that an area can include. In addition, shopping centers must provide parking for disabled shoppers, so wider stalls and access ramps are needed near building entrances. Traffic flow (circulation patterns) and ingress/egress are other concerns.

The shopping center parking plan must also consider the needs of specific retailers. For example, supermarkets may require a drive-up lane for loading. Video stores and fast food restaurants require more parking spaces because of the frequent turnover of their customers. Shopping centers that include offices must provide long-term parking for employees of both the offices and the stores in addition to parking for customers. Certain retailers within the center may have more extensive parking requirements than others, or they may have a higher demand for parking at particular times during the day or week. Cinemas in shopping centers pose a different problem. Parking for nighttime showings will not conflict with regular daytime customer parking, but matinees require additional parking—at the expense of parking for shoppers.

Retail Tenant Selection Criteria

- Merchandise category and pricing—fit with consumer demographics and psychographics
- Retailer's reputation—how it treats customers
- Merchandise presentation
- Financial stability—including the parent company
- Tenant requirements—amount of space, visibility, special needs
- Tenant mix of the center—match of merchandise types and price lines
- Tenant placement in the center

Tenant Selection

In choosing tenants[1] for retail space, the manager weighs many factors. Apart from consumers' natural curiosity, the shopping center manager must anticipate what will actively attract customers to the shopping center. The ideal tenant will offer appealing merchandise whose price and quality are a good match with the goods and services of the other tenants. In addition, the ideal tenant's merchandise should fill a need in the market that competing shopping centers do not meet. All of these factors are in keeping with the demographic and psychographic profiles of the trade area. The manager must scrutinize the retailer's reputation and financial status to determine the prospect's quality, responsibility, and ability to pay the rent. Requirements for store space and support services as well as products or services that the retailer offers must also be considered—particularly as they affect where the retailer can or will be located in the center.

Reputation.   One of the most important factors to consider when choosing a retail tenant is reputation. Because reputation results from public perception, learning how a retailer treats customers is important. This is easy to ascertain for a store that is part of a franchise or chain or one that is planning to move from one site to another. Assuming the role of a customer and making a purchase, then asking to return or exchange the item, will reveal the quality of a retailer's *customer service*. Observation of the treatment of other customers in the store and asking them about their perceptions of the store can give insights as to how the prospective tenant conducts business.

A consideration in addition to customer service is *merchandise presentation*. A slim inventory of dusty items suggests a poor sales record; fresh

---

1. As mentioned previously, the names of all corporate officers, business partners, and sole proprietors who apply for a retail lease must be checked against the Specially Designated Nationals and Blocked Persons list (SDN). (Chapter 1 discusses the SDN.)

merchandise presented carefully implies the opposite. Salespeople who know their stock and present themselves well in both dress and attitude are an asset to the retailer and will be the same for the shopping center. How much the retailer advertises indicates what it is doing to establish and maintain its reputation.

The inclusion of a unique business in a shopping center whose other tenants are well-known can give the center a competitive edge. While the risks involved with a new business are greater, the rewards may outweigh the risks. An innovative enterprise may quickly gain a healthy customer base because of its difference from established retailers and chains. A new or developing enterprise may not have an identifiable reputation, but finding out how it will operate is not impossible. An individual or company that presents a clear plan of action for developing a new business, including an investment in inventory and a pricing structure that is in line with the demographic and psychographic profiles of customers in the trade area, will probably be a better prospect than one whose plans are vague. A knowledge of its probable clientele and an understanding of its competition are also important. Prior retailing experience is almost essential.

Financial Integrity.   There was a time when the decision to accept a prospective tenant could be based primarily on reputation—the name "Bloomingdale's" was once sufficient to solidify a deal. In an age of buyouts and takeovers, however, shopping center managers should carefully investigate the financial health of all prospects. While an established store in a chain may be doing exceedingly well, that one store may not be an accurate reflection of the success of its parent company or the parent company's parent company. If the related enterprises are foundering, the parent company may sell the individual store to raise cash. While such an occurrence may not affect a prospective tenant's business, any change in the ownership of a complex retailing operation increases the risks to the individual store and may create a vacancy in the shopping center.

The greatest cause of business failures is undercapitalization, which is one reason for carefully investigating new or proposed retail businesses. The costs of operating a retail business include not only rent, utilities, and maintenance of the store area, but also inventory, payroll, store design, fixtures, and advertising. For an established business, moving costs and the loss of business resulting from the move must be considered as well. Prospects should have sufficient reserve funds to be able to weather an initial lean period after they relocate.

Tenant Requirements.   The retail tenant's primary concerns will be the availability of adequate space for its business, visibility of its location, and the volume of customer traffic a shopping center generates. In addition, some tenants will have special requirements. Food service operations have unique garbage disposal and pest control problems that must be addressed. Furniture and appliance stores require specialized loading docks. Supermarkets need large areas for short-term parking. A bank may want to provide drive-up services for its depositors. Whether and how these unique tenant requirements can be met are the subject of lease negotiations. However, the shopping center manager must know in advance what types of accommodations are possible so he or she does not make unrealistic promises during prospecting.

Special services arranged for one tenant that are beyond those normally provided can lead to a concern on the part of other tenants, even if the tenant that needs the special service pays for it. The best way to counter these concerns is by explaining positive outcomes. For example, if a movie theater in a shopping center has a last showing that begins at what is closing time for the other stores in the center, the common areas leading to the theater must remain open so its patrons can exit after the show. Even if the entrances to the stores are closed and locked, tenants whose stores are adjacent to the theater may be fearful that late-hour theater patrons may damage their stores. The shopping center manager should understand this concern and act on it. One approach is to make it a condition of the theater's late showing that the theater provide a security officer until all of its patrons leave. Limiting access to the shopping center to a single entrance during the late hours is also helpful. The manager should point out to other tenants that the theater's last showing may be responsible for a swell in business before the stores close because theatergoers may arrive early to do some incidental shopping.

Tenant Mix and Placement.   The combination of retailers and service vendors that lease space in a shopping center constitutes its *tenant mix*. A shopping center anchored by an upscale department store will attract shoppers that seek—and can afford—its lines of merchandise. A center anchored by a discount department store will attract people seeking bargains. The best tenant mix for each shopping center will follow the anchor's lead. In other words, the merchandise of the ancillary tenants must not clash with that offered by the anchor tenants. For example, a furrier probably will not succeed in a shopping center anchored by a supermarket or a hardware store. On the other hand, a dry cleaner may flourish in such a center because it, too, serves immediate needs.

Another consideration that relates tenant mix to merchandise is *destination shopping* versus *impulse shopping*. People usually have a specific purpose in mind when they are visiting an optical shop or a luggage store in a shopping center; their search for a particular item or service has led them there. If they buy an ice cream cone in the process of going to or coming from their destination store, that is an impulse purchase. A good tenant mix serves both destination and impulse shoppers and increases sales of the center as a whole.

Shopping centers that have more than one anchor tenant must ensure that the merchandise offered by each of them is a good match and is complementary to the offerings of the ancillary tenants. An effective way to create a workable tenant mix is to view the specialty shops and department stores in the shopping center as parts of one big store.

Where the tenants are located in relation to each other in the center is also vital. Shoe stores are a natural complement to retailers that sell men's or women's clothing. An ice cream parlor often does well next to a sandwich shop. When developers build new shopping centers, they pay careful attention to the positioning of tenants in order to maximize their potential to attract customers to and through the shopping center as a whole.

Retail Rent

Rents for retail space are based on the gross leasable area (GLA) of the individual spaces. Like offices, stores are usually rented as open *shell space* (sometimes called a *vanilla box*). Contrary to the practice in office buildings, the tenant, not the owner, is usually responsible for completing the interior beyond the shell stage (subject to the owner's preapproval of plans as well as other parameters).

Base Rent.   Shopping center leases state rent for the space as base rent. *Base rent,* also known as *minimum rent,* is usually calculated on a per-square-foot-per-year basis and is commonly stated in the lease as equal monthly incremental amounts. Base rent assures the property owner a minimum income regardless of the merchant's sales success. In addition, retailers usually pay *pass-through charges* that cover the cost of operating the center (including taxes and insurance) plus *common area maintenance* (*CAM*) charges.

Percentage Rent.   In a larger shopping center, retailers may also pay a portion of their sales revenue as *percentage rent.* When percentage rent is charged, the property owner shares in the success of the retailers that lease space in the property. Percentage rent is generally based on gross annual sales, but most tenants pay percentage rent monthly, except anchor tenants who pay it annually. Because this type of rent is based on the retailer's sales volume, the amount can fluctuate significantly from month to month, so percentage rent is usually paid *in addition to* base rent. Some retailers may be able to negotiate to pay percentage rent only, but owners rarely make this exception and then only for large establishments with very high sales levels.

There is no universally applied percentage rent rate—it depends on the type of business and the locale—but there are accepted ranges of percentage rent.[2] For example, supermarkets have a very large sales volume and very low profit margins, yet 1 percent of their gross sales will yield a large amount of percentage rent. Conversely, gift shops have comparatively small sales volumes but high profit margins, and 10 percent of their gross sales may be appropriate.

The actual percentage is always negotiated. It is usually collected on sales in excess of the amount of base rent and referred to as *overage rent*. In other words, the base rent for a store may be $120,000 a year, payable in equal monthly amounts of $10,000; if the percentage rent is 5 percent of gross sales, the tenant's gross sales must exceed $200,000 a month before percentage rent applies ($10,000 ÷ 0.05 = $200,000). The tenant pays the greater of the percent of gross sales or the base rent.

In the preceding example, the $200,000 a month in sales is the *natural breakpoint*. If the store produces $250,000 in gross sales in a month, its rent will be the $10,000 base rent plus 5 percent of sales above the natural breakpoint—in this case, 5 percent of $50,000, or $2,500, meaning the total rent for that month will be $12,500. However, the prospective tenant or the property owner may negotiate an *artificial breakpoint* to use as the threshold for paying percentage rent. The artificial breakpoint may be higher or lower than the natural breakpoint—a downward adjustment of the breakpoint would increase the owner's income. An artificial breakpoint can accelerate payback to the owner of funds advanced for tenant improvements.

Pass-Through Charges and Net Leases.   As in office leasing, under a *gross lease* for retail space, all operating expenses are the responsibility of the property owner who must recover them fully in the rent. However, most retail tenants have *net leases,* meaning that *some expenses of operating the property are passed through to the tenant.* The type of net lease the owner offers determines what the tenant pays, and pass-through charges are prorated based on the GLA of the individual store as a percentage of the GLA of the shopping center as a whole. The types of net leases follow:

- *Net lease.* The tenant pays a prorated share of real estate taxes only.

- *Net-net lease.* The tenant pays a prorated share of real estate taxes and insurance costs.

- *Net-net-net lease.* All operating expenses including real estate taxes, insurance, utilities, common area maintenance (CAM), and various

2. The Urban Land Institute publishes percentage rent rates in its publication *Dollars and Cents of Shopping Centers.*

Clauses Unique to Retail Leases

- Use
- Exclusive use
- Radius
- Store hours
- Common area maintenance (CAM)
- Tenant's pro rata share of expenses
- Advertising and signage
- Tenant improvement allowance (TIA)
- Continuous occupancy
- Continuous operation
- Alterations (to the store space)
- Insurance (required of the tenant)
- Parking
- Marketing fund or merchants' association
- Percentage rent
- Sales reporting
- Auditing sales

---

fees are prorated and passed through to the tenant. Under a *modified triple-net lease,* which some shopping centers may use, the owner is responsible for structural repairs to the building and for payment of management fees for the common areas.

Numerous other—mostly regional or local—definitions exist of the expenses that are passed through to the tenant under a particular type of net lease, so delineation of the pass-through charges is essential when describing a type of net lease.

Major retail tenants may also negotiate with property owners to set a *cap* (an *expense stop*) on certain expenses, most often on common area expenses. This ceiling assures that the retailer will pay only a certain dollar amount per year for the particular pass-through expense or expenses to which the cap applies. Unlike an expense stop in an office lease, which sets a ceiling on how much the property owner pays, a cap in a retail lease defines a limit on how much the tenant pays.

Escalations. Because retail leases have long terms (a 20- or 30-year lease for an anchor tenant is common; ancillary tenants' leases usually have 3- to 10-year terms), escalations have to be written into the lease in order for them to take effect automatically. As in leases for office space, provisions for rent increases may be negotiated as a periodic percentage increase, or they may be based on an index such as the Consumer Price Index (CPI). Base year and expense-stop provisions are also used.

An escalation provision typically applies only to the base rent; however, escalation provisions sometimes apply to expense stops or base year expenses. The lease for an anchor tenant whose sales generally surpass the agreed-upon breakpoint may mandate an escalation in base rent only once every five years. Ancillary tenants' leases usually call for annual increases. The specifics depend on market conditions at the time the lease is negotiated.

The Retail Lease

The standard lease form for a shopping center includes a number of clauses that are specific to this type of property. It addresses concerns and contingencies that can arise over the number of years covered by the lease. (The lease for a freestanding store or for space in a small convenience shopping center may not have such specific provisions.) In addition to the specific clauses and considerations described in this section, the lease specifies rental rates and other charges and states when and how payments are to be made.

Use.   A shopping center is carefully designed and leased to appeal to a specific market in a specific location. If any tenant were to change its merchandise or its image (e.g., specialty lines to general merchandise, upscale to discount), that could alter the tenant mix of the center. A use clause prevents a tenant from using the premises in a different way than originally intended.

Exclusive Use.   A prospective tenant may seek a clause covering *exclusive use* to prohibit other tenants in the shopping center from selling a similar product—in other words, to minimize competition. However, some competition within the center is generally beneficial, and an exclusive use clause can be counterproductive. It may also violate antitrust laws enforced by the Federal Trade Commission, which make restraint of trade illegal. However, temporary limits on certain product lines or on competing store sizes may help a retailer meet its lease obligations (e.g., rent) or give a new business a head start. Because it is desirable to have several types of tenants in each retail category in a regional or larger center, and because the merchandise carried by each retailer in a category tends to complement the others' merchandise rather than compete with it, owners rarely grant exclusive use.

Radius.   The *radius clause* prohibits a tenant from operating a similar store or from developing a similar chain of stores within a certain distance from the shopping center—typically three to five miles. Its intent is to prevent the tenant from directing customers to a nearby store in order to reduce percentage rent. The owner and tenant may negotiate a compromise in which the tenant agrees to include in the percentage rent calculation part or all of its gross receipts from a permitted nearby store.

Store Hours.   Among tenants of the same shopping center, variation in store hours should be minimal. This clause authorizes the management of the property to set store hours for the center as a whole. Some anchor tenants such as supermarkets or large drugstores may remain open 24 hours a day. These stores are usually located in open shopping centers where the ancillary tenants maintain their own hours. A *store hours clause* may also include provisions for seasonal adjustments and special hours for holiday shopping periods.

Common Area Maintenance.   The *common area maintenance (CAM) clause* specifies exactly what constitutes the common area of the shopping center and what expenses the tenant will pay. In addition, it spells out the property owner's responsibility to maintain the common areas and repair any damage to them. It also gives the owner the right to expand, reduce, or otherwise alter the common area. The common area in an enclosed mall includes the mall corridors, parking lots, escalators, landscaped areas, and other parts of the property that the tenants use in common. (In a neighborhood shopping center, the common area may be limited to the parking lot and landscaped areas.) In addition to maintenance and upkeep of the common areas, CAM charges include expenses for security personnel and alarm systems that protect the shopping center, its tenants, and their customers. They also include fees for management of the common area.

   As noted earlier, CAM fees are normally prorated based on the percentage of gross leasable area of the center the individual store occupies. On that basis, a store with 3,000 square feet of GLA in a 300,000-square-foot (GLA) shopping center would pay 1 percent of the center's CAM costs. (A separate clause usually specifically states the tenant's *pro rata share* of CAM and other expenses.)

Advertising, Signs, and Graphics.   The property owner retains the right to restrict the size, location, lettering, and language of all signs in the shopping center. Large malls establish uniform graphic images and seek to maintain consistency in the caliber of signage. This is especially important for signs that are permanently mounted on the exterior of the building or are placed in the center's interior. Tenants may be required to spend a certain percentage of their gross income on advertising to promote their stores—and the shopping center.

Marketing Fund versus Merchants' Association

In order to promote a shopping center to consumers, the retail lease contains a *marketing clause* that requires tenants to provide funds for center-wide marketing efforts by participating in either a marketing fund *or* a merchants' association.

Marketing Fund. This is an account specifically for funding center promotions and advertising that is *controlled by the property owner.* All tenants in the center must contribute a predetermined amount stated in their leases; the amount is based on their GLA (an amount per square foot). The owner's contribution may be a percentage of the tenants' total contributions, and it may take the form of salaries and benefits for marketing personnel, insurance, and office space.

Merchants' Association. This is an organization *controlled jointly by the owner and the tenants* that plans promotions and advertisements for the center as a whole. It is established as a legal, usually nonprofit, corporation with bylaws and a budget. Both tenants and owner pay dues—tenants contribute a pro rata share based on their GLA or a percent of their annual gross sales; the owner provides a percentage of the total budget, often based on the amount collected from the tenants.

The merchants' association is an older concept. Most shopping centers developed since the early 1980s have adopted the marketing fund approach to underwriting shopping center marketing costs.

Concessions.   As in office leasing, a shopping center owner may offer concessions to secure a new lease or to retain an established tenancy. Because concessions are a special part of the lease negotiation process, they are usually stipulated in the applicable clauses rather than included as a single specific clause, or if there is no applicable clause to amend, they may be listed in separate documents incorporated into the lease by reference (addenda). Ideally, any concession granted will not lower the quoted rent. It is important to remember that any reduction in rent also reduces the value of the property (see chapter 8).

One type of concession, a *tenant improvement allowance* (*TIA*), is money the owner provides for modification of the leased space before the tenant moves in. This may be a dollar amount per square foot, and the tenant may have to repay this as *additional rent* prorated over the lease term. Store space is typically leased as a "vanilla box" consisting of a storefront, demising walls, and HVAC. Depending on the area of the United States and market conditions, the demised premises may include (or specifically exclude) other items such as utility lines to the interior of the space, a dropped ceiling, and a restroom. Tenants usually finish the interiors of their store spaces and install appropriate display fixtures themselves. (Unlike in office buildings, retail tenants' improvements rarely have direct impact on structural components or mechanical systems of the shopping center building.) However, the tenant will be required to submit a construction or remodeling plan for the property owner's approval before work begins.

Other concessions include payment of a new tenant's moving expenses, a higher artificial breakpoint for percentage rent, or a period of free rent.

Other Clauses.   Requirements for *continuous occupancy* (staying in business for the full term of the lease) and *continuous operation* (keeping the business operating smoothly and consistently) are common clauses in retail leases. Shopping center owners usually include *sales reporting and sales auditing clauses* to ensure that tenants report and pay percentage rent accurately and on time. Provisions regarding *alterations* to the store space, *insurance* coverage for the retailer's business, ADA compliance, and related indemnification are also common. *Parking* is a concern for some businesses, and a separate clause may address the tenant's specific rights and limitations.

Most large shopping centers have promotional campaigns for the center as a whole, and to support those campaigns, they may require tenants to participate in a *marketing fund* or *merchants'association*, usually through a specific lease clause. Options similar to those described for office leases—to renew, to expand, to cancel—may also be a part of retail lease negotiations.

Shopping Center Management

Management of a shopping center requires intensive work and a tireless staff. In addition to ensuring that the center is up-to-date, clean, and safe, the shopping center manager must deal with the tenants and their concerns. The tenants' economic survival depends on customers coming to the shopping center and patronizing their stores. Competition among tenants is sometimes intense and can result in strained relations unless the shopping center manager serves all of them in a fair and consistent manner.

Retailers experience competition from the Internet. However, many established retailers use the Internet as an adjunct to their brick-and-mortar stores. This may become an issue for negotiation of retail leases so that tenants do not direct sales away from store locations to reduce their obligation to pay percentage rent.

In addition to the physical and financial management of the property, shopping center managers become intensely involved with the marketing of the site and, therefore, with the marketing of each store. In general, managers of shopping centers are more involved with the ongoing activities of their tenants than are managers of office buildings or residential or industrial properties. Shopping center management can be as dynamic as retailing itself. To be successful, shopping center managers must have a knowledge of retailing and merchandising that is comparable to their knowledge of real estate management.

For thousands of shoppers to visit every day is not unusual. Their continued patronage will be assured by careful attention to their comfort while they shop in the hope that they will leave with a favorable impression. However, such large numbers of people can lead to concerns about crime, and shopping centers are vulnerable to many forms of criminal activity. Some anchor tenants may employ their own security forces, but most shopping centers of significant size contract with a security agency to guard the premises. While such personnel are important, the efforts of the shopping center manager should focus on educating tenants and their employees about ways to prevent crime and reduce opportunities for criminal activity.

OTHER COMMERCIAL PROPERTIES

Professional real estate managers are also involved in the management of a variety of other types of commercial space. Leases for those properties include clauses similar to office and retail leases as well as clauses specific to the particular use.

Property Types

Other professionally managed commercial properties include medical buildings, industrial sites, and warehouses. Each poses distinct challenges to the real estate manager because of the unique requirements of its tenants.

Medical Buildings.   Buildings whose space is leased primarily to medical and dental professionals must be modified to meet those tenants' needs for additional (sometimes specialized) plumbing and electrical wiring. The nature of their clients (patients who may be ill) and the services they provide mandate special care in cleaning and waste disposal—bloodborne pathogens and other hazards (e.g., radiation). The lease must address those issues. Entrances and other common areas—including parking—must accommodate disabled and ailing individuals.

In addition to doctors and dentists, other possible tenants for a medical building include pharmacies, biomedical laboratories, physical therapists, optical services, and health maintenance organizations.

Industrial Properties.   Industrial properties include large single-user buildings, incubator space for small business start-ups, multi-tenant business parks, self-storage facilities, and business continuity services (records maintenance). They often have a mix of uses that combines office, retail, light manufacturing, distribution, and storage at a single site.

Technology has affected industrial users' space needs as it has those of office and retail uses. Manufacturers can often maintain minimum stocks of raw materials, parts, and packaging because computer inventory systems coupled with overnight shipping services allow *just-in-time delivery* that keeps pace with their production levels.

Most new industrial rental space consists of single-story structures that can be configured to accommodate a single tenant or multiple tenants (*flex space*). Often built in a business park setting, such spaces have no lobbies or fancy fixtures, and they have no load factors or add-on charges. Rents are lower, and parking is ample. Tenants can be companies that need large blocks of inexpensive space (e.g., Internet, e-commerce, and telecommunications firms setting up data centers) or firms that need their offices in the same building as their manufacturing or warehouse operations.

Research facilities and factories are often built to tenants' specifications (*build-to-suit lease*). Truck access and rail lines may be among their requirements along with reliable sources of electricity and other utilities (gas, water). Existing commercial facilities that are open to the public as well as renovations and new construction are required to meet accessibility requirements of the Americans with Disabilities Act (ADA).

Businesses (and individuals) may choose to store and secure their goods themselves in *self-storage facilities* that resemble rows of attached garages. Many of these facilities include living quarters for an on-site manager. Some storage areas do not have insulation, and therefore storage is at the tenant's risk. Newer self-storage facilities have insulation and provide climate and humidity controls.

Warehouses.   *Warehouses* may exist in city or suburban areas. Their space is leased for storage of inventory, records, excess raw materials, and the like. Warehouse management services may include shipping and receiving, with charges based on gross weight of materials handled or the number of packages shipped and received. The storage environment (e.g., control of temperature and humidity) is critical for many materials, and federal and other laws mandate labeling to identify specific hazards of materials transported in interstate commerce. These requirements may affect management procedures.

Lease Considerations

Industrial leases include many clauses similar to those in office and retail leases. To maintain the owner's control over the property, the *use clause* should be specific about the tenant's type of business. The tenant often has direct responsibility for maintenance, especially if a single tenant is in a building.

Storage is another important consideration. Industrial tenants often use hazardous materials that require special storage facilities and special waste disposal equipment and procedures. To reduce risk and protect the value of the property, the leases of such tenants should require an annual environmental inspection of their leased spaces (at the tenant's expense). The *insurance clause* will usually be specific as to type and amount of coverage the tenant must maintain.

Tenants in a *research and development park* or similar campus-style property may establish a tenants' association to oversee road maintenance and groundskeeping, budgeting, and collection of fees for common area operations and maintenance, and any other routine management activities. In a *master-planned development,* tenants in a single-use building are offered some form of net lease. In *multi-tenant properties,* the tenant is responsible for maintaining the interior of the leased space, including the HVAC.

Generally, the owner is responsible for the roof, structural elements, and common areas. The owner bills the tenants (large and small) for their pro rata share of common area maintenance (CAM) charges plus real estate taxes and property insurance.

MARKETING COMMERCIAL SPACE

Businesses are not inclined to move very often. When one does, it usually intends to remain at its new location for a long time. Because of the infrequency of moves, and because a multiple-year lease translates into many thousands or millions of dollars in rent over its term, commercial tenants are commonly recruited directly, although conventional advertising and promotion cannot be overlooked.

Prospecting for Tenants

To ensure optimum occupancy, a property representative must make direct calls on potential tenants. This is particularly important for proposed developments; lending institutions usually require a certain percentage of a planned property to be *preleased* (leased before construction of the building begins or while the construction is taking place) before construction loans will be approved.

A property or a management firm may employ a leasing agent (either temporarily or permanently) or contract with a leasing agent whose sole purpose is to seek out potential tenants. The leasing agent accomplishes this through a process known as *cold calling* or *prospecting,* which involves direct calls on the principals of businesses (individuals or corporations) to discuss the possibility of moving their operations to the subject property. In order to achieve success with such a program, the leasing agent must conduct research on various businesses to ensure that his or her efforts are directed toward the most likely prospects. This is especially important for retail properties that seek specific types of tenants to fill a particular product or service niche in the tenant mix of a large shopping center.

Information regarding businesses that may be considering a move can come from many sources, including the chamber of commerce, company annual reports, and referrals from business acquaintances. The most likely prospects are businesses that anticipate expansion and those whose leases are nearing expiration. Use of the Internet facilitates recruiting on a nationwide basis. Leasing agents can learn of retailers' plans to expand, and prospective tenants can find listings of available space.

Real estate managers or leasing agents use a *prospect report* that records information about prospective tenants for office space, their space needs, current space and lease expiration data, how they were contacted, whether they were qualified for tenancy, and their status as prospects (received brochure, given a tour of the property). This is a cumulative record of the prospects brought to a building by a particular leasing agent. For retail space, information about the type of business, expected lease terms, and tenant improvement work is similarly documented along with the source of the contact and the status of individual prospects (lease under negotiation, dead deal). Such records determine the leasing agent's commission (especially when outside brokers are used) as well as the overall progress in leasing available space.

Marketing on Value

Unlike residential property, which is usually marketed on personal appeal, the marketing emphasis for commercial space is usually on the dollar value the prospect will receive for the rent paid. In this case, value directly affects the prospect's profit margin. The four principal ways to market space based on value are to emphasize price advantage, improved efficiency, increased prestige, and economy.

1. *Price advantage.* Well-managed businesses always strive to improve net profits. If a leasing agent can demonstrate a price advantage in a location that fully meets the prospect's expectations or prerequisites, the likelihood of at least stimulating preliminary interest is great.

2. *Improved efficiency.* Convenient access for employees or customers, low utility costs, and excellent tenant services are some attractions that may turn a prospect into a tenant. Better operating efficiency is also a form of price advantage. Space plans and layouts or other visual aids can illustrate the expectation of more efficient operations. A demonstration of space adaptability is a tangible and especially strong incentive. Such a demonstration, coupled with data on the

probable reduction of expenses, may justify the prospect's move. In addition, with increasing dependency on technology, many businesses relocate to buildings that have superior mechanical and electrical systems so they can upgrade their operations and equipment.

3. *Increased prestige.* In terms of business value, prestige is a marketable commodity. The rent for prestigious space will certainly be higher, but greater visibility may increase the prospect's business so the amount of rent as a percentage of gross income may actually be lower. Prestigious locations can also help attract employees.

4. *Economy.* When price advantages are mentioned, a lower cost on a comparable item is implied. In commercial space, however, economy refers to space that is lower in price but not necessarily equivalent to the space currently occupied. Sometimes a business located in a Class A office building could just as well have part or all of its operations in less-expensive space without compromising its strength or reputation. During periods of inflation or slow business activity, a prospect may consider less-luxurious space or outlying locations to control occupancy costs.

Leases for residential property may involve some negotiation, but negotiations with commercial prospects are commonplace. The property owner and the tenant may specifically negotiate many lease clauses. Negotiation of leases for commercial space is complex because the financial risks are greater for both the tenant and the property owner.

INSURING COMMERCIAL PROPERTIES

When an investor makes a "small investment" in commercial property, the purchase price of the store or office building may be several million dollars. "Large investments" do not necessarily have upper limits, but property valued between $100 million and $1 billion is available in most major U.S. cities. Whether the investment is small or large by industry standards, the expectation is for the property, over its lifetime, to generate income well in excess of its purchase price. In fact, the purchaser's ability to retain ownership usually depends on the periodic income the property generates.

Owner's Insurance

If the lifespan of the property ended abruptly because of damage, even a so-called small investment could bankrupt the investor. *Comprehensive insurance coverage* provides protection from financial ruin due to the loss of use of the property. However, no single policy can completely protect the investor; even if such a policy were available, the premium cost would be prohibitive.

As with income-producing residential property (see Chapter 9), the owner insures commercial property against loss of income, structural damage, and liability. The policy identifies the owner as the named insured party and lists the manager as an additional named insured. A major difference for commercial property, however, is that insurance premiums are an operating expense that the owner may prorate and pass through to the tenants.

While almost anything can be insured, the owner must balance the cost of the premium against the risk of leaving all or part of the value uninsured. To illustrate, windows are easily broken and expensive to replace, so most basic insurance policies exclude plate glass windows from coverage or limit the amount paid in any year for window breakage. If every policy included this coverage and placed no upper limit on the amount the insured could claim, owners of skyscrapers that may replace numerous windows in a year because of breakage would benefit at the expense of owners of buildings that have few windows that they rarely have to replace. The insurer would have to charge high premiums in order to pay the claims, and the cost to insure a small building would be prohibitive. To avoid such an inequity, insurers exclude plate-glass coverage from basic policies altogether. However, a separate plate-glass policy can be purchased, or an endorsement can be added to the primary policy to pay for plate-glass damage. The owner of a building that has thousands of windows probably would investigate the value of paying for the coverage. For a smaller building, the owner might leave the windows uninsured and pay for the occasional replacement as an operating expense.

In the wake of September 11, 2001, owners and managers of commercial buildings in New York City, in particular, discovered that their insurance coverage did not include acts of terrorism, and their claims were denied. Subsequently, Congress passed the *Terrorism Risk Insurance Act (TRIA)*, which requires insurers to make that coverage available (see also chapter 9). Insurers sell terrorism insurance coverage separately from other coverages, and the premiums are expensive. However, owners of commercial properties, especially properties located in urban centers, should at least consider purchasing it. Lenders are likely to require such coverage if the building is mortgaged. The owner's insurance agent can advise on how much coverage would be appropriate.

Tenant's Insurance

Because insurance for the property as a whole does not cover the contents of tenants' individually leased spaces, most commercial leases require tenants to carry enough insurance to cover their inventory and whatever furnishings and equipment they have in their leased space. The commercial tenant's insurance coverage should be sufficient both to preserve the business and to meet the obligations of the lease in case of disaster. Tenants may need other types of insurance as well (e.g., crime coverage). Commercial tenants are usually required to carry their own liability insurance, and the lease may obligate them to list the owner of the property as an additional named insured party. Retail leases may specifically require tenants to have insurance against plate-glass damage and business interruptions. (Federal law requires that employers carry workers' compensation insurance to cover on-the-job illness and employee injury.)

The relationship of an insurance company with its customers technically gives it the right to sue an entity in the name of the insured party in order to recover a settlement it has paid if evidence shows that the other entity may be liable. This right is called *subrogation*. Suppose, for example, that an electrical fire damages a building, and the property owner's insurance pays the claim. If later evidence proves that a tenant's employee left a space heater on overnight and it ignited the carpeting, the owner's insurance company might file a suit against the tenant or its insurance company to recover the amount of the claim. The existence of this right can make obtaining insurance very difficult for both the tenant and the owner, so both parties are usually obligated to sign a *waiver of subrogation* to prohibit the exercise of this right.

SUMMARY

Leased retail properties are available in ground floor spaces in apartment and office buildings, in shopping centers, and in a variety of other commercial spaces. Rentable space that is not solely for residential use is considered commercial space.

Shopping centers are the most common form of professionally managed retail property. They are located in suburbs and in cities. Each shopping center is planned as a single project. Shopping centers usually have a unified image and provide on-site parking in suburban centers. Shopping centers are classified by size and by types of tenants. The types of shopping centers are constantly evolving. As with office buildings, shopping center rent is based on the square footage of the leased space, and some operating expenses of the shopping center are passed through to the tenants as a separate charge in addition to base rent. Retailers may also pay a percentage of their gross sales as additional rent.

Other types of commercial real estate that professional real estate managers may manage include medical buildings, industrial properties, storage facilities, and self-storage facilities. Along with the financial and administrative issues, managers of these types of properties must often deal with issues relating to storage and disposal of hazardous materials as well as tenants' special needs.

Marketing is more aggressive for commercial space than it is for residential property. The real estate manager or leasing agent targets specific businesses as prospective tenants and calls on them directly to sell the benefits of relocation to the property he or she represents.

All property owners, real estate managers, and commercial tenants must have insurance to protect their own interests and to protect the interests of all others involved with the property. As with residential space, the diversity of commercial property types does not permit development of a definitive insurance policy to cover all of the damage that may occur at an individual property. When planning a unique combination of policies and endorsements, the property owner and the real estate manager must balance the premiums against the cost of self-insuring in order to design an insurance program that is economical and effective.

12

The Business of Real Estate Management

Those who choose real estate management as a profession often begin their careers with an established management firm. To develop a complete perspective on this specialized profession, the manager must understand how a real estate management business is acquired, how management fees are determined, how a real estate management office is organized, and the types of collateral services that a management company may offer its clients.

HOW MANAGEMENT BUSINESS IS ACQUIRED

A substantial portion of the executive manager's time—at least 20 percent—should be spent in acquiring new accounts. This is necessary just to maintain the same volume of business because accounts are lost due to changes in property ownership, assumption of management by ownership, or transfer of management to another firm when the management agreement term expires. Expansion of the business requires even more attention.

Recruitment of prospective clients is similar to seeking prospective tenants. Management firms may attempt to specialize their services based on the type of client, the type of property, or both. Such specialization tends to minimize the increase in administrative duties as the firm's portfolio grows. The difference between managing one office building or two, for example, is not necessarily a doubling of the overall workload. Site management responsibilities may double, but the similarity of administrative tasks reduces the cost of establishing procedures and reports for each property.

Identifying Prospective Clients

Any individual or organization that owns income-producing real estate is a potential client of a management firm. However, not all of them are legitimate prospects. The real estate manager should study the types of owners and the reasons they are most likely to seek professional management. This identification process will enable the firm to concentrate on a particular type of client and may aid in specializing the business by property type.

Quite often, new management business arises from problem properties. If a property is not profitable, it becomes a liability to the owner instead of an asset, and the owner will investigate alternatives to strengthen the return on the investment. One of these alternatives may be new management. The owners of properties undergoing a downturn are therefore a potential market for professional management. Telltale signs of financial hardship are the loss of a major tenant, a vacancy rate higher than that in comparable properties, bankruptcy, or foreclosure. Evidence of deferred maintenance may also indicate an opportunity. Even though such conditions may provide an opportunity to acquire a new client, the manager and the firm should proceed with caution. Thorough analysis is necessary before making any promises or proposals. If space in a property is not leasable, any investment in such a property by a management firm can divert attention from other clients and properties that will benefit from dedicated management.

New buildings present a different type of management opportunity. A developer often contracts a management firm before ground is broken, and the manager is involved in the planning process early. Research of zoning changes, demolition permits, and sales of vacant land, coupled with insights from the media, colleagues, and acquaintances can identify such opportunities so the management firm can promote itself for consideration to manage a new property.

Some types of owners naturally seek professional management, primarily to free themselves from the responsibility of caring for the property. In most cases, management firm clients can be categorized either as owners by choice or as owners by circumstance.

Owners by Choice.   Individuals, partnerships, limited liability companies, corporations, real estate investment trusts (REITs), foreign investors, and others who invest in real property (institutions such as insurance companies and pension funds) are owners by choice. Their goals for an investment may differ, but all such owners offer distinctive and profitable opportunities for the real estate manager.

Individuals who actively engage in their own professions may have

Potential Management Clients

Owners by Choice
- Individuals
- Partnerships
- Limited liability companies (LLCs)
- Corporations
- Foreign investors
- Institutional investors
    —Insurance companies
    —Pension funds
    —Real estate investment trusts (REITs)
- Common interest realty associations

Owners by Circumstance
- Individuals/estates (inheritance)
- Businesses (merger; buyout)
- Financial institutions (foreclosure)
    —Banks
    —Trust companies
    —Mortgage banks
- Governmental agencies (foreclosure; seizure)

neither the time nor the inclination to collect rents, handle leasing activities, perform maintenance, or do any of the other tasks that are essential to effective real estate management. Sole proprietors who do not reside or work in the immediate area of their investment properties almost always require the services of local managers.

Partnerships are groups of investors who seek profit from a real estate investment but who may require professional guidance and attentive property administration to achieve their goal. A management firm may create a partnership (a syndicate in such a case) to purchase a property in order to manage it. Other forms of multiple ownership (REITs, joint ventures, and other investment-based ownership arrangements) almost invariably seek professional management of their properties. (However, major players typically self-manage their properties.)

Some corporations own and are responsible for operating income-producing property, but they are not large enough to create an organization for that purpose. Corporations sometimes erect buildings to house their own operations and build much larger structures than they need. They may do that to gain rental income or provide space for future expansion, or merely for prestige. To operate such a building, the corporation may hire a real estate manager as a staff member, but many engage a management firm.

The owners' association of a condominium or cooperative is usually a corporation, but the individual owners may not have the ability to supervise the property in which they live, let alone an interest in doing so. Nonprofit corporations such as colleges and universities often hire managers to operate and maintain their academic and residential buildings. They may also own income-producing property acquired through bequests, and those properties require management as well.

Foreign investors commonly rely on professionals to manage their real property holdings in the United States. This dependence stems from more than geographic distance; foreign investors rely on the native real estate manager to advise them on the legal and cultural implications of actions involving their property. Naturally, this requires the manager to understand the laws and culture of the foreign investor's homeland as well.

Owners by Circumstance.   Sometimes individuals and institutions become owners of real property that they did not purchase. These owners by circumstance may be geographically removed from their property, unwilling, or unable to manage it themselves. An individual who inherits an apartment building in another state is an example. Owners by circumstance present a unique opportunity for professional management.

Estates themselves are another source of management opportunity. Whether a property is put in trust after its owner's death or is held by the estate for some other reason, professional management may be necessary to maintain the value of the property, assure a regular income, or both. Lawyers who represent owners or estates that have properties requiring administration occasionally assume the management of those properties, but most engage a professional manager.

Financial institutions (banks, trust companies, mortgage banks, investment houses) and other sources of investment capital (insurance companies, pension funds) are other potential clients. They are among the large group of investors classified as *institutional owners*. They may also become the owners of real property because of a mortgage foreclosure. They will often try to sell such a property as quickly as possible to reduce their loss. However, a property they cannot sell must be managed to retain its value and, if possible, generate income in order to meet specific financial obligations (i.e., taxes). Because they do not seek to hold a foreclosed property for a long period, financial institutions rarely seek to improve such property or increase its market value unless improvements are necessary to sell the property and repay the loan.

Federal, state, and local governments are important factors in the local real estate economy and are therefore prospective clients for real estate managers. A housing authority may acquire property or, as a principal lender, may become the owner of foreclosed property. Other agencies or departments become owners of real property through seizure. Property may be seized because the taxes were not paid, because the money used to purchase the property was obtained illegally, or because the financial institution holding the property was declared insolvent and its assets were seized to liquidate the institution. Regardless of how they become owners of income property, most governmental agencies engage private professional real estate managers rather than set up their own management departments.

Litigation in the courts involves naming receivers or trustees, and the professional real estate manager is qualified to fill these roles. The manager who is acquainted with the local heads of agencies that own real property and with the courts that have jurisdiction over properties in receivership is a likely candidate to manage them.

Promoting the Management Firm

Identifying potential clients is just the beginning. The challenge is to convert those prospects into clients of the management firm. Most prospects become clients because of direct solicitation, established reputation, personal referral, institutional advertising, and good public relations.

Direct Solicitation.   The best way to acquire business is to ask for it. However, before asking for management business, the manager should become familiar with a specific property or an owner's portfolio as well as that owner's investment goals. Based on that information, the manager should prepare a brief proposal stating the general advantages of professional management as well as the specific advantages of management for the particular property or portfolio. This means that before contacting a prospect, the manager will have carefully examined the building and evaluated its operations. The proposed service must understandably be justified. The manager should also know as much as possible about the owner. When the real estate manager finally contacts the property owner, the prospect should receive an appealing and clearly understandable presentation packet that outlines the qualifications of the management organization and the kinds of services it offers.

Direct solicitation requires persuasion and perseverance. A prospect's property is a major investment, and it is unlikely that an owner will award a management contract to a new manager after only one call; usually many calls are required. Managers who solicit business directly must understand that rejection is more common than acceptance. However, the reasons for rejection can become obsolete over time, and repeated follow-up can lead to success because an owner may eventually be willing to reconsider a manager who previously presented a proposal.

Reputation.   One of the most important ways to achieve success in real estate management is to establish a favorable reputation. *Professional repu-*

tation is the overall opinion of the business community regarding the character and capability of the manager or the management firm. This opinion is based on successful results and on personal and business characteristics such as ethical practices. While a good reputation in the community is important to a management firm, it is also important for the individual manager. Personal reputation is the cornerstone on which an individual manager can build his or her own management company. Neither management firms nor individuals can rest on their laurels for long. An accomplished manager must work as hard to preserve a good reputation as a newcomer must work to create one.

An owner turns a property over to a management firm because he or she trusts the integrity and capability of that firm. Establishing his or her worthiness of that trust should be the highest priority in the real estate manager's efforts to obtain business—and retain it. The manager does this in part by developing as many solid credentials and good references as possible. The CERTIFIED PROPERTY MANAGER® (CPM®) designation and the AC-CREDITED MANAGEMENT ORGANIZATION® (AMO®) accreditation from the Institute of Real Estate Management (IREM®) are two such credentials.

Referral. The adage "nothing succeeds like success" certainly applies to expanding the business of a real estate management firm. A proven record of managerial success and a reputation for diligence can lead satisfied clients and other business acquaintances to recommend the manager and the firm to owners who could benefit from their services. They may also identify prospects directly to the management company or the individual manager. Licensed real estate agents who sell various types of income property naturally encounter new owners and established investors, and they are important sources of referrals, as are professional real estate managers who do not manage the type of property or who do not manage in the city in which the property is located. (Real estate agents customarily receive a referral fee if a management agreement is signed because of their referral.)

Institutional Advertising. Advertising can effectively promote management services. However, institutional advertising is usually designed to increase name recognition and build reputation rather than to promote a specific service. Four types of institutional advertising have proved effective.

1. *Display advertising* in community newspapers reaches a wide circulation and, if handled effectively, enhances an organization's prestige. However, advertising in a newspaper reaches its entire readership, most of whom are not in the market for real estate management. Because those who own property or who have control of property in some manner are the potential prospects, advertising in the real estate, business, or financial section of a newspaper may be more

cost-effective. Display advertising in real estate and other investment-related periodicals is another, often more-effective, way to direct the message to an appropriate audience.

2. *Direct-mail advertising* promotes the firm exclusively to those who are likely prospects for management. The promotional material should be of superior quality and should be personalized as much as possible. The quality of the presentation and the care with which the mailing list is created and maintained determine the success of direct-mail advertising. Regular mailing of a client newsletter published by the management firm is another direct-mail strategy that many firms use successfully.

3. *Signs* on buildings the firm manages are a significant source of new business. Prospective clients are influenced by the judgment of other building owners. The buildings a management firm manages are direct evidence of the quality of service it offers. In this regard, building signs should be carefully designed, and the signs as well as the buildings must be meticulously maintained.

4. *Web sites* are an increasingly important form of advertising for real estate management companies. Most do significant institutional advertising on their Web sites. In addition, the firm's Web page can include display advertisements, the contents of direct-mail promotions, and news releases that have been sent to the media. The Web site provides a continuous marketing effort.

Public Relations.   In addition to purchased advertising, a thoughtfully conceived public relations program is a valuable promotional adjunct. *Public relations (PR)* relates to public knowledge, approval, confidence, and preference. An effective PR program acquaints as many people as possible with the existence of the management company—what it does and what it stands for—and encourages general acceptance of the company. Because a real estate management firm provides a service, a sound public relations program is very important. People usually give more credibility to what they read or hear if the source of the information is not an advertisement, so a management firm should take every opportunity to garner favorable *publicity*. Familiarity and cooperation with members of the press can help in this regard, especially when the firm issues a press release about a new contract, a new major tenant, changes in management personnel or practices, or any other newsworthy item. The management firm's public includes its clients, and copies of press releases can be used to promote new or expanded services to established (and prospective) clients—another direct-mail advertising strategy. Note, however, that most companies distribute press releases via e-mail and then put them up on their Web pages.

The management firm should continually monitor its promotional efforts and measure their success. Cataloging the source of each business contact is the primary method of identifying the most effective public relations activities. Some firms require their real estate managers to make a prescribed number of cold calls each week, and they pay a bonus for new business obtained from this activity.

Good PR also requires introspection in regard to the office environment, personnel, and clients' properties. The firm should review its operations regularly and make appropriate changes as necessary. The buildings a firm manages are also a reflection on it, so the company's management portfolio requires periodic review. As part of prospecting for clients, buildings selected for management should be a credit to the firm.

Ultimately, responsibility for establishing public acceptance rests with the personnel of the organization. Personnel represent the company, so they should reflect well on it. Their duties and responsibilities should be reviewed in terms of their PR impact. They should be able to communicate effectively to bring credit to themselves and their company. Individuals within the firm should be encouraged to establish themselves as respected authorities in particular fields by speaking to civic and business organizations, publishing articles, and participating in related professional activities. They should also be encouraged to participate in community affairs, and, when they do, to perform the duties they accept. The management firm should consider issuing a press release and placing an announcement on the company's Web site regarding such public service activities and any awards the company or individual employees garner.

HOW MANAGEMENT FEES ARE DETERMINED

Before a real estate management firm considers acquiring the management of a particular property, the manager must estimate the amount of income the property can potentially generate. The manager negotiates a specific fee with the property owner, and the amount depends on the type and extent of services provided.

Basic Fee Structures

In most circumstances, the management firm receives a percentage of the property's gross receipts (the total amount collected during a reporting period—the effective gross income). The management agreement sometimes states a minimum monthly amount to ensure compensation for services regardless of the property's income. A management fee of three percent of gross receipts with a minimum monthly fee of $3,000 would require the property's gross receipts to be less than $100,000 a month for the minimum fee to apply.

Individual real estate managers may be employees of an institutional owner or of a management firm and may receive a regular salary. An independent real estate manager (one who is not employed by a management firm) can contract to manage properties himself or herself on a percentage-fee basis. Percentage fees usually apply only when rents are the principal source of income.

Compensation for management of condominiums or other association-operated properties is commonly a flat fee. Those properties do not have rental income as such; resident-owners are assessed a prorated amount to maintain the property.

Additional Fees

In addition to a management fee, the real estate firm or manager may seek separate compensation for other specific services such as lease-up of a new building. However, normal (turnover) leasing activity in an existing apartment building is usually included in the regular management fee. Construction oversight (supervision of contractors rehabbing a residential property or building out tenants' spaces in commercial property) is often compensated separately. Leasing agents for commercial space usually work on commission, although some brokerage firms offer the option of a salary plus a bonus. The manager of the property may handle renewal of commercial leases; that may or may not warrant an additional fee.

The management agreement should itemize the services the management fee covers so the owner understands that a request for other types of services will result in additional charges. Some firms establish a schedule of fees for services not included in the management contract. For example, standard procedure may be to provide one copy of a financial status report to the owner each month, in which case, a charge for additional copies or more frequent reporting would be appropriate. Such a schedule of fees may be incorporated into the management agreement by reference and by attaching a copy of the schedule to the agreement.

THE REAL ESTATE MANAGEMENT OFFICE

Many of the same criteria that make real property desirable (location, amenities) also affect the value of a real estate management business. The company office should be convenient and comfortable for the firm's clients, the tenants of the properties it manages, and its employees. The people in charge must be conscious of the clients' perceptions, in particular, because clients entrust their investments to the firm. An office with stacks of paper,

---

Common Client Expectations of Real Estate Management Firms

- Ethical practices
- Confidentiality regarding client information
- Qualified, experienced personnel
- Detailed reporting
- Thorough long-range planning
- Sophisticated financial accounting
- Thorough analysis of a property's performance
- Frequent communication
- Rapid response time
- High net operating income
- Knowledge of physical maintenance

---

mismatched furniture, tattered carpeting, and dingy walls will not inspire a prospective client to sign a management agreement. On the other hand, an office in the most prestigious building in town may raise other concerns. Because management fees pay for the company's office space, clients may think the firm's fees are too high if the offices are luxurious—even if the fees are competitive with those of other firms. Successful management companies understand what their clients expect and reflect that in their own offices.

Location

Two elements of location are most important for real estate management firms to recognize—where the on-site office is located in a building and where the management firm's central office is located with respect to the buildings it manages. Not all management firms have multiple offices; some may have all operations in one on-site office or they may have an on-site office in each property they manage. A management firm could have a central office in addition to on-site offices, or if the firm has only small properties in its portfolio, it may have only a central office and no on-site locations.

Most new apartment buildings have space planned and designated as an on-site office. Smaller buildings may have an on-site manager living on the premises who conducts business out of his or her apartment. Otherwise, management business is conducted from the main office of the management company.

An on-site office in commercial property should be easily accessible to visitors and tenants, but it need not be a ground-floor location. The manager must evaluate the potential loss of rental income before choosing a location for the office. Management offices in retail properties are often

Management Office Space Planning

The management office should be well designed, with consideration given to the business activities that will be conducted there. While accounting and record keeping are major functions—in fact, the primary if not the exclusive activity of a small company—a large firm will need to provide work spaces for a personnel function (human resources) and supervisory staff. Since employees will also be dealing with suppliers and tradespeople as well as prospective tenants and clients, a conference room is appropriate. This can also be used for staff meetings.

Office furniture should be selected with comfort and the job function in mind. Adequate lighting appropriate to the task is imperative. Offices and workstations should be configured for computers and any other equipment a worker's job requires. Shared equipment (e.g., computer peripherals) should be readily accessible. Files and storage cabinets should be convenient.

Groups of people who need to work together should have a work area designed to facilitate teamwork. Employees whose tasks include placing and receiving numerous telephone calls or who work with noisy office equipment should not be near accounting personnel who need a quiet area where their concentration is less likely to be interrupted. Good space planning accounts for the people, the equipment they use, and the way they do their work.

adjacent to but not in the midst of primary traffic areas. At large industrial parks, a management office may be in office space on-site; smaller properties are often managed off-site. In all types of properties, directional signage is necessary to guide people to the management office.

Under ideal circumstances, the central office or headquarters of a large management firm is located close to many of the properties it manages. However, that may not always be possible. A firm that manages residential property exclusively may have its main office in another part of town because of zoning restrictions where the apartment buildings are located. Some management companies have offices in buildings they own, which may not be near their clients' buildings. Working for clients whose properties are in other cities may necessitate opening branch offices or assigning regional managers who are based at the headquarters office but periodically visit the out-of-town properties.

Call center-based management is a recent management approach still under testing. A regional call center equipped with the latest technology allows the management of projects/properties from anywhere an Internet connection is available. Managers can monitor and manage security systems, access control, and the building's physical systems and equipment over the Internet. Current clients are large institutional owners of real estate whose portfolios are located throughout the world.

Office Procedures and Equipment

Clients expect that a management firm's personnel will know how to manage their properties efficiently and effectively. This requires the firm to have in place specific policies and procedures that instruct the staff how and why tasks are performed a certain way and establish responsibility and authority for getting the job done. Standardization of operating procedures ensures consistency in the services provided to clients and establishes the parameters within which the company's business is conducted.

Having the right tools to perform the tasks is also important to fulfilling clients' service expectations. A vast array of equipment is available to perform an equally vast array of office functions. However, efficiency and economy should be major criteria for selecting office equipment, and the manager must remember that the most sophisticated models are not always the most appropriate ones.

Office Procedures. The real estate management firm should develop standard operating policies and procedures for the management office. These should be compiled and published in an *operations manual.* The management firm should also develop policies and procedures for each managed property and compile them in a *property operations manual.*

Operations Manual. The management firm's operations manual should include background information on the company as well as a declaration of its dedication to ethical practices. That is usually at the beginning of the manual, and it provides a basis for the policies and procedures that follow.

Policies and procedures should address all aspects of operating the business, including a job description for each position in the management firm. The manual should include copies of the various forms used for accounting and record keeping. If a property's expenses are submitted to the central office for payment, they should be matched to a purchase order or a contract and approved by the manager of the property.

The manual should address the use of office equipment and business services. While office machines can save time and money, overusing them can reduce efficiency. Establishing specific procedures for routine business activities and setting limits on the use of more expensive systems and services can help control costs. The policies and procedures should also address the issue of business and personal use of e-mail—the company's name or acronym is usually included as a domain name—and the Internet.

Specific policies and procedures should address marketing and leasing, including qualification of prospective tenants; tenant service requests and work orders for maintenance and repairs; and hiring, evaluating, promoting, and terminating personnel. The manual should detail when and how management reports are prepared and sent to owners and who is responsible for approving finished reports.

The operations manual should declare how the company handles illegal or unethical practices. This section should include prohibitions on *commingling* of funds, price-fixing in setting rents, and discriminatory practices in marketing and leasing, in hiring, or in other interactions with employees. The manual should address other legal issues or questionable practices as necessary and appropriate.

An operations manual should also include potential risks and liabilities that arise when company policies and procedures are not followed. (Management firms should carry *comprehensive general liability insurance* to cover unforeseen risks, and they must carry *workers' compensation insurance* for their employees. Professional liability insurance is discussed later in this chapter.) The manual should also spell out requirements for bonding individuals in positions that handle the company's and its clients' funds.

Property Operations Manual.   Policies and procedures in the property operations manual may duplicate or only slightly modify many of the firm's operational policies, especially those regarding administrative and personnel functions. The property manual should specify records that are to remain at the site, and it should include job descriptions and other particulars related to on-site staff (e.g., maintenance workers) and contracting for specific services.

Maintenance schedules and procedures will be specific to the property—they should be based on or refer to the owners' manuals for equipment the property uses. Safety issues and *emergency and evacuation procedures*[1] will be property-specific as well (these may be addressed separately and distributed to tenants as well as employees).

Property features and amenities require special attention. Leasing practices and marketing strategies must also be tailored to the property. A residential property will need policies regarding compliance with *fair housing laws;* a commercial property may need to address environmental compliance. The property operations manual may also address an owner-client's requirements for the managed property.

Computers.   Computers dominate most office functions, and the real estate management office is no exception. The ability to transmit data between computers is particularly important for real estate management firms because it facilitates sharing information between on-site offices and the central office. Computers also allow real estate managers to transmit data or reports to clients electronically (in addition to or instead of paper reports).

1. The Institute of Real Estate Management has published a comprehensive guideline for emergency planning. Titled *Before Disaster Strikes: Developing an Emergency Procedures Manual,* it addresses management company and property-specific concerns and covers a wide array of emergencies from fire and power outages to weather-related emergencies and other types of disasters.

For institutional owners or other clients who prefer to have reports prepared in formats and programming they use, the electronic transfer of files expedites the entire process.

Hardware peripherals expand the computer's capabilities. Printers, scanners, and digital cameras help management office staff efficiently generate reports, management proposals, brochures, and other print documents such as marketing materials. Handheld computers offer a variety of capabilities, including the ability to evaluate financial and real estate investments.

In real estate management, accounting, word-processing, and maintenance management software programs are essential. A spreadsheet program facilitates the preparation of budgets. Database management software organizes information about clients and tenants and generates mailing lists. Many firms use desktop publishing software to format complex documents and promotional materials as well as to prepare company and property (tenant) newsletters.

Specialized programming allows development of forms that can be filled in on a computer and printed out as completed documents. However, numerous forms used in real estate management continue to be completed by hand, among them building inspection reports, tenant service requests, and maintenance work orders. Prospect cards used by leasing agents and leasing traffic reports are other examples. The way forms will be used should be kept in mind during the design process.

Computer capabilities expand continually as new software becomes available. Mapping software facilitates locating prospective clients' properties (or those under management) and their competition within specific geographic areas for preparation of management plans or management proposals. Demographic data is available as digital files to be used for regional and neighborhood analyses as components of such plans and proposals or for ongoing market analysis of properties under management.

Backing up the real estate management firm's computer files is extremely important. Records can be copied to a variety of digital media. A number of factors determine which files to back up and how often. Software usually does not require backing up. However, if it was not downloaded from the Internet, the original delivery media should be retained so the programming can be reinstalled directly from them. Since digital files use up memory, periodically deleting files and data is also advisable. Policies must be in place regarding which data can be deleted and which are important records that must be retained on storage media as archives.

A back-up copy of all essential information should be maintained on-site in case a computer (or network) crashes and reinstallation of software and recovery of document files become necessary. Another copy should be stored in a secure off-site location. In addition to back-up files (both paper and digital archives), the management company should have a plan for disaster recovery so it will be able to resume operations in a timely fashion after a fire, a flood, or any other major disaster that may have destroyed company records.

The Internet.   Real estate management companies increasingly use the Internet as a marketing vehicle to promote the management company to prospective clients. High-speed wireless connections are rapidly becoming standard. The firm's Web page presents information about the company and its services. Employees, clients, and tenants communicate directly with the company and with each other via e-mail. The management firm may create a Web page for each managed property as a means of communicating information to tenants and as a way for tenants to submit e-mail requests for maintenance and other property services. Management firms also use the Internet for transmitting data and purchasing (and selling) products and services, as well as marketing space for lease.

Because of their ease of use and the ability to retain a long chain of messages, e-mail files have replaced hard-copy files for some kinds of correspondence, and they often contain important and valuable information regarding management company business. The management company should have in place and enforce electronic record retention policies that specifically identify the types of records that must be retained, those that should be deleted, and when the files should be destroyed. The policy should classify different types of business documents and detail the retention period for each type of document.

Communication Equipment.   Telephone communication is another area in which technology is developing rapidly, and the array of available equipment and services is ever changing. Communication between the central office and on-site personnel is especially important. A management firm that has numerous remote offices may be able to improve efficiency by using e-mail and fax machines to avert lengthy (or missed) telephone calls. The management office must have a telephone message system—voice mail, an answering service, or a calling center—for when the management office is closed or when on-site staff are not available. A toll-free incoming telephone number may be efficient and cost-effective if remote properties do not have on-site management.

Cellular telephones have revolutionized interpersonal communications, and they can be extremely useful to managers in the field. Many have direct Internet access, picture, and text messaging capabilities. Most cellular companies offer large time packages and competitive rates for volume and long-distance usage.

Management offices increasingly use pagers, cell phones, two-way radios, and other electronic devices to communicate with on-site maintenance personnel. Such a system can ensure prompt service, but it has the potential to cause delays if the staff experiences constant interruptions. Two-way radios may be more efficient because they allow immediate communication without taking the worker away from the task. (Some cellular services include two-way radio communications within the phones.)

Accounting Systems and Equipment.   Much of the activity in a real estate management office involves the management of funds collected for the properties. Each property may have one bank account for security deposits and one for general operating funds. Such separation of funds may be mandatory, especially if security deposits are required by law to be held in escrow. The size of the property, the owner's requirements, and applicable laws determine how many bank accounts a specific property needs. Limitations on federal deposit insurance coverage of accounts may also be a consideration.

In some situations, separation of clients' funds may be accomplished solely through accounting and bookkeeping procedures. If the firm uses separate accounting instead of separate bank accounts, the manager must take extreme care to avoid using one owner's funds for another owner's property. In addition, owners' funds should not be commingled with the management firm's funds. *Commingling* owner and agency funds is unethical and illegal.

The equipment necessary to operate an accounting department efficiently depends on the number of accounts maintained. This, in turn, depends on both the number of properties managed and the number of accounts maintained for each property. Separate bank accounts distinguish security deposits from operating funds. As income is deposited into and expenses are paid out of the operating fund each month, the specific amounts are recorded as a type of income or expense that is identified in the *chart of accounts* (see chapter 5).

A new management firm may initially rely on other businesses that provide accounting and reporting services (i.e., service bureaus). As the firm grows, it may purchase computer hardware and software as its income stream and/or capitalization permit. As detailed in chapter 5, most accounting functions are increasingly computerized.

Accuracy is of the utmost importance in accounting. No matter what system a firm may use or how well-qualified the staff may be, mistakes can occur. The management firm can protect itself against financial liability from an administrative oversight by carrying professional liability (*errors and omissions*) insurance. That type of insurance is very expensive because of the size of the financial awards that may result from the adjudication of specific claims. In order to exclude small claims, errors and omissions coverage usually has a high deductible, and the policy carefully delineates what constitutes an error or omission.

ADDITIONAL CLIENT SERVICES

The real estate management firm that offers a wide variety of services is attractive to many property owners. Typical offerings include property appraisal, management and investment consultation, corporate fiscal service, tax assistance, and insurance services as well as real estate brokerage and financing assistance. All of these services can command separate, additional fees and are therefore good sources of income for a management firm. Because so many of these services are necessary during the purchase of a property, offering them is a good way to build management business.

The demand for *asset management* is increasing, and many collateral offerings of a real estate management firm may lead to providing this service. The objective of asset management is similar to that of conventional real estate management. However, asset managers may also oversee the financial operation of an investor's entire real estate portfolio, which may involve investigating and recommending financing alternatives and participating in real property acquisition, development, and divestiture. The asset manager may also assist a client in defining his or her short- and long-term goals for real property investment. An asset manager's investment responsibilities exceed the normal involvement with maximizing net operating income and property value, but those real estate management objectives are basic to asset management. Even though asset managers may be more attuned to the financial investment an owner has in a property than to its day-to-day management, asset managers who possess strong site management skills in addition to investment ability are more likely to maximize the value of an investor's portfolio.

Yet another opportunity for professional real estate management is *facility management*. Companies that own real property and occupy all or part of it may prefer to contract with a real estate management firm to maintain the property rather than to manage it with in-house personnel. Governmental agencies and universities often contract for facility management as well.

Appraisal

Real estate management and real estate appraisal can be closely linked activities. Real estate managers are expected to exercise business and economic judgment in the interest of their clients. Property owners ask about the future of their properties and wonder what they should do with their real estate investments. An *appraisal,* which is an estimate of the property's value, may provide a partial answer to those questions. Appraisal involves gathering information to determine the highest and best use of the property and its value at a specified time. To arrive at an estimate, the real estate manager must review data on competitive properties, economic conditions and trends, population movement, neighborhood trends, and market conditions in addition to conducting an in-depth analysis of the property itself. Since an appraisal is an opinion regarding a property's value, its validity depends on the qualifications of the individual who performs it.

Real estate professionals recognize four methods of estimating property value.

1. The *cost approach* estimates property value based on the value of the land plus the cost of replacing the improvements on it. In this approach, the cost of construction is adjusted to reflect observed or measured depreciation of the existing improvements as well as the owner's intent, which may be to *replace* the building with a similar facility (using modern materials) or to *reproduce* it (build an identical facility using precisely the same materials). The manager estimates the value of the land based on sales of nearby vacant property or comparable properties.

2. The *market approach* (also called the *sales approach*) establishes value by comparing the subject property with similar properties that have sold recently. Similarities in terms of location, lot size, construction materials, zoning, physical condition, and other factors are important to the comparison because the appraiser must make substantial adjustments of the value for differences in these elements. The appraiser must obtain as much information as possible about the comparable sales to perform a market approach appraisal with accuracy.

3. The *income capitalization approach* bases value on the net operating income (NOI) from the property. For an appraisal of income-producing property, this is a major consideration. The real estate manager may use the income capitalization approach to calculate estimated current value and to project estimated future value.

4. The *discounted cash flow method* arrives at the present value of a property by discounting all the future fiscal benefits of the real estate (cash flow, appreciation, equity buildup) over a projected holding period.

The projection that shows the greatest income that the property can potentially generate indicates the property's *highest and best use.* Such projections are central to any recommendations to alter, rehabilitate, modernize, or otherwise change a building or its operation. The length of time the owner expects to own the property and the payback period that a change would require also influence such recommendations.

Usually no single approach is sufficient to accurately estimate the value of an income-producing property, nor does averaging the results of those different appraisal methods accomplish that goal. However, for income-producing real estate, the appraiser gives more emphasis to the results of the income capitalization approach and the discounted cash flow method unless several recent sales of very comparable properties have taken place.

Because the analytical methods used by the real estate manager and the appraiser are similar, a management business and an appraisal business may operate from the same office. The two activities can be interrelated because real estate taxes, estate tax appraisal, condemnation appraisal, and other special-purpose appraisals are necessary for professionally managed real estate. Management of real property provides numerous opportunities to solicit appraisal jobs, assuming the manager or another individual in the management firm is qualified to conduct appraisals. (Real estate appraisal as a business activity generally requires professional certification, and it may require state licensing.) It is important to note, however, that appraisers are often expected to be independent—i.e., have no monetary interest in the property appraised. Therefore, a real estate manager who also performs appraisals must exercise care to disclose any affiliation with the property he or she appraises.

Management Consultation

Some property owners do not require ongoing management service, but they may seek professional advice about specific problems. Real estate managers can accommodate these owners by offering consulting services.

Based on experience in the real estate industry, a manager can advise owners on ways to manage their properties to achieve maximum profits. Most consulting work relates to converting property to other uses or enhancing the investment through rehabilitation or modernization. At other times, owners who wish to buy, sell, or refinance property—or lenders granting a loan—may request a due diligence report, management plans, proposals, or budgets. Developers sometimes call on real estate managers to assist in determining the feasibility of a proposed project. A developer may also hire a real estate manager to recommend rental schedules, marketing programs, and leasing policies for proposed projects. Common interest realty associations that do not require full-time management may occasionally consult a professional real estate manager to ensure sound operation of their properties.

The changing U.S. economy and the increasing complexity of real estate transactions have created an environment in which demand for such consultation will continue to grow. Potential clients for management consulting services include buyers and sellers, investors, developers, home-owners' associations, corporate owners of real estate, financial institutions, and other lenders.

Real Estate Investment Counseling

Successful real estate managers usually have an intimate knowledge of the real estate market in the region. They often know which investors want to buy property and which are likely to sell. They know what property is available in the market, the level of demand for it, and its probable future value. Understanding the market and knowing the investment profiles of their management clientele, real estate managers are in a position to counsel clients on potential real estate transactions and sometimes to participate in them.

In addition, lawyers often call upon real estate managers to testify as expert witnesses in court cases involving real estate. Managers charge an agreed hourly rate for reviewing the court case documents, preparing to testify, and testifying in court.

Investment Partnerships.   A real estate manager may form and promote a limited partnership to acquire, develop, manage, operate, or market real estate or to undertake any combination of those activities. (A limited liability company may be formed for the same purpose.) In such an arrangement, the real estate manager assumes the role of the general partner. The manager who forms a limited partnership must be familiar with the laws (both federal and state) that govern real estate investment and operation.

The risks inherent in participating in a limited partnership can be substantial, especially if the real estate manager recruits current clients to participate in the venture with the manager and the investment property operates at a loss. The other participants' confidence in the real estate manager may weaken; they may hire new management for their other properties and leave the real estate manager with the responsibility of the faltering property the partnership owns. To minimize the risks, a professional appraiser should carefully appraise the subject property, and the real estate manager should prepare a detailed management plan and a thorough financial analysis before presenting the opportunity to any investors.

Joint Ventures.   Another means by which a real estate manager can participate in the ownership of a property he or she manages is a *joint venture*—an association of two or more persons or legal entities conducting a single business enterprise for profit. Real estate enterprises that require large amounts of investment capital frequently operate as joint ventures. Such an arrangement creates a pool of equipment, skill, knowledge, talent, and financial resources. A real estate manager may participate in a joint venture by offering professional management skills in exchange for the opportunity to share in the property's success.

Acquisitions for Clients.   Property owners may seek additional property for their investment portfolios, and they may hire a real estate manager or a management firm to find suitable investments. Compensation for this service is usually a brokerage fee; a broker's or sales license may be necessary to accept a brokerage fee. The manager may charge a separate fee for preparing a management plan, proposal, or budget. Unless the property is located in an area that creates a burden (e.g., legal limitations), the management firm is also likely to manage the property.

In order to acquire property for clients, the real estate manager must know what the client is seeking from the investment. A property that is suffering from obsolescence or deferred maintenance may be a suitable short-term holding if repair, rehabilitation, or modernization will lead to a rapid appreciation in value. Investors who prefer long-term ownership may desire a property that is in good physical condition and has a proven record of market strength. The type of property may be another consideration. Some investors may want to diversify the types of properties they own, and others may choose to divest themselves of one type and reinvest in an entirely different type. Acquisition as a management activity is often a function of asset management, which is discussed later in this chapter.

Corporate Fiscal Service

The real estate manager or management firm employed by a corporation must often be prepared to administer not only the property owned by the corporation but other corporate affairs as well. The latter involves responsibilities beyond those inherent in the management of real property. The management firm that provides complete fiscal service may have to plan meetings of the corporate board of directors. It may also be required to send a representative to the meetings to furnish information and advice on a property's operations. Stockholders in real-estate-owning corporations often have questions about the properties, and the management firm that is providing fiscal service may handle their inquiries.

The management firm may also have complete charge of the books and records of the corporation. This accounting activity transcends the maintenance of operating records on the buildings the corporation owns and may involve supervision of the filing of capital stock tax returns and income tax returns as well as preparation and filing of other taxes and government forms.

Tax Service

The scope of real estate management has expanded as real estate transactions have become more complex, and investors are increasingly likely to turn their real estate investments over to a real estate management firm for complete administration, including collateral services such as payment of taxes associated with real property. The firm must keep appropriate records so it can file tax reports for clients, and it should develop tax calendars and reserves to ensure the availability of funds and prompt payment of the taxes involved. The scope of tax service varies with the size of the management firm and the expertise of its staff.

Real Estate Tax.   Real estate tax is an *ad valorem tax,* which means it is based on the value of the real property. The local tax assessor's office periodically reassesses the property to adjust the tax according to the property value. Therefore, analyzing the real estate tax bill is important, especially if it has changed from the previous year. The manager verifies the measurements, the age of the property, the amount of depreciation allowed, the classification of the property, and the unit replacement cost. He or she compares the assessed value to the estimated market value. Then the manager validates the computations of the total tax by applying the tax rate to the assessed valuation. If this analysis indicates excessive assessment, there may be reason to protest. The real estate manager should prepare and submit such a protest to the tax assessor's office, or, with the owner, contract a professional agency or a law firm to file the protest. If the protest is disallowed, an appeal to the next higher authority may be justified.

A primary duty of a real estate manager who handles the taxes of the property is to make sure that adequate funds are available to pay real estate taxes by the due date. Whenever possible, the manager should establish a reserve fund for that purpose. Otherwise, he or she should specifically budget real estate taxes by setting aside a prorated amount each month.

Special Assessments.   The local real estate taxing body levies special assessment taxes. Such assessments are common when public improvements (sidewalks, curbs, or other infrastructures) are necessary within a small area. Only the properties that directly benefit from the improvements are assessed the tax.

The taxing body may levy another type of special assessment. In dense urban areas, owners of buildings within a narrowly defined area (a single block or several blocks along a thoroughfare) may band together to form a nonprofit corporation with a specific purpose. That purpose may be to clean up the area, to increase security, or simply to give the area a specific identity (e.g., using signs or banners).

Such activities are beyond the services the city would ordinarily provide and therefore collected real estate taxes do not cover them. The city usually has to agree to the arrangement and may designate the area as a *special improvement district*. The building owners within the defined district join the corporation or other organization, control what it does, and set up a budget for it, but the city may actually collect the assessments. The amount of the assessment may be a percentage of the real estate taxes on a property, but sometimes other formulas are used.

The real estate manager often represents the owner's interests in the corporation and may actually have the owner's proxy vote and attend the organization's meetings. Real estate managers sometimes help review budgets, set up plans for the special improvement district, and provide services to the association.

Personal Property Tax.   Where personal property taxes are imposed locally, the manager may have to file a schedule of personal property (vehicles, building furnishings, and the like) that is subject to the tax with the tax assessor's office. To do that, the real estate manager must understand both local laws and accepted practices. Here again, the manager is responsible for timely payment of the tax.

Federal Income Tax.   Most individual property owners handle their own income taxes and include the earnings or losses from real property on their personal returns. Corporations, however, may rely on the accounting department of the real estate management firm to prepare and file federal income tax schedules on their real estate holdings.

All real estate managers should be familiar with state and federal income tax laws. In a large management firm, at least one individual should know the income tax rules related to real estate investment. However, real estate management professionals should stay within the bounds of management responsibilities. They should refer accounting or legal issues to qualified accountants or attorneys.

Payroll Tax.   The management firm may file tax payments as well as the appropriate forms for some of the property owner's employees in addition to those for its own employees. To file those forms and make those tax deposits, the real estate manager must have power of attorney from the owner.

Excise Tax.   Managers of office buildings and other large properties may have to collect federal excise taxes that are levied on the production, sale, or consumption of certain commodities. These are indirect taxes on the ultimate consumer. When the management of a building includes the operation of separate merchandise or service departments (restaurants, bars, drugstores), management should investigate its responsibility concerning excise taxes.

Sales Tax.   When taxable sales are transacted in states and cities where sales taxes are imposed, a return must be prepared and the tax must be paid. These taxes may apply to electricity resale; hotel, food, and beverage operations; gasoline and oil sales; and other types of sales (i.e., all taxable goods sold in subsidiary operations under the manager's direct administration). A real estate manager should check sales tax regulations when he or she assumes management of property in which goods are sold.

Insurance Service

The risks of real estate ownership vary in different localities and under different operating conditions, so clients customarily expect the real estate management firm to determine the extent of the risks involved and to know with which agency or corporation these risks may be safely and adequately insured. That level of involvement has prompted some real estate managers to write insurance as a service to clients. However, the manager should consult with other, more-experienced insurance professionals when writing specialized policies (e.g., terrorism insurance).

Although the real estate manager may be an insurance broker, he or she *always* represents the insurance buyer. In this capacity, the manager determines the risk from the buyer's point of view, investigates the insurance market for the best and most economical protection, and then recommends the proper insurance for the client to purchase.

While added services may increase the manager's income, they also increase his or her responsibility. The duties of representing a client in insurance matters are extremely important. The real estate manager must carry them out with the utmost care to avoid a conflict of interest. The manager must have sufficient knowledge of all aspects of insurance underwriting to provide the client with the fairest and most economical insurance coverage possible. He or she is also responsible for keeping records of the policies so that renewals can be handled in a timely manner. Knowing the expiration dates far enough in advance permits the manager as insurance broker to continually research other agencies and companies for more economical coverage.

Regardless of whether the real estate manager is also an insurance broker, he or she must have enough familiarity with the policies and their limitations to ensure the client constant and adequate coverage. To accomplish this effectively, the manager must establish schedules to inspect clients' properties to determine whether any changes have occurred that may increase the risk that is underwritten. This is especially true in the case of retail and industrial properties, where changes in types of merchandise carried or kinds of goods manufactured may alter the coverage cost or jeopardize the effectiveness of the coverage. The same considerations apply if the manager is writing insurance for the occupants (tenants) rather than the owners of the property.

SUMMARY

Real estate managers often start their careers with established management firms. Understanding how clients are acquired, how fees for the firm's services are determined, and how a management office is organized is essential to gaining a complete perspective on the profession of real estate management.

Management firms must promote themselves to acquire new business and to retain established clients. Promotion encompasses much more than advertising. Direct solicitation and a good reputation are often the definitive factors in successfully promoting a management firm. Other means of obtaining clients are personal referrals and public relations.

When prospects become clients, a management fee must be negotiated. Owners of rental property usually pay a percentage of gross receipts for management services; the management agreement may state a minimum fee as well. Other management arrangements are compensated by a flat fee.

The offices of the management firm must be conveniently located, carefully planned, well maintained, and conservative in decor. Standard operating policies and procedures are necessary to ensure consistent business practices. They should be compiled in a company operations manual and in separate operations manuals for individual managed properties. Appropriate office equipment can improve efficiency and reduce the cost of administrative functions. Personal computers, fax machines, photocopiers, cellular telephones, and the Internet are common office tools.

The complexity of real estate management often creates opportunities for a firm to diversify its business and offer collateral services to its clients. Appraisal, management consultation, investment counseling, corporate fiscal service, specialized tax services, and insurance brokerage are possible related services. These services need not be restricted to management clients. Owners who do not require ongoing management of their properties but do need occasional advice may seek such consultation services.

Glossary

absorption rate   The amount of space of a particular property type that becomes leased compared to the amount of that same type of space available for lease within a certain geographic area during a given period.

accelerated cost recovery   Type of depreciation in which the government allows a larger deduction during the early years of the depreciation period. (See also *depreciation*.)

ACCREDITED MANAGEMENT ORGANIZATION® (AMO®)   A designation conferred by the Institute of Real Estate Management on real estate management firms that are under the direction of a CERTIFIED PROPERTY MANAGER® and meet and comply with stipulated standards as to accounting procedures, performance, and protection of funds entrusted to them.

ACCREDITED RESIDENTIAL MANAGER® (ARM®)   A professional service award conferred by the Institute of Real Estate Management on individuals who meet specific standards of experience, ethics, and education.

accrual-basis accounting   The method of accounting that involves entering amounts of income when they are earned and amounts of expense when they are incurred—even though the cash may not be received or paid. (Compare *cash-basis accounting*.)

actual cash value (ACV)   Insurance that pays a claim based on the purchase price of the item, usually allowing for depreciation because of age and use. (Compare *replacement cost coverage*.)

adaptive use   The recycling of existing structures through a change of use.

add-on factor   An amount added to the base rent to account for the proration of the common areas among individual commercial tenants. Also called *load factor.* (See also *base rent.*)

adjustable-rate mortgage (ARM)   A type of variable-rate mortgage (loan) for which the interest rate can be adjusted (raised or lowered) at specific intervals (e.g., semiannually or annually). The adjustment is based on a predetermined index or formula, such as the prime rate plus 2 percent. (Compare *variable-rate mortgage.*)

ad valorem tax   A tax levied on the basis of the value of the object taxed. Most often refers to taxes levied by municipalities and counties against real property and personal property.

Age Discrimination in Employment Act (ADEA)   The federal law that prohibits discrimination against older workers.

agent   A person who enters a legal, fiduciary, and confidential arrangement with a second party and is authorized to act on behalf of that party.

aging in place   The behavior of persons of retirement age who remain in their present residences, whether they own or rent.

allodialism   A system under which an individual can own land independently without being subject to rent, service, or acknowledgment of a superior (e.g., sovereign). (Compare *feudalism.*)

American Society of Heating, Refrigerating, and Air-Conditioning Engineers (ASHRAE)   Professional association that provides information on refrigerant chemicals and equipment modifications and costs.

Americans with Disabilities Act (ADA)   A federal law passed in 1990 that prohibits discrimination in employment on the basis of physical or mental disability and requires places of public accommodation and commercial facilities to be designed, constructed, and altered in compliance with specified accessibility standards. The accessibility requirements may also apply to common areas of residential properties (e.g., rental offices).

amortization   Gradual reduction of a debt, usually through installment payments.

anchor tenant   A major shopping center tenant that draws the majority of customers.

ancillary tenant   A shopping center tenant that occupies a smaller space and a location that is secondary in relation to the anchor tenant.

annual budget   The most common form of operating budget. Projects the entire year's income and expenses for each account. There are two types: a *historical budget* based on a review of income and expenses from previous years; a *zero-based budget* that consists solely of projections and ignores past operating expenses. (See also *operating budget.*)

appraisal   An opinion or estimate of the value of a property. An estimate of value that is (usually) prepared by a certified or accredited appraiser. Four methods of appraisal are common—the *cost approach,* based on the estimated value of the land plus the estimated cost of replacing the improvements on it less depreciation; the *market approach* (also called *sales approach*), based on a comparison to similar properties in the market that have been sold recently; the *income capitalization approach,* based on the net operating income of the property; and the *discounted cash flow method,* which discounts all future fiscal benefits of an investment property over a predetermined holding period. All four are used to estimate value if sufficient information is gathered in each approach to do so.

appreciation   The increase in the value of an asset over time.

articles of incorporation   Document that states that a condominium association is a corporation under the laws of the state.

artificial breakpoint   See *breakpoint.*

asbestos   A fibrous mineral formerly used in buildings for flooring, insulation, and fireproofing later determined to be a health hazard.

assessment   An amount paid by each owner or tenant of a property to fund its operation; also used in referring to local (municipal) taxes.

asset management   A specialized field of real estate management that involves the supervision of an owner's real estate assets at the investment level. In addition to real estate management responsibilities that include maximizing net operating income and property value, an asset manager may recommend, be responsible for, or participate in property acquisition, development, and divestiture. An asset manager may have only superficial involvement with day-to-day operations at the site (e.g., supervision of personnel, property maintenance, tenant relations).

assignment   The transfer of one person's interest or right in a property (e.g., a lease) to another; the document by which such an interest or right is transferred.

assisted living facilities   Housing intended for seniors who need assistance with most (or all) daily living tasks—because of age or frailty but not because of illness.

at will   Employment in which either the employee or the employer may terminate the relationship at any time for any reason (with or without cause). Important exceptions are antidiscrimination (protected classes) statutes, antiretaliation (whistleblower) statutes, and specific contractual arrangements, including collective bargaining agreements.

balloon mortgage   A loan with a constant monthly rate of repayment and a much larger (balloon) payment at the end of the term to fully amortize the loan.

bankruptcy   A state of financial insolvency (liabilities exceed assets) of an individual or organization; the inability to pay debts.

base rent   The minimum rent as set forth in a (usually commercial) lease.

base year   In an office lease, the stated year that is to be used as a standard in determining rent escalations. During the next year, operating costs are compared with the base year, and the difference (higher or lower) determines the tenant's rent adjustment.

blanket policy   Insurance coverage that insures several properties under one policy. May offer more favorable premiums than individual policies.

board of directors   The elected governing body of any corporation, including condominium and other home-owners' associations. (See also *corporation.*)

bodily injury insurance   Type of coverage that protects against liability for damages arising out of injury or death occurring on a property.

boiler insurance   Type of coverage that pays for any damage resulting from a boiler malfunction.

BOMA Standard Method   See *Building Owners and Managers Association International.*

breakpoint   In retail leases, the point at which the tenant's percentage rent is equal to the base rent and beyond which the tenant will begin to pay overages; also called *natural breakpoint.* Sometimes a tenant and owner will negotiate an *artificial breakpoint* that requires the tenant to begin paying percentage rent before or after the natural breakpoint is reached.

budget   An estimation of income and expenses over a specific period for a particular property, project, or institution. (See also *capital budget* and *operating budget.*)

Building Owners and Managers Association International (BOMA)   A trade association that serves the commercial real estate building industry and provides operational statistics for office buildings. The *BOMA Standard Method* computes a tenant's rentable area by multiplying the tenant's usable area by an *R/U ratio,* which is the rentable area of a floor divided by the usable area of that same floor. A pro rata share of the building's common areas is then added to the basic rentable area to arrive at the tenant's total rentable square feet.

building standard   A uniform specification that defines the quantity and quality of construction and finish elements a building owner will provide for build-out of space leased to commercial tenants. (See also *tenant improvement allowance.*)

build out   In retail leasing, to construct the tenant's space.

build-to-suit   An arrangement in which a landowner constructs (or pays for constructing) a custom building on the land, and both land and building are leased to the tenant; a frequent arrangement in shopping centers (e.g., for *pad* or *outlot* spaces) and industrial properties.

business cycle   Four successive stages (recession, depression, recovery, and prosperity) that businesses experience during periods of inflation and deflation of an economy.

bylaws   Regulations that provide specific procedures for handling routine matters in an organization—e.g., a home-owners' association.

call center-based management   Management approach in which a regional call center equipped with the latest technology allows the management of projects/ properties from anywhere an Internet connection is available.

cap   See *expense stop.*

capital budget   An estimate of costs of major improvements or replacements; generally a long-range plan for improvements to a property.

capital improvement   A structural addition or betterment to real property that increases its useful life; the use of capital for a betterment that did not exist before.

capitalization   The process employed to estimate the value of a property by the use of a proper investment rate of return and the annual net operating income produced by the property, the formula being expressed as follows:

Net Operating Income ÷ Rate = Value (I/R = V)

capitalization rate (cap rate)   A rate of return used to estimate a property's value based on that property's net operating income. This rate is based on the rates of return prevalent in the marketplace for similar properties and is intended to reflect the investment risk associated with a particular property.

cash-basis accounting   The method of accounting that recognizes income and expenses when money is actually received or paid. (Compare *accrual-basis accounting*.)

cash disbursements report   A chronological record of payments for operating expenses that lists the vendor, the amount, and the check number for all payments and includes items that are not operating expenses (debt service, payment for capital expenditures); also called *check vouchers.*

cash flow   The amount of cash available after all payments have been made for operating expenses, debt service (mortgage principal and interest), and capital reserve funds; also called *pretax cash flow* to indicate that income taxes have not been deducted.

cash-on-cash return   See *return on investment.*

C corporation   See *corporation.*

central business district (CBD)   The concentration of high-rise buildings within a community.

CERTIFIED PROPERTY MANAGER® (CPM®)   The professional designation conferred by the Institute of Real Estate Management on individuals who distinguish themselves in the areas of education, experience, and ethics in property management.

chart of accounts   A classification or arrangement of account items.

Check 21 Act   Federal legislation that became effective in October 2004; allowed banks, retailers, and others with whom consumers do business to speed the transfer of funds through a process called *electronic check conversion.* The act created a new negotiable instrument called a *substitute check,* which is a paper copy of an original check that becomes a vehicle for electronic funds transfer. Banks are not required to accept checks in electronic form, but they must accept substitute checks.

chlorofluorocarbon (CFC)   Refrigerant chemical that contains two types of halogens—chlorine (Cl) and fluorine (F). It is being phased out and replaced with similar compounds that do not include chlorine.

Civil Rights Act (Title VII)   Prohibits discrimination in employment—hiring, compensation, promotion, termination; enforced by the United States *Equal Employment Opportunity Commission* (*EEOC*).

cold calling   Telephoning or personally calling on commercial prospects with whom the leasing agent has had no previous contact in order to interest them in leasing space.

collateral   Property pledged as security for a loan or debt.

commercial property   All real estate development that is not exclusively residential.

commingle   To mix or combine; to combine the money of more than one person or entity into a common fund. A prohibited practice in real estate.

common area   Area of a property that is used by all tenants or owners. In a condominium, the areas of the property in which the unit owners have a shared interest (e.g., lobbies, laundry rooms). In an enclosed mall, the mall corridors, parking lots, escalators, landscaped areas, and other parts of the property that the tenants use in common.

common area maintenance (CAM) clause   Lease clause that specifies exactly what constitutes the common area of the shopping center, what expenses the tenant will pay, and what rights and responsibilities the property owner has. (See also *common area.*)

common interest development (CID)   See *common interest realty association.*

common interest realty association (CIRA)   Real estate that is operated for the mutual benefit of the owners; also called *common interest development* (*CID*). Condominiums, cooperatives, gated communities, and planned unit developments (PUDs) are examples.

common law   Court interpretation based on precedent—the inherent beliefs of the society and previous court decisions. (Compare *statute law.*)

community shopping center   A shopping center usually anchored by a junior or discount department store, supermarket, or large hardware store. The 25 to 40 ancillary tenants may include men's and women's apparel stores, bookstores, card shops, family shoe stores, and fast food operations. Community shopping centers range in size from 150,000 to 400,000 square feet of GLA and usually require a population of 100,000 to 150,000 to sustain them.

comparison grid   A form for price analysis in which the features of a subject property are compared to similar features in comparable properties in the same market. The price (or rent) for each comparable property helps to determine an appropriate market price (or rent) for the subject.

concession   An economic incentive granted by an owner to encourage the leasing of space or the renewal of a lease.

condominium   A multiple-unit structure in which the units and pro rata shares of the common areas are owned individually; a unit in a condominium property.

condominium association A nonprofit corporation comprised of the unit owners of a condominium that governs its operation. Also called *home-owners' association.*

congregate housing For those who want to remain independent but require some assistance with daily tasks, these arrangements include meals, transportation, and some housekeeping services.

Consolidated Omnibus Budget Reconciliation Act (COBRA) Federal law that requires employers to offer employees an opportunity to continue their group health care coverage for a time by paying the premiums themselves when they are terminated or leave their jobs.

Consumer Price Index (CPI) A way of measuring consumer purchasing power by comparing the current costs of goods and services to those of a selected base year; sometimes used as a reference point for rent escalations in commercial leases (i.e., as a measure of inflation). (Compare *Producer Price Index.*)

continuous occupancy clause Retail lease clause in which the tenant agrees to stay in business for the full term of the lease.

continuous operation clause Retail lease clause in which the tenant agrees to keep its business operating smoothly and consistently for the full term of the lease.

convenience shopping center Shopping center type that usually has a convenience market or a combination gas station and food store anchor and 2 to 10 stores. Most are open all day and all night. Other tenants may be card- or coin-operated laundries, barbershops, dry cleaners, or liquor stores. Also called *strip shopping centers.* Usually has 5,000 to 30,000 square feet of GLA. Typical trade area comprises the immediate neighborhood of the site and the traffic on the street. A convenience center can succeed in an area with a population of 1,000 to 2,500.

conversion ratio The average number of prospects who visit a rental property compared to the number who sign a lease.

cooperative Ownership of a share or shares of stock in a corporation that holds the title to a multiple-unit residential structure. Shareholders do not own their units outright but have the right to occupy them as co-owners of the cooperative association under *proprietary leases.*

corporation A legal entity that is chartered by a state and is treated by courts as an individual entity separate and distinct from the persons who own it. The federal government classifies most corporations *C corporations.* The entity pays income tax and has no restrictions on the number of shareholders it can have or the types of stock it can issue. An *S corporation* combines the ownership features of a corporation with those of a partnership. It does not pay federal income tax; profits (and losses) pass directly to the shareholders.

corrective maintenance Ordinary repairs that must be made to a building and its equipment on a day-to-day basis. (See also *deferred maintenance* and *preventive maintenance.*)

cost approach See *appraisal.*

cost-benefit analysis   A method of measuring the benefits expected from a decision (e.g., a change in operating procedures) by calculating the cost of the change and determining whether the benefits justify the costs.

cost recovery   See *depreciation.*

curb appeal   General cleanliness, neatness, and attractiveness of a building as exemplified by the appearance of the exterior and grounds and the general level of housekeeping.

custodial maintenance   The day-to-day cleaning and other work that is essential to preserving the value of a property; also called *janitorial maintenance* or *housekeeping.*

debt service   Regular payments of the principal and interest on a loan.

declaration   A legal document that creates a condominium. The document describes the property, defines the method of determining each unit owner's share of the common elements, and outlines the responsibilities of the owners and the association. (See also *condominium association.*)

deductible   In insurance, a specified amount the insured party must pay before the insurer pays on a claim.

deed of trust   Instrument some states use in place of a mortgage. The deed pledges the property as collateral—the buyer holds title to the property as a warranty deed, and the financial institution and the buyer execute a note as evidence of the debt. A mortgage requires a court order for foreclosure, but a deed of trust does not. (Compare *mortgage.*)

default   Failure to fulfill an obligation; the nonperformance of a duty.

deferred maintenance   Ordinary maintenance of a building that, because it has not been performed, negatively affects the use, occupancy, and value of the property. (See also *corrective maintenance* and *preventive maintenance.*)

deflation   An economic condition that occurs when the money supply declines in relation to the amount of goods available, resulting in lower prices. (Compare *inflation.*)

demand   The availability of purchasers for a given amount of goods or services.

demised premises   That portion of a property covered by a lease agreement; usually defined by the walls and other structures that separate one tenant's space from that of another.

demographic profile   A compilation of social and economic statistics (including population density, age, education, occupation, and income) for a specific population, usually within a geographic area (as a neighborhood or region). (Compare *psychographic profile.*)

Department of Housing and Urban Development (HUD)   A department of the U.S. government that supervises the Federal Housing Administration (FHA) and other agencies that administer housing programs.

depreciation Loss of value due to all causes, including physical deterioration (ordinary wear and tear), structural defects, and changing economic and market conditions (see also *obsolescence*). The tax deduction that allocates the cost of an asset over its useful life; also called *cost recovery*.

disability A physical or mental impairment that substantially limits one or more major life activities, a record of such impairment, or being regarded as having such an impairment.

discounted cash flow method See *appraisal*.

discretionary income Money available for spending after physical needs (food, clothing, shelter) have been met and taxes have been paid.

disposable income The amount that is left over after personal income taxes have been subtracted from personal income. The amount of money that consumers actually have available to spend or save.

Drug-Free Workplace Act The federal law that requires employers who contract with the U.S. government to certify that they maintain a drug-free workplace and have a published statement notifying employees that drug activity is prohibited in their workplace and specifying the actions that will be taken against those who violate the prohibition. Employees must abide by the terms of the employer's drug free workplace policy as a condition of their employment.

Economic Growth and Tax Relief Act of 2001 The federal law that lowered individual tax rates. (See also *Jobs and Growth Tax Relief Act of 2003*.)

economic obsolescence See *obsolescence*.

economic shift Fluctuation in real estate sales prices and rental rates. (Compare *population shift*.)

economic vacancy The percentage of rental units that are not producing income. Includes unoccupied units, leased space that is not yet producing income, delinquencies and leasable space that is used for other purposes or is otherwise unleasable.

effective gross income The total amount of income actually collected during a reporting period; the gross receipts of a property. Gross potential rental income *less* vacancy and collection losses *plus* miscellaneous or unscheduled income.

effective rent The cumulative rental amount collected over the term of a lease expressed as an average monthly rental (residential) or an annual rate per rentable square foot (office, retail, industrial).

electronic check conversion See *Check 21*.

eminent domain The right of a governmental body to acquire private property for public use through a court action called condemnation. The court also determines the compensation to be paid to the owner.

Employee Polygraph Protection Act (EPPA) The federal law that prohibits the use of lie detector tests in most business situations; in the event of an economic loss, it allows the use of polygraph tests, subject to notification and other restrictions.

Employee Retirement Income Security Act (ERISA)   The federal law that safeguards employees' rights to benefits under a company's pension.

Employment Eligibility Verification form (form I-9)   Federal form that verifies the employee's identity and right to work in the United States. Employees can present a number of documents to verify their identity and right to work. Employers should retain I-9 forms in the employee's personnel file for at least three years.

endorsement   An attachment to an insurance policy that provides or excludes a specific coverage for a specific portion or element of a property; also called a *rider.*

entertainment shopping center   Shopping center type that typically consists of entertainment, dining, and other retail stores. Most have a GLA in the range of 150,000 square feet up to 300,000 square feet, but some are much larger. The trade area varies, depending on the location of any other similar center or competition.

Environmental Protection Agency (EPA)   The agency of the U.S. government established to enforce laws that preserve and protect the environment.

Equal Employment Opportunity Commission (EEOC)   A U.S. governmental body created under Title VII of the Civil Rights Act of 1964 to end discrimination in the workplace.

equity   The interest or value that an owner has in real estate over and above the mortgage against it.

errors and omissions insurance   See *professional liability insurance.*

escalation clause   In a lease, a provision for increases in rent based on increases in operating costs, sometimes based on a standard index such as the Consumer Price Index (CPI) to account for inflation.

eviction   A legal process to reclaim real estate, usually from a resident's or a commercial tenant's failure to perform under the lease (*for cause*). The two types of causes are monetary (nonpayment of rent) and nonmonetary (breach of a lease covenant).

eviction notice   A written notice to a tenant to cure a breach of the lease immediately or vacate the premises within a specified period.

exclusive use clause   In a retail lease, clause that prohibits other tenants in a shopping center from selling a similar product in order to minimize competition.

Executive Order 13224   See *U.S.A. Patriot Act.*

executive summary   A section at the beginning of a management plan that highlights the information presented in the report.

exempt status   See *Fair Labor Standards Act.*

expense cap   See *expense stop.*

expense stop   In an office lease, a clause obligating the property owner to pay operating costs up to a certain amount per square foot per year; tenants pay their pro rata share of any costs in excess of that amount. When used in a retail lease, a clause obligating the tenants to pay a pro rata share of operating expenses up to a certain amount (*expense cap, cap*) per year; the owner pays any costs in excess of that amount. An expense stop in an office lease sets a ceiling on how much the property owner pays; a cap in a retail lease defines a limit on how much the tenant pays.

extended coverage (EC)   An endorsement to a standard fire insurance policy that adds coverage against financial loss from certain other specified hazards.

facility manager   A type of real estate manager who, when employed directly by a corporation that owns real estate incidental to its primary business, may be responsible for acquisition and disposition in addition to physical upkeep of the property, record keeping, and reporting on its management, although a corporate asset manager is likely to handle acquisition and disposition. More broadly, the responsibilities involve coordinating the physical workplace with the people and purpose of the organization.

Fair Credit Reporting Act (FCRA)   A federal law that gives people the right to see and correct their credit records at credit reporting bureaus. It also requires real estate managers to inform rental applicants if a credit bureau is contracted to investigate their credit (and to obtain the applicant's written authorization to do so), advise them in writing if a lease is denied because of a poor credit report, and identify the source of credit information that resulted in their being denied a lease.

Fair Debt Collection Practices Act (FDCPA)   A federal law that created a series of guidelines for debt collectors to follow. Designed to prevent collection agencies from harassing debtors, the law was later expanded to include any organization that collects consumer debt (including real estate managers). The law is governed and regulated by the Federal Trade Commission (FTC).

fair housing laws   Any law that prohibits discrimination against people seeking housing. There are federal, state, and local fair housing laws. Specifically, Title VIII of the U.S. Civil Rights Act of 1968 prohibits discrimination in the sale or rental of housing based on race, color, religion, or national origin. It was amended in 1974 to include sex as a protected class; the Fair Housing Amendments Act of 1988 further prohibits discrimination on the basis of familial status (children) or mental or physical disability.

Fair Labor Standards Act (FLSA)   The federal law that regulates hourly workers' wage rates and the number of hours worked and requires overtime compensation for time worked in excess of 40 hours per week. Employers must pay workers for all hours worked, including work performed at home and travel as part of the job. Employees (usually salaried) who do not have to be paid for overtime work are considered to have *exempt status*. New rules issued in 2004 require employers to pay some formerly exempt employees overtime based on a minimum salary requirement and specific guidelines for determining exempt status. In addition to hourly workers, white-collar employees whose annual salaries are less than a certain dollar amount ($23,660 in 2005) must be paid overtime when they work more than 40 hours in a workweek. This act is frequently referred to as the federal *Wage and Hour Law*.

fair market value   The price paid, or one that might be anticipated as necessarily payable, by a willing and informed buyer to a willing and informed seller (neither of whom is under any compulsion to act), if the object sold has been reasonably exposed to the market.

familial status   The presence in a household of children under age 18 living with parents or guardians, pregnant women, or people seeking custody of children under age 18.

Family and Medical Leave Act (FMLA)   The federal law that requires employers to grant eligible employees up to 12 weeks of unpaid job-protected leave in the event of a serious health condition or to care for a family member. To be required to participate, the firm must have at least 50 employees within 75 miles.

Federal Housing Administration (FHA)   An agency that is part of the U.S. Department of Housing and Urban Development (HUD). It administers a variety of housing loan programs.

Federal Insurance Contributions Act (FICA)   The federal law that requires employer and employee to contribute funds equally based on the employee's income to the Social Security fund and Medicare.

Federal Unemployment Tax Act (FUTA)   The federal law that requires employers to contribute funds to compensate employees who are laid off or terminated. The employer alone makes the contributions, and the amount or rate is based on the number of employees and the number of claims made.

Federal Wage and Hour Law   See *Fair Labor Standards Act.*

fee simple ownership   The investor purchases both the underlying land and the improvement. (Compare to *leasehold interest.*)

feudalism   A period that lasted from the ninth to the fifteenth centuries in Europe during which time the king was the principal landowner in any sovereign state. (Compare *allodialism.*)

fidelity bond   A *surety* issued by a third party (usually an insurance company) that protects one individual against financial loss that might result from dishonest acts of another specific individual.

fiduciary   One charged with a relationship of trust and confidence, as between a principal and an agent, trustee and beneficiary, or attorney and client, when one party is legally empowered to act on behalf of another.

financing   The availability, amount, and terms under which money may be borrowed to assist in the purchase of real property, using the property itself as the security (*collateral*) for such borrowing.

fire insurance   Coverage on property against all direct loss or damage by fire.

fixed-rate mortgage   A loan for real property in which the interest rate is constant over the term of the loan.

flex space   Single-story commercial structure that can be configured to accommodate a single tenant or multiple tenants or to have varying proportions of office and warehouse or manufacturing space according to tenants' needs.

floor area   See *gross leasable area.*

floor plate   Rentable floor size.

for cause   See *eviction.*

foreclosure   A court action initiated by the mortgagor, or a lienor, for the purpose of having the court order the debtor's real estate sold to pay the mortgage or lien.

formaldehyde gas   A foaming agent once used in foam insulation and still present in adhesives used in making pressed-wood products. Its presence in a building can be harmful.

form I-9   See *Employment Eligibility Verification form.*

functional obsolescence   See *obsolescence.*

garden apartment building   A low-rise building designed for multifamily living, usually located in a suburban area.

general partnership   The business activity of two or more persons who agree to pool capital, talents, and other assets according to some agreed formula, and similarly to divide profits and losses, and to commit the partnership to certain obligations. General partners assume unlimited liability. (Compare *limited liability limited partnership* and *limited partnership.*)

government-assisted housing   Any residential rental property in which the property owner receives part of the rent payment from a governmental body. As a rule, governmental housing subsidies are either resident based or property based. Also called *subsidized housing.* (Compare *public housing.*)

Gramm-Leach-Bliley Act (GLBA)   Federal law under which property owners fall within the definition of "financial institutions" because they collect personal and financial information from prospective tenants; information that must be safeguarded to protect both prospects and tenants from identity theft.

great room   A living space that combines the living room, dining room, and kitchen.

gross domestic product (GDP)   Measure of productivity used in the United States since 1991. It indicates the market value of all final goods (tangible objects such as canned food and automobiles) and services (intangible objects such as entertainment activities and transportation) produced *only within the United States* in one year's time. (Nearly all other countries measure productivity as GDP, so use of GDP facilitates comparisons of U.S. economic activity with that of other countries.) (Compare *gross national product.*)

gross leasable area (GLA)   The total square feet of floor space in all store areas of a shopping center, excluding common area space; also called *floor area.* The size of a retail tenant's area of exclusive use in a shopping center, usually expressed in square feet.

gross lease   A lease under the terms of which the property owner pays all operating expenses of the property and the tenant pays a fixed rent. (Compare *net lease*.)

gross national product (GNP)   The market value of all final goods (tangible objects such as canned food and automobiles) and services (intangible objects such as entertainment activities and transportation) produced by an economy in one year's time. It measures output attributable to U.S. residents *regardless of their geographic location*. (Compare *gross domestic product*.)

gross potential rental income   The sum of the rental rates of all spaces available to be rented in a property, regardless of occupancy; the maximum amount of rent a property can produce.

habitability   A state of being fit for occupancy (e.g., sanitary, safe, in compliance with applicable codes).

heating, ventilating, and air-conditioning (HVAC) system   The combination of equipment and ductwork for producing, regulating, and distributing heat, refrigeration, and fresh air throughout a building.

highest and best use   The use of real property that will produce the highest property value and develop a site to its fullest economic potential.

high-rise apartment building   A multiple-unit dwelling that has 10 or more stories.

historical budget   See *annual budget*.

hoteling   A company's practice of setting aside one or more spaces for staff members who only need to work in the office periodically rather than maintaining office space for a particular employee.

home-owners' association   See *condominium association*.

home purchase clause   Residential lease clause that allows the resident to break the lease in the event a purchase transaction is closed before the lease term ends.

household   All persons, related or not, who occupy a housing unit.

housekeeping   See *custodial maintenance*.

Housing and Community Development Act   The 1974 federal law that authorized the Housing Assistance Payments Program commonly referred to as the *Section 8 Housing Choice Voucher Program*. The program provides rental assistance nationwide to low-income families and elderly and disabled individuals. *Public housing agencies (PHAs)*, which receive funds from the U.S. Department of Housing and Urban Development, locally administer housing choice vouchers.

Immigration Reform and Control Act (IRCA)   The federal law that requires the employer to verify an *only within the United States* employee's identity and eligibility to work in the United States. Employees must complete Immigration and Nationalization Service (INS) form I-9.

income capitalization approach   See *appraisal* and *capitalization*.

income statement   See *statement of operations*.

individual tax identification number (ITIN)   Identification number the Internal Revenue Service issues to a noncitizen who needs to report income for tax purposes but is not eligible for a Social Security number.

indoor air quality (IAQ)   An environmental concern specifically related to the work environment. Problems can arise in any type of building, but office buildings are the most susceptible. That is partially because their centralized HVAC systems serve such a large space and partially because they are built new or retrofitted as entirely enclosed systems (the windows cannot be opened), which results in poor air circulation.

inflation   An economic condition occurring when the money supply increases in relation to the amount of goods available, resulting in substantial and continuing increases in prices. (Compare *deflation*.)

initial investment basis   The difference between the loan amount and the purchase price of a property (i.e., the owner's initial equity).

Institute of Real Estate Management (IREM®)   A professional association of men and women who meet established standards of experience, education, and ethics with the objective of continually improving their respective managerial skills by mutual education and exchange of ideas and experience. The Institute is an affiliate of the NATIONAL ASSOCIATION OF REALTORS®. (See also *Certified Property Manager®*.)

institutional owner   A financial institution (bank, trust company, mortgage bank, investment house) or other source of investment capital (insurance companies, pension funds) that invests in real estate.

insurance   An agreement by one party (the insurer, carrier, insurance company) to assume part or all of a financial loss in the event of a specified contingency or peril (e.g., liability, property damage) in consideration of a premium payment by a second party (the insured).

International Council of Shopping Centers (ICSC)   The worldwide trade association of the shopping center industry, dedicated to advancing the development of the industry.

janitorial maintenance   See *custodial maintenance*.

Jobs and Growth Tax Relief Act of 2003   The federal law that lowered individual tax rates, including reducing the long-term capital gains tax rate from 20 percent to 15 percent. (Those capital gains rate cuts were to be effective for the tax years ending on or after May 6, 2003, through December 31, 2008.)

joint and several liability   A situation in which all the participants in a legal agreement are individually responsible for performing the obligations of the agreement and one or more or all of them can be sued for a breach of the agreement. In real estate management, when a lease is signed by unrelated adults who agree that they are all individually, and as a group, responsible for rent payments and other duties of the tenant.

joint tenancy   Ownership by two or more persons specifically designated as joint tenants, with the right of survivorship—upon the death of one joint tenant, ownership is passed to the other joint tenant(s). (Compare *tenancy in common.*)

joint venture   An association of two or more persons or businesses to carry out a single business enterprise for profit.

just-in-time delivery   A system manufacturers use to allow them to maintain minimum stocks of raw materials, parts, and packaging by using computer inventory systems coupled with overnight shipping services to supply the materials they need to keep pace with their production levels.

landlord   One who owns real property that is leased to a tenant; a property owner. (See also *lessor.*)

landlord-tenant law   Laws enacted by various jurisdictions that regulate the relationship between property owner and tenant.

lead-based paint   Type of paint used in housing built prior to 1980 that poses a serious lead-poisoning hazard to resident children. (Its use in the United States was outlawed in 1978.)

leaking underground storage tank (LUST)   Many older buildings used to maintain their own fuel supply for their boilers, usually in storage tanks on the premises. The threat of contamination of groundwater has led to regulations requiring inspection and replacement of tanks that are still in use. Those no longer in use may have to be removed.

lease   A contract, written or oral, for the possession of part or all of a property for a stipulated period of time in consideration of the payment of rent or other compensation by the tenant. Leases for more than one year generally must be in writing to be enforceable. A residential lease is sometimes called an *occupancy agreement.*

leasehold interest   An ownership type in which the investor owns only the improvement (the building) outright; the underlying land is leased from another owner. (Compare to *fee simple ownership.*)

leasing agent   A person who is directly responsible for renting space in assigned properties.

lessee   The tenant in a lease.

lessor   The property owner in a lease.

liability insurance   Insurance protection against claims arising out of injury or death of people or physical or financial damage to property.

lien   The legal right of a creditor to have his or her debt paid out of the property of the debtor.

lifestyle shopping center   A shopping center type that has anchor tenants such as Ann Taylor, Barnes and Noble, and Pottery Barn. These shopping centers have few small shops because they lack the traditional anchor tenants. The trade area may vary greatly from one center to another, depending on the local competition. They generally have 250,000 to 500,000 square feet of GLA.

limited liability company (LLC)   Created by state statute, a business ownership form that functions like a corporation—its members are protected from liability—but for income tax purposes is classified as a partnership. Income and expenses flow through to the individual members. The arrangement offers considerable flexibility in its organization and structure.

limited liability limited partnership (LLLP)   A form of limited partnership that limits the liability of the general partners. (Compare *general partnership* and *limited partnership*.)

limited partnership (LP)   A partnership arrangement in which the liability of certain partners is limited to the amount of their investment. Limited partnerships are managed and operated by one or more general partners whose liability is not limited; limited partners have no voice in management. *Private limited partnerships* have 35 or fewer investors and usually do not have to register with the Securities and Exchange Commission (SEC), although they may have to file a certificate with state authorities. *Public limited partnerships* have an unlimited number of participants and must register with the SEC when the number of partners and the value of their assets reach certain levels. (Compare *general partnership* and *limited liability limited partnership*.)

load factor   See *add-on factor*.

locator service   A business in a major city or other large community whose sole objective is matching prospective tenants with rental spaces.

long-range budget   A budget that illustrates the relationship between operating income and expenses over five or more years in the life of a property. (See also *budget*.)

low-rise apartment building   Multiple-unit residential dwelling of three or fewer stories. (See also *garden apartment building*.)

M1   See *money supply*.

M2   See *money supply*.

management agreement   A contractual arrangement between the owner(s) of a property and the designated managing agent, describing the duties and establishing the authority and compensation of the agent and detailing the responsibilities, rights, and obligations of both agent and owner(s).

management fee   The monetary consideration paid monthly or otherwise for the performance of management duties.

management plan   An outline of a property's physical and fiscal management that is directed toward achieving the owner's goals.

manufactured housing   A dwelling that is built in a factory, transported to and anchored on a site, and used as a year-round residential unit. All manufactured homes must be in compliance with the federal Manufactured Home Construction and Safety Standards Act of 1974 (the HUD code) which became effective in 1976. (Usage note: The term *mobile home* is commonly used to identify all manufactured housing even though the legal nomenclature is "manufactured homes" for units built after the enactment of the HUD code.)

market analysis   An evaluation of supply and demand conditions in a particular area for a particular type of goods or services. In real estate management, the process of identifying the specific group of prospective tenants for a particular property and then evaluating the property by that market's standards for rental space.

market approach   See *appraisal.*

marketing   All business activity a producer uses to expose potential consumers to available goods and services, including selling, advertising, and packaging. For rental property, methods used to attempt to lease space.

marketing fund   In a shopping center, an account controlled by the landlord that is specifically for funding shopping center promotions and advertising. Merchants and the owner of the shopping center contribute to this fund based on a predetermined amount stated in their leases. (Compare *merchants' association.*)

material safety data sheet (MSDS)   A compilation of information regarding the hazardous properties of chemicals. Usual information includes composition, physical and chemical properties, and known hazards (e.g., toxicity, flammability, explosion potential); recommended cautions for handling (e.g., protective clothing and devices), storage, and disposal; clean-up procedures, and first aid treatment in the event of exposure. An MSDS is provided when chemicals (e.g., solvents, cleaning compounds) are shipped in bulk in pails or drums and when the information does not fit on the labels of small containers. Maintenance and other on-site personnel must retain these documents for reference.

megamall   A giant shopping center that may contain five million or more square feet of GLA. Such malls are often connected to or contain hotels, amusement parks, or nightclubs in addition to numerous anchor tenants and hundreds of ancillary tenants.

Megan's Law   In 1996, the federal government passed legislation called Megan's Law, which requires disclosure to the public of the presence of convicted sex offenders (names and addresses). This information is available from a variety of sources, including local police departments and the Internet. As interpreted up to 2005, the federal law does not address the responsibility of a property owner to a tenant regarding disclosure.

merchants' association   An organization formed in shopping centers and controlled jointly by the property owner and the tenants to plan promotions and advertisements for the good of the center as a whole. Usually all tenants are required to participate and both tenants and property owner pay dues. (Compare *marketing fund.*)

micro-market   The neighborhood of an office building.

mid-rise apartment building   A multiple-unit dwelling ranging from four to nine stories tall.

miscellaneous income   Income a property produces from sources other than rent, such as coin-operated laundry equipment, vending machines, and late fees; also called *unscheduled income.*

mixed-use development (MXD)   A single property, often found in central business districts, that has more than one use, including retail, office, and hotel space, among other possibilities.

mobile home   See *manufactured housing.*

modernization   The process of replacing original or outdated equipment with similar features that are of up-to-date design.

money supply   All of the printed currency and coinage in circulation outside of banks, plus those bank deposits that are immediately convertible to cash (savings and checking deposits owned by individuals but held in banks), plus other negotiable instruments such as traveler's checks, credit union share-draft balances, and negotiable order of withdrawal (NOW) accounts. This amount of money, referred to as *M1,* is the most frequently cited measure of the U.S. money supply. More broadly, the money supply includes less liquid funds such as money market mutual fund shares and small time deposits (e.g., certificates of deposit) on which penalties are imposed for withdrawal before a specified maturity date. Those less liquid funds are added to M1, and the result is called *M2.*

mortgage   A conditional transfer or pledge of real property as security for the payment of a debt. The document used to create a mortgage loan. (Compare *deed of trust.*) (See also *collateral.*)

mullion   A vertical bar that separates the panes of glass in a window. In newer buildings that have expansive windows, the spacing of the mullions usually determines the placement of the walls.

narrative report of operations   A report that explains any differences or variances between the actual income and expenses and the amounts projected for them in the budget.

National Apartment Association (NAA)   A professional association that compiles statistics on rental apartments.

National Association of Industrial and Office Properties (NAIOP)   A professional association that provides operational statistics for industrial properties.

natural breakpoint   See *breakpoint.*

negotiation   The process of bargaining that precedes an agreement; in commercial leasing, the bargaining to reach a mutual agreement on rental rates, term of the lease, and other points.

neighborhood analysis   A study of a neighborhood and comparison with the broader economic and geographic area of which it is a part to determine why individuals and businesses are attracted to the area.

neighborhood shopping center   A shopping center type in which the most common anchor tenant is a supermarket, a super drugstore, or a combination of the two. This type of center usually has 15 to 25 small shops. Ancillary tenants include dry cleaners, bank branches, beauty salons, and card and gift shops. The GLA of a typical neighborhood center is between 30,000 and 150,000 square feet. A neighborhood shopping center usually thrives in an area with a population of 5,000 to 40,000.

net lease   A lease that requires the tenant to pay a share of specific property operating expenses in addition to base rent. Three types of net leases are common: *net* (or *single-net*), *net-net* (or *double-net*), and *net-net-net* (or *triple-net*), depending on the extent of the costs that are passed through to the tenant. Used most often for commercial tenants, the definitions of the terms vary with location and types of property—e.g., office, retail, industrial. (Compare *gross lease*.)

net operating income (NOI)   Total collections (gross receipts) less operating expenses.

new urbanism   See *urban village*.

no-cause action   Termination of a tenancy by a property owner without stating a cause if the tenant has a month-to-month lease.

obsolescence   Lessening of value due to being out-of-date (obsolete) because of changes in design and use; an element of *depreciation. Physical obsolescence* is a condition of aging (wear and tear) or deferred maintenance of a property; *functional obsolescence* is a condition of obsolete design or use of a property; and *economic obsolescence* is a loss of value due to external causes (e.g., market conditions) such that the property cannot generate enough income to offset operating expenses.

occupancy agreement   See *lease*.

Occupational Safety and Health Act (OSHA)   A law passed in 1970 requiring employers to comply with job safety and health standards issued by the U.S. Department of Labor. It mandates use of protective clothing and devices for certain types of tasks.

office condominium   An office space that a business purchases as an alternative to leasing. The most common purchasers are medical and dental practitioners, real estate firms, financial planners, entrepreneurs, and small companies that need 1,000 to 10,000 square feet of space. (See also *condominium*.)

office park   A discrete business center near an airport, major highway, or other suburban attraction.

off-price center   See *outlet shopping center*.

operating budget   A listing of all anticipated income from and expenses of operating a property, usually projected on an annual basis. (See also *annual budget*.)

operating expense   Any expenditure made in connection with operating a property with the exception of debt service, capital reserves (and/or capital expenditures), and income taxes.

operations manual   An authoritative collection of information that describes the organization and its goals, explains policies that guide its operations, outlines specific procedures for implementing those policies, assigns responsibility for performing various functions, and contains the various documents (forms) for performing the work; also called *standard operating procedures manual.* (Compare *property operations manual.*)

option   The right to obtain a specific condition within a specified time. An option is often written into a lease as an addendum.

option to cancel   An option that grants the tenant the right to cancel the lease before its expiration and, if granted, usually requires a financial penalty.

option to expand   An option that requires the property owner to offer specific additional space at a stated time in the future, often at the end of the lease term.

option to renew   An option that allows a tenant to renew a lease on the same terms and conditions as the original lease.

outlet shopping center   A shopping center in which at least 50 percent of the stores are factory outlet stores. They may include off-price and discount merchants. At an *off-price center,* retailers offer name-brand merchandise at well-below-normal retail prices. Outlet centers may attract customers from a radius of 20 miles to as far away as several hundred miles in rural areas. They traditionally require a minimum population of 200,000.

outlot   In a shopping center, a separate site that is not attached to the main center. Also called a *pad.* Banks, restaurants, automotive service centers, and movie theaters are common tenants for these spaces.

overage rent   See *breakpoint* and *percentage rent.*

owner, landlord, and tenant (OLT) liability insurance   Type of insurance that covers claims against a property owner, a landlord, or a tenant arising out of injury to a person or persons on the property.

pad   See *outlot.*

parking area ratio   The relationship between the size of the parking area and the size of the building it is intended to serve.

parking index   For a retail property, the number of spaces per 1,000 square feet of GLA.

partnership   See *general partnership* and *limited partnership.*

passive activity income   See *Tax Reform Act of 1986.*

passive loss rules   See *Tax Reform Act of 1986.*

pass-through charges   In commercial leasing, operating expenses of a property that are paid by the tenants, usually on a pro rata basis and in addition to base rent.

payback period   The amount of time required to recover the cost of a capital investment.

percentage rent   In retail leasing, rent that is based on a percentage of a tenant's gross sales (or sometimes net income or profits), often set against a guaranteed minimum or base rent and referred to as *overage rent*. (See also *breakpoint*.)

physical obsolescence   See *obsolescence*.

physical vacancy   The percentage of units (apartments, office suites, store spaces) that are unoccupied and available for lease.

planned unit development (PUD)   A zoning classification that allows flexibility in the design of a subdivision, usually setting an overall density limit that allows clustering of units to provide for common open space. A PUD is a departure from conventional residential zoning; therefore, the term *planned unit development* also refers to a special zoning apparatus that permits the undertaking.

point   One percent of the total loan amount.

polychlorinated biphenyl (PCB)   A chemical present in electrical transformers that is relatively harmless if left undisturbed. However, if a PCB-containing transformer leaks or burns, lethal *dioxin* gas may be released. Local or state law may require removal of PCBs during rehabilitation.

population shift   A fluctuation in numbers of individuals in different age and income groups and changes in household sizes. (Compare *economic shift*.)

power shopping center   A type of super community shopping center. Several large, strong, high-volume, heavy-advertising retailers occupy most of the space. Home furnishings, office supplies, sporting goods, home improvements, toys, and consumer electronics (computers, major appliances) stores are common anchor tenants in these centers. Power centers have GLAs ranging from 200,000 to 600,000 square feet and at least four category-specific off-price anchors, each occupying 20,000 or more square feet of GLA. The trade area may extend up to 30 miles, depending on local competition; they need a minimum population of 150,000.

prelease   To lease before construction of a building begins or while the construction is taking place. For proposed developments, lending institutions usually require a certain percentage of a planned property to be leased before construction loans will be approved.

pretax cash flow   See *cash flow*.

preventive maintenance   A program of regular inspection and care that allows potential problems to be prevented or at least detected and solved before major repairs are needed. (See also *corrective maintenance* and *deferred maintenance*.)

prime interest rate   The lowest interest rate available from banks for short-term loans to their most creditworthy customers.

primogeniture   A rule of inheritance in which estates could be passed to descendants.

principal   In real estate, one who owns property; in real estate management, the property owner who contracts for the services of an agent; in finance, the amount of money that is borrowed in a loan as distinct from the interest on such loan.

private limited partnership   See *limited partnership.*

Producer Price Index (PPI)   A measurement of inflation at the wholesale level. (Compare *Consumer Price Index.*)

professional liability insurance   In real estate management, insurance to protect against liabilities resulting from honest mistakes and oversights (no protection is provided in cases of gross negligence); also called *errors and omissions insurance.*

professional real estate management   The profession of conducting a property's management, operations, marketing, leasing, and financial reporting to meet the objectives of the owner. It also involves planning for the future of the property by proposing physical and fiscal strategies that will enhance the value of the real estate.

progressive discipline   A system of employee reprimand that provides ample opportunity for the employee to change or correct his or her behavior; such a system usually involves verbal warnings, written warnings, probation, and termination.

Project-Based Rental Assistance   HUD Section 8 program under which HUD makes up the difference between the rent a low- or very low-income household can afford and the approved rent for an adequate housing unit in a multifamily project. Eligible renters pay rent based on their income.

property analysis   A study of a property referring to such items as deferred maintenance, functional and economic obsolescence, land location and zoning, exterior construction and condition, plant and equipment, unit mix, facilities, and expected income and expenses.

property damage insurance   Coverage that protects against liability for damage to the property of others that occurs on the insured property.

property management   See *real estate management.*

property operations manual   A manual that a real estate manager or management firm develops for a specific managed property. Some policies and procedures may duplicate or only slightly modify many of the firm's operational policies, others will be property-specific. (Compare *operations manual.*)

proprietary lease   See *cooperative.*

pro rata   Proportionately; in real estate ownership and leasing, based on the size of individually owned or leased spaces in relation to the whole. Condominium owners and commercial tenants commonly pay proportionate shares of operating expenses and other costs.

prospect   A potential tenant or management client.

protected class   See *fair housing laws.*

psychographic profile   An analysis of a retail trade area that goes beyond the numbers to examine the interests and shopping habits of the people who live in the shopping center's trade area. (Compare *demographic profile.*)

public housing   Housing owned by and/or managed for a local or state governmental agency; the principal form of low-income housing available in the United States. (Compare *government-assisted housing*.)

public housing agency (PHA)   See *Housing and Community Development Act.*

public limited partnership   See *limited partnership.*

qualification   The process of judging a prospective tenant's financial status or creditworthiness. In real estate management, the process of determining whether a prospect can afford the rent on the unit applied for and has a good history of bill payments.

radius clause   A provision in a retail lease that prevents a retailer from opening and operating a similar—and therefore competitive—business within a certain radius from the shopping center.

radon   A colorless, odorless, tasteless gas that occurs naturally in the radioactive decay of radium and uranium. It became a problem with the advent of energy-efficient buildings that allow only minimal transfer of air between the building's interior and exterior.

real estate   Land and all improvements in or on it.

real estate cycle   Recurring periods of high and low activity in real estate markets. The cycle has four components: overbuilding, adjustment, stabilization, and development. They generally follow their business cycle counterparts.

real estate investment trust (REIT)   An entity that sells shares of beneficial interest to investors and uses the funds to invest in real estate or mortgages. Real estate investment trusts must meet certain requirements such as a minimum number of investors and widely dispersed ownership. No corporate taxes need to be paid as long as a series of complex IRS qualifications are met. (See also *shares of beneficial interest.*)

real estate management   A profession in which someone other than the owner (a real estate manager) supervises the operation of a property according to the owner's objectives or consults with the owner on the definition of those objectives and the property's profitability.

receivership   Court-ordered turnover of a property to an impartial third party (receiver) so that it may be preserved for the benefit of the affected parties.

regional analysis   A detailed study of a region, usually the area surrounding and including one or more neighboring cities, to determine the force of various factors affecting the economic welfare of a section of the region, such as population growth and movement, employment, industrial and business activity, transportation facilities, tax structures, topography, improvements, and trends.

regional mall   A large shopping center that has one or more full-line department stores as anchor tenants. The presence of a department store tends to attract such ancillary tenants as men's and women's apparel stores, optical shops, electronic equipment stores, and jewelers. Many include small fast food outlets arranged in a food court. Some also have cinemas. Regional malls contain 400,000 to one million square feet of GLA. Their trade area has a radius of 7 to 10 miles, and they usually serve a population of 150,000 to 300,000.

rehabilitation The process of renewing the equipment and materials in the building; entails correcting deferred maintenance.

rent In real estate, payment made for the use of space; periodic payments made under a lease.

rentable area The area in an office building on which rent is based and which generally includes the space available for tenants' exclusive use plus identified common areas less any major vertical penetrations (air shafts, stairways, elevators) in the building. The term is applied to the building as a whole, to individual floors, and to portions of floors. (Compare *usable area.*)

rental agreement See *lease.*

rental ledger A record of rent received, date of receipt, period covered, and other related information for each individual tenant. (Compare *rent roll.*)

rent control Laws that regulate rental rates, usually to limit the amount of rent increases and their frequency.

rent loss insurance Coverage that protects the owner from loss of income resulting from damage that makes all or part of the property unleasable.

rent roll A listing of all rental units, showing the rental rate, tenant's name, and lease expiration date as well as the status of rent and other payments. (Compare *rental ledger.*)

replacement cost coverage Insurance to replace or restore a building or its contents to its preexisting condition and appearance. (Compare *actual cash value.*)

reserve account transactions report A report that lists deposits to and withdrawals from the reserve fund.

reserve fund Money set aside to provide funds for anticipated future expenditures.

resident One who lives (or resides) in a place. Many real estate professionals prefer to refer to residential tenants as "residents." (Compare *tenant.*)

Resident-Based Rental Assistance HUD Section 8 program. The individual or family who receives a housing voucher is responsible for finding a suitable housing unit. The public housing agency pays the subsidy directly to the property owner on behalf of the participating renter. The renter then pays the difference between the amount subsidized by the program and the actual rent charged by the owner (usually limited to 30 percent of the renter's adjusted monthly income).

Residential Lead-Based Paint Hazard Reduction Act The federal law that requires owners and managers of apartment buildings constructed before 1978 to give renters (1) a disclosure form detailing the presence of lead-based paint; (2) a government pamphlet on lead paint hazards; and (3) a copy of any existing reports that describe lead paint hazards at the property.

residential manager   One who manages a residential property or properties.

resident manager   See *site manager.*

retrofit   To replace fixtures or facilities in a building with new equipment that is more efficient, usually in terms of energy consumption, fire protection codes, or accommodations for new technology.

return on investment (ROI)   A measure of profitability expressed as a percentage and calculated by comparing periodic income to the owner's equity in the property. (income ÷ equity = % ROI) It can be calculated either before or after deduction of income tax. (Also called *cash-on-cash return.*)

rider   See *endorsement.*

right of first offer   As an alternative approach to granting an *option to expand,* a tenant may be granted a first choice to rent a particular space subject to availability of that space.

right of first refusal   An option that gives a tenant the first choice to lease contiguous space or other space in the building when it becomes available. The lease clause specifies the area.

right of reentry   The property owner's right to enter an occupied apartment to make repairs, provide agreed-upon services, and show the apartment to prospective tenants and others, subject to certain limitations.

R/U ratio   See *Building Owners and Managers Association International.*

sales approach   See *appraisal.*

S corporation   See *corporation.*

Section 8 housing   Privately owned residential rental units that participate in the low-income rental assistance program created by the 1974 amendments to Section 8 of the 1937 Housing Act. Under this program, the U.S. Department of Housing and Urban Development (HUD) pays a rent subsidy to the property owner on behalf of qualified low-income residents so they pay a limited portion of their incomes for rent.

Section 202   Federal housing program that covers supportive housing for the elderly.

Section 811   Federal housing program that covers supportive housing for the disabled.

security deposit   An amount of money advanced by the tenant and held by an owner or manager to ensure the faithful performance of the lease terms by the tenant. Part or all of the deposit may be retained to pay for rent owed, miscellaneous charges owed, unpaid utility bills, and damage to the leased space that exceeds normal wear and tear. Limitations on withholding may be imposed by local and state ordinances.

self-storage facilities   Storage facilities that resemble rows of attached garages in which individuals and businesses store and secure their goods themselves. Many of these facilities include living quarters for an on-site manager.

shares of beneficial interest   Shares sold by real estate investment trusts (REITs); they are traded on the stock markets similar to corporate common stock. (See also *real estate investment trust.*)

shell space   Condition in which new office space and store space is commonly leased—enclosed by outside walls and a roof, with a concrete slab floor and utilities brought in. The plumbing and electrical installations are unfinished, and the space has no partitioning walls, ceiling tiles, wall coverings, or flooring.

shopping center   A generic term applied to a collection of retail stores enclosed in one building or adjacent to each other in separate buildings. Shopping centers are categorized based on their gross leasable area, type of tenancy, and the extent of their geographic trade area (customer base).

single-family home   A residence that has its own entry. Townhouses, which by definition share a common wall but have private entrances, are also classified as single-family homes.

site management   A profession that involves maintaining the physical structure of a property as well as maintaining and updating property-related documents and information.

site manager   An employee who oversees and administers the day-to-day affairs of a property in accordance with directions from the property manager or the owner. For residential properties, the manager may live in the building he or she manages (*resident manager*) or off-site. For commercial properties, the manager may occupy an office on-site or off-site.

sole proprietorship   A business enterprise carried on by one person.

space planning   The process of designing an office configuration for maximum functional efficiency based on a prospective tenant's space utilization needs, aesthetic requirements, and financial limitations.

special assessment   A special tax levied by a local government to fund public improvements (sidewalks, curbs, or other infrastructure) within a small area; only properties directly benefiting from the improvements are assessed the tax. In a condominium, monies collected from owners to fund a capital expenditure (e.g., roof replacement) when reserve funds are insufficient. This is in addition to the regular assessment for maintenance of common areas. (See also *assessment.*)

special form insurance   Coverage that pays for all losses except those that are specifically excluded in the policy. (Formerly *all-risk insurance.*)

Specially Designated Nationals and Blocked Persons (SDN) list   See *U.S.A. Patriot Act.*

specialty shopping center   A dominant theme or image characterizes this type of shopping center. Those in downtown areas are often the result of adaptive use of a historic building. They do not always have an anchor tenant, and many rely on tourists for most of their sales. Their uniqueness is their main attraction. They usually vary in size from 25,000 to 70,000 square feet, although some of these centers can be as large as 375,000 square feet of GLA. The specific use defines the trade area, and it may extend beyond the radiuses usually associated with centers of this size. Specialty shopping centers require an area population in excess of 150,000 to survive.

standard operating procedures manual   See *operations manual.*

standard tenant improvement allowance   See *tenant improvement allowance.*

statement of operations   An at-a-glance view of the property's gross amounts of income and expenses for a period. It emphasizes the cash flow paid to the owner. Also called an *income statement.*

statement of receipts report   Chronological report of rents and income from sources other than rents that identifies the source and amount of all monies received.

statute law   Written law enacted by a governmental body. (Compare *common law.*)

steering   An illegal discriminatory practice that encourages a prospective tenant to look at another site for housing or conceals vacancies from a prospect.

store hours clause   A retail lease clause that authorizes the management of the property to set store hours for the center as a whole. It may include provisions for seasonal adjustments and special hours for holiday shopping periods.

strip shopping center   A shopping center designed in a line. The term is sometimes used for convenience shopping centers and can refer to other types of centers as well.

sublet   The leasing of part or all of the premises by a tenant to a third party for part or all of the tenant's remaining term.

sublet clause   A clause in a residential lease that states that, in order for the resident to vacate the premises before the end of the term, he or she must find a suitable resident to sublet the space for the remainder of the lease obligation. The manager must approve that person, and the resident or the subtenant must pay for the credit check.

submarket   A segment of the overall market that is limited by a particular market influence.

subrogation   The substitution of one creditor for another such that the substituted person succeeds to the legal rights and claims of the original claimant; in insurance, the right of an insurer to attempt to recover amounts from an at-fault third party for claims paid to the insured party.

subsidized housing   See *government-assisted housing.*

substitute check   See *Check 21 Act.*

super regional mall   A large shopping center that includes four or more full-line department stores and 100 to 150 small shops. May include *outlots* or *pads*. It usually has one million to three million square feet of GLA. Its trade area has a radius of 10 to 20 miles, and it serves a population of 300,000 or more.

supply   The availability of goods and services.

surety   A formal guarantee.

syndicate   A type of professionally managed limited partnership formed to invest in different types of real estate.

syndication   A method of selling property in which a sponsor sells ownership interests to investors.

tax   An amount assessed by government for public purposes, usually based on the relative value of property or income.

Tax Reform Act of 1980   Federal legislation that offered numerous incentives for real estate investment and fueled unprecedented development. (See also *Tax Reform Act of 1986*.)

Tax Reform Act of 1986   Legislation that restructured federal income tax and its associated deductions. Of primary importance in real estate are its definitions of *passive activity income* (and loss), which include real property income, and its restrictions against using passive losses to offset active income—i.e., salary. (The Technical and Miscellaneous Revenue Act of 1988 delineated technical corrections to the Tax Reform Act of 1986.)

telecommute   To work at home using a computer linked to an employer's location via a telephone network.

tenancy in common (TIC)   Ownership by two or more persons in which each holds an undivided interest in the property. Upon the death of one tenant, that tenant's interest in the property passes to his or her heirs—not to the other tenant(s); the right of survivorship does not apply. A tenancy in common is a fractionalized fee-simple interest in real property used in certain tax-deferred exchanges. While technically a real estate transaction, TICs are in fact sold as securities. (Compare *joint tenancy*.)

tenant   One who pays rent to occupy real estate. Real estate managers often limit the use of the term "tenant" to commercial tenants and refer to residential tenants as "residents." (See also *lessee* and *resident*.)

tenant improvement allowance (TIA)   In commercial leasing, an amount a landlord agrees to spend to improve the leased shell space for a tenant before move-in or as a condition of lease renewal. A *standard tenant improvement allowance* is a fixed dollar amount allowed by the owner for items that may be installed in the leased premises at no charge to the tenant. Payment for tenant improvements is part of the lease negotiations. (See also *building standard*.)

tenant mix   The combination of types of businesses and services that lease space in a shopping center or office building or (sometimes) industrial park.

term   The duration of a tenant's lease; the duration of a mortgage (e.g., a 30-year term).

terrorism   As defined in the U.S. Code of Federal Regulations, the unlawful use of force and violence against persons or property to intimidate or coerce a government, the civilian population, or any segment thereof, in furtherance of political or social objectives.

Terrorism Risk Insurance Act (TRIA)   This federal legislation requires insurers to offer terrorism insurance to commercial industry and provides a federal backstop to support the insurance industry in the event of catastrophic terrorist attacks. Congress signed TRIA into law in 2002. The act was scheduled to expire at the end of 2005, but legislation was introduced to extend the act for two years.

timeshare   A specialized form of condominium found mostly in resort areas. As the name implies, the owner has the right to occupy the unit for a specific period.

time value of money   The assumption that a dollar today is worth more than a dollar at some future date. The basis of compounding to determine future value or discounting to determine present value.

Title VIII   See *fair housing laws.*

trade area   The geographic area from which a shopping center obtains most of its customers, its size depends on the type of center, location of competition, and other factors. A trade area is generally divided into primary, secondary, and tertiary zones based on distance from the shopping center, travel time, and other factors.

traffic report   A record of the number of prospects who visit or make inquiries at a property and the factors that attracted them to it.

transfer clause   A residential lease clause that allows the resident to break the lease without penalty in case of a job transfer.

umbrella liability insurance   Extra liability coverage that exceeds the limits of a basic liability policy.

unemployment rate   The number of unemployed divided by the number in the labor force (the number of employed plus the number of unemployed).

unit deed   A document that legally transfers title to a condominium unit and a share of the common areas from one owner to another.

unscheduled income   Income that may be unanticipated and/or not planned for.

The Urban Land Institute (ULI)   An independent nonprofit research and educational organization dedicated to improving the quality and standards of land use and development. It publishes comparison data on shopping centers and multifamily housing.

urban renewal   A federal program that opens land in cities to development or redevelopment and new uses.

urban village   A parcel of land that was previously home to an industrial use or an apartment complex that is redeveloped to incorporate a variety of residential and commercial uses into a "pedestrian-friendly" neighborhood. This phenomenon, called *new urbanism,* includes higher-density development with narrow streets complemented by wide sidewalks. This strategy is revitalizing urban areas and creating an identifiable downtown in suburbs that do not have one.

usable area   The area in an office building that is available for the exclusive use of a tenant. (Compare *rentable area*.)

U.S.A. Patriot Act   This federal legislation, along with Executive Order 13224, has increased federal government scrutiny of financial transactions, including real estate transactions. The purpose is to curb and prevent business interactions with terrorist organizations. Commercial property managers in particular should periodically check the *Specially Designated Nationals and Blocked Persons* (*SDN*) list to ensure that current and prospective tenants are not on that list. Residential property managers should also check prospects and existing residents against the list since known terrorists have leased apartments in the United States.

U.S. Civil Rights Act of 1968   See *fair housing laws.*

use clause   In a retail lease, a clause that prevents a tenant from using the premises in a different way than originally intended.

valuation   An estimation or calculation of the worth of an object or service; the process of determining an object's or service's worth.

variable-rate mortgage   A mortgage in which the lending institution can raise or lower the interest rate of an existing loan depending on prevailing loan rates or a prescribed index. (Compare *adjustable-rate mortgage.*)

Wage and Hour Law   See *Fair Labor Standards Act.*

walk-up   An older four-story apartment building that has stairs only.

Worker Adjustment and Retraining Notification (WARN) Act   The federal law that requires employers of large numbers of workers to give affected workers 60 days' advance notice of a layoff if it impacts 33 percent of the employer's workforce, provided that at least 50 employees are to be laid off.

workers' compensation insurance   Coverage obtained by an employer to pay compensation and benefits awarded to an employee in the event of employment-related sickness or injury.

zero-based budget   See *annual budget.*

zoning   Regulation of the character and use of property by areas or "zones," usually by local (municipal) government.

Index

A

Absorption rate, 84, 319
Accelerated cost recovery, 58, 319
Accessibility
    of office building, 249–250
    of shopping center, 274–275
Accounting
    accrual-basis, 110, 319
    cash-basis, 110, 323
    for income and expenses, 109–118
    methods of, 110–111
    outsourcing, 134
    software for, 118–119
    systems and equipment, 109–111,
        309
Accredited Management Organization®
    (AMO®), 13, 299, 319
Accredited Residential Manager®
    (ARM®), 13, 319
Accrual-basis accounting, 110, 319
Acquisitions for clients, 313–314
Active income, 7
Actual cash value (ACV) insurance,
    243, 319
Adaptive use, 319
    in analysis of alternatives, 87

Additional rent, 284
Add-on factors, 258, 320
Adjustable-rate mortgage (ARM), 54,
    320
Adjustment, 46
Administrative costs, 112
Ad valorem tax, 43, 315, 320
Advertising, 116–117
    billboard, 184
    broadcast, 187
    calculating in terms of cost per
        prospect, 192
    classified, 183
    direct-mail, 300
    display, 183–184, 299–300
    fair housing law and, 217
    help-wanted, 136
    institutional, 299–300
    newspaper, 183–184
    property, 96
    radio, 187
    for shopping centers, 283
    television, 187
Advertising agency, use of, 182–193
Aesthetic appeal of shopping center,
    274–275

Age Discrimination and Employment
     Act (1967) (ADEA), 148, 320
Agent, 15, 320
   in management agreement, 91
Aging in place, 237, 320
All-cash purchase, 52
All-inclusive rent, 265
Allodialism, 2, 320
Amenities
   in apartments, 8
   custodial maintenance of, 160
   recreational, 116
   residential, 241
American Housing Survey, 70
American property law, basis of, 1–2
American Society of Heating, Refriger-
     ating, and Air-Conditioning Engi-
     neers (ASHRAE), 169, 170, 320
Americans with Disabilities Act (ADA)
     (1990), 148, 220, 260, 268, 287,
     320
Amortization, 53, 320
Analysis of alternatives
   changes in, 87
   in management plan, 85–89
Anchor tenants, 271, 279, 320
Ancillary tenants, 271, 272, 282, 320
Annual budget, 123, 320
   items common to, 124
Antennas, 162
Apartment guides, 184
Apartments, 211–213
   amenities in, 8
   garden, 212, 331
   high-rise, 212, 332
   low-rise, 212, 335
   management of, 213
   mid-rise, 212, 336
   types of, 212
Appearance of office building, 250
Applicants, recruiting, 135–138
Applications
   bandwidth-intensive, 252
   employment, 137–138
   rental, 215, 216
Appraisals, 310–312, 320–321
   cost approach to, 311
   discounted cash flow approach to,
     311

income capitalization approach to,
     311
   market approach to, 311
Appreciation, 31, 53, 321
   capital, 56
Articles of incorporation, 230, 321
Artificial breakpoint, 280, 321, 322
Asbestos, 45, 168, 321
Assessments, 230–231, 321
   special, 231
Asset manager, 16, 17
Assets
   illiquid, 52
   liquid, 52
Assets management, 17, 310, 321
Assignment, 321
Assisted living facilities, 237, 321
At will employment, 150, 321
Audits
   provision for, 95
   of sales in retail lease, 285
Automobile insurance, 117

B
Baby Boomers, 37
Back rent, 201
Balloon mortgage, 54–55, 321
Balloon payment, 55
Bandwidth-intensive applications,
     252
Bank accounts
   establishment of, 93–94
   records on, 121
Bank Holding Company Act, 30
Bankruptcies, 39, 105, 203, 321
Base rent, 111, 279, 320, 321
Base year, 48, 263, 321
*Before Disaster Strikes: Developing an
     Emergency Procedures Manual,*
     306n
Benefits, 142
Billboards, 184
Bill of Rights, 1
Biometric identification, 173
Blanket policy, 118, 322
Board of directors, 322
   working with, 234
Bodily injury insurance, 117, 322
Boiler insurance, 117, 322

Bonds
  fidelity, 117–118
  fiduciary, 138
Boundary definition in neighborhood
    analysis, 72
Branch banking, 30
Branch savings and loan associations
    (S&Ls), 30
Breakpoint, 322
  artificial, 280, 322
  natural, 280, 322
Broadcast advertising, 187
Brochures, 185–186
  computer-generated, 186
Budgets, 322
  annual, 123–124
  capital, 124–125
  in financial management, 121–125
  historical, 123
  long-range, 125
  operating, 122–123
  quarterly, 123–124
  zero-based, 123
Building activity, 48–49
Building common areas, 258
Building managers, 16
Building Owners and Managers Asso-
    ciation International (BOMA), 70,
    71, 258, 322
  Standard Method, 258, 322
Building services, 114
Building size in property analysis, 73
Building standards, 260, 322, 347
Building-to-land ratio in property
    analysis, 74
Build out, 257, 261, 322
Build-to-suit lease, 287, 322
Business cycle, 33–39, 322
  real estate cycle and, 46
Business-to-business services, 195
Bylaws, 230, 322

C

Call center-based management, 304, 322
Cap, 281
Capital
  foreign, 65–66
  pooled, 3
Capital appreciation, 56

Capital budget, 124–125, 323
Capital expenditures, 108
Capital improvements, 323
  as reason for investing, 57–58
  reserve fund for, 107–108
Capitalization, 323
Capitalization rate (cap rate), 106–107,
    323
Capital preservation, 55–56
Cash-basis accounting, 110, 323
Cash disbursements journal, 110
Cash disbursements report, 120, 323
Cash flow, 57, 104–105, 323
  calculating, 103
Cash flow chart, 100–105
Cash-on-cash return, 104. *See also*
    Return on investment (ROI)
Cash receipts journal, 110
Casings
  custodial maintenance of, 160
  preventive maintenance of, 162
C corporations, 63, 64. *See also*
    Corporations
Cellular telephones, 308
The Census Catalog and Guide, 70
Central business districts (CBDs), 42,
    246–247, 261, 323
Certified Property Manager® (CPM®),
    12–13, 299, 323
Chart of accounts, 109, 309, 323
  common categories for, 110
Check 21 Act (2004), 31–32, 323
Chicago commodity markets, 22
Chlorofluorocarbons (CFCs), 168, 169,
    323
Civil Rights Act (Title VII, 1968), 148,
    216, 324
Class A office buildings, 247, 248–249,
    253, 290
Class B office buildings, 247, 248, 249,
    253
Class C office buildings, 247–248, 249,
    253
Classified advertising, 183
Cleaning, 113
Clients
  acquisitions for, 313–314
  identifying prospective, 295–298
  recruitment of prospective, 294–295

Client services, 310–317
Code of Professional Ethics, 12
Cogeneration equipment, preventive
    maintenance of, 164–166
Cold calling, 288, 324
Collateral, 52, 324
Collection policies in tenancy cycle,
    200–205
Collection system, 202
Commercial properties, 270, 286–288,
    324
  insuring, 290–292
  lease considerations, 287–288
  market analysis of, 77, 79
  marketing of, 288–290
  on-site office in, 303
  sources of income at, 111
  types of, 286–287
Commingling of funds, 306, 309, 324
Common area maintenance (CAM),
    111, 265
  charges for, 279
  clause on, 288, 324
Common areas, 324
  building, 258
  condominium, 229
  custodial maintenance of, 160
  in property analysis, 73–74
  shopping centers, 271
Common interest developments
    (CIDs), 10–11, 324
Common interest realty associations
    (CIRA), 324
  in residential property management,
    229–235
Common law, 2, 324
Communications, 143–144
  equipment for, 308–309
  with maintenance personnel, 155
Community shopping center, 272, 324
Comparison grid in market analysis,
    79–82, 324
Compensation
  for employees, 141–143
  for management services, 98, 302
Competition, defining, in market
    analysis, 75–76
Compliance status in property
    analysis, 74

Comprehensive general liability insur-
    ance, 306
Comprehensive insurance coverage,
    290–291
Computer-aided design (CAD) equip-
    ment, 261
Computer-generated brochures, 186
Computer networks, 163
Computers, 25–26, 306–308
Concessions, 324
  as marketing incentive, 189–190
  in office leases, 265–266, 284
Condition
  of building, in property analysis, 73
  of premises, 223–224
Condominium association, 229–230,
    242, 297, 325
Condominium conversion
  in analysis of alternatives, 87–88
  demolition for new development in,
    88–89
Condominiums, 6, 229–231, 324
  manufactured housing, 237
  office, 268
  owners' association of, 229–230,
    242, 325297
  time-share, 182
Congregate housing, 237, 325
Consolidated Omnibus Budget Recon-
    ciliation Act (COBRA), 149, 325
Construction oversight, 302
Consumer Price Index (CPI), 28–29,
    264, 282, 325
  rent and, 48
Continual training, 144–145
Continuous occupancy clause in the
    retail lease, 285, 325
Continuous operation clause in the
    retail lease, 285, 325
Contract for labor as needed, 130
Contract laborer, 130
Contractors, 133–134, 174–175
Contracts, employment, 139
Contract workers, on-site, 133–134
Convenience shopping center,
    271–272, 325
Conversion ratio, 192, 325
Cooperatives, 231–232, 325
  owners' association of, 297

Corporate fiscal service, 314
Corporations, 63–65, 325
  as real estate owners, 64
Corrective maintenance, 154, 325
Corridors in office building, 251
Cost approach of appraisal, 311
Cost-benefit analysis, 86, 89, 326
Cost-benefit ratio, 256
Cost recovery, 57. *See also*
      Depreciation
Credit card debt, 39
Credit reports, 219
Curb appeal, 326
  in property analysis, 74
  of residential property, 159, 242
Current management in property
      analysis, 74
Custodial maintenance, 154, 159–160
  amenities in, 160
  common areas in, 159
  driveways in, 159
  elevators in, 159
  exterior walls and components in,
      160
  grounds in, 159
  interior walls in, 160
  lobbies in, 159
  parking areas in, 159
  walks in, 159
  windows and casings in, 160
Customer service
  reputation and, 276
  strategies in retaining tenants, 207
Cycle of tenancy. *See* Tenancy cycle

D
Data evaluation in neighborhood
      analysis, 72–73
Debt service, 43, 52, 53, 104, 105, 326
Declaration, condominium, 230, 326
Deductibles, 243, 326
Deed of trust, 53, 326
Default, 29, 326
Deferred maintenance, 326
  budget constraints and, 155
  defined, 154
  evidence of, 295
Deflation, 27, 326
Delinquency, 201–202

Demand, 326
  effect on price, 23
  real estate value and, 69
Demised premises, 326
Demising walls, 258
Demographic profile, 69, 274, 326
Demographics, 70
  sources of, 70–71
Demolition for new development,
      88–89
Depreciation, 30, 31, 57, 327, 338
Depression, 36
Deregulation, 30
Destination shopping, 278
Development, 47
  demolition for new, 88–89
Dioxin gas, 169
Directional signs, 185
Direct mail, 186, 300
Direct solicitation, 298
Disability, 327
Discipline
  employee, 145–147
  progressive, 146–147
Discounted cash flow method of ap-
      praisal, 311
Discount rate, 11, 31
Discretionary income, 327
Dismissal of employee, 146, 150–151
Display advertisements
  in developing marketing program,
      183–184
  in real estate management, 299–300
Disposable income, 327
Dot-com companies, 10
Downspouts, preventive maintenance
      of, 162
Driveways
  custodial maintenance of, 159
  preventive maintenance of, 161
Drug-Free Workplace Act, 149, 327
Drug testing, 138–139
Dun & Bradstreet rating, 254

E
E-commerce, 8
Economic Census, 70
Economic growth, population growth
      and, 37

Economic Growth and Tax Relief Act (2001), 29, 327
Economic indicators, 33
Economic obsolescence, 249, 338
Economics
  basic, 21–22
  defined, 21
  real estate, 39–49
  trends in, 21
Economic shifts, 73, 327
Economic vacancy, 101, 327
Economy, 27–33
  business cycle in, 33–39
  marketplace in, 22–27
  role of government in, 27–33
Effective gross income, 102, 327
Effective rent, 190–191, 327
Elderly, housing for, 237–238
Electrical network, preventive maintenance of, 163–164
Electric utilities, deregulation of, 267
Electronic check conversion, 32. *See also* Check 21
Elevators
  custodial maintenance of, 160
  in office buildings, 250–251
  preventive maintenance of, 162–163
E-mail, 187
Emergency and evacuation procedures, 306
Eminent domain, 3, 327
Employee manual, 140–141, 146
  contents of, 140
Employee Polygraph Protection Act (EPPA), 149, 327
Employee Retirement Income Security Act (1974) (ERISA), 6, 149, 328
Employees. *See also* Staffing
  compensation for, 141–143
  discipline in, 145–147
  dismissal of, 146, 150–151
  of management firm, 130–133
  performance reviews of, 141
  prospective, 139
  retaining valuable, 141–145
  selecting, 138–140
  temporary, 133
  termination of, 147–151

Employee-screening service, 139
Employer
  liability of, 151
  of on-site staff, 129
Employment. *See also* Unemployment
  at-will, 150
  changes in levels of, 27
  federal laws that affect, 148–149
  full, 24
Employment agencies, 136
Employment application, 137–138
  contents of, 137
  verifying information provided on, 139
Employment contracts, 139
Employment Eligibility Verification form (form I-9), 139, 328
Employment levels, 24–25
Employment policies, 146
Enclosed shopping malls, 42
Encryption software, 8
Endorsements, 244, 328
Energy conservation tactics, 171–172, 172
Entertainment shopping center, 273, 328
Environment, protecting, 168–171
Environmental Protection Agency (EPA), 168, 328
Equal Employment Opportunity Commission (EEOC), 140, 328
Equal opportunity housing, 217
Equity, 53, 328
Errors and omissions insurance, 309. *See also* Professional liability insurance
Escalation clauses, 48, 328
  in office leases, 263
  in retail leases, 281–282
Estates, management opportunity for, 297
Eviction, 202, 328
  proceedings in, 203–204
  types of, 204–205
Eviction notice, 202–203, 328
Excise tax, 316
Exclusive use in retail lease, 328
Executive Order 13224, 11, 220, 349

Executive property manager, 16
Executive summary, 328
Exempt status. *See* Fair Labor Standards Act (FLSA)
Exit signs, lights in, 165
Expense cap. *See* Expense stop
Expenses
  accounting for, 109–118
  categories, 111–118
  payment of, 94
  reporting on, 118–121
Expense stop, 264, 281, 328–329
Extended coverage (EC) insurance, 117, 243, 329
Exterior maintenance, 250
Exterior walls and components
  custodial maintenance of, 160
  preventive maintenance of, 161

F

Facility management, 17, 310
Facility managers, 17, 329
Fair Credit Reporting Act (FCRA), 197, 219, 329
Fair Debt Collection Practices Act (FDCPA), 201, 329
Fair Housing Act (1968), 216
Fair Housing Amendments Act (1988), 217
Fair Housing laws, 45, 216–218, 306, 329
Fair Labor Standards Act (FLSA), 141–142, 148, 329
Fair market value, 330
Familial status, 330
Family and Medical Leave Act (FMLA) (1993), 148, 330
Federal Bankruptcy Act (2005), 203
Federal Deposit Insurance Corporation (FDIC), 30
Federal funds rate, 11
Federal Housing Administration (FHA), 330
Federal income tax, 29, 316
  changes in laws on, 29–30
Federal Insurance Contributions Act (FICA), 148, 330
Federal programs, 142–143

Federal Reserve Bank, 32–33
Federal Savings and Loan Insurance Corporation (FSLIC), 8, 30
Federal Unemployment Tax Act (FUTA), 142–143, 148, 330
Federal Wage and Hour Law. *See* Fair Labor Standards Act (FLSA)
Fee simple ownership, 2, 330
Feudalism, 2, 330
Fidelity bonds, 117–118, 330
Fiduciary, 15, 91, 330
Fiduciary bonds, 138
File backup system, 119
Financial institutions, 297
Financial Institutions Reform, Recovery, and Enforcement Act (FIRREA), 30
Financial integrity
  in property analysis, 74
  in tenant selection, 277
Financially distressed property, managing, 105
Financial management, 18–19, 99–126
  accounting for income and expenses, 109–118
  budgeting in, 121–125
  evaluation of operating funds, 99–108
  reporting on income and expenses, 118–121
  responsibilities of real estate managers, 93–95
  role of real estate managers in, 99, 100, 104, 118
  training in, 149
Financial reasons to invest in real estate, 56
Financial regulation, 30–32
Financing, 52–54, 330
Fire extinguishers, 166
Fire insurance, 117, 243, 330
Fire safety, 165
  preventive maintenance of equipment in, 164–166
  training program, 165
Fiscal affairs, residential property and, 235
Fixed annual increase, 264–265
Fixed-rate mortgage, 54, 330

Flex space, 262, 331
Floor area. *See* Gross leasable areas
    (GLAs)
Floor area ratio (FAR) in property
    analysis, 74
Floor plate, 255, 331
Food court, 272
Food service operations, 277–278
For cause. *See* Eviction
Foreclosure, 331
Foreign capital, 65–66
Foreign investors, 297
Formaldehyde gas, 170, 331
Form I-9. *See* Employment Eligibility
    Verification form (form I-9)
Foundations, preventive maintenance
    of, 161
Full employment, 24
Functional obsolescence, 338
Funds
    commingling of, 306, 309, 324
    marketing, 284, 285
    operating, 99–108
    pension, 6, 7
    reserve, 104, 107–108, 231
    separation of, 94

G
Garden apartments, 212, 331
Gas lines, preventive maintenance of,
    164–166
Gas utilities, deregulation of, 267
Gated (common interest) communi-
    ties, 11
General ledger, 110
General partnerships, 60–61, 331
General property management,
    96–97
Generational groups, 37
Generation X, 37
Geographic information system (GIS),
    71
Global reliance on technology, 8–9
Goodwill, building, in tenancy cycle,
    207
Governing documents, 230
Government
    real estate and, 43–45

    role of, in economy, 27–33
    subsidy programs of, 44
Government-assisted housing, 213–
    215, 331
Gramm-Leach Bliley Act (2001)
    (GLBA), 197, 331
Great Depression, 5
Great rooms, 8, 331
Grievances, 144
Gross domestic product (GDP), 28, 33,
    331
Gross floor area, 271
Gross leasable areas (GLAs), 271, 272,
    273, 279, 331–332
Gross lease, 199, 332
Gross national product (GNP), 28, 332
Gross potential rental income, 100–
    101, 332
Grounds
    custodial maintenance of, 159
    preventive maintenance of, 161
Groundskeeping, 115
    expenses in, 114
Gutters, preventive maintenance of,
    162

H
Habitability, 226, 332
Hazardous materials in buildings, 169
Heating, ventilation, and air-condition-
    ing (HVAC) system, 332
    preventive maintenance of, 163
Help-wanted advertisements, 136
Highest and best use, 21, 68, 311, 332
High-rise apartment buildings, 212, 332
High-rise office buildings, 247, 260
    staffing for, 130
Highways, impact on real estate mar-
    ket, 42
Historical budget, 123
Home offices, 25
Home-owners' association, 229, 235.
    See also Condominium association
    management for, 98
Home purchase clause in residential
    lease, 224–225, 332
Hoteling, 25, 256, 332
Household, 332

Housekeeping. *See* Custodial maintenance
Housing and Community Development Act (1974), 213, 332
Housing and Urban Development (HUD), U.S. Department of, 326
Housing Assistance Payments Program, 213
Housing authority, 297
Housing for elderly, 237–238
  in residential property management, 237–238

I

Identification signs, 185
Illiquid asset, 52
Immigration Reform and Control Act (IRCA), 148, 332
Impulse shopping, 278
Incandescent lamps, types of, 171
Incentives, 223
  offering marketing, 189–191
  tax, 57
Income, 23
  accounting for, 109–118
  categories of, 111
  collection of, 94
  reporting on, 118–121
Income capitalization approach of appraisal, 106, 311
Income-producing properties, sources of income for, 99
Income-property ownership, principal forms of, 58–66
Income sources of residents, 218–219
Income statement, 121. *See also* Statement of operations
Income taxes, 57, 104, 107
Independent contractor, 91*n*
Index of leading indicators, 33
Individual tax identification number (ITIN), 197, 333
Indoor air quality (IAQ), 170, 333
Industrial leases, 287–288
Industrial properties, 286–287
Industry, effect on real estate market, 40–41
Inflation, 11, 27, 29, 333

Inflation offset, 264
Informational signs, 185
Initial investment base, 54, 333
Inspection reports, 155–156
Institute of Real Estate Management (IREM®), 70, 299, 333
  founding of, 12–13
  Management Agreement form of, 92
Institutional advertising, 299–300
Institutional owners, 297, 333
Insurance, 117–118, 153, 333
  actual cash value (ACV), 243
  automobile, 117
  blanket policy, 118
  bodily injury, 117
  boiler, 117
  choice of packages, 244–245
  clause on, in industrial lease, 288
  comprehensive, 290–291
  comprehensive general liability, 306
  errors and omissions, 309
  extended coverage, 117, 243
  fire, 117, 243
  issues in residential property management, 241–245
  liability, 244
  owner, landlord, and tenant liability, 117
  owner's, 290–291
  professional liability, 309
  property damage, 117
  rent loss, 117
  special form, 117, 243
  tenant, 291–292
  terrorism, 220, 243, 291, 317
  umbrella liability, 117, 244
  workers' compensation, 143, 292, 306
Insurance service, 317
Interest rates, 32–33
  prime, 32
Interior painting and decorating, 115–116
Interior walls, custodial maintenance of, 160
Internal promotion, 135–136
International arena, money and, 31

International Council of Shopping
    Centers (ICSC), 70, 333
Internet, 8, 26, 187–188, 308
Intrinsic value, 55–56
Inventory control system, 178
Investment
    basis of value, 53
    means of, 51–55
    reasons for, 55–58
Investment partnerships, 313
Investment property, 14

J
Janitorial maintenance. *See* Custodial
    maintenance
Job descriptions, 136, 144, 145
    contents of, 136
Jobs and Growth Tax Relief Act (2003),
    29, 333
Joint and several liability, 60, 222, 333
Joint tenancy, 60, 334
Joint ventures, 65–66, 313, 334
Journals, 110
Just-in-time (JIT) delivery, 287, 334

L
Labor Statistics, Bureau of, 24
Land, 39
Landlord, 334
Landlord-tenant laws, 334
    compliance with, 226–228
Land value, 40
Late fees, 201
Layoffs, 148–150
Lead-based paint, 168, 169–170, 334
Leading indicators, 33
Leaking underground storage tanks
    (LUSTs), 171, 334
Lease(s), 197, 334. *See also* Residential
    leases; Retail leases
    build-to-suit, 287
    defined, 221
    duration of, 198–199
    executing, 96
    fundamental elements of, 198–199
    gross, 199
    importance of, 221–222
    industrial, 287–288

negotiation of, in office building
    management, 262–268
net, 200
office building, 262–268
parties to, 222–223
percentage, 200
proprietary, 231
renewal techniques for, 207–208
residential, 221–229
term of, 223
types of, 199–200
Lease, office, 263–265
Lease document in tenancy cycle,
    197–200
Leased premises, 165
Leased retail space, 270
Leasehold interest, 2, 334
Leasing, outsourcing, 134
Leasing agents, 96, 134, 181, 195, 334
Leasing and tenant management, 19
Leasing commission, 188
Legal expense, 115
Legionnaires' disease, 170
Legionnnella bacteria, 170
Lessee, 197, 334
Lessor, 197, 334
Liability, 244
    employer, 151
Liability insurance, 244, 334
    comprehensive general, 306
    owner, landlord, and tenant, 117
    professional, 309
    umbrella, 117, 244
Lien, 334
Lifestyle shopping center, 273, 334
Lights in exit signs, 165
Limited liability company (LLC), 63,
    313, 335
Limited liability general partnerships
    (LLGPs), 61
Limited liability limited partnership
    (LLLP), 61, 335
Limited partnerships (LP), 61–62, 313,
    335
Liquid assets, 52
Load factor, 320
Loans, 53
    treatment of, 95

Lobbies
  custodial maintenance of, 160
  in office buildings, 250
Location, 181, 192
  elevators and, 250
  factors that influence quality of,
    83–84
  importance of, 68–69
  of office buildings, 248–249
  of real estate management office,
    303–304
  of shopping center, 274–275
Locator services, 335
  referrals and, 188–189
London Inter-Bank Offering Rate
  (LIBOR), 31
Long-range budget, 125, 335
Low-rise apartment buildings, 212, 335

M
M1, 26
M2, 26
Mailroom supervisor, 133
Maintenance, 153–179. *See also* Cus-
    todial maintenance; Preventive
    maintenance
  contracting for, 133
  controlling energy consumption,
    171–172
  corrective, 154
  custodial, 154, 159–160
  deferred, 154, 155, 295
  issues in residential property man-
    agement, 238–241
  janitorial, 159
  in maintaining property security,
    172–173
  managing, 97, 173–178
  objectives of, 154
  on-site work for, 130
  preventive, 154, 160–167
  protecting environment, 168–171
  record keeping in, 175–178
  for rental housing, 211
  repairs and, 113–114
  of residential properties, 234–235,
    238–241
  safety and, 167–168

  schedules and inspections in,
    155–159
  service request for, 175
  staffing for, 174–175
Mall manager, 16
Managed properties
  proximity of, to each other, 132
  size and tenancy of, 131–132
Management
  of apartments, 213
  of condominium, 231
  of cooperative, 231
  of manufactured housing commu-
    nity, 237
  of office buildings, 246–269
  of rental housing, 233–235
  of residential property, 210–245
  of shopping center, 285–286
  of subsidized housing, 214–215
Management agreement, 68, 91–98,
    302, 335
  basic components of, 92–93
  responsibilities of manager, 93–97
Management consultation, 312
Management fees, 98, 112, 335
  determination of, 301–302
Management firm, employees of,
    130–133, 174
Management information systems
  (MIS) specialist, 133
Management offices
  in retail properties, 303–304
  in space planning, 304
Management plan, 67–91, 335
  adaptive use, 87
  analysis of alternatives, 85–89
  changes in use, 87
  condominium conversions, 87–88
  defined, 68
  demolition for new development,
    88–89
  market analysis in, 75–85
  neighborhood analysis, 71–73
  operational changes in, 86
  property analysis in, 73–75
  regional analysis in, 69–71
  structural changes in, 86–87
Management reports, 119–121

Management services, compensation
  for, 98
Manager(s). *see also* Real estate
  managers
  asset, 16, 17
  building, 16
  executive property, 16
  facility, 17
  mall, 16
  as owner's agent, 92
  portfolio, 16
  property, 16, 132
  of real property, 21
  regional, 16
  residential, 16
  site, 16
Manager member, 63
Manufactured housing, 335–336
  in residential property management,
  236–237
Market, 22
Market analysis, 336
  in management plan, 75–85
Market approach of appraisal, 311
Marketing, 336
  approving of prospect, 195, 197
  broadcast advertising in, 187
  brochures in, 185–186
  of commercial space, 288–290
  concessions in, 189–190
  developing program for, 182–189
  direct mail in, 186
  effective rent in, 190–191
  incentives in, 189–191
  Internet in, 187–188
  locator services and referrals in,
  188–189
  measuring effectiveness of, 191–194
  newspaper advertising in, 183–184
  offering incentives in, 189–191
  press releases in, 186–187
  print media in, 184
  sales techniques in, 194–195
  signs in, 184–185
Marketing fund, 284, 285, 336
Marketplace, 22–27
Market size, factors that determine, 181

Master-planned development, 288
Material safety data sheet (MSDS), 168,
  336
Mechanical systems in office buildings,
  252–253
Medical buildings, 286
Megamall, 273–274, 336
Megan's Law, 220, 336
Members, 63
Merchandise presentation, 276–277
Merchants' association, 284, 285, 336
Mercury vapor lamps, 171
Metal halide lamps, 171
Metropolitan statistical areas (MSAs), 48
Micro-market, 72, 336
Mid-rise apartment building, 212, 336
Military base, 44
Millennials, 37
Minimum rent, 279
Miscellaneous cash receipts, 120
Miscellaneous income, 102, 120, 337
Miscellaneous receipts, 120
Miscellaneous services, 114
Mixed-use development (MXD), 17, 88,
  89, 337
Mobile home, 337
Mobile home parks, 236
Model units, 101
Modernization, 86, 337
Modified triple-net lease, 281
Mold and mold-like substances,
  170–171
Money, 26–27
  function of, 22
  international arena and, 31
Money supply, 26, 337
  M1, 26
  M2, 26
Monthly planning, 123
Montreal Protocol, 169
Morale, promoting, 144
Mortgage, 52–54, 337
  adjustable-rate, 54
  balloon, 54–55
  deductibility of interest, 57
  fixed-rate, 54
  variable-rate, 54

Mortgage foreclosures, 49
Mortgage lending, 48
Move-in/move-out inspection form, 241
Mullions, 252, 337
Multiple-owner properties, 6
Multisorted office buildings, 250
Multi-tenant properties, 288

N

Narrative report
  in market analysis, 84–85
  of operations, 121, 337
National Apartment Association (NAA),
    71, 72, 337
National Association of Building Own-
    ers and Managers, 12
National Association of Industrial and
    Office Properties (NAIOP), 71–72,
    337
National Association of Real Estate
    Boards, 12–13
  Property Management Division, 12
National Register of Historic Places, 88
Natural breakpoint, 280, 322
Negative balance of trade, 10
Negligent hiring, 151
Negligent retention, 151
Negligent supervision, 151
Negotiable order of withdrawal (NOW)
    accounts, 26, 30
Negotiation, 337
  lease, 262–268
Neighborhood, 71
  analysis of, 71–73, 337
Neighborhood shopping center, 272,
    337–338
Neighbors, respect for, 221
Net leases, 200, 265, 280–281, 338
  types of, 265
Net-net lease, 264, 265, 280
Net-net-net lease, 264, 265, 280–281
Net operating income (NOI), 338
  appraisals and, 311
  cost-benefit analysis and, 89, 100,
    103–106
  efforts to increase, 68
  operating budget and, 122

Newsletters, 143
Newspaper advertising, 183–184
New tenants, tenancy cycle welcom-
    ing, 206
New urbanism, 88, 338
New York Stock Exchange (NYSE), 22
No-cause action, 338
Nonpayment, 203

O

Obligations of owner, 97
Obsolescence, 338
  economic, 249, 338
  functional, 338
  physical, 338
Occupancy agreement, 222. *See also*
    Lease
Occupancy in property analysis, 74
Occupancy levels, 47
Occupancy rate, 68
Occupational Safety and Health Act
    (OSHA), 149, 167, 338
Office buildings
  appearance of, 250
  Class A, 247, 248–249, 253, 290
  Class B, 247, 248, 249, 253
  Class C, 247–248, 249, 253
  criteria for classifying, 248–253
  high-rise, 130, 247, 260
  management of, 129, 246–269
    class of structure, 247–248
    criteria for classification, 248–
      253
    leases and lease negotiation in,
      262–268
    property analysis for, 246–254
    service requirements in, 256–257
    space requirements in, 255–256
    tenant options in, 266–267
    tenant selection, 254–257
  market for, 25
  multisorted, 250
  tenant options in, 266–267
Office condominiums, 268, 338
Office expenses, 112
Office interiors in office building,
    251–252

Office leases
  base year in, 263
  escalation, 263
  expense stop, 264
  fixed annual increase, 264–265
  inflation offset, 264
  operating expense, 263
  pass-through charges, 265
  past-through charges, 264
Office parks, 249, 338
Office rent, 257–262
  establishing rates, 259–261
  measuring rentable and usable
    space, 257–259
  space planning, 261
  tenant improvements, 261–262
Office space
  demand for, 6
  market for, 25
Office usable area, 257
Off-price center, 273. *See also* Outlet
    shopping center
On-site contract workers, 133–134
On-site office in commercial property,
    303
On-site signage, 184
On-site staff, 128–130, 174
  employer of, 129
  size of, 132
Open-door policy, 144
Operating budget, 122–123, 338
Operating expenses, 102–103, 120,
    153, 263, 338
Operating funds, evaluation of, 99–108
Operating procedures, standardization
    of, 305
Operational changes in analysis of
    alternatives, 86
Operations manual, 305–306, 338–339
Options, 339
  to cancel, 267, 339
  to expand, 266, 339
  to renew, 208, 267, 339
Orientation of new personnel, 140–141
Outlet shopping center, 273, 339
Outlots, 272, 339
Outside contractors, 128
Outsourcing, 134

Overage rent. *See* Breakpoint; Percent-
    age rent
Overbuilding, 45–46
Owner, landlord, and tenant (OLT)
    liability insurance, 117, 339
Owners
  by choice, 295–297
  by circumstance, 297–298
  manager as agent of, 92
  obligations of, 97
  relations, 233–234
  reports to, 95–96
Ownership, pride of, 58
Owner's insurance, 290–291

P
Pads, 272. *See also* Outlots
Parking
  availability of, 249–250
  for shopping centers, 275
Parking area ratio, 275, 339
Parking areas
  custodial maintenance of, 159
  preventive maintenance of, 161
Parking index, 275, 339
Parking ratios, 275
Parties in residential leases, 222–223
Partnerships, 60–63. *See also* General
    partnerships; Limited partnerships
    (LP)
  limited, 313
Passive activity income, 7. *See also* Tax
    Reform Act (1986)
Passive loss rules. *See* Tax Reform Act
    (1986)
Pass-through charges, 265, 280–281, 339
Pass-through clauses in long-term
    leases, 56
Pass-through operating expenses, 102
Payback, calculation of, 172
Payback period, 86, 89, 339
Payroll
  hiring staff and administering, 97
  related expenses and, 112–113
Payroll tax, 316
Pension funds, 7
  role of, 6
Percentage lease, 200

Percentage rent, 111, 279–280, 340
Performance reviews, 141
Performance reviews of employee, 141
Periodic return, 57
Permanence potential, 221
Personal property tax, 316
Personal referrals, 137
Personnel management, 17–18
Pest control, preventive maintenance
   for, 166–167
Pet policy in residential lease, 224, 225
Petty cash, 111
Physical inspection in neighborhood
   analysis, 72
Physical obsolescence, 338
Physical vacancy, 101, 340
Planned unit developments (PUDs), 9,
   232–233, 340
Plumbing, preventive maintenance of,
   163–164
Point, 54, 340
Policy manual, 143
Polychlorinated biphenyls (PCBs), 168,
   169, 340
Pooled capital, 3
Population, impact on real estate mar-
   ket, 41–42
Population growth, economic growth
   and, 37
Population shifts, 72–73, 340
Portfolio manager, 16
Portfolio supervisor, 16
Power shopping centers, 8, 273, 340
Prelease, 340
Premises, condition of, in residential
   leases
Press releases, 186–187
Prestige of office building, 250
Pretax cash flow, 107. *See also* Cash flow
Preventive maintenance, 154, 340
   cogeneration equipment in, 164
   driveways in, 161
   electrical network and plumbing in,
      163–164
   elevators in, 162–163
   exterior walls in, 161
   fire prevention and safety equipment
      in, 164–166

foundations in, 161
gas lines in, 164
grounds in, 161
gutters and downspouts in, 162
heating, ventilating, and air-
   conditioning equipment in, 163
parking areas in, 161
pest control in, 166–167
roof in, 162
stairways in, 163
walks in, 161
windows and casings in, 162
Price, 22
   laws and supply and demand rela-
      tive to, 23
Price advantage in marketing, 289
Price controls, 27
Pride of ownership, 58
Primary trade area, 274
Prime interest rate, 32, 54, 340
Primogeniture, 2, 340
Principal, 53, 340
Print media, 184
Private limited partnerships, 61. *See*
   also Limited partnerships (LP)
Private property, 1, 3
Probation, 147
Producer Price Index (PPI), 28, 341
Productivity, measures of, 28
Professionalism, real estate manage-
   ment and, 11–19
Professional liability insurance, 309
Professionally managed housing,
   211
Professional real estate management,
   1, 341
Professional reputation, 298–299
Progressive discipline, 146–147, 341
Project-Based Rental Assistance, 214,
   341
Promotion, 116–117
   internal, 135–136
Property
   advertising, 96
   marketing, 180–197
   respect for, 221
   security of, 172–173
   type of, 181

Property analysis, 341
  in management plan, 73–75
  for office buildings management,
    246–254
  for shopping centers, 271–275
Property damage insurance, 117, 341
Property management. *See* Real estate
  management
Property manager, 16
  size and experience of support staff,
    132
Property operations manual, 306, 341
Property owners
  common law and, 2
  goals of, 128
Property tax, 3
Property valuation, 106–107
Property value, preservation and
  enhancement of, 153–154
Proprietary lease, 231
Pro rata share, 258, 341
  of common area maintenance, 283
Prospect card, 194, 195, 196
Prospecting, 188
  expenses for, 116–117
  for tenants, 288–289
Prospect report, 289
Prospects, 341
  approving, for tenancy, 195, 197
Prospect-to-tenant ratio, 192
Prosperity, 36–39
Protected class. *See* Fair housing
  laws
Psychographic profile, 274, 341
Public housing, 213, 342
Public housing agencies (PHAs),
  213–214. *See also* Housing and
  Community Development Act
  (1974)
Public limited partnerships, 61. *See also*
  Limited partnerships (LP)
Public relations, 300–301
Purchase order, 111, 178

Q
Qualification of tenants, 197, 342
Quarterly budget, updates for, 123–124

Quiet enjoyment, 224
Quotations, 174

R
Radio advertising, 187
Radius clause in retail lease, 282–283,
  342
Radon, 168–169, 342
Real estate, 342
  defined, 14
  government and, 43–45
  means and reasons for investing in,
    51–58
Real estate cycles, 45–49, 342
Real estate economics, 39–49
Real estate investment counseling,
  313–314
Real estate investment trusts (REITs), 6,
  7, 10, 65, 213, 342
Real estate management, 1–19,
  294–318, 342
  acquisition of, 294–301
  determination of fees, 301–302
  documents in, 68
  effects of 9/11 on, 11
  evolution of, 3–11
  historical perspective of, 1–3
  identifying prospective clients,
    295–298
  positions in, 16
  as profession, 1, 11–19
  promoting firm, 298–301
  recruitment of prospective clients,
    294–295
  skills in, 13–14
Real estate management office, 22,
  302–309
  appraisals by, 310–312
  client services of, 310–317
  consultation, 312
  corporate fiscal service, 314
  insurance service, 317
  investment counseling, 313–314
  location of, 303–304
  procedures and equipment, 305–
    309
  tax service, 314–316

Real estate managers
  accounting systems and, 109
  budgeting and, 121
  cash flow and, 104–105
  current and future challenges for, 9
  debt service and, 104
  expense categories and, 112
  financially distressed property and,
    105
  goals of, 128
  knowledge of tax laws, 108
  primary responsibilities of, 14–19,
    93–97, 127–128, 315
  of public or government-assisted
    housing, 215
  reports of, 119–121
  role of, in financial management, 99,
    100, 104, 118
  security and, 114–115
  security deposits and, 108
Real estate market, 40–43, 75
Real estate owners
  corporations as, 64
  tax advantages of, 58
Real estate syndicate, 62–63
Real estate taxes, 107, 116, 315
Real property
  goal of managing, 21
  historical perspective on, 1–3
Receipts reports, 120
Receivership, 105, 342
Recession, 34–36
Recognition agreement, 231
Record keeping, 175–178
Recovery, 36
Recreational amenities, 116
Recyclables, 115
Redevelopment, 88
Referrals, 188–189, 299
Refundable deposit, 197
Regional analysis, 342
  in management plan, 69–71
Regional mall, 272, 342–343
Regional manager, 16
Regulatory compliance, 154–155
Rehabilitation, 86, 343
Renewals, encouraging, 228–229

Rent(s), 199, 343
  additional, 284
  all-inclusive, 265
  back, 201
  base, 111, 279
  Consumer Price Index (CPI) and, 48
  effective, 190–191
  minimum, 279
  office, 257–262
  percentage, 111, 279–280
  set, 82, 84
  for shopping centers, 279–282
Rentable area, 257, 343
Rentable space, 258
Rental agreement. *See* Lease
Rental application form, 215, 216
Rental collection, 200–205
Rental housing
  apartments as, 211–213
  government-assisted, 213–215
  maintenance for, 211
  residential lease, 221–229
  in residential property management,
    210–229
  selecting qualified residents,
    215–221
Rental income, 153
  gross potential, 100–101
Rental inquiry, 194
Rental ledger, 120, 343
Rental price, 47–48, 182
Rental retail space, 6
Rental schedule, 82
Rental space, 23–24
  impact of technology on, 25
  size of, 181
Rent bills and receipts, 120
Rent controls, 44–45, 343
  laws on, 227–228
Rent due date, 200–201
Rent loss insurance, 117, 343
Rent-paying ability, 218
Rent roll, 120, 343
Replacement cost coverage, 243, 343
Reputation
  of management firm, 298–299
  in tenant selection, 276–277

Requests, handling, in tenancy cycle, 206–207
Research and development park, 288
Reserve account transactions report, 120, 343
Reserve funds, 104, 107–108, 231, 343
Reserve ratio, 31
Resident-Based Rental Assistance, 214, 343
Residential amenities, 241
Residential Lead-Based Paint Hazard Reduction Act (1978), 220, 343
Residential leases, 221–229
　compliance with landlord-tenant laws, 226–228
　condition of premises in, 223–224
　defined, 221
　encouragement of renewals in, 228–229
　home purchase clause in, 224–225
　importance of, 221–222
　parties to, 222–223
　pets in, 224, 225
　principal clauses of, 222–226
　right of reentry in, 224
　rules and regulations, 226
　subleasing in, 224–226
　term of, 223
　transfer in, 224
　utilities in, 226
Residential managers, 16, 344. *See also* Site manager
Residential markets, market analysis of, 76
Residential property
　curb appeal of, 242
　maintenance of, 234–235
Residential property management, 210–245
　common interest realty associations in, 229–236
　housing for elderly in, 237–238
　insurance issues in, 241–245
　maintenance issues, 238–241
　manufactured housing communities in, 236–237
　rental housing in, 210–229
　single-family homes in, 236

Residential rentals, laws that affect, 220
Residential unit make-ready report, 239–240
Residents, 343
　encouraging renewals by, 228–229
　individual spaces in property analysis, 74
　selecting qualified, 215–221
Resident's handbook, 226
　information in, 227
Resolution Trust Corporation (RTC), 8
Respect for property and neighbors, 221
Retail leases, 282–283, 282–285
　clauses unique to, 281
　exclusive use, 282
　radius, 282–283, 342
　use, 282
Retail properties, management offices in, 303–304
Retail rent for shopping centers, 279–282
Retail space, leased, 270
Retail store, 22
Retention, tenant, 153, 205–207
Retrofit, 172, 344
Return on investment (ROI), 104, 344
Revolutionary War, 2–3
Riders, 244, 328
Right of first offer, 266–267, 344
Right of first refusal, 266, 344
Right of reentry in residential lease, 224, 344
Right of survivorship, 60
Risk-free rate of return, 31
Roof, preventive maintenance of, 162
Rubbish removal, 115, 153
R/U ratio, 258. *See also* Building Owners and Managers Association International (BOMA)
Rust Belt, 40

S
Safety, 154
　elevator service and, 251
　maintenance and, 167–168
Sales approach, 311
Sales auditing clause in retail lease, 285

Sales reporting clause in retail clause, 285
Sales tax, 316
Sales techniques, tenancy cycle using, 194–195
Satellite dishes, 162
Satisfaction, tenant, 153
Savings and loan associations (S&Ls), 7, 30
    failures of, 7–8, 30
Scanners, 173
S corporations, 63–64. *See also* Corporations
Secondary trade area, 274
Section 8 Housing, 344
    Choice Voucher Program, 213
    Project-Based Rental Assistance, 214
Section 202 program, 214, 344
Section 811 program, 214, 344
Security, expenses for, 114–115
Security deposits, 108–109, 344
    handling of, 226
    maintenance of, 108
    in tenancy cycle, 205
Self-storage facilities, 287, 344
Semimonthly payroll system, 112–113
Senior citizens, housing alternatives for, 237
Senior property manager, 16
September 11, 2001
    effects of, on real estate management, 10, 11
    security following, 173
    tenant selection and, 254–255
Service, insurance, 317
Service requirements in office building management, 256–257
Set rents in market analysis, 82, 84
Sewers, 115
Shares of beneficial interest, 345
Shell space, 257, 345
Shopping centers, 270–286, 345
    advertising, signs, and graphics, 283
    classification of, 271
    common area maintenance, 283
    community, 272
    concessions, 284–285
    convenience, 271–272

entertainment, 273
lifestyle, 273
management of, 285–286
megamall, 273–274
neighborhood, 272
outlet center, 273
parking for, 275
power, 273
property analysis, 271–275
radius, 282–283
regional mall, 272
retail rent for, 279–282
specialty, 272–273
staffing for, 129, 130
store hours, 283
super regional mall, 272
tenant mix for, 278–279
tenant selection for, 276–279
Sick building syndrome (SBS), 170
Signs, 184–185, 300
    directional, 185
    identification, 185
    informational, 185
Single blanket policy, 244
Single-family homes, 11, 236, 345
    in residential property management, 236
Site management, 15–17, 345
Site manager, 16, 345
Skyscrapers, 4
Smoke alarms, installation of, 165
Social Security/Medicare, 143
Social Security number (SSN), 197
Sodium vapor lamps, 171
Software
    accounting, 118–119
    encryption, 8
Sole proprietorship, 59–60, 345
Space adaptability in marketing, 289–290
Space planning, 261, 345
Space requirements in office buildings, 255–256
Special assessments, 231, 315–316, 345
Special form insurance, 117, 243, 345
Special improvement district, 315
Specialization, 130

Specially Designated Nationals and Blocked Persons List (SDN), 11, 254–255, 276*n*, 349. *See also* U.S.A. Patriot Act

Specialty shopping center, 272–273, 345–346

Speed, elevator service and, 251

Sprinkler systems, 165

Stabilization, 46–47

Staffing, 127–152
   communications, 143–144
   compensation, 141–143
   continual training, 144–145
   contractors, 133–134
   determining adequate size, 134–135
   developing talents, 145
   dismissing employee, 146, 150–151
   employee discipline, 145–147
   employees of management firm, 130–133
   employee termination, 147–151
   employer liability and, 151
   facing layoff, 148–150
   hiring, and administering payroll, 97
   hiring qualified personnel, 135–140
   maintenance, 174–175
   orientation of new personnel, 140–141
   promoting morale, 144
   in property analysis, 74
   recruiting applicants, 135–138
   requirements, 128–135
   retaining valuable employees, 141–145
   selecting employees, 138–140

Stairways, preventive maintenance of, 163

Standardization of operating procedure, 305

Standardized measurement, 258

Standard Method for Measuring Floor Area in Office Buildings, 258

Standard operating procedures manual, 305–306, 338–339

Standard tenant improvement allowance, 347

Statement of condition, 223–224

Statement of operations, 121, 346

Statement of receipts report, 120, 346

Statistical Abstract of the United States, 70

Statute law, 2, 346

Steering, 217, 346

Stock market crash (1929), 5

Storage, 287–288

Store hours in retail lease, 346

Strip shopping center, 271, 346

Structural changes in analysis of alternatives, 86–87

Sublet, 346

Sublet clause in residential lease, 225–226, 346

Submarket, 75, 346

Subrogation, 292, 346

Subsidized housing. *See also* Government-assisted housing
   management of, 214–215

Substitute check. *See* Check 21 Act (2004)

Sunbelt, 40–41

Super regional mall, 272, 346

Supplies, 22, 114, 347

Supply and demand, 22
   impact on real estate market, 42–43
   laws of, 26

Surety, 118, 347

Swimming pools, custodial maintenance of, 160

Syndicates, 5, 347

Syndication, 62–63, 347

T

Taxes, 29–30, 347
   ad valorem, 315
   advantages of real estate ownership, 58
   excise, 316
   federal income, 316
   income, 107
   payroll, 316
   personal property, 316
   real estate, 107, 116, 315
   sales, 316

Tax Reform Act (1980), 7, 347

Tax Reform Act (1986), 7, 29, 58, 347

Tax service, 314–316

Technological change, 25–26
Technology
  by-products of, 26
  effects on retailing, 8
  global reliance on, 8–9
Telecommunications industry, de-
    regulation of, 267
Telecommuting, 256, 347
Telephone expense, 113
Telephone systems, 163
Television advertising, 187
Temporary employees, 133
Tenancy cycle, 180–209
  building goodwill in, 207
  collection policies in, 200–205
  handling requests in, 206–207
  lease document in, 197–200
  lease renewal techniques in,
    207–208
  marketing incentives in, 189–191
  marketing property in, 180–197
  measuring marketing effectiveness
    in, 191–194
  prospect approval in, 195, 197
  retaining tenants in, 205–207
  sales techniques in, 194–195
  security deposits in, 205
  welcoming new tenants in, 206
Tenancy in common (TIC), 60, 347
Tenant improvement allowance (TIA),
    260, 261, 284, 347
Tenant improvements, 257, 261–262
Tenant insurance, 291–292
Tenant mix, 347
  in office building, 253
  in shopping centers, 278–279
Tenant reps, 186
Tenant requirements, 277–278
Tenants, 347
  anchor, 271, 279
  ancillary, 271, 272, 282
  options in office building manage-
    ment, 266–267
  prospecting for, 288–289
  qualification of, 197
  retention of, 153, 205–207
  satisfaction of, 153
  welcoming new, 206

Tenant-screening services, 139
Tenant selection, 254–257
  business reputation and financial
    status in, 254–255
  for shopping centers, 276–279
Tenant services in office buildings, 252
Tennessee Valley Authority (TVA),
    27–33
Term, 347
  of residential leases, 223
Termination, employee, 147–151
Terrorism, 347–348
  insurance for acts of, 243, 317
Terrorism Risk Insurance Act (TRIA),
    220, 291, 348
Tertiary trade area, 274
Thermal scan, 162
Thermostats, 172
Thrifts, 7
  failures of, 7–8
Timeshares, 231, 348
  condominium, 182
Time value of money, 348
Title VIII. *See* Fair housing laws
Townhouse communities, 11
Town square market, 22
Trade area, 72, 271, 348
  analysis of shopping center, 274
Traffic flow, 275
Traffic report, 192, 193–194, 348
Training
  continual, 144–145
  in financial management, 149
  in fire safety, 165
Transfer clause in residential lease,
    224, 348
Tuck-pointing, 161

U
Umbrella liability insurance, 117, 244,
    348
Unemployment, 24
  changes in levels of, 27
  rate of, 24, 348
Unemployment compensation, 151
Unit deed, 230, 348
United States Constitution, 1
Unit make-ready report, 238, 239–240

Unit preparation in residential properties, 238–241
Unscheduled income, 102, 348
Unsolicited applications, 137–138
Urban Land Institute (ULI), 71, 275, 348
Urban land use, trends affecting, 3
Urban living, trends toward, 10
Urban renewal, 44, 348
Urban village, 88, 348
U.S.A. PATRIOT Act, 11, 197, 220, 349
Usable space, 258, 349
Use clause in retail lease, 282, 349
Useful life, 57
Utilities, 113, 153
    for amenities, 116
    in residential lease, 226

V
Vacancies, 202
    collection loss and, 101–102
    economic, 101
    physical, 101
Vacant property, oversupply of, 7
Valuation, 349
    property, 106–107
Value, marketing on, 289–290
Vanilla box, 279, 284
Variable-rate mortgage, 54, 349
Verbal warnings, 147
Video-conferencing, 252
Video stores, 26
Vintage property, 211–212
Virtual businesses, 26, 41
Volatile organic compounds (VOCs), 170

W
Wage and Hour Law. *See* Fair Labor Standards Act (FLSA)
Wages, 141–142
Waiver of subrogation, 292
Walks
    custodial maintenance of, 159
    preventive maintenance of, 161
Walk-up, 212, 349
Wall Street Journal, 31
Warehouses, 287
Warranty deed, 53
Water, 115
Web page, 308
Website, 187–188, 300
Windows
    custodial maintenance of, 160
    preventive maintenance of, 162
Wireless connections, 308
Worker Adjustment and Retraining Notification (WARN) Act, 149, 150, 349
Workers' compensation insurance, 143, 292, 306, 349
Work force, reduction of, 24–25
Work log, 175, 176, 177
Work order, 175, 176
Work rules, 146
Written warnings, 147

Z
Zero-based budget, 123. *See also* Annual budget
Zoning, 349
    manufactured housing and, 236–237
    ordinances on, 43